D1365261

pl-

THE PEOPLE
AND THE
CONSTITUTION

THE PEOPLE
AND THE
CONSTITUTION

Being a History of the
Development of the People's Influence
in British Government

BY

CECIL S. EMDEN

SECOND EDITION

OXFORD
AT THE CLARENDON PRESS

Oxford University Press, Amen House, London E.C.4

GLASGOW NEW YORK TORONTO MELBOURNE WELLINGTON
BOMBAY CALCUTTA MADRAS KARACHI KUALA LUMPUR
CAPE TOWN IBADAN NAIROBI ACCRA

FIRST EDITION 1933
SECOND EDITION 1956
REPRINTED LITHOGRAPHICALLY IN GREAT BRITAIN
AT THE UNIVERSITY PRESS, OXFORD
FROM SHEETS OF THE SECOND EDITION
1959

PREFACE TO SECOND EDITION

THE issue of a new edition has enabled me to bring this book up to date. I have added a considerable amount of new matter; and, at the same time, occasional abridgement has proved desirable. Several modifications in the sub-headings of the chapters are intended to facilitate the book's usefulness.

For some time now the two-party system has been once more operative, with consequent improvement in the outlook for our democracy. In certain respects, however, the recent history of the people's influence on government has been disappointing. I have included some remarks on these developments; and I hope that this edition may help to attract increased attention to a subject which is vital to the cause of freedom in this country.

C. S. E.

PREFACE TO FIRST EDITION

DURING recent years the people have acquired a new status in the sphere of politics. They have become a deciding factor in the choice of Ministries; and their 'mandate' is said to be necessary for important changes in national policy. Now that the entire body of citizens may be regarded as having been admitted to a share in the control of public affairs, it seems proper to enlarge the scope allowed to writers on constitutional history.

In the present attempt to trace the development of the people's part in English government, I have preferred to divide the chapters of the book into subjects rather than periods. I trust that any disadvantages that some recapitulation and discontinuity may involve will be thought to be outweighed by advantages.

There was an obvious inducement to adopt a middle course. A turning-point in the constitutional history of the people occurred just a hundred years ago; and it would not have been altogether impracticable to have divided the book into two periods, that which led up to the great Reform Bill, and that which followed it. This course would, I think, have been an artificial one. It would certainly have proved difficult to accomplish.

If I seem to be guilty of having devoted a disproportionate amount of space to certain topics, perhaps the contribution of fresh information will serve as an extenuation. And, as regards omissions, it is true that less notice than might have been expected has been given to the history of representation and to some aspects of the influence of public opinion; but these are matters which have been dealt with fully elsewhere.

Two sources, political tracts and parliamentary debates, have yielded a larger amount of material, useful to my purpose, than anticipated at an early stage of preparation. I hope that the frequent citations made from these sources will be considered as adding weight, and not heaviness.

It is a great pleasure to have this opportunity of expressing my indebtedness to Professor J. L. Brierly for the encouragement that he has given me during several years. The book has much benefited by the kindly and valuable criticism and advice received from Mr. Keith Feiling, Student of Christ Church, and Mr. F. H. Lawson, Fellow of Merton College. And I am deeply grateful to my brother, who has been an unsparing critic in a double sense: he has spared neither himself nor the manuscript.

I wish I could have done more to justify the time and thought that those who have read the book in manuscript have expended on it, and to deal adequately with an important branch of constitutional history.

C. S. E.

CONTENTS

CHAPTER I

INTRODUCTORY

ONLY a little more than a century ago democracy, as it is understood in this country today, was unpractised: three centuries ago it was hardly imagined. The people had no effective part in the management of national affairs. But, after political representation became democratic, they gained a new and direct influence on the course of politics, so that nowadays their power is occasionally exercised otherwise than through representatives. Although the essential object of general elections is the choice of members of Parliament to act on the people's behalf, votes have in recent times been interpreted as deciding political issues.

During the last hundred years and more, the direct participation of the people in politics has developed side by side and in close connexion with representative democracy. An investigation, therefore, of the way in which the people's share in government has come to be enlarged will be rendered easier, if certain outstanding incidents in the history of representation in England are first recalled.

At the time when the principle of representation was in its infancy, those who were chosen did not act on behalf of the people, but in respect of property. They had duties rather than rights; and, even after it became recognized that they attended in Parliament as much for the object of consulting on national affairs as for that of supplementing the financial resources of the Crown, their influence remained for a long time very slight.

After the decay of feudalism the character of representation changed, and the representation of property gave way to that of the aristocracy. Members of Parliament began to exercise a genuine influence on national affairs; but this influence was exercised on behalf of a limited class. As late as the eighteenth century there was no real departure from aristocratic rule. Admittedly politicians and others, both in writing and in public speeches, discussed 'the representation of the people', claimed efficacy for the people's voice, and asserted that the good of the people was the true aim of government. But popular influence was only

effective sporadically, through the casual action of public
opinion.

It was not until 1776 that Wilkes had the distinction of
moving in the House of Commons 'that leave be given to
bring in a Bill for a just and equal Representation of the
People of England in Parliament', and of being the first to
make a proposal in the House of Commons for Reform,
which was inspired by democratic principles. He not only
proposed a redistribution of seats, but he told the House that
'every free agent in this Kingdom' was entitled to be represented, and that 'the meanest mechanic, the poorest peasant
and day-labourer' had a right to a share in the making of
laws.[1]

Schemes for Reform, which were advanced towards the end
of the eighteenth century, were chiefly concerned with the
redistribution of seats, and not with any general extension of
the franchise. Only after the spread of Thomas Paine's doc-
trines and the stimulating effect of the French Revolution
was any large interest awakened in the possibilities of democratic representation. Even then there were many who did
not see that a radical change in the character of representation was inevitable.

The official definition of the object of the Reform Act of
1832, as given in its full title, was 'to amend the Representation of the People'. This terminology was new to the statute-
book; and its employment may be regarded as attesting the
victory of a constitutional principle more revolutionary in its
implications than the enlargement of the electorate introduced by the Act itself. The admission of the new voting
qualifications was of greater importance than the increase
in the number of voters. With the passing of the Act there
finally disappeared the rigid principles of preceding centuries.
Redistribution of seats was but the rectification of an anomaly
which, by itself, would have left standing the barriers between the privileged and the unprivileged. The adoption of
enlightened principles for widening the franchise not merely
enabled the ancient barriers to be shifted—at first, it is true,
only a little—but rendered inevitable the subsequent revision
of the whole political structure.

By the middle of the nineteenth century modern views of
representation were expressed in the works of writers on the
Constitution. Representative government was regarded as

[1] 18 *Parl. Hist.* 1287–97.

coincident with representative democracy. The old ideas of representation had become obsolete. Lord Brougham, in his book on *The British Constitution* (1861), described popular choice as an essential condition of representative government, in contrast to the choice of the aristocracy, which had been effective prior to 1832. He regarded representative democracy, namely the system by which 'the body of the people, either in whole, or in a considerable proportion of the whole, elect deputies to a chamber of their own', as 'the great invention of modern times'.[1]

Some years passed, however, before it was admitted that the whole people, and not merely a select number, should possess the franchise. Gladstone caused consternation in 1864 by announcing in the House of Commons that 'every man who is not presumably incapacitated by some consideration of personal unfitness or of political danger is morally entitled to come within the pale of the Constitution'.[2] Palmerston was shocked by this announcement; and, as Prime Minister, he wrote to Gladstone, a member of his Ministry, protesting against what seemed to him to be an assertion of the doctrine of universal suffrage. 'What every man . . .', he said, 'has a right to is to be well governed and under just laws.'[3] In the following year, 1865, Disraeli, when commenting on Gladstone's dictum, spoke of the suffrage as a privilege 'to be gained by virtue, by intelligence, by integrity'; and he expressed much doubt whether a democracy was a type of government suitable to this country.[4]

These selective principles were left far behind in the extensions of the franchise of 1884 and after. When he was about to introduce the Bill of 1884, Gladstone declared that it was no longer a question of nice calculations. He took his stand, he said, 'on the broad principle that the enfranchisement of capable citizens . . . gives an addition of strength to the State'. And the Opposition as a whole did not display any marked interest in the meaning of the expression 'capable'.[5] When the vast extension of the electorate was undertaken in 1918, but small attention was paid to any need for justifying the full application of the democratic principle. The chief reason for the widening of the franchise

[1] *The British Constitution*, 2nd ed., pp. 29, 31, 89.
[2] 175 *Parl. Deb.*, 3 s., 324.
[3] Morley, *Life of Gladstone*, vol. ii, pp. 128–9.
[4] 178 *Parl. Deb.*, 3 s, 1702.
[5] 285 *Parl. Deb.*, 3 s., 107; 286 *Parl. Deb.*, 3 s., 1827.

was given by the Prime Minister of the day, Lloyd George, as the necessity for allowing those who had taken a part in the War to have a voice in the national counsels.[1] Sir George Cave, the Minister chosen to move the second reading of the Bill in the House of Commons, remarked that the addition which was proposed to the number of voters 'excites no emotion whatever, except a feeling of satisfaction that, by making this addition, we shall approach nearer to the ideal of representative government, namely to make Parliament a mirror of the nation'.[2] There was but slight opposition to the main proposals of 1884, and none to those of 1918. In the more recent measures, the legislature has, wisely or unwisely, thrown off the old attitude of circumspection and restraint in dealing with the problem of the extension of the franchise.[3]

During the period of its enlargement, which has been briefly outlined in the preceding paragraphs, the electorate secured the ability to influence the course of politics otherwise than through the agency of its representatives. It has come to be recognized that the choice of the Ministry and the undertaking of important legislative changes are in some degree dependent on the disposition of the people, as expressed by their votes at general elections. This kind of development need not raise the apprehension that representative government is in the process of being superseded by direct government. The people's power has not become sufficiently extended to prevent their representatives from using a considerable discretion in the application of the general principles approved by the electors. The representatives retain their responsibility for government. But, in so far as the people acquire the capacity to influence policy, to that extent representative government is modified.

It is difficult to imagine any arrangement by which the people of a large State could take more than an extremely limited share in governmental activities. Apart from the choice of the party from which Ministers are to be drawn, direct government cannot extend beyond decisions on the outlines of policy. The whole political organization would have to be drastically revised before it would be possible for government by means of representatives to be superseded.

[1] 92 H.C. Debt, 5 s., 489.   [2] 93 H.C. Deb., 5 s., 2134 ff.
[3] In round figures the Representation of the People Acts raised the numbers of the electorate as follows: 1832, to 1,000,000; 1867, to 2,500,000; 1884, to 5,000,000; 1918, to 21,000,000; 1,929 to 29,000,000.

The steps leading up to the direct intervention of the people in politics are not easy to trace. Although it was not until the nineteenth century that the Government was recognized as being pledged to follow the preferences expressed by the people at general elections, there was at a much earlier date a considerable use of individual pledges by parliamentary candidates. The second half of the seventeenth century may be taken as the approximate period at which Parliament began to secure a place in what Burke called 'the standing government of this country'. Almost as soon as this stage had been reached, the desire of constituencies to exercise control over the votes of individual members on political questions became manifest. The first sign, then, of the people as a whole becoming articulate can be discerned in occasional attempts of constituencies to dictate to members what their attitude should be on matters of policy.[1]

So long as members of Parliament continued to be regarded essentially as local representatives, whose duty it was to speak for their constituents only, it was difficult for the sum total of individual pledges to be interpreted as one general pledge, involving the Government in a liability to pursue a particular course of action. But during the eighteenth century members came increasingly to be regarded as representing the whole nation and not merely a locality; and this change of view helped to prepare the way for the new era which was to begin with the passing of the Reform Bill of 1832.

At the same time that the relations of members and constituents were developing in a manner which was to facilitate the increase of the power of the people as a whole, the period, say, of the four Georges, respect was occasionally being paid by those in authority to movements of public opinion. Why this was so it is not easy to say, for there were no recognized sanctions available, as there are in a system of government that is genuinely democratic. The Ministry did not depend on the votes of the people. The ultimate sanction of physical force probably provided a part of the explanation; and doubtless an increased understanding of the proper principles of government had its effect among both the politicians and the people at large.

The influence of public opinion at that period was less direct in its action than it is today. When party allegiances

[1] See Chapter II (Influence of Constituents on Members).

were insecure and majorities unstable, Ministers were more inclined to watch the attitude of members of Parliament than that of the people. But towards the end of the eighteenth century public opinion began to operate more as it does today, by inducing Ministers to follow the wishes of the people, regardless of the attitude of their representatives.

Even during recent years, when the enfranchisement of a large proportion of the inhabitants has rendered it advisable for party politicians to pay careful attention to public opinion, it has been difficult to ascertain the true state of the public mind. It was doubly difficult to do so in earlier periods. Opinions might be gathered in particular localities; but it was hardly possible to form any judgement of national opinion. As, however, methods of communication improved, the circulation of newspapers increased, and education was more widely diffused, both the scope and the activity of public opinion were enlarged. This course of events contributed to the feasibility of ascertaining the wishes of the people by means of their votes at general elections.[1]

Before general elections were construed as decisions by the people, the most prevalent methods by which public opinion could be expressed were petitioning and the holding of public meetings. It is difficult to estimate the effect of these popular demonstrations; but it seems that, until the early part of the nineteenth century, they frequently received but slight attention. They were followed by the formation of political and other associations. These more highly organized mediums of public opinion were more effective than petitions and public meetings, and are still widely employed.[2]

Not only is it necessary for the attitude of the people to be prepared, so that they may make decisions, but the questions for decision must be prepared for them. In the eighteenth century there was no machinery for the requisite submission of issues. The party system, as then operative, was too undeveloped and insufficiently imbued with public spirit to perform this function. Party principles, in the modern sense, were non-existent; and any central organization of parties was of a rudimentary character, and, therefore, limited in its efficacy.

There was, moreover, a large number of members who

[1] See Chapter III (Public Opinion and Government).
[2] See Chapter IV (Public Opinion and Government (cont.)).

did not own allegiance to party, and who acted and voted according to their own ideas or interests at any particular juncture. The electors were often ignorant of the political leanings, such as they were, of parliamentary candidates; and when a new Parliament was elected, it usually happened that only a rough estimate could be made of the number of votes obtainable, on one side or the other. In these circumstances, general elections were incapable of being used for the purpose of interpreting the wishes of the electors.[1]

Very soon after the first extension of the franchise, in 1832, party organization improved rapidly; and this improvement led to the acceptance of uniform programmes and uniform pledges by party candidates. Towards the end of the nineteenth century party organization had become so fully developed that the federation of local associations occasionally influenced the construction of programmes. Electors throughout the country, who were members of a party, were thus enabled to express their views on the selection of issues for determination at elections.[2]

The two kinds of decision in which the people now take a part—regarding the choice of Ministries and regarding policy—are usually closely associated. It was approximately during the same period, in the nineteenth century, that the ability to make both kinds of decision came to be recognized. But their two histories can be traced separately with advantage. They each disclose points of interest in the development of the relations of the Sovereign, Parliament, and the people.

The later Stuart sovereigns not only retained an unfettered ability to choose their Ministers; they sometimes changed the composition of the Ministry immediately before a general election. This practice, combined with the automatic majorities obtained by the Crown, excluded any power in Parliament or the people to influence the choice of Ministries. The free choice by the Sovereign was challenged by the House of Commons during the Georgian period. But, soon after the House of Commons had established its claim that Ministries were dependent on support in the House, the people began to be courted by party leaders, who knew that a redistribution of political power was inevitable. As a result, it was accepted, in the later nineteenth century, that

[1] See Chapter V (Parties and the People).
[2] See Chapter VI (Party Organization and Policy).

the choice between alternative Ministries could be directly inferred from the results of general elections. It became necessary, too, for a Ministry, newly appointed during a period of Parliament, to obtain the approval of the electorate, through the election of a majority in its favour.[1]

A few years after the Revolution of 1688, although the Sovereign's ability to choose his Ministers remained undiminished, there was some evidence of a slight connexion between the results of general elections and the course of policy. Progress in this direction was hindered, first, by royal and other intervention in election contests, and, secondly, by the inadequate representation of the people in Parliament, and their consequent failure to have issues submitted to them or to take an interest in politics.[2]

It was not until 1832 that the principle of the peoples' mandate was first genuinely operative. The passing of the great Reform Bill demonstrated how the election of a majority of representatives, pledged to a particular measure, could be interpreted as imposing an obligation on the Government to introduce it. Politicians saw the advantage, from the point of view of securing a majority in Parliament, of inviting the new electorate to exercise its judgement in public affairs. With each extension of the franchise and with the disappearance of the old types of corruption, this advantage became more obvious. The electors were treated as capable, not merely of electing members, but of making decisions on vital political questions, such as the maintenance of free trade, or the disestablishment of the Irish Church.[3]

The undertaking of important legislative programmes, in which Ministries were involved in the course of the nineteenth century, prompted by unprecedented industrial and commercial developments, necessarily placed the Cabinet in a position of enhanced importance. When the House of Commons was more powerful than the Ministry, the constituencies did no more than attempt to control individual representatives. But, when the Ministry became more powerful than the House of Commons, it was the former rather than the latter that the people wished to control.[4]

Even Sir Henry Maine, who displayed an attitude of sus-

---

[1] See Chapter VII (The Choice of Ministries).
[2] See Chapter VIII (Prelude to the Mandate).
[3] See Chapter IX (The People and Policy).
[4] Cf. Lowell, *Government of England*, vol. i, pp. 421 ff.

picion regarding democratic progress, recognized, as early as 1885, that, owing to recent developments, 'the electoral body must supply the House of Commons with a mandate to alter the Constitution'.[1] And, shortly afterwards, James Bryce, when comparing the Constitutions of the United States of America and of England, described a general election in England as having become 'an expression of popular opinion on the two or three leading measures then propounded and discussed by the party leaders, as well as a vote of confidence or no confidence in the Ministry of the day'.[2]

Although no striking advance in the accession of the people to political power has been made since 1888, when Bryce wrote the above-quoted passage, the change which he mentioned has been confirmed and consolidated as a result of the experiences of subsequent general elections. Professor Dicey, in 1910, described Bryce's remarks as 'characteristically moderate'. The modification of the supremacy of the representative chamber by the interposition of the people's influence, which was, at the time when Bryce wrote, partially effective, had become, Dicey said, completely effective in 1910. 'The time has arrived for the formal recognition of a principle which, in fact, if not in theory, forms part of our constitutional morality.'[3] Dicey himself was not a person whose opinions on such a subject were likely to be exaggerated. An important part of his contribution to the understanding of the practice of government was his explanation of the way in which the conventions of the Constitution become absorbed into Constitutional Law, and in which *de facto* authority develops into authority *de jure*. He was, therefore, peculiarly qualified to verify the impression that the 'practical mastery' of the people was in the process of ripening into legal authority.

The above-quoted observations of eminent constitutional lawyers, which carry unquestionable authority in their own sphere, may well prompt inquiry regarding the views of practical politicians. The latter, it may be suggested, do not exhibit the same unanimity regarding the development of

---

[1] *Popular Government*, p. 118, Maine, like others of his period, did not welcome the use of the term 'mandate', which seemed to him to be adapted from the *mandat impératif*, which obliged a French representative to act in accordance with the instructions of his constituents. The term is undoubtedly open to objection as having too autocratic a flavour. But it is difficult to find a better. Perhaps 'commission' would do.

[2] *American Commonwealth*, 1st ed. (1888), vol. ii, p. 71; 3rd ed. (1893), vol. i, pp. 466–7.   [3] 212 *Quarterly Review* (1910), p. 550.

the people's powers. Although, with the exception of one or two Liberals of the old school, no leading politician of the last half-century has questioned the principle of mandate, pressure of circumstances has caused party leaders to take divergent views in varying circumstances on the extent to which it is applicable. Politicians, although endeavouring to pursue a consistent course, would be more than human if, from time to time, they were not found trimming their sails according to the prevailing wind. An instance of this inclination to opportunism, which will require further notice in a later chapter, may be briefly mentioned here.

Gladstone, after the election of 1885, suddenly announced his intention to make proposals for the introduction of Home Rule for Ireland. As a result, he lost the support of a section of his party under the leadership of the Marquis of Hartington, who maintained that Gladstone had no right to initiate legislation on a subject of so great importance without first consulting the opinion of the electorate, and that the irregularity of the proposed course was aggravated by the shortness of the interval between the announcement of the new policy and the preceding general election.[1] Gladstone replied, unconvincingly as it seems, that no mandate was required to keep the law, by which he implied that the state of politics in Ireland fully justified measures of the kind which he had proposed and did not necessitate submission to the people. When, however, a fresh general election, within a year of the last, became inevitable, Gladstone, who realized that every effort must be made by him to secure the support of the country, placed the Home Rule issue unequivocally before it. He declared in plain terms that the people were called upon to decide by their votes at the election whether or not the policy of Home Rule for Ireland was to be adopted.[2]

These incidents of 1885 and 1886 are typical of the attitude which has been adopted on various occasions by the Ministry and the Opposition respectively. It will be seen that, as a general rule, a Ministry in office which retains a majority is disinclined to recognize that its proposals involve the necessity of an appeal to the people, while the party in op-

[1] 304 *Parl. Deb.*, 3 s., 1241–2.
[2] See, for example, his speech at Edinburgh on 18 June 1886, and the terms of the Queen's Speech prior to the dissolution of 1886, which are quoted on p. 287 below.

position frequently maintains that the Ministry is transgress-
ing constitutional usage by introducing important legislation
which has never formed the subject of an issue at a general
election.

Not only have questions of expediency given rise to
differences of opinion regarding the applicability of the
principle of mandate, but problems regarding the nature
and the extent of the authority to be obtained have puzzled
those who are anxious to see that the people's newly acquired
political capacity has a fair chance of being exercised.

Any attempt to investigate constitutional development in
this country is rendered difficult by the large element of
unpremeditated modification to which the mechanism of
government is subject. One of the necessary sequels to the
operation of our informal Constitution, as opposed in some
respects to a formal one, is the difficulty of detecting the
course of its evolution. New conventions become established,
and the distribution of power is varied without a full recognition of the extent of the change. If, therefore, the people are
to have enlarged powers, we must be prepared for consequen-
tial changes in the powers of other branches of the constitutional machinery.

Not long ago the dominant position of the House of
Commons in the British Constitution was the pride of the
nation and the envy of foreign observers. The supremacy of
the House of Commons was proverbial. In Victorian times,
Bagehot described the Cabinet as 'a combining committee—
a hyphen which joins, a buckle which fastens the legislative
part of the State to the executive part of the State'. Since the
time when Bagehot wrote, the situation has, as we shall see in
later chapters, greatly altered. Today there are some who think
that the powers of the House of Commons have been so much
reduced that its functions are chiefly confined to the ventila-
tion and crystallization of public opinion. The House of
Commons might now be described as being so much reduced
in status that it is in effect a link between the Cabinet and
the people, both of whose powers have expanded considerably. An extensive view of constitutional history is desirable in
order to appreciate the significance of changes such as these.

CHAPTER II

INFLUENCE OF CONSTITUENTS ON MEMBERS

§ 1. *Instructions and pledges at elections*

THE medieval member of Parliament, grudgingly elected, went to the place of assembly conscious that he would more certainly consent to the taxation of his constituents than obtain any advantages for them. His chief function was to consent. He was unable to exert much influence on financial policy, and legislation was not a matter for him to discuss. He was regarded in all respects as a local representative, national affairs being outside his scope. And if, as is unlikely, his electors expressed to him their notions on governmental concerns, he was not in a position to do anything effective to forward them. But, as medieval grew into more modern times, there is some evidence of electors communicating their interest in general politics to their representatives; and, by the latter part of the seventeenth century, means were found of informing parliamentary candidates or newly elected members of the wishes of their electors. During the critical years of 1640 to 1649, the interest of the people expressed itself in 'instructions' to members by freeholders, requesting the intimation of their complaints to Parliament on such matters of grievance as monopolies and ship-money.[1] This method was used as an alternative to that of petition by counties to Parliament. It is to be observed that the members were not asked to take any action beyond that of communicating the grievances to the Legislature. They were not instructed to vote in any particular way.

An interesting broadsheet, which was printed in connexion with the campaign preceding the election to the Convention Parliament in 1660, provides an early example of common-form instructions to members to undertake a particular line of policy. They did not merely intimate the wishes of constituencies, but required that the wishes should be carried out. The broadsheet was evidently published in the hope that it would be utilized by many constituencies

---

[1] e.g. 2 *Parl. Hist.* 652; Rushworth, *Hist. Coll.*, Part III, vol. i, pp. 30–31.

and that parliamentary candidates would be confronted with
it and made to subscribe to its purport. The author was
probably a reclaimed Commonwealth man. After reciting
the sad experiences of the preceding years and the need for
a happy settlement of differences, he asserted that members
elected to the ensuing Parliament were 'obliged in point
of duty and conscience' as 'publick servants and proxies,
vigorously to pursue all such just prescriptions for the common
welfare and establishment of our native country' as the electors 'shall present to them'. It was proposed to the electors
that they should 'earnestly desire and require' their newly
elected members to restore 'the antient Constitution' and
'the antient fundamental regal government', to advance
trade, to regulate all exorbitant taxes, and to obtain a
general Act of Indemnity. In so far as evidence is available
to disclose the circumstances of the election of 1660, it appears
to be unlikely that there was any organization to enable
these instructions to be very widely employed.[1]

A few years later a form of instructions, prepared, it seems,
by the Earl of Shaftesbury for the election preceding the
Parliament summoned for March 1681,[2] was probably circulated among the county constituencies by the vigorous
agents of the Earl, with the object of being used as widely as
possible in the election campaign. The instructions required
the member to insist on a Bill to exclude the Duke of York
and on 'an adjustment between the King's prerogative of
calling, proroguing and dissolving Parliaments and the rights
of the people to have annual Parliaments'.[3] The Earl of
Shaftesbury adopted several new electioneering schemes; and
it is likely that the design of securing the ends of his party by
pledging newly elected members to uniform lines of policy,
although not originated by him, was first utilized on any
considerable scale at his instigation. If party organization
had remained sufficiently active and competent to ensure, by
the distribution of common-form instructions, that the issues
of general elections were uniformly defined, the people's
control over policy and legislation might have been expe-

[1] Although it is tedious in style, this broadsheet has a special interest in
view of its early date and its comparability with later common-form instructions. It is accordingly reproduced in Appendix II.
[2] B. Martyn, *Life of Shaftesbury*, vol. ii, p. 266.
[3] The instructions are reproduced in Appendix III. Cf. also Burnet, *History
of My Own Time* (ed. Airy), vol. ii, p. 281. With regard to the probability of
instructions being in common form, see 45 *E.H.R.*, p. 573.

dited by many years. In fact, however, the device was not continued to any appreciable extent, with the result that individual constituencies were left to prescribe the pledges to be obtained from their particular members.

Not only was the election of 1681 memorable for the use of general instructions, but also for the use of instructions prepared locally in separate constituencies. At first, directions by constituencies were confined to the time immediately after election; and it is necessary to distinguish between these instructions—sailing orders, so to speak—and those which were given as and when emergencies arose, during the period of a representative's commission. It is apparent that, while the former type is capable of justification, the latter may result in the member being degraded to the position of a mere agent or instrument.

As regards the former type, it seems that the only sensible way of ensuring that the wishes of the electors are followed by their representatives is to insist on a promise prior to election. Instructions, as first used, had no such business-like basis. Perhaps the undertakings were postponed in deference to constitutional propriety. However this may be, it is likely that the electors realized that the sanction for enforcement was the same whether the transaction took place immediately before or after the election. In either instance, the remedy for breach of faith was postponed to the next election, since the possibility of calling upon the member to resign his seat had not then been realized.

The instruction of members by constituencies with Whig majorities in regard to the exclusion of James, Duke of York, in 1681 appears to have been general.[1] In the directions given by the County of Middlesex, the phraseology is suggestive of the novelty of the expedient. They were as follows:

The Address of the Freeholders of the County of Middlesex, made and delivered in writing the third day of this instant March, 1680 [1681] at Hamstead Heath, unto Sir William Roberts, Knight and Baronet, and William Ranton Esquire; after they were declared to be elected Knights to represent the said County of Middlesex in the next Parliament to be holden at Oxford the one and twentieth of this instant.

Gentlemen, we the Freeholders of this County have (in great

[1] See *Vox Patriae . . . being a True Collection of . . . Addresses . . . to . . . Representatives* (1681). The Tories also used a similar form; see, for instance, *The Bristol Address* (1681).

confidence of your integrity, wisdom and courage) now chosen you, to represent us in the next Parliament, to be holden at Oxford on the 21st day of this present March. And although we do not in the least question your faithfulness to the true interest of this nation; nor your prudence in the management thereof. Yet esteeming it greatly our duty, in this unhappy juncture, wherein our religion, lives, liberties, properties, and all that is dear to us, are in such eminent danger, to signifie our pressing dangers unto you. And accordingly we do request, that in the next Parliament wherein we have chosen you to sit and act, that you will, with the greatest integritie and most undaunted resolution, join with and assist the other worthy representatives and patriots of this nation in the searching into, and preventing the horrid and hellish villanies, plots and designs of the wicked and restless sort of people the Papists, both in this and the neighbouring Kingdoms . . .

In securing to us the enjoyment of the true protestant religion, and the well established government of this Kingdom . . .

In asserting the people's unquestionable right of petitioning . . .

In preventing the misery, ruine, and utter destruction which unavoidably must come upon this and the neighbouring nations, if James, Duke of York, or any other Papist, shall ascend the royal throne of this Kingdom.

A note is appended to the effect that the address was very gratefully accepted by both the elected members, 'and their answer returned to the great content of the Freeholders'. Instructions of other counties and of one or two boroughs, given at the same election, have been preserved. They resemble in their purport those of the County of Middlesex.[1]

It is obvious that this development in the relations between electors and members would be first observable on occasions of intense political agitation; and the practice of giving instructions at election time is accordingly again found in operation at the election of November–December 1701, with the outburst of patriotic excitement exhibited as the result of the intervention of the French King into English politics. The County of Bucks asked its newly elected members 'to support the King [of England] with the most effectual and equal supplies; to restore and keep the credit of the nation; heartily to concurr in such alliances as his majestie has or shal make for putting down the exorbitant power of France'. The members of the City of Westminster were 'to endeavour to support his majesties title, and defend the nation against the

[1] See, for instance, Bodleian Library, Ashm. 1681, 85, 88, and 89: *Calendar of State Papers, Domestic, 1680–1*, p. 203.

French King, who threatens to give a King to England, as
he has done to Spain'. This was the substance of the instructions; but considerable variation was shown in their
form. Some constituencies merely besought or recommended
their members to do this or that; others stated that they
expected such and such a policy to be pursued; the City of
London went so far as to say: 'We earnestly desire and charge
you'; while Bristol was bolder still with: 'We do direct and
require you.'[1]

In more than one instance the instructions contained some
attempted justification of the new departure. The City of
Westminster talked of its 'undoubted rights', as also did
Gloucester; Bristol had 'no doubt that we have a right to
direct our representatives and give them our advice what is
most necessary for them in our judgments, to promote and
carry on in Parliament'. On the other hand, the County of
Sussex disclaimed any right. 'It is not', said the electors,
'that we think we are able to instruct or direct you our
representatives, how to discharge that high trust which we by
our choice have called you to.'

This practice of issuing instructions was repeated in 1705
and 1715;[2] and the City of London, at least, continued
it far into the eighteenth century. Horace Walpole was
shocked, in 1761, when the City of London, some months
after the elections, but prior to the Session, gave instructions
to its members to promote an inquiry into the disposal of the
money which had been granted in connexion with the war,
and to consent to no peace, unless all, or very nearly all, the
conquests were retained. Thus, said Horace Walpole, the
City of London usurps the right of making peace and war.[3]

Members were still primarily regarded as local representatives, and the idea of the majority of Parliament representing
the majority of the people had not yet developed. In so far
as the practice of giving instructions at election time did not
compromise the reasonable freedom of the member by the

[1] Luttrell, *Brief Relation of State Affairs* (1857 ed.), vol. v, pp. 115, 119; *The Electors' Right Asserted, with the Advices and Charges of Several Counties, Cities and Boroughs in England to their respective Members of Parliament, &c.*, 1701; *The Cornish Hug . . . being Instructions of the County of Cornwall*, 1701; *The Postman* for 25–7 Nov. 1701. See also Daniel Defoe, *The Original Power of the Collective Body of the People of England, examined and asserted*.
[2] *The History of the Reign of Queen Anne digested into Annals, Year the Fourth* (Boyer), p. 15; *The Political State of Great Britain*, vol. ix, pp. 163 ff.
[3] *Gentleman's Magazine*, May 1741; Sharpe, *London and the Kingdom*, vol. iii, p. 70; *Horace Walpole's Letters* (ed. Toynbee), vol. v, p. 138.

use of too particular and peremptory expressions, it was capable of justification. It evidenced a more lively interest of the people in public affairs, and it provided an obvious precedent for the exaction of election pledges, a practice which prepared the way for the development of the principle of mandate in the nineteenth century.

The exaction of election pledges, or promises prior to election, soon followed and became prevalent at the elections of 1774 and 1780; and it was possibly in use as early as the election of 1768. The City of London and the County of Middlesex were pioneers; and Wilkes, at a meeting of the freeholders of Middlesex in 1774, engaged himself to promote Bills for the shortening of Parliaments, the exclusion of placemen, and the reform of the representation. Four out of five candidates for the City of London signed pledges to work for a Bill to enable the American colonists to tax themselves. The fifth refused on the ground that he objected to the principle of pledges.[1] The innovation was evidently regarded as a dangerous one; and many members at once took a firm stand and refused to accept such obligations. Burke was among the number; and his well-known remarks on this subject[2] were also made in 1774. Even the leaders of the Whigs disclaimed pledges as 'derogatory to their characters as senators, and restrictive of their rights as men'. At a Westminster election, early in the nineteenth century, Hobhouse, whose views were not regarded as illiberal, refused a request to pledge himself to the ballot, the abolition of house and window taxes, of the newspaper stamp-duty, and the repeal of the Septennial Act, remarking that 'my whole public life is the best pledge that can be offered'. Sir Francis Burdett, whose reputation as a consistent reformer was unimpeachable, described pledges as 'a system of self-deception by which knaves are taught to catch fools'. These words may have suggested to Francis Place his better-known remark, to the effect that 'none but fools demand pledges and none but knaves give them'. Prominent Radical candidates, like Joseph Hume, adopted a similar line.

The unexampled nature of the Reform issue in 1831, which marked the development of the particular pledge between constituency and representative into that of a general pledge

---

[1] Cooke, *History of Party*, vol. iii, pp. 201–2; *Lloyd's Evening Post*, 3–5 Oct. 1774.   [2] Quoted on p. 23 below.

between people and Parliament, brought about a complete
change in the attitude of candidates. Conscientious objections
to the impropriety of pledges were swept away. The Duke
of Wellington mournfully admitted that 'there was scarcely
an election, even in a corrupt borough, in which the candidates were not called upon to give pledges, and did not pledge
themselves to vote for Reform', while Lord Eldon expressed
his 'deep sense of humiliation' at the conduct of the members
of the Lower House in this respect.[1]

During the debates on the great Reform Bill in 1831,[2]
Lord Lyndhurst said that 'the members of the present House
of Commons can scarcely be considered members of a de-
liberative assembly, but delegates sent out by the people for
an especial purpose'. That they were sent out by the people
for a special purpose was obvious; but they were not mere
local delegates, proxies, or agents, in the phraseology adopted
by the Radicals. Parliament was for the first time charged
by the people with the carrying out of a specified policy. It is
sufficient, in the present chapter, to take note of the sequence
by which the relations of constituents and members formed
the basis of the new relations of people and Parliament.
From 1832 onwards there has been a growing tendency for
pledges to be uniform party pledges and not merely individual ones; but a discussion of the development of the history of the general pledge or mandate is reserved for later
chapters.

§ 2. *Instructions between elections*

The issue of instructions by constituencies to members at
times other than election times was a serious extension of
the practice which has been mentioned in the preceding
section. It was much more likely to debase the status of the
member. It seems to have been an extension rather than a
separate development, since there is very little evidence of
this type of instruction before the eighteenth century. The
so-called instructions of the middle of the seventeenth century,
some of which seem to have been given between general
elections, were messages rather than directions.[3]

Andrew Marvell's letters to his constituents at Hull have

[1] For the extreme attitude taken by the City of London, see *Annual Register*
for 1832, Part I, p. 300.   [2] 8 *Parl. Deb.*, 3 s., 285.
[3] Cf. p. 12 above; and see *The Humble Petition of the County of Kent . . . with
certain Instructions* (1642), and *Instructions from the Honourable House of Commons . . .
to the Committee in Kent . . . Likewise certain Instructions from the said County* (1642).

been quoted as proving that instructions were given to him during the course of Parliaments. His close relations with the Corporation of Hull are a matter of very common knowledge; but the instructions he received from time to time are of a local character; and his letters to that body regarding questions of general policy do not appear to evince more than a habit of reporting fully and frequently on the business before the House and the state of commerce at the time. It is true that on one occasion, in 1670, he wrote: 'What is your opinion at Hull of the Bill from the Lords for general naturalisation of all Forainers that shall take the oaths of allegiance and supremacy?' But there is little, if anything, else in the letters of a similar kind. As one of Marvell's editors has aptly observed, the inquiry regarding naturalization must have puzzled the Corporation. The truth seems to be that Marvell's anxiety to improve the political education of his constituents not unnaturally led him occasionally to assume in them a higher capacity than was warranted.

The extreme popular interest aroused by the Excise Scheme of 1773 was the occasion for the first important instance of instructions between elections; and many constituencies, including the City of London, sent formal instructions to their members to oppose any extension of the excise laws.[1] The member for Carlisle, Colonel Charles Howard, was among those who received instructions; and the description given by him, in a letter to his father, the Earl of Carlisle, of his reply to his constituents proves how difficult an intelligent and conscientious member found it to reconcile these instructions with his duties as a representative. He wrote from London on the 3rd of March:

I . . . told them that, as I was ignorant what the proposal would be, I believed they, at a greater distance, could not be much less so; that if the scheme was right, to prevent frauds without detriment to the fair trader, or the liberty of the subject, their directions would prevent my giving my concurrence to it; if on the contrary it was attended with any of these inconveniences that alarmed them . . . it would have met with my negative, had I not received their instructions; so I desired to know, whether they expected me to oppose it, in what light soever it appeared to me.

[1] *Hist. MSS. Comm., 15th Report*, Appendix, Part VI (Carlisle MSS.), p. 95; Lord Hervey, *Memoirs* (ed. Sedgwick), vol. i, p. 134; Lord Mahon, *History of England*, vol. ii, p. 244; R. R. Sharpe, *London and the Kingdom*, vol. iii, p. 36.

This protest was effectual in inducing the constituents to withdraw their instructions and leave the member free to act as he thought right.[1]

The borough of Colchester put its request to its members to oppose the Excise Scheme in strong terms; and, when one of its members protested, it told him that:

if you vote for a Bill of that nature, even in the shape you seem to be pleased with or in any other, you can't reasonably expect our approbation since we are fully convinced that all excise laws are destructive to trade, innovations on our ancient rights, and altogether inconsistent with the true interest of a free people.[2]

A political tract, which is thought to have been written by old Horatio Walpole,[3] described this novel method of giving instructions to members as subversive of the Constitution. The author described the making of representations by constituents as proper and legitimate. But injunctions and positive commands, he said, involved a transference of the legislative power from Parliament to the people.

In 1739 and 1740 a large number of counties, cities, and boroughs issued instructions as a result of the agitation for legislation to limit the number of placemen in the House of Commons. The City of York, for instance, wrote:

We are sensible that the spirit of a British Parliament can only be exerted in an assembly of men uncorrupted and independent; we do therefore insist and require you our representatives to join with those who shall be willing to promote a Bill to reduce and limit the number of placemen in the House of Commons.[4]

Some members appear, on this occasion also, to have objected to receiving instructions on a matter affecting the general public.[5]

[1] Hist. MSS. Comm., 15th Report, Appendix, Part VI (Carlisle MSS.), pp. 102, 103.   [2] Excise: being a Collection of Letters &c., 1733.
[3] The Rise and Fall of the Late Projected Excise Impartially considered by a Friend to the English Constitution, 1733.
[4] 58 Political State of Great Britain, p. 424; 59 Political State of Great Britain, pp. 47, 127 ff., 133.
[5] The following letter was, it seems, sent by a member to a constituency in the north of England: 'In answer to yours of the 23rd of last month, as I have the honour to be one of your representatives, I shall always be ready to take your directions in every thing brought into Parliament, wherein your Corporation is particularly concerned; if I am convinced that it is for the benefit of it. But in matters of general nature, you'll allow me to judge what is best to do, a confidence I take to be reposed in every member of Parliament by their electors. As to what your letter refers to, I don't know of any such Bill to be brought in, more than common report; if there is, when I see how it's framed, I'll act therein as I think most for the good of the public.' (Great Britain's Memorial containing a Collection of the Instructions &c., 1741.)

Walpole's resignation, in 1742, was the signal for a further use of this method, many constituencies recommending a strict inquiry into past measures, and pressing for triennial parliaments and the enactment of a measure dealing with placemen. The City of Bath concluded the instructions, which it sent to its members at this time, with what appears to be a thinly veiled threat. 'These are our sentiments, ye are our representatives, and we are your electors.'[1]

The climax in the use of this kind of instructions was, perhaps, reached in 1756 and the following years of patriotic enthusiasm. Inquiry into the loss of Minorca and the situation in America was urged by the City of London and many influential constituencies.[2] In the agitation regarding Wilkes and the Middlesex election of 1769 the City of London was again in the forefront and referred, not only to its 'indispensable duty', but also to its 'undoubted right'. London and other constituencies issued instructions in respect of the rights of electors, the preservation of the Habeas Corpus Act, and the reform of the law of libel.[3] At a great meeting, held in February 1769, Beckford, one of the members for the City of London, declared that, if he received instructions directing him to take a course opposed to his convictions, he would consider himself bound to follow them. But there was a considerable body of feeling opposed to this enthralment of the member of Parliament. The conclusion was reached, in some quarters, that the more proper method of the electors advancing their political opinions during the period of Parliament was that of petitioning. Burke was among those who expressed this view.[4]

[1] 12 *Parl. Hist.* 416 ff.; *Catalogue of Prints and Drawings in the British Museum*, vol. iii, p. 458. A tract, entitled *Faction detected by the Evidence of Fact*, by John Perceval, afterwards Lord Egmont, first appeared at this time. It obtained very wide and favourable notice and ran into several editions. It dealt sternly with the issuing of instructions by constituents; and it might be inferred that the author regarded Walpole's resignation as their first occasion. He described the instructions of the City of London 'not only as a direct and scurrilous libel on the administration, but the most seditious instrument that ever was penned and very little short of treason both against the King and Constitution '(pp. 96–97). The views expressed in this tract have a special interest, since Perceval had been an ardent opponent of Walpole and had supported an inquiry into the late administration, a course which was insisted upon in the instructions of 1742. Cf. Lecky, *History of England in the Eighteenth Century*, vol. i, p. 467.

[2] *The Voice of the People*, 1756; 25 *London Magazine, passim*. For instructions regarding the Jews Naturalization Act, 1753, see 23 *Gentleman's Magazine*, pp. 467 ff., and 22 *London Magazine, passim*.

[3] *Instructions given to Sir Robert Ladbroke, &c.*, 1769; 3 *Political Register*, p. 101; 4 *Political Register*, pp. 65 ff., 191–2.

[4] Cf. Burke's *Correspondence*, vol. i, p. 181.

Extreme Radicals continued to court and obey instructions; and an example of their attitude is provided by John Jebb, who drew up the following declaration for the use of candidates at the Westminster election of 1782: 'I do declare upon my honour that I will either act in conformity to their instructions or embrace the first opportunity of resigning my seat.' But, in the early nineteenth century, the Whigs were as much opposed to these notions as the Tories. Romilly, for instance, though an advocate of parliamentary reform, refused to bind himself to support it; and other Whig members studiously and openly repudiated liability to follow the views of their constituents. Even philosophical Radicals, like James Mill and John Stuart Mill, argued in favour of the necessity of the representative retaining full freedom to act in any circumstances as he might deem proper.

The common failure to discriminate between the two classes of instructions to members, which have been discussed in this and the preceding section, may to some extent be explained by the repetition of instructions to newly elected members which were first given in the periods between elections; but the very real difference between the two is worth emphasizing. The position of a member who undertakes on his election to accept his commission on certain principles is distinguishable from that of a member who is expected to obey the orders of his constituents from time to time on various questions as they arise during the period of his membership. In so far as the subject of the present study is concerned, the former class is important as marking a stage in the development of the constitutional position of the people as a whole; whereas the interest of the latter is more confined to a history of the relations of the member and his constituents, to which further consideration must be given in the remainder of this chapter.

§ 3. *National representation*

Credit has chiefly been allowed to Burke as the originator of the doctrine that a member of Parliament, when elected, represents, not his constituents, but the whole community. His insistence on the dangers of treating a representative as a mere delegate, expressed in his *Speech at the Conclusion of the Poll*,[1] has been quoted hundreds of times. Every one knows

[1] *Works* (1826 ed.), vol. iii, p. 19. See also his distinction between 'individual

that Burke, in this speech, condemned the use of 'authoritative instructions, mandates issued, which the member is bound implicity to obey', and that, in arguing for national as opposed to local representation, he observed: 'You choose a member indeed; but, when you have chosen him, he is not a member of Bristol, but he is a member of Parliament.'

The principle of national representation was a frequent factor in the arguments against the admissibility of the class of instructions which have just been mentioned; and, for this and other reasons, it will be well to obtain some idea how it developed.

Mr. Porritt, in his *Unreformed House of Commons*,[1] says that 'the idea expressed by Burke was not new. It had, he noticed, been put forward in Parliament as early as 1745 by Sir William Yonge, in a speech in opposition to annual Parliaments. But it can, in fact, be traced back more than a century farther, at least as far as Coke's *Fourth Part of the Institutes of the Laws of England*, which was written before 1630. Coke remarked, in his first chapter, that 'though one be chosen for one particular county or borough, yet when he is returned, and sits in Parliament, he serveth for the whole realm, for the end of his coming thither, as in the writ of his election appeareth, is general'. It is not easy to appreciate Coke's object in making this observation; but he may have been more concerned in magnifying the function of the member than in opposing claims of constituencies to control those whom they elected.

Towards the end of the seventeenth century the principle is again asserted by Algernon Sidney, in his *Discourses concerning Government*, which were first printed in 1698, but which were written a few years earlier.[2] 'It is not', he said, 'for Kent or Sussex, Lewis or Maidstone, but for the whole nation, that the members chosen in those places are sent to serve in Parliament'; and, though they might listen to the opinions of their electors, they were responsible to the nation alone.

It is tolerably clear that Burke's expresssion of opinion on this matter owes something to Sidney's statement, in form as well as in matter. Sidney's views, which might have been expected to favour the rights of constituents, resemble those of a more orthodox person, namely Edward Chamberlayne,

representation' and 'equal representation', made in 1784. *Speeches*, vol. iii, pp. 43–54.
[1] Vol. i, p. 271.   [2] 1698 edition, p. 451.

the author of *Angliae Notitia*, the Whitaker's *Almanack* of the
day. The number for 1679 and some subsequent numbers
of this handbook contain remarks on national representation.
Chamberlayne, while he regarded the members as each
representing the whole kingdom, admitted that they should
pay special attention to the needs of the constituencies by
which they were elected.[1]

The same principle is advanced from time to time through
the eighteenth century, in such periodicals as the *Freeholders'
Journal*,[2] and *The Craftsman*,[3] and also in speeches in Parliament by, for instance, Sir William Wyndham in 1733,[4] and
Sir William Yonge in 1734 and 1745.[5] It was also mentioned
by Charles James Fox in 1797. When speaking on Grey's
motion for a Reform in the Representation, Fox admitted
that, on the question of instructions, he leaned to the opinion,
that, having to legislate for the Empire, members ought not
to be altogether guided by instructions that may be dictated
by local interests. And later in the same year, having observed that it was popularly held that a member should consider himself as the representative of the people at large, he
acknowledged the impropriety of members complying with
the wishes of their constituents, if that action should result
in the prejudice of the whole nation.[6]

A century ago Brougham, in his treatise on the Constitution, pointed out that a member 'represents the people of
the whole community'; but works on Constitutional Law do
not nowadays enlarge on this doctrine. The prevalent tendency for constituencies to press their members to advocate
local interests was in a large measure responsible for the repeated insistence on national representation. Now that the
member of Parliament is much less concerned than he was
with legislation of a local character, the need for emphasiz-

---

[1] 1679 edition, Part II, p. 55. His remarks respecting attention to local
requirements were omitted in the number for 1723 and subsequent numbers.
 Charles Davenant, the political economist, while maintaining, in or about
1704 (*Essays upon Peace at Home and War Abroad, Political and Commercial Works*
(1771 ed.), vol. iv, pp. 267 ff.) that constituents have a right to give instructions
to their members, added the qualification that 'these are not such dictates, as
their members must not depart from', since political representation was
national and not merely local.   [2] 7 Mar. 1722.
[3] No. 350, Mar. 1733. The principle was also relied upon in the famous tract
by John Perceval, entitled *Faction detected by the Evidence of Facts* (1743), 2nd
ed., p. 101, and in earlier tracts, e.g. *The Freeholder's Plea against Stock-jobbing
Elections of Parliament-Men* (1701) [by Daniel Defoe].   [4] 8 *Parl. Hist.* 1210.
[5] 9 *Parl. Hist.* 450; 13 *Parl. Hist.* 1078. Yonge, in 1734, described the principle
as not 'altogether new'.   [6] 33 *Parl. Hist.* 728, 1111.

ing the principle is correspondingly reduced. But the subject may regain prominence, in the event of sectional interests being more generally promoted by members.

Although the principle of national representation was chiefly used to counteract an undue attention to the local aspect of a member's functions, its admission must have contributed to the increase in the control of the people as a whole over national policy, which is discussed in later chapters. It has already been remarked that the obligations of individual members arising as a result of separate pledges to their constituencies developed into the obligations of Parliament by reason of the separate pledges becoming general ones of a uniform character. The influence of the principle of national representation operated in a different way. It helped to establish that the obligations of members were due, not merely to separate constituencies, but to the people as a whole.

§ 4. *Obligations of Members to constituents*

Relations between members and their constituents cannot, as such, come under the jurisdiction of the Courts of Law. There are, however, occasions when the position of a member in regard to a political association may raise questions of legality. If bodies of constituents should propose to bind their members contractually to act from time to time as directed by them or their nominees, it is probable that such an arrangement would be unenforceable. There have been instances of attempts by trade unions (who occupy, for some purposes, the position of political associations) to bind members paid by them to vote as directed by the Labour party organization. If a contract of this character is illegal, similarly a contract to the same effect between other associations of persons and members of Parliament would also be illegal.

The maintenance of the freedom of action which is inherent in the position of a parliamentary representative was treated incidentally in a leading case on the law respecting trade unions, *The Amalgamated Society of Railway Servants* v. *Osborne*.[1] A trade union made it part of its arrangement with candidates whom it adopted and financed that they 'must sign and accept the conditions of the Labour Party and be subject to their whip'. In other words, the members of Parliament

[1] [1910] A.C. 87.

promoted by the trade union in question had to undertake to enter into a contract to do what they were told in their capacity as representatives. They had to give a pledge to follow instructions. Lord Shaw, in his judgement in the House of Lords, regarded this arrangement as illegal. He said that a member of Parliament

is not to be the paid mandatory of any man, or organization of men, nor is he entitled to bind himself to subordinate his opinions on public questions to others, for wages, or at the peril of pecuniary loss; and any contract of this character would not be recognized by a Court of Law, either for its enforcement or in respect of its breach.

Obiter dicta of some of the judges in the *Osborne* case indicate the extent of the danger to constitutional propriety which might follow if the essential freedom of action of a representative is unduly restrained as a result of pecuniary considerations. Lord Shaw, who dealt more vigorously than any of the other judges with this aspect of the case, pointed out that the use of capital funds of trusts and other organizations to procure the subjection of members of Parliament would imperil the whole prospects of parliamentary government.

Besides questions of legality, members of Parliament have from time to time been faced with moral problems when they have deviated from their party allegiance. Constituencies, though they no longer wish to treat their members as proxies, retain a close interest in the votes and speeches of their representatives in the House of Commons. A change of circumstances in politics during the period of a Parliament may bring the views of a member and his constituents into collision; or a member may indulge in a political volte-face without any external provocation. In the course of the last century or more, he has often had to consider whether he was under a moral obligation to resign his seat, and possibly to seek re-election.

Wilberforce, speaking in the House of Commons in 1802, asserted that representatives should agree with constituents in the great principles of political conduct and in the general line to be pursued in any given conjuncture of affairs, but that the constituents ought not too scrupulously to look for an exact coincidence in every individual vote, and on every particular question;[1] and Canning, in an address given to his

---

[1] Cobbett, *Political Register*, 1802, vol. ii, p. 1617.

constituents at Liverpool at the election of 1812, reviewed
the whole problem so fairly that, after more than a century,
there seems little in his remarks that the most conscientious
candidate of the present day could wish to amend.[1]

It may happen [he said] that your own judgement may
occasionally come in conflict with my own . . . In all such cases,
I promise you not indeed wholly to submit my judgement to
yours; . . . but I promise you that any difference of opinion
between us will always lead me to distrust my own views, carefully to examine, and, if erroneous, frankly to correct them.

And he added that,

if, unfortunately, occasions should occur . . . on which there
should arise between us, on points of serious importance, a radical
and irreconcilable difference of opinion, I will not abuse my
trust, but will give you the earliest opportunity of recalling or
reconsidering your delegation of it.

A convention has grown up, though it is not altogether of a
rigid character, for members to retire or to seek re-election,
if they change their party allegiance or their view regarding
some vital political issue. As regards change of party, it may
be noticed that the representative in this country is more in
the position of a delegate than in, say, France, where it is
easy to move from one political group to another without
disturbing the relations between deputy and constituency.
This difference is, of course, largely attributable to the existence in continental countries of many small parties of different shades of political colour.

Even in the eighteenth century, conscientious scruples
occasionally led members to resign their seats on altering
their political tenets. Wedderburn, who was elected to represent Richmond in Yorkshire as a Tory in 1768, felt himself
in honour bound to resign his seat in 1769, on going over
to the popular side and espousing the cause of Wilkes. But
the first person of eminence to resign his seat after altering
his attitude on a subject of prime importance was Peel,
who yielded up his place as member for the University
of Oxford at the time of his conversion to the need of concession to the Roman Catholics. He was aware that his
constituents were, as a whole, hostile to concession at the
time they elected him; and he regarded himself as pledged
to them to oppose a relief measure. He did not succeed in

[1] *Speeches*, vol. vi, pp. 326-7.

obtaining re-election at Oxford University, but immediately gained a seat elsewhere.

Peel's resignation was criticized by his friend Croker as 'a democratical and unconstitutional proceeding, and a precedent dangerous to the independence of the House of Commons'; but it was Croker who, in the Reform election of two years later, pressed Peel to pledge himself against Reform.[1] It was certainly unusual for members, other than those of a Radical tendency, to act, prior to 1832, as if bound by pledges to their constituents; and Peel, when afterwards reviewing his behaviour of 1829, said that he vacated his seat 'upon the impulse of private feelings, rather than upon a dispassionate consideration of the constitutional relation between a representative and his constituents'. He even suggested that his example was not one which ought to be regarded as a precedent.[2] It was, in fact, followed in 1833 by Sir J. Hobhouse, Chief Secretary for Ireland, who considered himself under an obligation, by reason of his election declarations, to oppose taxes which the Liberal Government were about to introduce. Hobhouse resigned and sought re-election in the same constituency. His high moral sense did not, however, obtain immediate recognition, since he was not re-elected. Another example of conscience enforcing resignation was that of Lord Ashley (afterwards the Earl of Shaftesbury) in 1846. Ashley regarded himself as having been elected as a protectionist. He was converted in 1844 to the principles of free trade. Although, as he said, 'no pledges were given or asked', he felt that there was an 'honourable understanding'. Resignation was particularly galling to him because it disabled him at a very late stage from the conduct of his Ten Hours Bill.[3]

This problem in the relations between constituencies and members has presented itself on many occasions in recent years. At the outbreak of the South African War in 1899, a few Conservative members took a view opposed to hostilities. In one or two instances suggestions of resignation by local associations were ignored. In the instance of Sir Edward Clarke, however, a definite request was complied with. On other occasions, members, who have crossed the floor of the House without seeking re-election, have been refused renomination by their local associations. One of the best re-

[1] *Croker Papers*, vol. ii, pp. 7 and 101.   [2] *Memoirs*, vol. i, pp. 311–12.
[3] E. Hodder, *Life and Work of the Seventh Earl of Shaftesbury*, vol. ii, p. 127.

membered instances of a change of party allegiance without resignation was that of Winston Churchill in 1904. In the spring of that year he declared himself to be an opponent of the Conservative party, since he was unable to obtain assurances satisfactory to him respecting the adoption of tariff reform; and his adherence to the principles of free trade led him to decide to attach himself to the Liberal Opposition. He recognized, as he stated in the House of Commons, that his constituents were entitled to be consulted in regard to his change of allegiance. If they desired him to resign and submit himself for re-election, they had only to call upon him to do so. But he desisted from disorganizing the local party association in view of the probable imminence of a general election.[1] As matters proved, however, the dissolution of Parliament did not occur until twenty months later.

There have been other occasions on which seats have been retained by members whose change of party has happened late in the life of a Parliament. In this situation, it may well be that the general understanding shall not apply, without any implication that the election of a member is for the whole of the ensuing Parliament regardless of his deviation from his political professions.

The course to be adopted by a member who goes into Opposition is made particularly difficult when his defection is due to the adoption by the Ministry of an entirely new policy which has never been in issue at a general election. He has, in these circumstances, some justification for arguing that the Ministry should go to the country and not the member, and that, if the Ministry has changed its main tenets, he at least should be allowed to retain the principles which he held when he last submitted himself for election. This was the attitude taken up by Joseph Chamberlain, when he broke away from Gladstone on the question of Home Rule in 1886. 'It is you who have changed, not I', he said, thereby implying that Gladstone's sudden conversion to a full programme of Home Rule, which only became generally known after the election of 1885, excused his leaving Gladstone's Ministry and going into Opposition. The question of his resigning his seat did not arise. He explained his position to his constituents immediately after parting with Gladstone; and they expressed their confidence in him. Indeed, he retained their confidence throughout his political transformation

[1] 132 *Parl. Deb.*, 4 s., 1023.

from a Radical to a Radical Unionist and from a Radical Unionist to a Conservative. Birmingham, in fact, always voted for Chamberlain as a 'Chamberlainite'.

In February 1931 Sir Oswald Mosley and five other members of the Labour party broke away and formed a 'New Party'. Although their withdrawal was strongly condemned in their constituencies, they did not consider it incumbent on them to resign their seats in Parliament.

If a dissolution of Parliament had not quickly followed, the problem would have had its most notable illustration in August 1931, when Ramsay MacDonald, who as leader of the Labour party had been Prime Minister, ceased to lead that party and formed a Joint or Coalition Ministry, the Labour party being in Opposition. His colleague, J. H. Thomas, stood by him. The view was expressed in local party meetings in the constituencies of the two Ministers that their action in breaking their party allegiance and in becoming members of the new Government necessitated the resignation of their seats. Both MacDonald and Thomas refused to take this course until the emergency in which the country was placed permitted it. Within a few weeks, however, they were re-elected at the general election.

The circumstances in which members change their party allegiances and political views admit of so many variations that it is impossible to discover any clear-cut rules of obligation. On the one hand, it is possible to agree with Macaulay that it is absurd to exact 'daily and hourly obedience'; and, on the other hand, it is indisputable that members cannot claim complete freedom of action regardless of their pledges on broad issues, which are the basis of the people's capacity to exercise a general control over changes in the policy of government. It must be remembered, however, that, owing to the ability of Ministries to remain in office for several years, during which many fresh political questions are bound to present themselves, and owing to the growing complexity of political issues, the ties of representation always tend to become more and more ineffective as the period of the legislature's life advances.[1] It has been truly said that any representation, which is not very transient, must necessarily imply a large element of licence.

[1] Cf. pp. 305–6 below.

CHAPTER III

PUBLIC OPINION AND GOVERNMENT

§ 1. *Early Stages*

TAXATION and other accompaniments of a war policy played an outstanding part in the early relations of constituents and members; and they were also productive of the first symptoms of the effective operation of public opinion. This is very natural: the type of citizen whose political interests are not primarily, or at any rate closely, concerned with his purse and his immediate convenience has yet to be discovered.

At the end of the reign of Queen Elizabeth I the popular feeling against the high scale of taxation and, in particular, against the 'enormous abuse of monopolies' expressed itself in an unmistakable way; but general interest, even in a matter so intimately affecting domestic politics, was regarded by those in authority as inappropriate. Robert Cecil complained in the House of Commons that 'parliament matters are ordinary talk in the streets!'[1] Elizabeth, however, seems to have had some regard for popular prejudices when she decided to adopt a conciliatory attitude respecting monopolies.

It is very easy to be misled into exaggerating the activity of public opinion at this stage. An eighteenth-century periodical, *Common Sense*,[2] had some remarks on the influence of public opinion in the time of Elizabeth, which illustrate the distorted impressions that were then current regarding those palmy days.

Queen Elizabeth's Ministers [it was said], before any new measure was taken, used to feel the People's pulse upon it, by causing a report to be spread, that such a thing was in agitation. If they found it well received, it was put in execution; if not, it was dropt. It was by these honest and laudable wiles that she grew so popular while she lived, and her memory has been so revered ever since.

A student of the period would, it seems, be hard put to it to discover much evidence in support of this happy phase in politics.

[1] Hayward Townshend (Heywood Townsend), *Historical Collections*, p. 251.
[2] 3 July 1738.

The people's interest took a fresh turn during the early Stuart period. The sublime disregard shown by Charles I, not only of his subjects' liberties, but also of their growing concern with public affairs, acted as a strong stimulus to a more intensified and enlightened public opinion. The struggle between King and Parliament on matters of prerogative which affected the rights of the people served to sharpen their powers of criticism and political insight. But the views of Charles I regarding the people's place in relation to government were inflexible. His speech on the scaffold, in which he asserted his respect for the people's liberty and freedom and, in the same breath, denied to them any 'share in government', proved him to be pitifully steadfast in his doctrinaire attitude.

It cannot be said that public opinion gained in efficacy during the period of the Commonwealth, though its subsequent development must to some extent be attributed to a reaction against Cromwell's autocracy, which certainly helped to prevent a repetition of the use of Parliament in wanton opposition to popular convictions.

Immediately after the Restoration public opinion exhibited some signs of returning vitality; and the evident and widespread desire for the disbandment of the army was, in the main, satisfied. Charles II's endeavours to rule without Parliament did not enable him to neglect the popular attitude towards such subjects as concessions to Roman Catholics. But he had no real sympathy with the people's political interests; and it must have been mortifying to him that his quarrel with Shaftesbury led to the latter's exploitation of the people as a power in politics by various novel devices.[1]

Soon after his dismissal Shaftesbury, in one of his political tracts,[2] gave an exaggerated picture of the people's capacity in regard to matters of government.

You have [he observed] in our English government the House of Commons affording the sense, the mind, the information, the complaints, the grievances, and the desires of all those people for whom they serve, throughout the whole nation. The people are thus secure, no laws can be made, no money given, but what themselves, though at home, fully consent and agree to.

This is a typical instance of the unreliability of passages dealing with the distribution of power in the State, which

---

[1] Cf. p. 15 above and p. 75 below.
[2] *Two Seasonable Discourses concerning the present Parliament*, 1675.

have been included in political tracts for the purpose of securing party ends. Bolingbroke, some few years later, wrote of the days of Charles II as more enlightened than the period of his mournful exclusion from politics. In the former period, he said, the character of Parliament was determined by the disposition of the people, and the actions of Parliament were always in consonance with 'the declared sense of the nation'.[1] But Bolingbroke, the disappointed man, had good reason for posing as *laudator temporis acti*.

Signs of the growth of the efficacy of public opinion were not regarded with complacency by the Ministries of Charles II. Immediately after the Restoration statutes were passed to prohibit tumultuous petitioning, and to disqualify persons who incited the people to hatred or dislike of the person of His Majesty or the established government.[2] The press became subject to a rigorous regulation and censorship. Later in the reign, a succession of proclamations were issued with the object of curbing free discussion of politics.[3] A proclamation of 1672 declared that

men have assumed to themselves a liberty, not onely in coffeehouses, but in other places and meetings, both public and private, to censure and defame the proceedings of State, by speaking evil of things they understand not, and endeavouring to create and nourish an universal jealousie and dissatisfaction in the minds of all His Majesties good subjects.

The publication of false news and the intermeddling with 'the affairs of State and government' were sternly prohibited. A similar proclamation appeared in 1674. And, in 1675, coffee-houses were suppressed by proclamation, because they were regarded as hot-beds of political unrest. It was stated in the proclamation that, as a result of meetings in coffeehouses, 'divers false, malitious and scandalous reports are devised and spread abroad, to the defamation of His Majesties Government, and to the disturbance of the peace and quiet of the realm'.

The neglect of popular aspirations in the sphere of politics by Charles II and James II did not sever the attachment of the people to the Stuart dynasty. In so far as it is possible to gauge the forces of public opinion, there is no reasonable

---

[1] *Dissertation upon Parties*, Letter 4.
[2] 13 Chas. II, c. 5; 13 Chas. II, c. 1, s. 2.
[3] References to these proclamations may be found in *A Bibliography of Royal Proclamations of the Tudor and Stuart Sovereigns* (Oxford 1910), vol. i.

doubt that, if a plebiscite had been taken in 1688 on the question of the substitution of William for James, the majority would have voted against the deposition of the latter. The Revolution was, as is often explained, not democratic; it was not the expression of public opinion; its drift was in the direction of a replacement of the absolutism of a king by a 'Venetian oligarchy' supported by the aristocrats. But the new régime of 1688 could hardly afford to neglect the obvious requirement of the mass of the people for a reasonable amount of freedom. The abolition of the unpopular hearth-tax in the first year of the Revolution must have been designed to conciliate the public; the Bill of Rights preserved the people's right of petitioning; and the press became emancipated from it censorship in 1695.

The turmoils of the years that followed gave public opinion full scope; and its exercise must have been effective in the reigns of William III and Queen Anne, since politicians began to find it worth their while to employ it in support of their designs. Harley was one of the first to realize the advantages of engaging the people on his side, and for this purpose he attached to his interest pamphleteers, like Swift and Defoe. It was becoming important, if not to instruct, at least to nurse and court public opinion. Ministers could easily realize this at a time when their identification with the Government was becoming more obvious and when the Sovereign's position was growing more detached. Walpole, in his early stages as a party leader, himself wrote political pamphlets, the first of which appeared in 1710, the year in which Swift effectively managed *The Examiner*. And there was a sudden increase in the issue of political periodicals in the reign of Queen Anne. Papers like *The Observator* edited by Tutchin, and Defoe's *Review*, biased though they were, doubtless helped to spread interest in political doings.[1]

As the pamphleteers became bolder, so the Ministry, towards the end of the reign of Queen Anne, proved itself indisposed to suffer free criticism. The press was subjected to a serious handicap by reason of the imposition of the newspaper stamp-duty, a duty which was later increased in amount and which was not removed, as will be noticed,[2] until 1855. In 1712 the majority in the House of Commons was so exasperated at the publication of a pamphlet reflecting on

---

[1] After 1712 the distinction between newspapers proper and political periodicals was less marked than before.   [2] See p. 62 below.

the proceedings of the House, that it resolved 'that the great liberty taken in printing and publishing scandalous and impious libels creates divisions among her Majesty's subjects, tends to the disturbance of the public peace, is highly prejudicial to her Majesty's Government, and is occasioned for want of due regulating the Press'.[1] But, instead of passing a statute to this end, it was thought that a 'more effectual way', would be to impose a duty on all newspapers and pamphlets. This duty was accordingly imposed by a section[2] included in a long statute concerned with duties on soap, silks, calicoes, &c. In consequence, the sale of pamphlets and periodicals was adversely affected.

As the century progressed, however, Ministers did not neglect to pay attention to the support of a Government press to combat the political tracts and periodicals of the Opposition. Walpole, when at the head of the Ministry, was active in this respect. He himself continued to compose political tracts. He wrote one, for instance, in defence of the Excise Scheme.[3] Government money was freely spent in subsidizing *The Free Briton*.[4] Later in the century Lord North used the *False Alarm* to bolster up the Ministerial policy; and even the autocratic tendencies of George III did not prevent his seeing the importance of securing the support of public opinion. He employed pamphleteers, like John Shebbeare and James Macpherson, to popularize a defence of the justice of the war with America.

But the proportion of the population touched by these methods cannot have been large. In Queen Anne's reign an official estimate of the circulation of all the principal newspapers was only forty-four thousand.[5] The circulation of the best-known political periodical of its day, *The Craftsman*, never seems to have risen above ten thousand. It must be remembered, however, that every copy was probably read by many persons.

§ 2. *The people inadequately informed*

Very little encouragement was given to the exercise of public opinion by the spread of authentic information regarding the course of politics. The official publication of 'votes',

---

[1] 4 *Chandler's Debates*, pp. 296, 297, 300.   [2] 10 Anne, c. 19, s. 101.
[3] *A letter from a member of Parliament to his Friend in the Country concerning the Duties on Wine and Tobacco* (1733).
[4] *Calendar of Treasury Books and Papers, 1731–4*, p. 581 and *passim*.
[5] *Calendar of Treasury Papers, 1708–14*, p. 235.

that is to say the determinations reached in proceedings in
Parliament, was to a limited extent in vogue between 1641
and 1681; but it was only in the latter year that a general
resolution was passed authorizing their publication. The
comment of Sir Leoline Jenkins on the occasion of this resolution expressed what must have been the attitude of other
members besides himself for some years to come. 'Consider',
he said, 'the gravity of this assembly. There is no great
assembly in Christendom that does it [publishes 'votes']. It
is against the gravity of this assembly, and it is a sort of appeal
to the people.' On the other hand, those in favour of publication argued that such a course 'is like true Englishmen, who
are not ashamed of what they do'; and that it was 'not
natural, nor rational, that the people who sent us hither
should not be informed of our actions'.[1]

The objection to publishing information on the ground that
it might imply an 'appeal to the people' recurred in succeeding
years. There was some dissension between the two Houses of
Parliament in the session of 1702–3 respecting public accounts
and respecting the Occasional Conformity Bill. The Commons adopted a motion that the votes of the House should
not be printed; and signs of disapproval were shown in
the country. The Lords, on the other hand, made a bid
for popularity and ordered their proceedings to be printed
forthwith. Whereupon the Commons, not to be outdone,
resolved to publish their proceedings likewise. Some of the
members of the House of Lords entered a formal protest
against publication, in which they asserted that the publication of proceedings would amount to 'an appealing to the
people', and would imply that the people had a right to
exercise judgement over Parliament.[2]

A distinction must be drawn between the publication of
'votes' and the publication of debates in Parliament. Although very summary reports or outlines of proceedings had
been published during the Commonwealth period, under
the title of *The Diurnall or The Heads of all the Proceedings in
Parliament* and similar titles, all reporting was forbidden at
the Restoration; and, for some years, it was only by means of
occasional illicit news-letters that the substance of the debates

[1] 4 *Parl. Hist.* 1306 ff.; *Report of the Select Committee on the Publication of Printed
Papers*, 1837.
[2] 6 *Parl. Hist.* 135; *The History of the Reign of Queen Anne digested into Annals,
Year the First* (Boyer), p. 222; *Protests of the Lords from 1624 to 1874* (ed. J. E. T.
Rogers), vol. i, p. 168.

in Parliament could be known to the outer world. Publication of debates was declared a breach of privilege in 1722; and the subject was again discussed in 1738, when the protest made by Pulteney included the same arguments as those which have just been quoted. He objected to a practice which would, as he alleged, involve appeals to the people regarding matters discussed in Parliament. In his contention publication of debates would have made members accountable 'without doors' for what they said within the House. Walpole and others based their opposition to publication chiefly on the alleged misleading character of the reports which usually appeared. Sir William Wyndham, on the other hand, said that a consideration which weighed heavily with him was the 'prejudice which the public will think they sustain, by being deprived of all knowledge of what passes in this House, otherwise than by the printed votes, which are very lame and imperfect'. He went farther, and suggested that the people might have a right to know somewhat more of the proceedings of the House than what appeared upon the votes. Publication of reports of debates was, however, declared 'a high indignity to and a notorious breach of the privilege of this House', which would proceed 'with the utmost severity against offenders'.[1]

The people were not so to be kept in the dark respecting the doings of Parliament. Imperfect reports of debates had appeared spasmodically in the seventeenth century[2] and with some regularity in Boyer's *Political State of Great Britain*, a publication which began in 1711. The *Gentleman's Magazine*, in 1731, and the *London Magazine*, soon after, published fairly full reports. The speakers were for some years given disguised names; but their identity was obvious to everyone. After the great quarrel over the privilege of the House of Commons in 1771 no further trouble was taken to maintain pseudonyms; and the breach of privilege was committed with impunity.

§ 3. *Walpole and the Pelhams*

(a) *Excise Scheme*

The eighteenth century did not progress very far before Ministers discovered that information on matters of vital

---

[1] 10 *Parl. Hist.* 800–12.

[2] The substance of debates on particular subjects was reproduced in tracts in 1681, and individual speeches were published before that date.

interest to the people travelled fast enought to prevent their acting in complete opposition to public opinion. When the people's pockets were affected or their patriotism aroused, they were particularly ready to make their wishes understood.[1]

Walpole's attention to any such symptoms was, it may be supposed, largely attributable to expediency. Lecky said that Walpole's withdrawal of Wood's halfpence, when they had excited the opposition of the Irish people, and his abandonment of the project of excise are examples of his constant respect for the wishes of the people. His leading principle was undoubtedly the avoidance of friction and dissension. But it is at least doubtful whether the wishes of the people were a primary factor, as is sometimes assumed, in his decision to withdraw his famous Excise Scheme in 1733.[2]

The violent antagonism which the Scheme aroused was to a large degree due to the intrigues of Walpole's enemies. They did not, it seems, imagine that the opinions of the public alone would deter Walpole from proceeding with his proposals; but they hoped that a sufficient number of his supporters in the House of Commons could be induced to desert him through fear of defeat at the general election which was due in the following year. In order to work upon the susceptibilities of members whose allegiance was insecure, they organized a campaign with the object of inspiring the public with apprehensions at the financial mischiefs which the Scheme would involve. And the divisions in the House, which pointed to the probability of progressive decreases in and even the disappearance of the majority of the Government, must have suggested that their hopes might well be realized.

In so far as the question of intimidation is concerned, Walpole could not fail to realize the risks of maltreatment by the crowd, which hustled and threatened him on more than one occasion during the period of the debates on the subject. But he was far from suffering from cowardly instincts; and it is not likely that direct threats of violence had much effect on him.[3] The possibility of his being actuated in his decision

---

[1] The recurrent apathy of the people towards political issues during the eighteenth century is mentioned on pp. 182-3 below.

[2] Cf. 42 *E.H.R.*, pp. 34 ff., an article by Raymond Turner.

[3] It is true that, in Feb. 1732, Walpole asserted, during a debate on the question of the revival of the Salt Tax, that, 'if there were any danger that the reviving of this tax would occasion murmuring among the people, I should be

by the demonstrations of the London mob at the time when
the Scheme was first introduced in Parliament may be discounted by reading his remarks in his speech on 14 March
1733. Sir William Wyndham had expressed surprise that the
Scheme had been introduced 'so much to the dislike and
dissatisfaction of the people in general' and had characterized
the proposal, after 'so many remonstrances against it', as
'most audacious' and 'in a manner flying in the face of the
whole people of England'. Walpole's reply to these denuncia-
tions is of importance in proving his knowledge of the lack
of spontaneity in the demonstrations against the Scheme,
especially those in London.

> As to these clamours [he said] which have been raised without
> doors, and which are now so much insisted upon, it is very well
> known by whom and by what methods they were raised, and it is
> no difficult matter to guess with what views; but I am very far
> from taking them to be the sense of the nation, or believing that
> the sentiments of the generality of the people were thereby
> expressed.[1]

And he informed the House that he was well aware of the
means by which the demonstrators had been induced to
collect at Westminster.

As regards the demonstrations emanating from the pro-
vinces, most of these seem to have been launched before the
speech, of which an extract has just been quoted, was made.
It is unlikely that there were a sufficient number of additional protests from the country, between the time of this
speech and the time of the decision to withdraw the Scheme,
materially to change Walpole's opinion regarding their
weight. The extent of the volume of protest from the pro-
vinces may be judged from one or two tracts composed
of letters of request to members of Parliament from constituencies, trading bodies, and others. It is clear that the
Opposition used every effort to collect all possible evidence
of antagonism to the Scheme. The tract with the largest
number of protests[2] was evidently published before the

---

as much against it as any man in this House'; 8 *Parl. Hist.* 969. But Walpole
must have realized, like any other statesman, that it is sometimes necessary to
carry through financial measures which are not popular, in the interest of the
nation.

[1] 8 *Parl. Hist.* 1305–6.

[2] *Excise: Being a Collection of Letters &c. containing the Sentiments and Instructions
of the Merchants, Traders, Gentry and Inhabitants of the principal Cities, Counties,
and Boroughs &c.* (1733). Cf. *A Collection of Letters from several Counties, Cities and
Boroughs containing Instructions to their Representatives in Parliament, &c.* (1733).

above-quoted speech was made. The list of constituencies
is not imposing. Only one county is mentioned; and only
some two dozen other constituencies seem to have sent official
requests to their members to oppose the Scheme. Similar
tracts, published in 1741, contain much more weighty lists
of constituencies, including many counties. Still, it must be
remembered that the City of London protested officially;
and this protest may well have had some influence on Walpole's decision.

There are, however, one or two circumstances which lend
some support to the view that Walpole was affected by the
popular agitation to a greater extent than by the unpromising
situation in the House of Commons; but, when they are
examined, they do not appear to be altogether convincing.

After a debate on the question of hearing arguments in
support of the petition of the City of London, Walpole only
narrowly escaped defeat. He had by that time privately
decided to drop the Bill; and he insisted that this decision
should not be made public until the hearing of the petition
was rejected. The reason given by him for this course was
his anxiety not to be 'seeming to yield . . . at the instigation
of the City'. If such were thought to be his attitude, there
would probably have followed more violent and effective
methods of agitation by this powerful body whenever any
future legislative project antagonized sections of the people.[1]
But the fact that Walpole displayed anxiety to avoid the
inference that he was actuated by public opinion does not
make it certain that the presssure of public opinion was the
main motive for his conduct.

Walpole is recounted by Coxe, his biographer, to have
explained to some of his friends that his action was guided
by the consideration that, 'in the present inflamed temper
of the people, the Act could not be carried into execution
without an armed force; and there will be an end of the liberty
of England if supplies are to be raised by the sword'.[2] Doubt
has been thrown on the genuineness of this story; but, even
if the story is true, it does not follow that the reasons given
to a group of supporters were the ones which moved him
most. Walpole would naturally refrain, before such an audience, from putting in the forefront lack of support in Parlia-

[1] *Lord Hervey's Memoirs* (ed. Sedgwick), vol. i, pp. 134, 135, 156, 157.
[2] Coxe took the view that 'dislike of counteracting public opinion' was
Walpole's main motive; see *Memoirs of Sir Robert Walpole*, vol. i, p. 403.

ment as the reason for withdrawal of the Scheme, for, if he had, he might have found some difficulty in recovering his normal majority.

The speech in which Walpole informed the House of Commons, on 11 April 1733, of the withdrawal of the Scheme is not reported in the *Parliamentary History*; and Lord Hervey, in his *Memoirs*, merely describes it as 'very long and artful'.[1] There is, however, an account of it in the diary of the Earl of Egmont,[2] who stated that Walpole gave three reasons for withdrawing his Scheme,

first the declension of the majority which shewed itself the first day, being 61, which last night he saw reduced to 17; secondly the clamours raised against it, which though artificially stirred up, yet it was not prudent to press a thing which the nation expressed so general a dislike to, however they were deceived; and thirdly, which was with him of most moment, the apprehensions which many honest and sincere friends of the Government had entertained of danger to his Majesty's person and Government from the disaffection which they supposed this Bill, however mistaken, might create in the abused people's minds, which alone was reason sufficient to justify his parting with the Bill.

There is no ground for doubting the substantial accuracy of this account; but it may not be necessary to conclude that the second and third reasons carried more weight than the first. Moreover, it is difficult to understand how circumstances had changed sufficiently by the 11th of April to make Walpole believe that the nation had expressed 'so general a dislike' for the Scheme. On the 14th of March he had, as noticed above, informed the House that he was satisfied that the clamours did not represent the sense of the people.

The available evidence, which is not conclusive in one direction or the other, leaves the impression that the withdrawal of the Excise Scheme did not follow mainly as a result of the direct operation of public opinion, but, to a large extent, as a result of indications in the House of Commons which were themselves produced by the action of public opinion, owing to the proximity of the expiration of the period of Parliament and of the general election. The truth seems to be that Walpole changed his plans for the immediate and compelling reason that he found it impossible to carry

---

[1] *Lord Hervey's Memoirs* (ed. Sedgwick), vol. i, p. 163, and see, with regard to the Scheme generally, vol. i, pp. 132–78 of this edition.

[2] *Hist. MSS. Comm., Diary of the Earl of Egmont*, vol. i, p. 360.

them in Parliament. Public opinion, in the days when party
loyalties were unreliable, affected the action of the Ministry
rather as a result of its influence on individual members than
by means of a direct influence on the Ministry itself.

(b) Anti-Jew agitation

The failure of the Ministry to gauge the latent antipathy
towards the Jews, at the time of the passing of the Jews
Naturalization Act of 1753, displays an insensitiveness to
popular prejudices not to be expected even from eighteenth-
century politicians. The Act, harmless enough in itself, was
passed some few months before the date at which a genderm
election was due. Again the Opposition adopted the stratageal
of raising the alarm. The Act, they said, would have the
result of depriving Christians of their religion; and, on
such a subject, the people were at that time easily provoked
to anger. The merchants of London became alarmed at
imaginary commercial advantages which the Jews were to
derive from the passing of the measure. It was even suggested
that the Jews would be put in a position to oust the nobility
and gentry from their estates and property. A popular
slogan was: 'No Jews, long beards, nor whiskers!' Fierce
opposition sprung up in every corner of the land, and it became plain that even the skill of the Pelhams in the management of elections might fail to overcome the infatuation of
the voters.

The Duke of Newcastle was chiefly responsible for the
change of policy by which the Act was repealed. The pressure of a fomented popular agitation deprived him of his
ability to refuse concessions. Chesterfield described him as
being 'frightened out of his wits at the groundless and sense-
less clamour against the Jew Bill'.[1] Newcastle required all
the specious explanations he could find to maintain his dignity. The measure, he said, was not a very important one
from the point of view of national interest, and, in consequence, he saw no harm in giving way and allowing its
repeal. Pitt, who at this stage gave his support to the Newcastle Ministry, likened the Government to an indulgent
father and the people to 'a peevish, perverse boy', who insisted
'upon something that was not quite right, but of such a
nature as, when granted, could not be attended with any very
bad consequence'. The wording of one of the recitals to the

---

[1] *Chesterfield's Letters* (ed. 1845), vol. iv, p. 94.

repealing Act bears witness to the futility of the proceeding.
'Whereas occasion has been taken . . .', it said, 'to raise discontents, and to disquiet the minds of many of His Majesty's
subjects: be it enacted . . .' It is odd that the Opposition,
which had been able to engineer the repeal of the Naturalization Act, was unable, although it objected to the terms of the
recital, to insist on its omission.

The repeal of the Jews Naturalization Act may have a
rather better claim than the withdrawal of the Excise Scheme
to be included among examples of the influence of public
opinion on the course of legislation; but it is an unsatisfactory one. The expression of opinion was not spontaneous:
it was provoked by unscrupulous and alarmist politicians
for their own party purposes at a time when a poor-spirited
Ministry was under strong temptation to accede to it. This
kind of surrender in the face of party machinations hardly
enables a true measure to be taken of the growth of the
recognition of the influence of the people.

There were, however, occasions when the people required
little or no stimulus from politicians to press for the removal
of grievances. Throughout the eighteenth century the interference with proper representation, as a result of the nomination by the King or the Ministry of placemen or pensioners
to seats in the House of Commons, raised genuine feelings of
indignation among the public. For many years the Ministry
was able to flout demands for remedy. But, in the reaction
after the fall of Walpole, a Place Bill became law in 1742.
Although it was far from satisfying the demands of reformers,
it had considerable effect by excluding inferior officers of
the Crown; and the achievement, in so far as it can so be
described, was one in which the people had an intimate
share.

(c) Foreign Politics

It was not only the passing or the repeal of legislation
that became subject to the people's influence. Questions
of peace and war and efficient leadership also aroused their
interest and became subject to popular pressure. Perhaps
the best instance of a declaration of hostilities being attributable to the influence of public opinion is that of the war
with Spain, commonly known as the 'War of Jenkins' Ear'.

The trade of Great Britain with the West Indies was,
towards the end of Walpole's régime, alleged to be impeded

by the interference of the Spaniards, and in particular by their exercise of claims to search and detain British ships. A sense of aggravation among the merchant classes developed into one of indignation among the citizens of the chief ports. In 1737 and 1738 organized expressions of feeling took shape in several petitions for redress by bodies of merchants; and, in the latter year, the Opposition leaders began to realize that the growing agitation might be exploited so as to make the position of Walpole's Ministry untenable. They tried to magnify the grounds for misunderstanding between the two countries with the object of rendering impracticable an adjustment of disputes. Their efforts to inflame the passions of the people were largely successful; and stories of the Spaniards' cruelties and insults to British sailors produced a widespread demand for war.

Walpole, who saw that a war with Spain would be contrary to the best interests of the nation, was able during 1738 to avoid a conflict. But when the terms of the Convention, designed to settle outstanding differences with Spain, were published in February 1739 it was immediately complained that some of· the chief grievances were unremoved; and further petitions poured in from the City of London and the merchants of many large ports of England and Scotland.[1] A widely distributed and effective pamphlet[2] claimed that less than ten thousand out of ten million citizens approved the Convention. There can, of course, have been no means of making any such calculation open to the author, although he had a considerable reputation as a mathematician. It is certain that Walpole was only able to organize a very small number of merchants to present counter-addresses in favour of peace. But it is unlikely that the inland counties and large towns, which were not immediately interested in the West India trade, displayed any extreme anxiety in regard to the situation, unless some account is to be taken of an incipient ardour for imperialistic expansion.

In March 1739 the Government only obtained a majority of 21 (95–74) in the House of Lords and of 28 (260–232) in the House of Commons, when the Convention was discussed. Pitt, making one of his early speeches in this debate, asserted in regard to the Convention that 'the voice of

---

[1] *Journals of the House of Commons*, vol. xxiii, pp. 53–55, 94–95, 247–52, 269–75.
[2] *An Address to the Electors of Great Britain, occasioned by the late Secession* (1739) [by Benjamin Robins], p. 4.

England has condemned it'. Still Walpole made every effort
to avoid war. For many months he had stood firm against
the pressure of the public outcry; and, in the debate on the
Convention, he declared that he was resolved 'to let no
popular clamour get the better of what I think is for my
country's good'.

Only a few weeks after making this remark, however,
Walpole's Ministry decided to declare war. The decision was,
according to Coxe, greeted 'with a degree of enthusiasm
and joy, which announced the general frenzy of the nation.
Bells pealed in all churches in London . . . the stocks rose . . .'.[1]
Coxe, who naturally regarded the agitation as fomented for
sinister reasons, would hardly have wished to exaggerate the
effect which the declaration of war produced. And there can
be no doubt that, in places like London and Bristol, the enthusiasm for war among the populace was unbounded.

The question, whether or not the war was undertaken as
the direct result of the pressure of public opinion, has been a
subject of full investigation by historians; and the weighty
opinion of Professor Temperley is to the effect that 'the old
contention of Burke, that the war was unjust, that it was provoked by Opposition clamour, and was "the fruit of popular desire" appears to be true'. Walpole was undoubtedly
affected, as he was in respect of the Excise Scheme, by the
dangers of the disappearance of his majority in Parliament;
and, if he had been properly supported by his own colleagues,
he would probably have taken the same view of the people's
influence as he had on other occasions, namely, that it should
be regarded as effective indirectly, through the channels of
Parliament, and not otherwise.

But there was a new factor which affected Walpole in
regard to the Spanish War, namely, the Duke of Newcastle,
who was a member of the Ministry. As in the instance of
the 'Jews' Bill', so also in 1738 and 1739, Newcastle was
palpably afraid of the mob; and Professor Temperley has
recognized in him one of the main explanations of the surrender of the Ministry. It is, in his view, impossible to attribute the decision to declare war to a change of attitude in
regard to, say, political relations with France, since

peace appeared to be almost certain until Parliament intervened.
Newcastle's deference to Parliament and to public opinion is too
obvious; the fateful dispatch of the counter-order coincides too

[1] Coxe, *Memoirs of Sir Robert Walpole*, vol. i, p. 617.

closely with the date of the parliamentary debate on the Convention to prevent any one denying that popular and parliamentary
agitation was the main factor in causing the war.[1]

§ 4. *The elder Pitt*

The observation of Dr. Johnson, to the effect that Walpole was a Minister given by the King to the people and
that Pitt was a Minister given by the people to the King, was
broadly true.[2] Pitt's arrival at a position of supremacy marks
a further and important stage in the history of public opinion,
though, here again, there were other influences at work
besides that of the people. Newcastle (at the head of the
Government) was seriously alarmed at the possible effect of
Pitt's patriotic oratory, and he fully appreciated the risk of
his going into opposition and so bringing about the defeat
of the Ministry.

By 1755 Pitt had secured the support of the Prince of
Wales's party at Leicester House; and there was no more
potent ally in a campaign against the Court. In the summer
of that year Newcastle made feverish efforts to obtain Pitt's
adherence, since it had become obvious that, if Pitt could
rally the Opposition with the cry of a mismanaged war, the
Ministry might well fall at the opening of Parliament. He
had steadily been increasing his hold on popular sympathies;
and, as Lord Rosebery said of him in his early parliamentary
career,

although Pitt's actual words reached the people late or not at all,
there was an echo which was audible, and made known all
through the three kingdoms, that there was within the walls of
Parliament an intrepid, unbribed, perhaps incorruptible orator,
who feared the face of no man, and who was embodying in fiery
words the antipathies and distrusts of the nation.[3]

The years 1756 and 1757 saw the triumph of Pitt's ambition
and the gratification of the insistence of the people. Widespread apprehension at the disastrous turn in national affairs,
the reverses in America, the failure of military efforts on the
Continent, the loss of Minorca, and the horrors of the Black
Hole of Calcutta, which was made plain in political tracts

---

[1] *Royal Historical Society Transactions*, 3rd series, 1909, vol. iii, pp. 227–30,
234–5.
[2] Dr. Johnson qualified his remark regarding Pitt by adding the words 'as
an adjunct'.
[3] Lord Rosebery, *Chatham, His Early Life and Connections*, p. 191.

and satires and in other ways, proved that salvation was, in the view of the nation, only to be found in a vigorous Ministry with Pitt at its head.

Newcastle was not only faced with clamour in the country; he suffered a serious blow in the desertion, at the moment of crisis, of both Fox and Murray. His majority was endangered; and he decided that resignation was the only possible course. After the King had indulged in some futile negotiations in search of an alternative, Pitt reached the dominant position which he justly regarded as his due. His appointment, as Secretary of State, was greeted with universal signs of approbation. *The Monitor*, a periodical which had recently been launched with the object of opposing and exposing Court intrigue, commented on the position more boldy than most of the periodicals of the time.

The good people of England [it said] have an undoubted right to the services of the brightest statesmen: therefore His Majesty has dismissed those servants, who had neither abilities to advise, nor resolution to execute the necessary measures for the honour and safety of his Crown and dominions; and has committed the care of the nation to men, who, in his greatest wisdom are accounted the most able to add splendour and dignity to our councils at home, and to give a check to the machinations of our enemies abroad; as soon as time and opportunity shall permit.[1]

Political versifiers were unable to restrain their glee at Pitt's appointment; and many ballads appeared showing that the masses understood what Pitt's appointment meant for them. A stanza of one of these ballads, entitled *The Ministry Changed or The Clean Contrary Way*, ran as follows:

Each dire oppression now shall cease
    'neath which the people groaning lay.
Each galling grievance be redressed—
    The clean contrary way.

Newcastle had none of Walpole's intrepidity. He was naturally of a nervous temperament. Horace Walpole, whose hatred for Newcastle was extreme, remarked that 'fear, a ridiculous fear was predominant in him';[2] and, in spite of the obvious prejudice, it is easy to believe it. He was even incapable of going to bed in a room which had no other occupant than himself. It may well be, therefore, that he was to some extent influenced by a feeling that public opinion

[1] *The Monitor*, 27 Nov. 1756.
[2] *Memoirs of the Reign of George II* (ed. Holland), vol. i, p. 166.

might take an ugly shape. Although his retirement cannot be described as having been precipitated by fear of force, that element probably played a part in his decision. Lampoons and ballads on him were hung at street corners, and he was pelted by the mob. A favourite ballad-song of 1756 had the refrain: 'To the block with Newcastle and yard-arm with Byng.'[1] It was Pitt himself who, on a later occasion, told Newcastle that they would not be safe in the streets if they opposed public opinion.

Although Newcastle was influenced by popular demonstrations, his eye was, it may be suspected, steadily directed on his majority in the House of Commons. The loosely attached members of the House might, as on other occasions in the eighteenth century, suddenly decide that their interests lay with politicians outside the Ministry. If a group of them were to desert Newcastle by reason of their anxiety to conciliate their patriotic electors, the Ministerial majority would disappear. It is likely, then, that the influence of the people on the change of Ministers was indirect as well as direct.

In 1757, at the time of Pitt's dismissal and prior to his reappointment to office in the same year, popular periodicals gave expression to the general eagerness that he should remain in control of the nation's fortunes. The *London Evening Post*[2] vindicated the people's right to influence the choice of Ministers. *The Monitor*[3] published a quaint sketch of the management of the ship of State, wherein the Captain in an emergency called upon 'Will' to take the helm; and 'Will' was described as putting the ship to rights. It was then disclosed that 'the Captain loves the old clan and does not like Will . . . The old clan are desperate and are resolved, rather than fail, to toss him overboard.' In various ways, the people displayed their indignation at the intrigue which led to the removal from office of the one man who had proved himself capable of averting disaster.

Pitt's difficulties in managing Parliament were as great, if not greater, than those of Newcastle. Horace Walpole wrote, regarding Pitt's first few months of office in 1756, that he was so little provided with interest in boroughs that the new Ministry was 'almost an administration out of Parliament'.[4]

[1] *Grenville Papers*, vol. i, p. 173; Brit. Mus. 1876, f. 1 (155).
[2] *Passim.* See especially Apr. 1757.
[3] 9 Apr. 1757 and 27 Aug. 1757.
[4] *Horace Walpole's Letters* (ed. Toynbee), vol. iv, p. 16; Horace Walpole, *Memoirs of the Reign of George II* (ed. Holland), vol. ii, p. 260.

Pitt fully realized his insecurity, in attempting to rely on public opinion to counterbalance the absence of a solid following in the House of Commons; and, in his second spell of office, on returning to power after a brief and fruitless effort on the part of the King to keep himself free of his demagogic Minister, he found that he would require the adherence of Newcastle's retinue as well as the support of the people in order to enable him to maintain his position. But he lost no opportunity of taking the people into his confidence, and of appealing directly to their patriotic instincts. He used, among other means, the King's Speech as a medium, and spoke of 'relying with pleasure on the spirit and zeal of my people', and of confidence in the bravery of the nation. In 1756 he remarked to the Duke of Devonshire, the nominal head of his first Ministry, in regard to the terms of the Speech on the opening of Parliament: 'I have drawn it captivating to the people'; and he reckoned that the Speech would 'go over the whole kingdom' and have the effect of spreading satisfaction.[1] One of his principles seems to have been that 'the public must be humoured'.[2] Nevertheless there had never before been a Minister who had thus affected to take the governed into partnership with the Government.

When he resigned, in 1761, on a disagreement with his colleagues regarding the necessity of a war with Spain, Pitt told them in Cabinet Council that he had been 'called to the Ministry by the voice of the people', a remark which drew from Newcastle a curious comment: 'When he talks of being responsible to the people he talks the language of the House of Commons and forgets that at this Board he is only responsible to the King.'[3] By 'the language of the House of Commons' he presumably meant the language that Pitt had been accustomed to use in that House to the discomfiture of those, like Newcastle, who feared any intrusion of the people into the political arena.

On the occasion of Pitt's admission to office, in contrast, for instance, to the agitation about the Excise Scheme, public

---

[1] MS. Letter, 15 Nov. 1756, quoted in Torrens, *History of Cabinets*, vol. ii, p. 343. It seems that the King refused Pitt's first draft, see C. P. Yorke, *Life of Hardwicke*, vol. ii, p. 373. He complained of its length and exclaimed 'stuff and nonsense' at some of its expressions; B. Williams, *Life of Pitt*, vol. i, p. 287.

[2] *Hist. MSS. Comm.* Report on MSS. of Mrs. Stopford-Sackville, vol. i, p. 304, Lord George Sackville to Prince Ferdinand, 23 Feb. 1759.

[3] *Annual Register*, 1761, Part I, pp. 43–44.

opinion acted with spontaneity. Instigation by an organized Opposition was not a factor in the undertaking, the object of which was eminently suited to the people's capacity. They were not in the least qualified to pronounce upon intricate questions of finance, such as were involved in the Excise Scheme. But, on a matter of choosing a vigorous and conscientious statesman in a national emergency, they were able to form an opinion and, as it proved, to enforce it.

It has been seen that, in three notable instances of change of policy, the influence of public opinion began to make itself felt, namely, the instances of the War with Spain in 1739, the repeal of the 'Jews' Act', and the inclusion of Pitt in the Ministry. In each of these incidents a large part was played by the timidity of Newcastle. It is likely that, if there had stood in his place a statesman of even average firmness of character, the exploitation of the people, in the first two instances, would never have had a chance of success, and that, if a reasonably competent Minister had been in charge in 1756, the people would never have had so early an opportunity of proving that their influence over the choice of Ministers was something which had to be taken into account.

Shortly after the Earl of Chatham had recovered from his long period of infirmity he was able to reappear in the House of Lords in January 1770, and to make two memorable speeches on the state of the nation, and, in particular, on the popular rights of election. The controversies surrounding the name of Wilkes had raised such loud and persistent clamour among the people that numerous addresses were presented censuring the attitude of the House of Commons. In the earlier speech, he emphasized the claim of public opinion to be heard; and he asked which were the more deserving of respect, the people's representatives or 'the collective body of the people'. He gave his answer in favour of the latter. In the second speech, he proposed as a cure for the discrepancy between the attitude of the people and that of their representatives, not the supremacy of public opinion by the subordination of the House of Commons, but reform of the legislature. 'The Constitution', he observed, 'intended that there should be a permanent relation between the constituent and representative body of the people. Will any man affirm that, as the House of Commons is now formed, that relation is in any degree preserved?' He added, however, that it was necessary to be cautious and not to resort to violent expedients. He advised 'gentler remedies', and he suggested that, by an increase in the number of the county members, the House of Commons could more truly reflect the opinion of the people than it did. In this way he imagined that the permanent relation would be maintained. But a mere increase in the number of county members and members of other large constituencies would have gone but a short way towards rectifying the evils he condemned.

The Earl of Chatham, in the first of these two speeches, regarded the effective exercise of public opinion as a compensation for the imperfections of a narrow representation; a few days afterwards, he prescribed a reform in the representation as the best method of compensation for defects in the exercise of public opinion. The two separate needs, respect for public opinion and a reform in the representation, were, in the course of these debates, as upon other occasions in the later eighteenth century, the subject of some confusion.

§ 5. *Burke*

Every student of Burke, who is not altogether captivated by his oratorical spell, has spent some effort in trying to reconcile his various interpretations of the people's liberties. His *Thoughts on the Present Discontents* was written at the beginning of 1770, about the time of the delivery of the two speeches of Chatham of which mention has just been made. Its object was to find a remedy for the abuses of faction, intrigue, and maladministration. His chief palliatives were the publication of parliamentary proceedings, so as to increase the capacity of the people to take an effective interest in politics, and the substitution of the true principles of party for the machinations of mere cliques, two subjects which are discussed elsewhere in this book. 'The virtue, spirit, and essence of a house of commons', he said, 'consist in its being the express image of the feelings of the nation.'[1]

By March 1770, however, before this pamphlet had left the printers, the City of London had prepared a remonstrance on the ungracious answer to a petition regarding the rejection of Wilkes, after his having been returned as a member for the fourth time by the electors of Middlesex. Burke's remarks in a debate in the House of Commons on this remonstrance are

---

[1] He expressed, however, his contempt for the politics of the uninstructed. He characterized 'the opinion of the meer vulgar' as 'a miserable rule even with regard to themselves, on account of their violence and instability'.

so markedly opposed to the principles advanced in his *Discontents* that the inconsistency can only be explained by his resentment at the City alleging that the House of Commons had ceased to be representative. He poured scorn on the notion that the City should regard some agreement between the House of Commons and the people as inherent in representation.

Let the people of the City of London [he is reported as saying], who are not so well instructed as we are in the principles of law, proceed by a sort of rough, vulgar, common sense of their own upon this question. To make the parliament the only representatives of the people they think there should be some agreement between it and the people; they think there should be some attention paid to their interests. We, Sir, know that this House is just as much the representatives of the people, as if we had the greatest connexion with their opinions: but we know this, because we are enlarged in our opinions; while they are confined.[1]

Ten years later Burke may be found, in carefully prepared statements on constitutional relations, repeating his liberal sentiments. In his *Letter to the Chairman of the Bucks Meeting* he remarked: 'It would be dreadful indeed if there were any power in the nation capable of resisting its unanimous desire, or even the desire of any great and decided majority of the people.' In the same year he exhibited equal fervour, during his *Speech on the Duration of Parliaments*: 'To govern according to the sense and agreeably to the interests of the people, is a great and glorious object of government.' But he qualified these words by saying that, although the people could judge in general whether a Ministry had done its work honestly and well, 'as to the detail of particular measures, or to any general schemes of policy, they have neither enough of speculation in the closet nor of experience in business to decide upon it'.

When the younger Pitt had, in 1784, adduced, with some justification, the support of the people as a ground for the dissolution of Parliament, which had the result of removing from Burke the hopes of political advancement, Burke seems to have been tempted to change his front. (As Lord Morley said of him, he 'changed his front, but never his ground'.) He introduced an elaborate motion in a speech which was listened to by the House with ill-disguised impatience. After admitting that the sense of the people, however erroneous,

---

[1] *Cavendish Debates*, vol. i, p. 544. The report is more likely to be accurate than most reports of the period.

must govern the legislature, he contended that it was sometimes the duty of the better informed and more enlightened
part of the community to resist the sense of the people, when
it appeared that the people were deceived or misled.

In reviewing Burke's attitude it is easy, as has been suggested, to seize upon apparent inconsistencies. Cartwright,
the Radical, charged him with talking of the people's liberties, and at the same time explaining away their rights. But
it must be remembered that, although he had a steady respect
for the aspirations of the people, he never pretended to a high
appreciation of their political capacity.

§ 6. *Fox and Pitt the Younger*

There were other prominent politicians besides Burke who
adopted the view that the representation of the people by
Parliament was absolute and plenary. At the opening of
his parliamentary career, Charles Fox employed the argument that the only proper method of ascertaining the opinion
of the people was by consulting the House of Commons.
When dealing with the question whether the people at large
were better judges of the public welfare than the House of
Commons, he described the latter as the only revealers of the
national mind, the only judges of what ought to be the sentiments of the Kingdom. There were many laws which were
highly necessary to the public welfare which did not obtain
popular approbation; and he declared, with youthful subli-
mity: 'I pay no regard whatever to the voice of the people:
it is our duty to do what is proper, without considering what
may be agreeable: their business is to chuse us; it is ours to
act constitutionally, and to maintain the independency of
Parliament.'[1] As a result of this speech, Fox was attacked
by a mob, as he drove down to the House, and was rolled in
the mud.

This phase soon passed; and Fox, when taxed, in 1780, with
having maintained that the voice of the people was only
to be collected in the House of Commons, excused himself
for allowing expresssions to drop which were 'loose and un-
defined' on the ground that he was only twenty-one years of
age at the time.[2] It was still his view, he remarked, that the
vote of the House of Commons was 'the most practicable and
expeditious means of declaring the sense of the people'; and

[1] 16 *Parl. Hist.* 1264; 17 *Parl. Hist.* 149.   [2] 21 *Parl. Hist.* 336.

he concluded his explanation, with considerable ingenuity, by pledging himself to the proposition that 'when the representative body did not speak the sense of the constituent, the voice of the latter was constitutional and conclusive'. But how is it to be known that Parliament does not speak the opinion of the people? This is a question upon which Fox's speech threw no light and which has given politicians, and will give them, scope for indefinite disputation. No arguments have been more frequently and more speciously employed than those which maintain the favour or disfavour of the people.

In the early months of 1784, when he was using every effort to dislodge the newly appointed and popularly supported Pitt from office, Fox again found it impossible not to qualify his recognition of the people's powers. While he admitted that the voice of the people should meet with attention, he claimed that it was not to be blindly followed, since the people, though they might be allowed to inflict small injuries on themselves, could not be allowed to condemn themselves to their own destruction.[1] Fox was forced by Pitt's well-timed dissolution of March 1784 to pay court to his constituency at Westminster, where he explained to his electors in non-committal terms, through his election address, that 'to secure to the people of this country the weight which belongs to them in the scale of the Constitution, has ever been the principle of my political conduct'.

Under Pitt's régime a closer attention was paid to the movements of public opinion. Pitt had, in 1791, entered upon preparations for hostilities against Russia. But, so strongly marked was the dislike of this policy shown by the people at large, he decided to relinquish his plan and to countermand the orders for the dispatch of the fleet, though he possessed what had proved for some years to be a safe majority in the House of Commons. This example of a sudden change of policy displayed the influence of the people working rather more in modern fashion than in the examples which have been cited to illustrate the earlier part of the eighteenth century. At the time of the dropping of the Excise Scheme, for instance, public opinion operated to a large extent indirectly, by diminishing a ministerial majority and so forcing the hand of the Minister. In the instance of Pitt and the armament against Russia, the chance of a defeat of the Government was more remote. Attention was probably paid

[1] 24 *Parl. Hist.* 647-8.

as much to the opinion in the country as to the chances of successful opposition in Parliament.

Pitt, however, seems to have regarded a defeat in the House of Commons as a possibility. He wrote a letter to the Minister at the Court of Berlin, in which he mentioned 'the effect which opinion and public impression' had in England, and remarked that the first discussions of the policy proved that the prospect of 'obtaining a support sufficient to carry this line through with vigour and effect was absolutely desperate'. If, he said, his plan had been pressed, it would either have not been carried or would have been approved 'by so weak a division as would nearly amount to defeat'.[1]

This letter was written with a view to mollifying the King of Prussia, an object which was necessary owing to Pitt's sudden withdrawal from an attitude of aggression to Russia. It is possible, therefore, that he expressed himself rather more vigorously regarding the weakness of his position in the House of Commons than he would have done if he had been writing a private memorandum.

Fox made a debate in the House in 1792, regarding the armament against Russia, the occasion for a full explanation of his matured views on the legitimate sphere of the operation of public opinion. A passage in his speech expresses an attitude which is as sensible today as it must have seemed at the time the speech was delivered.

It is certainly right and prudent [he said] to consult the public opinion; it is frequently wise to attend even to public prejudices on subjects of such infinite importance, as whether they are to have war or peace. But if, in the capacity of a servant of the Crown, I were to see, or strongly to imagine that I saw, any measures going forward that threatened the peace or prosperity of the country, and if the emergency was so pressing as to demand the sudden adoption of a decisive course to avert the mischief, I should not hesitate one moment to act on my own opinion. If the public opinion did not happen to square with mine; if, after pointing out to them the danger, they did not see it in the same light with me, or if they conceived that another remedy was preferable to mine, I should consider it as my due to my King, due to my Country, due to my honour, to retire, that they might pursue the plan which they thought better, by a fit instrument, that is, by a man who thought with them. Such would be my conduct on any great subject where conscientiously I could not surrender my opinion. If the case was doubtful, or the emergency

[1] Stanhope, *Life of Pitt* (ed. 1861), vol. ii, pp. 115–18.

not so pressing, I should be ready, perhaps, to surrender my opinion to that of the public; but one thing is most clear in such an event as this, namely, that I ought to give the public the means of forming an opinion.[1]

These sentiments have a genuinely democratic ring about them which was in advance of the times. But, acceptable as Fox's general views may be nowadays, they are coloured to some extent by the limitation of their period. Since the important change in the constitutional position, which began with the passing of the great Reform Bill, had not yet taken place, Fox, in dealing with the various circumstances which might lead a Minister to retire or to remain in office, could not envisage an appeal to the people at a general election with the object of settling whether one policy or another should be adopted. At the time of Fox and the younger Pitt, public opinion reached as wide an efficacy as it could before new social problems and new constitutional developments of the nineteenth century led to the enlargement of the methods of its operation and, on occasion, rendered it definitely ascertainable by means of the process of counting heads.[2]

§ 7. Modern times

(a) Influence on social legislation

Perhaps the most remarkable steps in the development of the influence of public opinion in the period following the Reform Act of 1832 are observable in connexion with the passing of the early measures of social legislation. These steps were largely the outcome of several new factors, of changes in industrial conditions and in notions regarding the proper sphere of State activities, and of progress in humanitarian ideas. The influence of public opinion on social legislation may, therefore, be justifiably selected for special notice before remarks are made regarding the various circumstances which

---

[1] 29 *Parl. Hist.* 974.

[2] It should be added that there were other instances, besides that of the armament against Russia, in which Pitt altered his policy in pursuance of the dictates of opinion 'out of doors'. He showed himself particularly responsive to the people's views in regard to taxation; and, on one or two occasions, he deemed it proper to withdraw proposals for imposts which proved to be unpopular. Examples are given in Lecky, *History of England in the Eighteenth Century*, vol. v, p. 302; and see *Hist. MSS. Comm.*, Report on MSS. of Mrs. Stopford-Sackville, vol. i, p. 48, Viscount Sackville to his son Charles, 17 June 1785.

enabled the people to take a more instructed interest than previously in public affairs.

The events leading up to the enactment of the first statutes for the amelioration of the conditions in factories and mines and of the state of sanitation in towns provide the best illustrations of the ways in which the new factors operated.[1]

It was during the last two or three decades of the eighteenth century that members of the labouring classes began to be engaged in factories for the purpose of tending machinery; and, before the end of that century, a few philanthropically minded persons evinced an interest in the question of the improvement of industrial conditions. Humanitarianism and social problems began to attract attention. A select number of master-spinners and factory-owners expressed their dissatisfaction at the employment of young children and at the number of hours worked by young persons. Early in the nineteenth century Robert Owen, the best known of the philanthropist mill-owners, after having regulated the conditions of work in his own mills on enlightened and humane principles, approached the Ministry with the object of securing the application of similar regulations to all the chief classes of factories. After long negotiations, a Bill of limited scope was passed in 1819, the chief merit of which was the setting up of some precedent for State regulation of conditions of labour.

Although there had been occasional signs of discontent among the workers for some years, it was not until about 1830 that they undertook for themselves a general agitation for the regulation of factory work. At the same time as the campaign for the great Reform Bill was raging, the textile workers of the north pressed for the limitation of working hours; and this agitation was supported by letters in the press, by inflammatory pamphlets, by large public meetings in the manufacturing towns of Yorkshire and Lancashire, and by the presentation of petitions. Extensive measures were taken to stimulate public opinion and to make it efficacious. The workers easily found leaders, both in and out of Parliament, who were ardent in pressing their claims.

In 1831 Michael Sadler, who took charge of the workers' cause in the House of Commons, introduced a Ten Hours'

---

[1] The comprehensive and masterly analysis of the relations between public opinion and legislation, supplied by Professor Dicey in his lectures on *Law and Public Opinion*, renders it superfluous to cover a wide field of illustration.

Bill. This Bill met with strong opposition by the manu-
facturer-members, who, it seems, thought that they could
best evade reform by insisting on an inquiry into the facts
by a Select Committee. When, however, the Report of
the Select Committee (presided over by Sadler) appeared,
it proved to be a document which, by the moving character
of its revelations and its vivid pictures of appalling hardships
and cruelty, would probably ensure a majority for the Bill.
The manufacturers proceeded to throw doubts on the reliability of the evidence brought before the Committee and
secured the appointment of a Commission, which was to
take fresh evidence. The Report of the Commission, while
in favour of reform, was in many respects more narrow in its
proposals than that of the Committee. It emphasized the
claims of the children rather than those of the adults. As a
result, Sadler's Bill gave way to a moderate Government Bill,
which became the Factory Act of 1833. This piece of legislation, though a sad disappointment to the workers, marked a
large advance in the progress towards a proper regulation of
factory conditions, particularly by the inclusion of provisions
for a centrally administered inspectorate.

The passing of the first measure for the regulation of conditions in mines illustrates the influence of public opinion
operating in a more direct, more rapid, and more effective
manner than it did in respect of the Factory Act of 1833. In
1840 Lord Ashley, in default of a favourable opportunity to
make progress in the House of Commons with his programme
of social legislation, obtained the appointment of a Royal
Commission to inquire into the conditions of children employed in mines. The Report of this Commission appeared
in 1842; and, by its means, 'a mass of misery and depravity
was unveiled, of which even the warmest friends of the labouring classes had hitherto but a faint conception'.[1] The substantial truth of the amazing disclosures of this Report was
unquestionable. It was described as taking the country by
storm. The case for reformation had the instant and energetic support of the whole of the press. Within a few weeks
of the appearance of the Report, Lord Ashley introduced his
Mines Bill, the object of which was to exclude from the pits
women, and girls and boys under thirteen years of age; and,
after some difficulties in the House of Lords, the Mines Act
of 1842 was passed without serious amendment.

[1] E. Hodder, *Life and Work of the Earl of Shaftesbury*, vol. i, p. 412.

Lord Ashley, who had been depicted as an aristocratic humanitarian, was, in fact, fully conscious of the necessity for reliance on public opinion. He spoke of the influence of 'benevolent and instructed' and 'enlightened' public opinion; and, when his Mines Bill was before the House of Lords and in some danger of defeat, he wrote in his diary: 'Now then I am impotent—nothing remains (humanly speaking) but public opinion—were it not for this I should not be able to carry one particle of the Bill.'[1]

Public opinion operated in connexion with the campaign for the improvement of sanitation in towns in much the same way as it did regarding mines. Interest in the subject of public health had not been general before Edwin Chadwick undertook his efforts for its improvement. It is true that the stimulus of successive epidemics of cholera at the end of the eighteenth century had incited a few local societies to press for remedial action. But it was the impression created by the figures published as a result of the passing of the Act for the Registration of Births and Deaths in 1837 which prompted Chadwick to obtain Reports on the results of fever epidemics and the possibility of diminishing their causes. It was due to his initiative that the Poor Law Commissioners were directed, in 1839, to prepare a general Report on public health; and, in 1842, the Report, chiefly the work of Chadwick, was published. It provided a convincing description of over-crowding, inefficient water-supply and drainage, and other scandalous conditions. It proved that a large proportion of total deaths were due to preventable causes.

In 1844 Peel, though unwilling to introduce legislation, appointed a Royal Commission on the Health of Towns, whose Report confirmed that of 1842. After a few years delay, due to the exclusion of interest from any other subject than that of Free Trade, the first Public Health Act was passed in 1848, largely as a result of the influence of public opinion aroused through the publication of Chadwick's Report and that of the Royal Commision. The Bill was in many respects unsatisfactory; but it was a beginning, and it was followed later in the century by more practical measures.

The preceding paragraphs, perhaps, sufficiently outline some of the factors which contributed to the enlarged

[1] Ibid., p. 430.

influence of public opinion as exemplified by the passing of the early measures of social legislation. The serious mischiefs, which arose as the result of rapid extension of industrial activities, not only stimulated a discontent among the workers, which was made public by various methods of agitation, but also evoked sympathy and practical interest among a growing number of humanitarians. It began to be widely realized that the individualistic point of view should be modified and that, if there was a general responsibility for the welfare of all members of the community, the State must become involved in the regulation of the conditions of life of those who were ill qualified to protect themselves. The principle of social solidarity was recognized. There were not lacking unselfish leaders, like Shaftesbury, Sadler, Oastler, and Chadwick, who were willing to advance the cause of those who needed protection. One of the most noteworthy factors affecting public opinion was the dissemination of information through the publication of Reports of Committees and Commissions. On more than one occasion, the opponents of reform secured the appointment of bodies of inquiry in the hope of delaying or defeating legislation. No device could have proved more futile. The rapid effect on the legislature of the disclosures made by Reports and their reception in the country is one of the outstanding features of the progress of social legislation in the nineteenth century.

(b) Aids to the understanding of politics

Although the above-mentioned instances of the influence of public opinion mark an important stage in the development of the people's part in government in modern times, they are not to be regarded as illustrating its full scope. The admission of the principles of State interference respecting conditions of employment and living was followed by that which Dicey calls 'equalization of advantages'. The passing of the Education Acts, of 1870 and after, is the most obvious example of the application of this latter principle; and public opinion played a large part in reinforcing the efforts of the educationalists. Public opinion, moreover, or, speaking more accurately, instructed public opinion, obtained further opportunities of gaining in efficacy not only by the enlargement of its range and intensity of general influence, but also by the exercise of its particular function of preparing the way for the decision of issues at general elections.

Various circumstances tended, from and after the later years of the eighteenth century, to enable the people to take an intelligent interest in many aspects of the business of government. It is not possible to do more than make a passing reference to the most notable methods of spreading information on politics.

General intelligence is, of course, an essential basis for the qualification of an efficient voter. During the last century instructed public opinion has been immensely reinforced as a result of the steady improvement and enlarged scope of public education. In recent decades the process has accelerated as a result of the increase in the numbers of young persons benefiting from secondary education. These factors, supplemented by adult education movements, have served both to multiply the number of voters having political intelligence and to improve their discrimination in regard to public affairs.

There was a period in Queen Victoria's reign and even a little later when some outstanding orator-statesmen of compelling personality toured the country so as to explain the political views which they wished to propagate in the public interest. Often politicians with contrary views followed in their wake. On these occasions large mass meetings were held in cities. Outstanding examples of such political orators were John Bright, Gladstone, and Joseph Chamberlain, all of a liberal tendency, and all having a sense of mission. These speech-making tours did much to stimulate interest in politics among a large number of citizens throughout the country, especially in the manufacturing districts.

The increase in circulation and improvement in the quality of the press, after the institution of such papers as *The Times* and the *Morning Post*, were conspicuous in promoting the people's political education. The set-back through the unfortunate repressive legislation following on the unrest induced by the French Revolution was only temporary. Lord John Russell, in proposing a motion for reform of the representation in 1822, gave figures proving the considerable augmentation in the circulation of newspapers in the preceding thirty or forty years, and spoke of the large number of books sold at cheap prices and the increase in the number of circulating libraries and book clubs.[1]

[1] 7 *Parl. Deb.*, 2 s., 56 ff.

The passing of the Reform Act of 1832 facilitated further advance. The newspaper stamp-duty was reduced from four-pence to one penny in 1836 and was abolished in 1855. The chief remaining obstacle to newspaper circulation, namely, the paper duty, was removed by Gladstone in 1861. At the time of the Reform Bill debates of 1866 and 1867 both Gladstone and Disraeli remarked on the improvements in the opportunities of the people to obtain political education. The former emphasized, among other factors, the institution of free libraries and institutes; and the latter discoursed on 'the increased application of science to social life', exemplified particularly by facilities for inexpensive travel.[1]

In recent years the circulation of newspapers has increased prodigiously. Some daily and Sunday papers have, each of them, circulations running into millions. Many of these pay too much attention to satisfying a widespread taste for sensationalism. National and international news tends, in these papers, to be coloured and even distorted by party bias or by the views of newspaper proprietors. Readers can hardly be said to be encouraged to form opinions on the politics of the day; they are presented with ready-made views, suitable for quick absorption rather than beneficial digestion. It is perhaps inapposite to direct adverse criticism at this kind of editorial practice. Newspaper proprietors want to make money; and, if they come to the conclusion that their readers require to be excited and entertained rather than informed and educated, their principles can at least be understood. On the other hand, the press may be thought to have a duty to the public which is not altogether to be governed by the tastes of the less educated of their readers.

There are newspapers, however, which display a high sense of responsibility in stimulating in their readers a genuine interest in politics and in encouraging the formation of individual opinions. Generally speaking these newspapers have much smaller circulations than those remarked upon in the preceding paragraph. There may be classed with the better daily papers some excellent weekly, monthly, and quarterly periodicals, whose circulation has increased in the last few years. Paradoxical as it may appear, there is much truth in the contention that the public-spirited periodicals with sales of only tens or hundreds of thousands have a greater influence on the policy of government than the dailies

[1] 182 *Parl. Deb.*, 3 s., 1132 ff.; 185 *Parl. Deb.*, 3 s., 219; 186 *Parl. Deb.*, 3 s., 7.

with phenomenally large circulations, because instructed public opinion is effective to a degree far beyond its numerical strength. The elimination of sensationalism and improvement in the standards of news-reporting and comment in some of the mass-circulation newspapers may well result from the steadily improving education of the people, leading in course of time to a more discriminating attitude in readers.

The increased demand for cheap, paper-covered, and other books of an informative kind has been rapid in recent years. This demand will doubtless continue to swell the ranks of the thinking public, and thus to enlarge the numbers of citizens who help to form that invaluable feature in national politics, instructed public opinion.

It is realized on all hands that the most extensive and the most beneficent influence for education in politics nowadays is broadcasting. The British Broadcasting Corporation has displayed a conscientiousness and a high ability in exercising this part of its function which it is hard to over-praise. Its complete impartiality enables it to ensure with unfailing uniformity that both sides of every political question are presented to listeners. As in election campaigns so at other times, broadcasting enables listeners to learn about political questions in a cool, detached frame of mind, without the mass-emotion sometimes engendered, even nowadays, at political public meetings. The B.B.C. never permits any incursion of the sensationalism that is the stock-in-trade of those whose primary aim is to sell millions of copies of newspapers.

In some respects the press and books have the advantage over broadcasting in the business of political education. The 'quality' periodicals provide a valuable forum of discussion, in putting on record the arguments for and against projects and policies, especially in correspondence columns. On the other hand, the skilful presentation of broadcast discussions held between distinguished controversialists in regard to political problems conduces to a wide habit of discussion among listeners. Indeed, any provocative broadcast talk is likely to stimulate discussion in the home and elsewhere; and it must be remembered that discussion is an almost essential prerequisite to the formation of public opinion.

The press and books have some advantage from the fact that their form is permanent. Printed matter can be read at any desired speed, at convenient intervals; and it can be re-read. Its substance can be pondered over at leisure. But a broadcast (unless printed in *The Listener*) is transient, and for that reason often fails to induce a profitable intellectual response.

We have already seen that it was by gradual steps that the claims of the people to information on the course of parliamentary business came to be admitted.[1] Even the conservative principles of Dr. Johnson enabled him to declare that every Englishman was entitled to expect that he should be kept informed of the course of national affairs, subject to the necessity of maintaining secrecy in regard to some aspects of future policy. Charles James Fox, whose views on the freedom of the press remained illiberal only for a short period, argued in 1778 that 'the public had a right to know what passed in Parliament'.[2] The public had, in fact, at the time when his remark was made, the opportunity of reading reports of debates in something like their modern form in such papers as the *Morning Post*, *Lloyd's Evening Post*, and *The London Courant*.

The nation owes a debt of gratitude to Cobbett, who, impressed by the importance of the wide publication of accurate reports of parliamentary proceedings, initiated his series of *Parliamentary Debates* in 1804, and who, in 1806, organized the production of his *Parliamentary History* comprising the best records of debates in the seventeenth and eighteenth centuries that were available to him. After the beginning of the nineteenth century due attention was paid to the verbal accuracy of the reports. This could be relied upon even before the recognition of parliamentary reporters by the Orders of the House of Commons came tardily in 1845. Perhaps, owing to the increased importance of the Ministry at the expense of Parliament and to the diversion of interest stimulated by platform speeches of party leaders, it may not now be correct to say, as was said by Lord Justice Cockburn in the leading case of *Wason* v. *Walter* (1868), that the reason for the people having the deepest interest in happenings in Parliament is that 'on what is there said and done the welfare of the community depends'.[3] Nevertheless public

---

[1] See pp. 35–37 above.   [2] 19 *Parl. Hist.* 648.
[3] *Wason* v. *Walter* (1868), 4 Q.B. 73, at p. 89.

opinion is still in a large measure fostered and directed through a general acquaintance with the reports of parliamentary proceedings. The Hansard Society has done much in recent years to enable the ordinary citizen to follow the activities of Parliament and to understand its role.

It was not until the early part of the nineteenth century that official publications were available to the general public. At that period, it seems, prints of Bills, Reports, and the like were officially circulated to local government officers and corporate bodies, as well as to public libraries, whenever it appeared that their subjects were likely to be of general concern.[1] Canning held enlightened views on the free circulation of State papers and the publication of a considerable amount of information regarding foreign politics. In 1835 a Select Committee of the House of Commons remarked that 'the advantage to the community by the diffusion of that information, which can, in the generality of cases, be obtained only through the House of Commons, must be evident to every member who had directed his attention to the subject'; and it recommended that 'Parliamentary Papers and Reports printed for the use of the House should be rendered accessible to the public by purchase at the lowest price they can be furnished'.[2] Very soon after this date the growth in the sales of Parliamentary Papers and Reports was pronounced. Its connexion with the passing of social legislation has been noticed at the beginning of the present section. And, since the middle of the nineteenth century, the number of sales of official publications, such as Reports of Royal Commissions, has continued to increase. The effect of this increase on the formation of public opinion must be considerable.

The vast extent to which the freedom and property of individual citizens are affected by regulations issued by Government Departments has prompted these Departments to publish explanations of the manner in which they intend to proceed. It is realized, not only by Ministers but by civil servants, that people co-operate more willingly in measures which they understand.

Before World War II one or two of the larger Government Departments had small 'public relations' staffs to explain

[1] Report of Select Committee on Printed Papers, 1837, evidence of L. G. Hansard.
[2] Report of Select Committee on Printed Papers, 1835; and see Report of Select Committee on Parliamentary Papers, 1853.

their activities to the press and thus to the public. But, during the war, it was widely recognized in ruling circles that many administrative measures would only be practicable if the people were fully informed about their intention and proposed opèration, and were, so to speak, made partners in the undertakings. Consequently the 'public relations' element in Government Departments was considerably enlarged, and it is now a matter of settled practice for the Government to ensure that it carries the people along with it in the putting into operation of measures that closely affect them. When the immensely important announcement was made in February 1955 that Great Britain was to begin the development and production of the hydrogen bomb, the Government statement ended: 'The Government believe that the country is entitled to know the gravity of the possible threat and to be given an indication of the lines on which they are working to meet it.'

Since the nationalization of railways, coal-mining, electricity, &c., the annual reports of public corporations have secured a good deal of interest among the more instructed sections of public opinion. These reports expressly take account of the fact that the people have a proprietary interest in the nationalized industries, and regard, or should regard, them as their special concern. Efforts are made by these Boards, in preparing the reports, to pay due regard to public criticisms and to explain their efforts to meet them.

There are a number of voluntary associations whose primary object is to provide political education, especially in regard to foreign affairs, by organizing lectures, training courses, discussion groups, conferences, and public meetings; and by issuing publications, periodicals, and visual aids (including films). Typical examples are the Bureau of Current Affairs, the British Society for International Understanding, and the United Nations Association.

(c) Consultations on proposed legislation

It has been freely admitted for many years that public opinion should have an influence, not merely on the broad principles of legislation, but also on some of its particular provisions, especially those of comprehensive measures the general objects of which are undisputed. During the last hundred years it has been customary for Bills to be published, so as to enable any marked attitude of public opinion in regard to them to be expressed before they are dealt with in Parliament. If features prove clearly to be opposed to popular feeling, steps are taken to have them amended.

By the middle of the nineteenth century a practice had grown up of allowing a sufficient period to elapse between the first introduction of a Bill into Parliament and its second reading to enable the views of the general public to be expressed in regard to it. Disraeli took occasion, in a debate on a Reform Bill in 1852, to urge on the Ministry of the day the observance of this usage. It was only fair, he said, that the opinion of the people should be ascertained in regard to the considerable alterations in the franchise, which were proposed and which were comprised in the Bill, prior to its second reading. He mentioned the circumstances of the introduction of the first Reform Bill and of the provisions for the repeal of the Corn Laws in support of his view of the proper practice.[1]

At the present day public bodies and associations sometimes assert that they should have an opportunity of discussing and commenting on the provisions of Bills in which they have a particular interest. When, in 1927 for instance, it was known that a new Unemployment Insurance Bill was shortly to be introduced, a member asked in the House of Commons whether the Bill would be printed and circulated in time for it to be discussed by trade union meetings which were shortly to be held.[2]

Further, matters have so far advanced in the consultation of interested and representative bodies during the period of preparation of legislation that Bills are frequently the outcome of accommodations reached by Ministers and those concerned. In pursuance of a recent development, it has occasionally been the practice for provisions of the annual Finance Bill to be settled by the Chancellor of the Exchequer after taking into account the views of persons representing big trading interests. Most of the legislation dealing with economic and social matters is drafted in the first instance in Government Departments; and Departments, such as the Ministry of Health, the Ministry of Education, the Board of Trade, and the Ministry of Labour, prepare Bills in consultation with local government associations, the General Council of the Trades Union Congress and individual trade unions,

[1] 119 *Parl. Deb.*, 3 s., 302.   [2] 209 *H.C. Deb.*, 5 s., 1216–18.

Chambers of Commerce, and employers' federations. When the Road Traffic Act was being prepared by the Minister of Transport in 1930, he announced that the Highway Code, being of direct or indirect interest to everybody, would be the subject of consultation with a large number of associations before the final draft was submitted for the approval of Parliament. 'I shall take into consideration', the Minister said, 'the views and criticisms of the press and the public, as well as the views of the wide range of representative bodies with whom I shall be in touch.' In 1932, the Minister of Agriculture met the representatives of the millers, the farmers, and the corn trade to discuss the terms of a Bill which had been drafted in his Department in order to encourage home-grown wheat. The object of this discussion was the agreement of amendments to the draft Bill, acceptable to all parties, before it was presented to Parliament. In 1946, the Minister of Health assured the House of Commons that, in the preparation of the comprehensive and important National Health Service Bill of that year, he had consulted the medical profession, the dental profession, the pharmacists, nurses and midwives, voluntary hospitals, local authorities, eye services, medical aid services, herbalists, insurance committees, and various other organizations. He certainly tried to cover the ground. This kind of consultation is now a matter of routine.

It is often pointed out, with much justification, that many modern statutes consist merely of skeleton provisions, to which are added powers to issue subordinate legislation, in the nature of orders and regulations. These orders and regulations are generally made by Government Departments. This tendency became marked towards the end of the nineteenth century; and, as a result of a general dissatisfaction at a large body of ordinances, many of which dealt with matters affecting the everyday life of the people, being launched without any previous warning, the Rules Publication Act, 1893, was passed. This Act was replaced by the Statutory Instruments Act, 1946, which did not attempt to ensure previous warning, but which relied on previous discussion with interested parties and prompt publication of delegated legislation so as to avoid possible injustice due to the ignorance of the public or to bureaucratic tendencies.

Several modern statutes include provisions for reference to consultative or advisory committees or to local authorities before regulations can be made by Government Departments under the powers conferred on them. These committees frequently include in their membership not only persons technically qualified, but also persons who represent the interests concerned in the widest sense.[1] But there is considerable difficulty in ensuring sufficient publicity, where the regulations relate to the general public and not to interests which are organized.[2]

(d) Ministries' reactions to public opinion

As a result of changes in political organization during the nineteenth century, it has been increasingly plain that public opinion influences the Ministry directly, rather than through its effect on individual members of Parliament. When Bagehot attributed the impossibility of 'a steady opposition to a formal public opinion' to a fear in the mind of each member that he might lose his seat, he was describing a situation which was passing away.[3] It is hardly expected nowadays that a member should change sides with changes of public opinion. He would be as likely to lose his seat if he forfeited the official sponsorship of his party organization as if he displayed a lack of independence.

The promptitude with which Ministries respond to movements of the public mind may vary according to circumstances. It will, perhaps, be less marked when there is a safe and solid majority to rely on than when there is not. But it has been proved that Ministries will involve themselves and their followers in certain defeat if they persist in neglecting obvious signs of warning from the sovereign people. The action of a representative assembly in which there is never a reliable majority (such as that of France) has been thought to assist the accurate reflection of public feeling. Whether or not political instability is, in the long run, conducive to democratic development is an interesting and difficult question.

There was in the nineteenth century considerable divergence in the views of leading politicians regarding the degree

[1] See, for instance, such provisions as Import Duties Act, 1932 (22 Geo. V, c. 8), s. 2; Education Act, 1944 (7 & 8 Geo. VI, c. 31), s. 4; National Health Service Act, 1946 (9 & 10 Geo. VI, c. 81), s. 2; National Insurance Act, 1946 (9 & 10 Geo. VI, c. 67), ss. 41, 77; Agriculture Act, 1947 (10 & 11 Geo. VI, c. 48), s. 77; Radioactive Substances Act, 1948 (11 & 12 Geo. VI, c. 37), s. 6. Cf. *Report of Committee on Ministers' Powers* (1932), Cmd. 4060, pp. 47–48.
[2] Ibid., p. 54.
[3] W. Bagehot, *The English Constitution* (1909 ed.), p. 241.

of attention to be paid to public opinion, although it became obvious that progressive extensions of the franchise would inevitably lead to an increased respect for the attitude of the people. It is a little difficult to accept word for word the estimate of Lord Salisbury (or Lord Robert Cecil as he then was), who wrote, in 1864, that 'any policy which is approved by the mass of the nation is certain to be promptly adopted by its rulers', and conversely that 'no Government could exist in England three months that was acting in the face of a decided national conviction'.[1] It is doubtful if this description could be accurately applied to the present time; but Lord Salisbury's biography, by his daughter, proves that he himself, when Prime Minister, was frequently influenced in his foreign policy by a sense of the probable attitude of public opinion; and he occasionally informed foreign diplomatists of the necessity of his being governed by this influence. How far this was part of his diplomatic technique must remain problematical.

Some of the most eminent and enlightened constitutionalists have held views not far removed from those of exclusive or absolute representation to which reference has already been made. If they did not think that all power was irretrievably surrendered during the life of a Parliament, at least they thought that Parliament in its wisdom was more likely to act for the essential well-being of the nation, when it could consider questions of policy unprejudiced by protest and clamour from without. Canning, in a debate on parliamentary reform in 1822, cited various instances where Parliament had proved right and the people wrong, where Parliament had either been more advanced or more cautious than the people, but with final justification; and he refused to admit that the legislature should necessarily and immediately reflect the apparent sense of the people. 'I do not believe', he observed, 'that to increase the power of the people—or rather to bring that power into more direct, immediate, and incessant operation upon the House . . . would enable the House to discharge its functions more usefully than it discharges them at present.'[2] Nevertheless, it has been said of him that he

did much to extend and create a popular interest in affairs by the liberal publication of State Papers, and by his popular progresses and circuits. He was the first Minister of importance who

[1] *Quarterly Review*, July 1864. Cf. some opinions expressed by him in 1872 and quoted on p. 216 below.   [2] 7 *Parl. Deb.*, 2 s., 133.

habitually delivered addresses to his constituents.[1] He was the first foreign secretary who elaborately explained and expounded his policy beyond the four walls of St. Stephens.[2]

It is not fair to charge statesmen with embracing particular views on the ground of a few extracts from their speeches isolated from their contexts; but Peel so frequently in the course of his career reiterated his preference for the opinion of Parliament to that of the people that he stands out as one of the chief exponents of what has been described as the principle of absolute representation. In a debate on Roman Catholic claims, some few years before his conversion to concession, he observed:

Much has been said of the opinions which prevail out of doors. Of these, or the impressions which they diffuse, I own that I am perfectly careless; . . . believing as I do, that the deliberate wisdom of Parliament is better calculated to weigh maturely the important bearings of any great question, than the general opinion of parties elsewhere.[3]

When opposing the great Reform Bill, he claimed that it was the duty of the representatives of the people not to be swayed by popular clamour, but to look prospectively to the true interests of the country.[4] And again, when speaking on a motion of want of confidence in the Ministry of Melbourne in 1841, he said that it was unwise to admit any other recognized organ of public opinion than the House of Commons. 'It is dangerous', he asserted, 'to set up the implied or supposed opinions of constituencies against their declared and authorized organ, the House of Commons.'[5]

Statements very like negations of the admissibility of public opinion, as a continuous influence on the course of public affairs, can be found as late as the present century. Asquith, in a speech on the Parliament Bill of 1911, said:

We all of us start from one common point—the assumption which lies at the root of representative government, that the House of Commons, itself a product of popular election, is, under normal conditions, a trustworthy organ and mouthpiece of the popular will. . . . How else are we to ascertain what the people think and desire?[6]

[1] Cf. his speeches at Leeds.
[2] H. W. V. Temperley, *Life of Canning*, pp. 100–2.
[3] 4 *Parl. Deb.*, 2 s., 1003.   [4] 4 *Parl. Deb.*, 3 s., 188.
[5] 58 *Parl. Deb.*, 3 s., 817.   [6] 21 *H.C. Deb.*, 5 s., 1748.

Expressions such as these are not inconsistent with democratic government; but, at the same time, there lurks in them a little of the outworn attitude, to the effect that public opinion is something, if not to be circumvented, at least to be appeased, rather than something which, if only it can be definitely ascertained, should promptly be followed.

Any student of contemporary politics must have noticed that, even in a supposedly developed democracy like ours, a Ministry with an adequate majority in the House of Commons is often tempted to disregard temporary movements of public opinion. It would not so act unless it believed, or at least hoped, that the movements would be short-lived. It can justify its disregard by an assumption, for instance, that the people are momentarily led away by excitement or emotion, or prejudiced by lack of discernment. But from time to time the expression of public opinion is so clear and so vigorous that the Ministry quickly recognizes the danger signal and complies with the bidding of its ultimate master.

In December 1935 the people were shocked and disgusted at the discreditable proposal of the Ministry to agree with France in allowing Italy to obtain practical control over Abyssinia after the Ministry had given entirely contrary undertakings at a general election a few weeks before. The people had been promised a 'League of Nations' policy, and the popular indignation at being flouted was so plain that the Baldwin Ministry at once gave way. Baldwin unqualifiedly admitted that he had been guilty of an error and assured the House of Commons that the proposals were 'absolutely and completely dead'. Public opinion thus won a rapid and resounding victory.

In May 1940 the public, being highly dissatisfied with the conduct of the early stages of World War II, were not merely insistent that the administration of the war should be changed, but that the Prime Minister should be changed also. This was an admirable instance of public opinion being plainly reflected in the demeanour of the House of Commons. Neville Chamberlain realized that the sudden decline in his majority in the House was symptomatic of the overwhelming loss of confidence in him in the country. He resigned, to be succeeded by Churchill, the leader in whom the nation's trust was so wisely reposed. In a national emergency, therefore, one of the ways in which the influence of the people's opinion can be made effective is through the interpretation of the votes of the people's representatives in the House of Commons.

(e) Public opinion and voting

It has already been remarked that the operation of public opinion has been to a large extent transformed since the general acceptance of the principle of mandate. The people have for about a century been treated as capable of deciding issues on the occasion of general elections. In so far as it is possible to place clear issues before the electorate, decisions so procured are more conclusive than inferences drawn from the observation of the workings of public opinion, the forces of which are difficult to measure. It may not be quite clear what is decided at a general election; but there is a numerical result. The clearer the issues, the stronger the claim to recognition. On the other hand, public opinion, free and at large, has more opportunity to display the movements of the mind of the nation unrestricted by issues specially prepared by party leaders and untrammelled by the misleading characteristics of mere numbers. Weight of opinion is given due effect.

But public opinion and voting are not in their essence two alternative means by which the people exercise their sway. The counting of votes is merely a formal means of ascertaining at intervals the state of public opinion, especially now that there exists an adequate system of representation. The recognition of voting as a decisive factor in politics only became feasible because public opinion had previously been active, and has shown informally, so to speak, the manner in which the people's influence could develop. And instructed public opinion, in its informal operation, has continued to prepare the way for its formal expression, even after that formal expression has become prevalent. Indeed, the degree in which inferences drawn from the results of general elections are useful is largely dependent on the extent of the preparatory action of public opinion.

CHAPTER IV

PUBLIC OPINION AND GOVERNMENT
(cont.)

A SKETCH of the influence of public opinion on government must include notice of the development of the various means, which are or have been habitual, if not recognized, of representing the views of sections of the people to their governors. The methods employed have changed in the course of the last two or three centuries, as a result of a combination of causes, the chief of which are the alteration in the distribution of political power, due mainly to the extension of the franchise, and the growth of the capacity of the people to understand questions of politics, following on improved education and distribution of information. The manner in which these methods have operated may best be noticed by dealing with them seriatim, although the periods of their employment have, in fact, overlapped.

§ 1. *Petitioning*

No general practice of petitioning in regard to the conduct of public affairs was apparent until the period immediately preceding the Commonwealth. Earlier petitions were, with the rarest exceptions, confined to the redress of private or local grievances or mischiefs. In 1640 several counties presented petitions complaining of the injustice of ship-money, monopolies, the Star Chamber, and other matters; and in the following years there was a constant flow of petitions asking for peace, the dispersal of the army, and for similar reliefs or remedies.[1] It was soon found by Parliament that these public petitions were a source, not only of civil commotion, but also of embarrassment to the Government. Often petitioners who lived near London advanced with much disorder to present their petitions in a body. Both Houses made declarations in 1648 against petitions being presented in a tumultuous manner.[2] Shortly after the

[1] 2 *Parl. Hist.* 542, 639 ff., and *passim*; 3 *Parl. Hist. passim*; Somers, *Tracts*, 2nd Collection, vol. ii (1750), p. 103; R. R. Sharpe, *London and the Kingdom*, vol. ii, p. 331; *The Journal of Sir Simonds d'Ewes* (ed. Notestein), pp. 5, 16.
[2] 3 *Parl. Hist.* 888.

Restoration a statute was passed regulating tumultuous petitions and providing that no petition should be presented by more than twenty persons unless with the consent of three or more justices of the peace.[1] The statute recited that the disorderly preparation of petitions was 'a great means of the late unhappy wars, confusions, and calamities in this nation'—a curious point of view.

For some few years the parliamentary history of petitioning consisted of attempts to regulate and curtail the practice, alternating with resolutions and protests in favour of it. In December 1679 Shaftesbury was astute enough to realize that petitions could be effectively used as a weapon in party warfare; and his Green Ribbon Club organized a vast campaign for the collection of signatures to petitions in favour of the assembly of Parliament. The petitions were not a spontaneous expression of national feeling; but they were portentous in their bulk; and they led to the issue of a proclamation prohibiting the agitation or promotion of petitions 'for specious ends and purposes to the publick', as tending to 'promote discontents among the people, and to raise sedition and rebellion'.[2] With the aid of promptings by the agents of the Crown, many addresses expressing 'abhorrence' of the petitions were presented. In the next year, however, Parliament resolved that 'it is and ever hath been the undoubted right of the subjects of England to petition the King for the calling and sitting of Parliaments and the redressing of grievances'.[3] The Bill of Rights of 1688 maintained that 'it is the right of subjects to petition the King, and all commitments and prosecutions for such petitioning are illegal'. But it was still necessary to provide against disorder in the manner of presentation of petitions; and the House of Commons framed orders, in 1689 and 1699, governing the presentation of petitions to the House. With the exception of petitions from the City of London, all petitions were to be presented by a member of the House.

The circumstances of the famous Kentish petition of 1701 illustrate the biased and prejudiced manner in which the

[1] 13 Chas. II, c. 5.   [2] See note on p. 33 above.
[3] 4 Parl. Hist. 1174. See also A Seasonable Memorial in some Historical Notes upon the Liberties of the Presse, &c. (1680), p. 21, in which it was contended that the multitude have no right to intermeddle in matters of State in which they have no skill, such as the calling and dissolving of Parliaments. It was suggested that porters and carmen might just as well petition for the better government of the herring-trade in Yarmouth.

Commons were apt to treat protests contrary to the feeling of the majority of members. At the time when this petition was presented, party feeling was running very high. The Tories, who were in power, were bitterly opposed to the King's war policy. The terms of the petition were not such as to merit ignominious treatment. It was temperate in matter and respectful in form. It humbly implored the House of Commons to enable the King to assist his allies before it was too late. But the House of Commons voted the presentation of the petition a breach of privilege, and ordered the imprisonment of the gentlemen who presented it, resolving 'that the said petition was scandalous, tending to destroy the constitution of parliaments, and to subvert the established government of these realms'. The Ministry was soon replaced by one more in sympathy with the national sentiments. Meanwhile, numerous tracts appeared in vindication of the right of petitioning. Two of them, Somers's *Jura Populi Anglicani or the Subjects' Right of Petitioning set forth* and Defoe's *Legion Memorial*, are as well known as any political tracts in the language.

About a year after the presentation of the Kentish petition the House of Commons was still, it seems, more interested in its own dignity than in the rights of the people. It adopted a set of resolutions respecting its liberties and privileges; and, apparently, it was only induced as an afterthought by the Marquis of Hartington to include a resolution similar in form to one passed twenty years before—that it was 'the undoubted right of the people of England to petition and address to the King, for the calling, sitting, and dissolving of parliaments, and for the redressing of grievances'.[1]

Throughout the eighteenth and much of the nineteenth centuries, petitions were frequently presented as a result of every kind of public grievance, not excluding grievances respecting impositions of taxation, although the House of Commons, for obvious reasons, made it a practice not to receive petitions against Money Bills.[2] When the acceptance of the petition of the City of London against the Excise Scheme of 1733 was debated in the House, the Ministry asserted that the petition was incapable of being received, and further alleged, absurdly enough, that no hardship would be suffered by refusing to receive it, because every petitioner

[1] 5 *Parl. Hist.* 1339–40.
[2] See a discussion in 1842, 62 *Parl. Deb.*, 3 s., 5 ff., 200 ff., 296 ff.

was represented in the House. The Excise Scheme never became law; but petitions against another financial measure, which was duly enacted by Parliament, succeeded in obtaining its repeal in 1766. Three years previously a tax had been imposed on cider and perry. All the cider and perry counties presented petitions against it; and, such was the character and extent of the agitation, that the imposition was forthwith removed.

The intensity of feeling in regard to the Middlesex Election in 1769 and 1770, and in regard to economical and parliamentary reform in 1779 and 1780, naturally had its counterpart in a free use of petitions. In the former instance, many constituencies begged the King to remove his Ministers and to choose new advisers.[1] In the latter instance, no less than twenty-four counties, as well as many other constituencies, presented petitions against the corrupt influence of the Crown. On the same day as that on which the House of Commons adopted Dunning's famous motion, that 'the influence of the Crown has increased, is increasing, and ought to be diminished', it resolved that 'it is the duty of this House to provide, as far as may be, an immediate and effectual redress of the abuses complained of in the petitions to this House from the different counties, cities and towns of this kingdom'.[2] Petitions, however, on such subjects as the war with America and parliamentary reform, were presented in the course of the following years with but small effect.

The right of petitioning was not directly restricted by the repressive legislation of the end of the eighteenth and the beginning of the nineteenth centuries, though some of the legislation placing restrictions on associations and public meetings must have had the effect of hampering the free use of this method of expression. Pitt, in a debate on the Seditious Meetings Bill in 1795, affirmed 'the right of the people to express their opinions on political men and measures, and to discuss and assert their right of petitioning all branches of the legislature'.[3] The effects of repression were, in fact, short-lived. The number of petitions in the five years ending in 1831 were twenty times greater than those in the last five years of the eighteenth century. Anti-slavery petitions were presented in 1814 and 1833, with about a million and a million and a half signatures respectively. These and the

[1] See *London Chronicle* and *Lloyd's Evening Post* for Nov. and Dec. 1769.
[2] 21 *Parl. Hist.* 367.
[3] 32 *Parl. Hist.* 274.

universal petitions in favour of reform, culminating in those of 1831–2, must be counted as the most signal examples of the use of petitioning as a means of popular agitation.

After the failure of the last of the monster petitions of the Chartists in 1848 Disraeli took the opportunity of justifying, in a speech in the House of Commons, the procedure and attitude of Parliament in regard to the acceptance of petitions. He obviously intended his remarks to be addressed to an audience beyond the limits of the House.

There is an idea [he said] that the presentation of a petition is an empty form—that it is ordered to lie on the table, and is never heard of again. Now it is as well that our constituents should know that every petition laid on the table is scrutinized by a select committee of the most experienced and influential members of this House—that every petition which, from the importance of its subject or the ability of its statements appears to merit particular notice, is printed at the public cost, and afterwards circulated among members; and I believe that at this moment the right of petition ... is a more important and efficient right than has ever been enjoyed at any time by the people of England in this respect.[1]

But the employment of this right, after reaching its 'peak' in the second half of the nineteenth century, has gradually declined towards desuetude, though giant petitions are still occasionally presented to Parliament with but small effect. Equal publicity could surely be obtained with less expense and trouble. This method of expressing general opinion has, in effect, been superseded by others. The House of Commons found, towards the middle of the nineteenth century, that a disproportionate amount of time was spent in debates on the presentation of petitions. It was accordingly provided that there should be no debate on the occasion of presentation except in urgent cases. This rule did not cause any immediate diminution in the number of petitions;[2] but its application, and the absence of publicity resulting from it, may well provide a partial explanation of the later decline in numbers.[3]

Many of the giant petitions, especially those from the Chartists, were proved to contain a large proportion of spurious signatures. The general failure of confidence thus

[1] 101 *Parl. Deb.*, 3 s., 673.
[2] The proportion of signatures to numbers of petitions decreased before the middle of the nineteenth century.
[3] After 1833 the proportion of petitions to be printed was much reduced; see *First Report of Select Committee on Publication of Printed Papers*, 1840.

engendered doubtless communicated itself to those who had
thoughts of organizing petitions. It was realized, too, that
many of the genuine signatures were those of persons who
could have very little interest in the subject-matter of the
petitions, since the expedients used for collecting or obtaining
signatures were frequently unprincipled and discreditable.
The authenticity of petitions was mistrusted at an early stage
in their use. In 1640 and 1641 it seems that unscrupulous
means were adopted in the collection of signatures.[1] And,
for a long time, only a small proportion of signatories can
have been capable of forming an opinion on any question
of politics. Dr. Johnson, deriding the value of petitions at
the time of the agitation respecting the Middlesex Election,
wrote in the *False Alarm*: 'One man signs because he has
vowed destruction to the turn-pikes; one because he owed his
landlord nothing; one because he is rich; another because he
is poor; one to show that he is not afraid, and another to
show that he can write.' When, however, in the nineteenth
century a more sensible view was taken of popular intervention in matters of government, it was seen that methods
which had frequently been proved to be open to suspicion
might fail to be effective.

But there are other, and more obvious, reasons for the
decline. Now that the representation of the people is adequately provided for by a very wide extension of the franchise,
there are no longer deficiencies to be mitigated by the presentation of petitions. The practice of petitioning was chiefly
suitable to a period in which the representation of the people
was defective, or in which the Government was unresponsive
to the views of the people. A Ministry's hopes of retaining
office do not depend, at the present day, merely on a limited
number of voters whose views might not be coincident with
those of the people in the broad sense of that term. They
depend on the votes of virtually the whole of the people. It is
obvious, therefore, that the Government will, as a general
rule, take pains to be susceptible to any clear movement of
public opinion. It is incomparably easier than it was for
general opinions to be collected and appreciated, owing to a
press of vast circulation and to amazing improvements in
means of communication. It is not, then, so necessary as it
was for the people to sign and present monster petitions in
order to propagate grievances, which, with modern methods,

[1] Clarendon, *History of the Rebellion* (ed. Macray), vol. i, p. 271.

can be made to echo through the land from end to end in a more expeditious and sensational manner.

Again, it would be something of an anachronism to petition Parliament at the present day, if this proceeding did not aim at the Ministry; for the time is now well past when Parliament can be regarded as ruling the country. For this reason, it is found that, even in the early stages of the nineteenth century, associations presented addresses to Ministers instead of petitioning Parliament. The Anti-Slavery delegates presented addresses to Ministers in 1833. The Anti-Corn Law League arranged for deputations in 1840 and the following years. It is evident that representations to the very individuals in whose power it was to give or to refuse what was desired seemed more likely to succeed than a formal approach to Parliament, which was beginning to lose its supremacy and which, notwithstanding the assurances of Disraeli that have just been quoted, often did nothing else but let the petition rest on the table.

Deputations, therefore, from many kinds of bodies, have waited on Ministers in regard to numerous subjects from Victorian times. In November 1841 a deputation from the Short Time Committees of the West Riding approached Peel and other Ministers to urge the importance of the limitation of working hours in factories and received a favourable reception, but no promises. Gladstone, in particular, was approached by organized bodies of every class. In 1886 the London Trades Council came to Gladstone in a deputation, asking him to take up the question of a legal eight-hour day. This plea proved unsuccessful. A famous deputation was one headed by Winston Churchill in July 1936 to make representations to Baldwin, the Prime Minister, about the inadequate state of our defences. No real satisfaction was obtained. Many deputations concern urgent matters of trade and industry. In March 1955 a deputation representing the Cotton Board was received by the Prime Minister. The deputation laid before him proposals for dealing with the anxious situation in the cotton trade. The Prime Minister assured the deputation that the Government would give 'urgent and earnest' consideration to the proposals. These are but isolated instances of a frequent practice which continues to the present day.

From two points of view deputations have advantages over petitioning. The members of deputations, although only representative of those having a grievance, can advance their case with more persuasiveness and authority than absent petitioners. Further, the Prime Minister or other Minister, who is the object of the deputation, if not more likely than Parliament to give a favourable answer, is more likely than Parliament to be in a position to give a prompt and definite one, based on an intelligent, and possibly sympathetic, consideration of the representations urged upon him.

§ 2. *Public meetings*

There were, from time to time, in early periods of English history, gatherings of people whose object was to demonstrate to their rulers by visual means the amount of support which existed, in numbers at least, for a change in law or government. Frequently these gatherings had no specific proposals to advance, and expressed no more than attempts to overawe the Sovereign or Parliament by suggestions of force. Others were merely musters of a rudimentary kind contrived by those who had some public grievance to which they wished to draw attention.[1] But meetings called in order to form, diffuse, and express the views of sections of the people on political subjects are characteristic of a fairly widespread education, and did not become habitual on a large scale, as a recognized means of expressing public opinion, until towards the end of the eighteenth century.

It is possible, however, to find instances at earlier dates of political meetings, not merely in connexion with the election of members of Parliament, but for the consideration and furtherance of proposals. There is some slight evidence of their happening so as to assist the preparation of petitions in the reign of Charles I;[2] and there were doubtless meetings preliminary to the presentation of petitions during the reigns of the later Stuarts.[3] In the course of the seventeenth century, meetings were evidently held with the object of promoting the designs of one or other of the opposing sides in politics.[4] During the agitation against the Excise Scheme at the end of 1732 'a great number of merchants, traders and citizens' met

---

[1] Even in quite recent times agitators have used such simple forms of political demonstration as the organized procession.

[2] Clarendon, *History of the Rebellion* (ed. Macray), vol. i, p. 271.

[3] *Chandler's Debates*, vol. v, pp. 134, 141.

[4] *Hist. MSS. Comm., 5th Report*, p. 346 (1642); pp. 300–1, 24 Mar. 1654, Cromwell to Justices of the Peace of Worcester; *3rd Report*, Appendix, p. 245, 27 May 1669, Arlington to Derby.

at the Swan Tavern in Cornhill and appointed representatives to wait on the members for the City of London, to request their opposition to the Scheme.[1] And in the early part of 1733 a large number of public meetings were held in various parts of the country with the intention of instructing members in the same sense.[2] In 1763 they were held in all the apple-growing counties to consider the presentation of petitions and other steps to secure the repeal of the cider tax;[3] and in 1769 and 1770 they were widely employed in important constituencies with the object of organizing protests on the matter of the people's right of election.[4] They were recommended by Burke, in his *Thoughts on the Present Discontents*, in 1770.

> Until a confidence is re-established [he said], the people ought to be excited to a more strict and detailed attention to the conduct of their representatives. Standards for judging more systematically upon their conduct ought to be settled in meetings of counties and corporations.

These instances, taken from different stages of the seventeenth and eighteenth centuries, have been mentioned because the use of public meetings for political purposes has sometimes been described so as to suggest that it began in 1779 and 1780.[5] This practice certainly became habitual to an extent that was unprecedented in those years. There were large assemblies in every county for the purpose of drawing up petitions.[6] Advertisements announcing them may be read in the daily press for December 1779 and January 1780. They were looked upon with intense suspicion by the Government; and Fox found it necessary solemnly to maintain in debate that 'the people out of doors . . . possessed a right to declare their opinion of men and things, in order to

---

[1] *Political State of Great Britain*, vol. xlv, p. 141.
[2] See tracts mentioned on p. 39 above.
[3] *London Chronicle*, July, Aug., and Sept., 1763.
[4] Wyvill, *Political Papers*, vol. i, pp. xvi, xxi; *London Chronicle*, Mar. 1770.
[5] Cf. May, *Constitutional History* (ed. Holland), vol. ii, p. 21, and 41 *Parl. Deb.*, 1 s., 1254.
[6] The 'county meetings', which were very generally held in the second half of the eighteenth century, for the purpose of passing resolutions or preparing petitions on matters of public interest, seem to have had a peculiar status. They may claim to be connected with the ancient shire moot or county court, although, being distinct from the gathering of justices, they formed no part of what is commonly understood to be local government. They were in most instances convoked by the High Sheriff; but, on one or two occasions, he refused to act. See S. and B. Webb, *English Local Government*, vol. i, p. 533 (note); Wyvill, *Political Papers*, vol. i, p. xxi.

do which they might meet and consult together, provided
they did it in a peaceable, orderly manner'. On a later occasion he described public meetings as 'not only lawful, but
agreeable to the very essence of the British Constitution'.[1]

The unrest following on the French Revolution of 1789
led, among other repressive legislation, to the passing of
statutes prohibiting seditious meetings and to the imposition
of stringent restrictions on meetings of any kind. The recitals
to an Act of 1795, and to later Acts in similar form, described
assemblies collected for the purpose, or under the pretext, of
agreeing on petitions as having been made use of 'to serve
the ends of factious and seditious persons, to the great danger
of the public peace, and to the production of confusion and
calamities in the nation'. There is still on the Statute-book
a curious relic of this phase of legislative restraint, namely,
a provision which prohibits gatherings of more than fifty
persons within a mile of Westminster Hall, when Parliament
or the Courts are sitting, for the purpose of presenting petitions or addresses on political matters.[2] The failure of the
Government to take effective steps towards the alleviation
of distress after the end of the war in 1815 and to exhibit any
confidence in the people was followed by a number of vast
meetings pressing for universal suffrage and other reforms,
and led, almost inevitably, to a tragedy of the magnitude of
Peterloo, which, in turn, brought in its train the Six Acts
of 1819, one of which[3] was designed to restrict the holding of
public meetings and was similar in its terms to Acts of 1795
and 1817. All meetings of more than fifty persons for political
and kindred purposes were prohibited, with the exception
of 'county meetings' called by the Lord-Lieutenant or Sheriff,
meetings of corporate towns called by the Mayor, meetings
called by five or more justices of the peace or those of
parishioners within their own parishes. The large unincor-
porated towns of the north suffered an unfair disadvantage.
This Act remained effective for five years.

At the time of the campaign for the great Reform Bill the
holding of public meetings for the purpose of influencing the
Government continued in vogue, and was doubtless a powerful factor in the success of the struggle. William IV, among
others at that time, was suspicious of the epidemic and
asserted that these demonstrations were not 'a just criterion

---

[1] 32 *Parl. Hist.* 278.   [2] 57 Geo. III, c. 19, s. 23.
[3] 60 Geo. III & 1 Geo. IV, c. 6.

of the sentiments of the people'. In his view their object, so far from being the championship of popular progress, was 'the promotion of discontent and the disturbance of the public peace'.[1] In 1832 and 1833 large meetings were held in Lancashire and Yorkshire by the factory workers to urge the passing of the Ten Hours' Bill. The Earl of Shaftesbury, when Lord Ashley, organized a rapid series of addresses to workers in the north in support of the same cause.

Public meetings played a considerable part in Victorian history; and the question of parliamentary reform again led to demonstrations of this kind in 1866. By this time, however, a more sensible view was taken of their propriety. Disraeli, as a Minister of the Crown, when suggesting to the Queen that some public places should be provided 'where the great body of the people . . . should have the right to assemble, and discuss, and express their opinion', observed that public meetings are 'the recognized and indispensable organs of a free constitution. They are safety valves.'[2] The right of holding public meetings in the Royal Parks in London, which was denied by the authorities in 1866, was treated in a manner not unsatisfactory to the people in 1872.[3] It was, however, stated in the *Trafalgar Square Case*[4] in 1888 that there is no right of public meeting in a public thoroughfare or place of public resort. Meetings in places of public resort are, nevertheless, allowed within prescribed limits and times, if no disorder is apprehended; and the fact that political gatherings are held on a highway does not necessarily make them unlawful.[5] The *Trafalgar Square Case* recalls the widely organized Socialist meetings of the latter part of the nineteenth century, which occupy a unique place in the history of this method of expressing general opinions. No other class of meetings, perhaps, has had a larger effect on the course of politics in this country.

The number of political gatherings, unconnected with parliamentary candidatures, has much diminished in the course of the last half century. The profusion of speeches arranged in the early days of the caucus and in Joseph Chamberlain's

[1] *Correspondence between William IV and Lord Grey*, vol. i, p. 98.
[2] Monypenny and Buckle, *Life of Disraeli* (new ed.), vol. ii, p. 184.
[3] See Paul, *History of Modern England*, vol. iii, p. 303; and The Parks Regulation Act, 1872 (35 & 36 Vict., c. 15), and regulations thereunder.
[4] R. v. *Cunninghame Graham and Burns* (1888), 16 Cox C.C. 420; and see debate in 322 *Parl. Deb.*, 3 s., 1879 ff.
[5] *Burden* v. *Rigler*, [1911] 1 K.B. 335.

later career was not long maintained. To some extent, the reasons for the decay in the practice of petitioning apply also to the decrease in the number of public meetings held for political purposes. Now that every adult has, in general, a capacity to take a share in the government of the country, the necessity for the use of unofficially organized methods of expression is lessened. The improvement in the means of the dissemination of information especially by means of broadcasting provides another reason for the change.

Those partaking in any form of political agitation have had to reckon with the provisions of the criminal law, especially respecting sedition and unlawful assembly, which, in times of unrest, have been interpreted with rigour. It was accepted law, in the seventeenth century, that any statement reflecting on the Government involved sedition; and this principle was applied as late as 1704, when the editor of the *Observator* was prosecuted for libel, because he had alleged that the Ministry was corrupt and the Navy ill managed. An extract from the charge to the jury of Lord Chief Justice Holt in that year gives a surprising view of the scope of this class of offence. He thus addressed the jury:

To say that corrupt officers are appointed to administer affairs is certainly a reflection on the Government. If people should not be called to account for possessing the people with an ill opinion of the Government, no Government can subsist. For it is very necessary for all Governments that the people should have a good opinion of it. And nothing can be worse to any Government, than to endeavour to procure animosities as to the management of it; this has always been looked upon as a crime, and no Government can be safe without it be punished.[1]

There were frequent instances of prosecution for sedition and breach of the peace in the late eighteenth and early nineteenth centuries. Many of the Chartists were indicted for unlawful assembly, that is to say, for meeting in such a manner as to cause reasonable apprehension that the public peace would be endangered, and for sedition, or imperilling the security of the State.

In 1839 one Vincent, together with other persons, who were members of a local Working Men's Association, which became affiliated to the Chartist Convention, were indicted for seditious conspiracy and unlawful assembly. The judge,

[1] *R. v. Tutchin* (1704), 14 *State Trials*, p. 1128.

in directing the jury, pointed out that, if it was the purpose of the defendants to obtain the five points of the Charter by reasonable argument and petition, there was no breach of the law. But if they had sought to effect the changes by physical force an offence had been committed. No civilized society could exist if changes were to be effected by force. The jury found all the defendants guilty of attending unlawful assemblies, and two of them of uttering seditious language.[1]

Another Chartist, who was indicted and found guilty of making a seditious speech and for taking part in an unlawful assembly, had described the Government as too contemptible to be recognized and as one which ought to be overthrown. Chief Justice Wilde (afterwards Lord Chancellor Truro) pointed out that the right of public meeting was one of the most valuable of our institutions, as also was the public discussion of actual or supposed grievances. But if, he said, the meeting was called for the purpose of speaking and hearing seditious language—language exciting persons to violence and resistance of the law—'there will be no doubt that the meeting is an illegal meeting, and that all that partook in the act of calling that meeting, and took part in those proceedings, which has such a tendency, will be guilty of an illegal meeting'.[2]

The present-day offence of sedition involves an intention

to bring into hatred or contempt, or to excite disaffection against the person of His Majesty, his heirs or successors, or the Government or Constitution of the United Kingdom, as by law established, or either House of Parliament, or the administration of justice or to excite His Majesty's subjects to attempt, otherwise than by lawful means, the alteration of any matter in Church or State by law established, or to raise discontent or disaffection among His Majesty's subjects, or to promote feelings of ill will and hostility between different classes of such subjects.[3]

In other words, it is unlawful to attempt to overthrow the Constitution or to use such unlawful means as force to obtain the alteration of the law; but reasonable criticism of the actions of the Government or of the laws of the land does not come within the definition. 'Every man has a right to give every public matter a candid, full and free discussion', pro-

[1] R. v. *Vincent and others* (1839), 3 *State Trials*, New Series, p. 1037.
[2] R. v. *Fussell* (1848), 6 *State Trials*, New Series, p. 723. See also R. v. *Burns and others* (1886), 16 Cox C.C. 355.
[3] Stephen, *Digest of Criminal Law*, 7th ed., p. 93.

vided that he does not do it in a way to excite tumult.[1] It is
well known that, in normal practice, proceedings are not
taken immediately some impetuous agitator oversteps the
limits of the legal definition. Broadly speaking, a revolutionary element must be manifest before a charge of sedition will
be brought, though the degree of strictness in the enforcement
of the law must almost necessarily vary according to the
political conditions at any particular time. In a prosecution
for sedition during the present century the judge described
the proceedings as 'somewhat of a rarity'. It is of interest, too,
that he informed the jury that they could take into account
the state of public feeling.[2] A public meeting, designed for the
purpose of making protests concerning the government of
the State or discussing changes in legislation will, if accompanied by a degree of tumultuousness calculated to excite
alarm, become an unlawful assembly. It will be held, that is
to say, to be an unlawful assembly when it has the effect of
giving firm and courageous persons in the neighbourhood
grounds to apprehend a breach of the peace. Such an assembly
will, as soon as its common purpose is put into effect, become
a riot. The classic definition of the difference between a riot
and an unlawful assembly is this:

If the parties assemble in a tumultuous manner, and actually
execute their purpose with violence, it is a riot, but if they merely
meet upon a purpose, which, if executed, would make them
rioters, and, having done nothing, separate without carrying
their purpose into effect, it is an unlawful assembly.[3]

If the purpose of an assembly includes an intention to interfere with and resist the free exercise by the Government of
its lawful powers, if, that is to say, the intention is sufficiently
general in its scope, those partaking in the assembly may commit high treason. 'Levying war against the King in his realm'
is a head of the offence of high treason which has been
broadly interpreted. It may cover an attempt to effect an
alteration in the law by force, which does not correspond
with the common description of war.

It is possible for the process of intimidation of the public
tending to an armed rebellion against the State to originate
in public meetings of privately organized armed forces.
Apprehensions of such possibilities arose in 1936, as a result

---

[1] R. v. *Collins* (1839), 9 C. & P. 456.
[2] R. v. *Aldred* (1909), 22 Cox C.C. 1.
[3] R. v. *Birt and others* (1831), 5 C. & P. 154.

of the activities of Sir Oswald Mosley and his uniformed 'Fascist' followers and led to the passing of the Public Order Act, 1936.[1] This Act made it an offence to wear in any public place or at any public meeting a uniform signifying association with a political organization. It was also made an offence to employ members of an association so as to enable them to usurp the function of the police or the armed forces of the Crown, or so as to use physical force in promoting any political object. General provisions for tightening police control over public meetings were also included. These were widely regarded as regrettable, though necessary.

Until modern times the provisions of the criminal law have been concerned with public meetings from the point of view of their possible danger to the community. But a few years ago a statute was passed which recognized the importance of protecting meetings for the free and undisturbed promotion and discussion of public questions. During the year or so preceding 1908 several political meetings, at which members of the Ministry were to make speeches, were interrupted by supporters of the women's suffrage movement. Chiefly owing, it may be presumed, to the disorders thus created, it was provided by an Act of Parliament[2] that 'any person who at a lawful public meeting acts in a disorderly manner for the purpose of preventing the transaction of the business for which the meeting was called together shall be guilty of an offence'. Not only, then, are persons punishable who misuse the right of public meeting to the danger of the State or of the public peace, but also those who interfere with that right, when it is being properly exercised.

The word 'public' in the expression 'public meeting' refers to the place and openness of the meeting and also to the subject-matter canvassed or discussed. The subject-matter must be of public interest or concern.[3]

§ 3. Organizations

(a) Political associations

The presentation of petitions and the holding of public meetings were often isolated acts, uncoordinated with any general scheme. Political associations betoken a more sustained and highly developed capacity in members of the

---

[1] 1 Edw. VIII & 1 Geo. VI, c. 6.
[2] Public Meetings Act, 1908 (8 Edw. VII, c. 66).
[3] See Public Order Act, 1936 (1 Edw. VIII & 1 Geo. VI), c. 6, s. 9(1).

public to organize their efforts, in order to secure the objects which they desire to attain. These associations have been able to collect and distribute information, rally the scattered forces of public opinion, educate their present and prospective adherents, regulate the presentation of petitions, and collaborate with each other.

The years 1779 and 1780 stand out as important dates in the history of political associations, as they also do in the histories of petitions and public meetings. Prior to those dates, the only instance worthy of notice in which these associations were active was connected with the invalidation of Wilkes's re-election. The Society for Supporting the Bill of Rights was formed under hopeful auspices; but it had a brief life, owing to its ultimate misuse by Wilkes's friends in the personal interests of the hero himself.

The twenty-six county associations of 1779–80, however, included many very respectable people, eager to organize the presentation of petitions for inquiry into the expenditure on the war, and, later, for reform of the representation and for shorter Parliaments. They were largely due to the initiative of Christopher Wyvill of the Yorkshire Association, which was the first and foremost of these associations. The appointment by these associations of delegates to meet and concert common plans of action was the design of a Radical element in their membership. It aroused considerable suspicion, especially in Ministerial circles. Rockingham told Shelburne that 'discretion and correctness have not predominated'.[1] Horace Walpole wrote to Sir Horace Mann:

> The Opposition . . . affected to transfer parliamentary power to the associations, who were very ready to affect parliamentary airs, and accordingly assumed cognisance of matters actually pending in Parliament. This has offended moderate men; and many, who approved the petitions, were alarmed at the associations.[2]

Freeholders of some of the counties actively disagreed with the policy of the twenty-six county associations and protested against their action. There was, for instance, a strongly supported protest from the county of Sussex, many of whose freeholders recorded that:

> We do most particularly protest against the resolutions of appointing a Committee of Correspondence, with the declared

---

[1] Fitzmaurice, *Life of Lord Shelburne*, vol. ii, pp. 73 ff.
[2] *Horace Walpole's Letters* (ed. Toynbee), vol. xi, p. 143.

purpose of forming general associations apparently tending to overrule the legislature and to introduce measures inconsistent with and subversive of our present excellent Constitution.

The county of Kent also was divided into two parties.[1] How far these protests were instigated by agents of the Government it is impossible to say.

The county associations had the sympathy of Fox and Shelburne. Fox led the defence of the propriety of the appointment of delegates, in the face of those who contended that these proceedings were in derogation of the rights and dignity of Parliament, and who were, perhaps, apprehensive that the new representative organization might become a challenge to Parliament itself.[2] Shelburne displayed his independent and advanced views and wrote: 'I cannot discover in the plan of the Yorkshire Association a single exceptional principle. General union is acknowledged to be essential to our success.'[3] And the younger Pitt, who was in a few years violently to oppose all political combinations, supported the activities of the associations that were interested in parliamentary reform, and enrolled himself as a member of the Society for Promoting Constitutional Information. When Pitt had produced his scheme of reform in 1785 and carried it to a division, the Yorkshire Association expressed itself as satisfied, and was dissolved in the following year.

The Protestant Association of that wild agitator, Lord George Gordon, does not throw much light on the development of political associations. But the lamentable occurrences of the uproar following the great meeting of 2 June 1780 led to a revulsion of popular feeling; and their formation became increasingly discredited.

Political associations based on class distinctions did not appear until the end of the eighteenth century. The first working-class association was the London Corresponding Society, which was founded in 1792 by Thomas Hardy. It was followed by other local corresponding societies. Their object was to secure parliamentary reform and adult suffrage; and, as their name implies, collaboration with each other was a leading feature in their organization. They existed chiefly to educate opinion; they eschewed any violent demonstrations; and, although they displayed republican sympathies,

---

[1] *Whitehall Evening Post*, 12 to 15 Feb. 1780; 37 *Commons Journals*, p. 761.
[2] 22 *Parl. Hist.* 97–98.
[3] Fitzmaurice, *Life of Shelburne*, vol. iii, pp. 73 ff.

they could hardly be described as seditious. Nevertheless, the over-cautious attitude of the Government prompted the attempt to obtain Hardy's conviction in 1794. The allegation of constructive treason was not sustained. But in 1799 an Act was passed suppressing the London Corresponding Society by name and all similar associations.[1]

Excessive caution on the part of the Government was equally clearly shown by its attitude to the harmless Friends of the People, also founded in 1792, an association of moderate views, which favoured parliamentary reform and which was supported by Fox, Grey, Sheridan, Erskine, Whitbread, Lambton, Tierney, and others. It was characterized by Ministers as revolutionary and seditious. No doubt the Government's sense of proportion was warped by apprehension that there might appear in England organizations as powerful and subversive as the Jacobin Clubs in France.

So far from showing signs of moderation after the peace of 1815, the governmental policy of repression was steadily pursued; and it renewed its vigour as a result of the agitation for Roman Catholic Emancipation. The Ministry decided that it must make every effort to check the activities of the Catholic Association, which had been formed by O'Connell in 1823 and which threatened to assume menacing dimensions. The gravamen of the charge against the association was that it threatened in its own sphere to compete with Parliament, and that its representative character constituted a challenge to the one body, which, it was said, was qualified and entitled to represent the people. A statute of 1817 evidenced the Government's suspicion of the appointment of delegates by political associations, for it enacted that any society electing delegates to meet with other societies or delegates should be deemed unlawful.[2]

After failing to succeed in prosecuting O'Connell on a charge of directly inciting rebellion, the Government took steps to suppress the organization itself. On 10 February 1825 the Chief Secretary for Ireland, Goulburn, introduced the Suppression of Unlawful Societies in Ireland Bill. The Bill was supported by Plunket, who had, on Grattan's death in 1820, become the foremost champion of Roman Catholic

---

[1] 39 Geo. III, c. 97.
[2] 57 Geo. III, c. 19, s. 25. This provision is still law, but is to a large extent treated as a dead letter, see *Luby* v. *Warwickshire Miners' Association*, [1912] 2 Ch. 371.

claims, and by Canning, who was a strong sympathizer with those claims. Plunket alleged that 'an association assuming to represent the people, and in that capacity to bring about a reform in Church and State, is directly contrary to the spirit of the British Constitution'. He expressly admitted the right of the people under a free constitution to meet for the purpose of promoting the redress of grievances by discussion or petition. But he denied that

any portion of the subjects of this realm have a right to give up their suffrages to others—have a right to select persons to speak their sentiments, to debate upon their grievances, to devise measures for their removal, those persons not being recognized by law. This was the privilege alone of the Commons of the United Kingdom; and those who trenched upon that privilege acted against the spirit of the British Constitution.

Canning's argument proceeded on similar lines.[1] The fear that the legislature might be endangered by the existence of some body, like the Catholic Association, with a representative organization was clearly very real; but the apprehensions of the Ministry were, it is obvious, stimulated by the evidences of unanimity of national feeling behind the Association.

The Anti-Slavery Association, which was formed in 1823, was political only in a limited sense. It might more properly be described as philanthropic; and it naturally did not arouse suspicions of seditious conspiracy when it organized a convention of delegates in London in 1833. Ministers received the delegates politely; and shortly afterwards the desired legislation was passed. This achievement was directly due to the vigorous campaign of the association. Stanley, in introducing the subject of abolition, opened with the remark that the increasing force of public opinion rendered it impossible to delay any longer the settlement of the question. He spoke of 'a growing determination on the part of the people of this country to put an end to slavery, which no one can deny or wisely despise'. It was, he said, a determination 'expressed in a voice so potential, that no Minister can venture to disregard it'.[2] The association is chiefly interesting, for the present purpose, because it provides an early instance of an elaborate and widespread effort to obtain general support for a project by educational methods. Never before had tracts been distributed on so vast a scale or the public support been so extensively canvassed.

[1] 12 *Parl. Deb.*, 2 s., 315, 316, 471.   [2] 17 *Parl. Deb.*, 3 s., 1194.

Similar in some respects is the history of the Anti-Corn Law League, which was active between 1838 and 1846. It brought a vast educational campaign to a successful issue. But it was more intimately connected with home politics; and loud cries were raised by Protectionists for its suppression. Some of them even described it as a seditious conspiracy.

The organization of the Anti-Corn Law League reached a very high pitch. Meetings, with competent speakers, were arranged in every part of the country. The circulation of information constituted a triumph of capacity and enthusiasm. In 1842–3 the League's methods of publicity reached heights which are astounding. Five million tracts were distributed to electors and nearly four million to non-electors. Nothing could stem the tide of progress of an organization such as this.

One of the methods adopted by the League was to obtain representation in Parliament for supporters of the campaign. Cobden and Bright were successful in bringing into the House a little band of Leaguers, not large enough to try conclusions with other parties, but capable of exercising an influence out of proportion to its size.

The Political Unions which agitated for Reform in 1831–2, many consisting exclusively of working-men, were little more than levies of the unrepresented who were prepared to urge a wider representation with every means available to them. A hundred and fifty thousand, for instance, met at Birmingham in November 1831, and threatened, like Hampden, to refuse to pay taxes. Meetings were vast and numerous, and many petitions were presented; but co-ordination was impeded by the repressive legislation regarding unlawful combinations which prohibited (and still prohibits) societies 'composed of different divisions or branches or of different parts'.[1] Nevertheless, the activities of these Unions aroused considerable uneasiness in the Ministry; and there was consequently issued, in November 1831, a Proclamation which declared them to be illegal and unconstitutional. Among those responsible for the issue of this Proclamation, there were some who had a few years earlier had intimate relations with similar organizations. But the Proclamation was only a timorous precaution; and its terms were not enforced.

When Reform was an accomplished fact, it was found by the working-men that they had been cruelly deceived. The

[1] 39 Geo. III, c. 79, s. 2.

effect of the Reform Bill was not what they had expected.
It was obvious that further agitation would be necessary if
their ideals were to be realized. There is, then, a connexion
between the Political Unions of 1831–2 and the Chartist
agitation, which opened in 1838. And the Chartists suffered
from the same disabilities in regard to their organization as
did their predecessors. The law made it difficult for them
to maintain a centralized body with branch societies. The
hopeless endeavour to press forward a national programme,
with local societies linked only by the visits of leaders and
speakers, soon drove the Chartists to form secret leagues, in
respect of which prosecutions for high treason followed. But
it was found possible in 1840 to form a National Charter
Association to assist in centralizing the movement; up till
then, apart from the efforts of leaders, the nearest approach
to a headquarters was the Convention or meeting of delegates.

The first Convention, which met on 4 February 1839, with
about fifty delegates, had as its chief object the presentation
of a giant petition, though there were some who advocated
more drastic methods. The attitude of a section of the
Chartists towards Parliament, as displayed at the Convention, was one of challenge. Some of the delegates imagined
that they were entitled to deal with Parliament on equal
terms. They said that they were really more representative
of the people than members of Parliament; and they wrote
the letters 'M.C.' after their names, signifying 'Member of
Convention'. When a resolution was passed that delegates
should wait on members of Parliament and endeavour to
induce them to support the National Petition and the terms
of the Charter, a few of them protested that this would imply
a recognition of the House of Commons as true representatives of the people. No doubt this element of challenge,
coupled with the suspicion that one of these Conventions
would claim to supersede Parliament and bring about a
revolution, alienated a large class of potential sympathizers.

The failure to secure any immediate result from the
Chartist agitation, which finally ceased in 1848, must be
ascribed as much to divided counsels, faulty leadership, and
legal obstacles to efficient organization as to causes inherent
in the objects of the campaign. The confinement of the movement to one class and the absence of any real representation
of supporters in Parliament also played their part. After the
fight for further reform was renewed in 1866, the successful

outcome could not be claimed by the National Reform League (a working-class body) alone. The National Reform Union, which consisted mainly of middle-class Radicals, was also striving for similar ends. This Union had means of influencing the legislature, which the League had not; and it subsequently survived as an auxiliary of the Liberal Party.

Since mid-Victorian times political associations have multiplied and flourished. It would be possible, if this were the suitable place, to describe the activities of a dozen of them which have played an important part in the history of the last hundred years. It is enough to remark here that they have ranged, in the character of their concerns, from the Fabian Society, supporting socialism, to the Women's Social and Political Union, supporting women's suffrage, and the Co-operative Movement advocating its principles of trading and other activities. Many voluntary associations, too, such as the Early Closing Association, whose objects have been the amelioration of social and industrial conditions, have helped to bridge the transition from individualism to socialism in its widest sense.

(b) Trades Union Congress

In the second half of the nineteenth century local political associations, formed chiefly for the purpose of organizing and supporting parliamentary candidatures, grew up universally within the ranks of the great parties. In this guise the political association comes under the heading of party organization, and, as such, is reserved for mention in the second part of Chapter VI. Trade unions, however, although they developed political activities, in addition to industrial and social activities, some fifty years ago, remained distinct from party organization until the advent of the Labour Representation Committee of 1900.

Trade unionism, in its political aspects, has not been open to the same disadvantages as those which handicapped the working-class bodies of the earlier nineteenth century. Whereas the failure of the Chartists was largely due to lack of organization and lack of influence in Parliament, the trade unions have succeeded in paying attention to both these factors, and, after some years, reached a position of unprecedented authority and influence.

The first Trades Union Congress, which developed out of the local trade councils, was held in 1868. It now meets annually. Its executive work was at first performed by a Parliamentary Committee and later by a General Council. This political executive of the movement was not able at first to do much more than arrange deputations to Ministers in support of resolutions of the Congress; and only subsequently was it able to act as an efficient co-ordinating body and to have a large influence on legislation affecting the working-classes.

The early Labour members of Parliament, mostly nominees of trade unions, did not, like the Anti-Corn Law Leaguers, stand aloof from all parties. They formed a group, which attached itself to the Liberals; but in 1900, as a result of a resolution of the T.U.C., the Labour Representation Committee or Labour party came into being. The Labour party rapidly developed into a fully efficient political instrument of the trade union movement; and the T.U.C. and its executive became to some extent an auxiliary organization. Indeed, it is regarded by some as an anomaly, if not a superfluity, since the periodical Labour party conferences necessarily cover much the same ground as the T.U.C. At the present time the Labour party and the T.U.C. work side by side in close co-operation. They have their joint departments for publicity, information, and research; joint meetings of the executives of the T.U.C. and the Labour party; and a National Council of Labour representing the T.U.C., the Labour party, and also the Co-operative Union.

The T.U.C., although it has millions of trade union members at its back, has never attempted to dominate the Labour party. It has rather had a stabilizing influence. Nevertheless it is in a position of immense power for it can if it so wishes immobilize nearly the whole of the nation's industrial machine. Potentially it is a giant 'pressure group'. It has, in the past, been able to use its power to threaten the Government that labour conditions would be disorganized unless its views on national policy were adopted. For instance, in 1920, when it was feared that the Government might involve Great Britain in a Russo-Polish war, the T.U.C., jointly with the Labour party, formed a council of action and held out menaces of 'any and every form of withdrawal of labour which circumstances may require', in the event of any and every form of military and naval intervention against the Soviet Government. Fortunately this action did not prove necessary. This holding of a pistol at the head of the Government was unconstitutional, as some of its advisers recognized later. It had, however, some justification from the fact that public opinion was largely in agreement with the views of the T.U.C. about Russia.

In 1926 the T.U.C. authorized a 'general' sympathetic strike in connexion with a dispute in a particular industry; and in the following year legislation was passed dealing with the relation of strikes to the safety of the State. The Trade Disputes and Trade Unions Act, 1927, declared strikes to be illegal which had any object other than or in addition to the furtherance of a trade dispute within the trade or industry in which the strikers were engaged, and which were designed or calculated to coerce the Government either directly or by inflicting hardship upon the community. Lock-outs were also declared illegal in similar circumstances. This Act was repealed in 1946.

Latterly the T.U.C. has come to the conclusion that it should confine itself to constitutional methods, and should not use the threat of a general strike to dictate governmental policy. In June 1934 the T.U.C., as part of the Labour Movement, formally repudiated the use of a general strike in an attempt to force the Government to withhold measures likely to lead to war. Nevertheless it continued to wield its immense influence respecting political questions coming within its ambit of interest. During the nineteen-thirties the T.U.C. more than once effectively thwarted measures proposed by the Government. In 1931, at the first impact of the economic crisis, it induced the Ministry to hold up its proposals for cuts in unemployment pay. In the spring of 1939 it successfully opposed the Government's proposals for partial conscription. Its views expressed on these occasions may have been right or wrong, but its intervention was justified since these matters closely concerned the organization of industry.

The T.U.C. did not during the troubled nineteen-thirties refrain from making representations to the Government in regard to international policy. In spite of its traditional bias towards avoidance of war at almost any cost, the T.U.C. called on the Government in September 1935 to take its part in checking Italian aggression and pledged its support. And again in September 1938, at the time of the Czech crisis, it called on the Government to take its part in resisting Nazi aggression, even at the risk of war. It had, however, consistently frowned on any large increase in expenditure on

H

national rearmament, so that it cannot be said to have helped to make resistance to aggression an easy policy for the Government to adopt in the period prior to World War II.

It is natural that the T.U.C. should take a close interest in the Budget of the Chancellor of the Exchequer, especially in regard to his proposals for taxation. Nowadays the T.U.C. adopts an annual practice of making representations to the Chancellor based on its special knowledge of the industrial situation. Its suggestions include such subjects as the taxation of profits.

With increased experience, and as a result of close relations with Governments and Government Departments, the T.U.C.'s policy in regard to expressing its views on national affairs has mellowed in recent years. Its tendency has been to seek co-operation with the Government rather than to be at loggerheads with it, and it has responded readily to the requests of whatever Government might be in power to help in promoting industrial efficiency. In spite of its close alliance with the Parliamentary Labour Party, the T.U.C. now recognizes that it must try to be on easy terms with Conservative Ministries. When Churchill took office in 1951, the T.U.C. intimated its willingness to support the new Conservative Ministry in searching for the solution of problems affecting the national interest. This co-operation with the Government of the day, whatever colour it may be, is much assisted by the T.U.C.'s representation on such vitally important Government bodies as the Economic Planning Board and the National Production Advisory Council.

(c) Miscellaneous

Associations of employers of labour, of which there are many, have no party in Parliament to represent them; they have, therefore, to use such means as they can, by communicating with members and by other means of exerting pressure, to influence Parliament in regard to objects in which they are interested. A notable example of this class was the Mining Association of Great Britain which fought a tenacious rearguard action against nationalization of coalmines for many years. There are, too, a variety of political associations that are concerned to influence Parliament in favour of objects that cut across the ordinary party divisions. There are such organizations as the Proportional Representation Society, the Free Trade Union, and others of a

similar kind. Again, there are a large number of voluntary
associations, whose objects can hardly be described as
political, which from time to time make representations to
Parliament or to Ministers on the subject of legislation,
bodies interested in philanthropic and scientific matters.
'Some of the most creative political proposals in modern
democracy originate, not with the Government, nor with the
permanent civil service, but with public-minded voluntary
groups, who have a public concern for this or that problem
and who have thought out a remedy for it.'[1] An early and
outstanding instance of the product of this class is the Anti-
Slavery legislation of the early nineteenth century, following
on the agitation already mentioned.

The risk of 'pressure groups', wielding an influence in
excess of parties and to the detriment of the party system and
overbearing the Government by the disproportionate use of
force or of money, has not at present loomed very large in
this country. It has been maintained that the organization
of the T.U.C. has taken excessive advantage of its influential
position. If this is true, it provides an example of the influence
of sheer numbers combined with a strong strategical position.
As regards money, it is easy to see that if, for instance, the
Anti-Corn Law League had been more largely supported
than it was by a number of wealthy persons, it might have
secured its ends regardless of what were the real opinions of
the majority of the people.

Occasionally during the last hundred years or so measures
of reform or changes in policy have been forced upon the
Ministry of the day as a result of public opinion being stirred
through important disclosures in the press. In several instances indefensible social conditions have been made the
subject of press campaigns. William Thomas Stead, the
enterprising and strenuous editor of the *Pall Mall Gazette*,
wrote in the eighteen-eighties articles or series of articles
advocating such reforms as the improvement of the conditions of the London poor and the removal of the scandal of
social vices. These campaigns can be paralleled by something
of the same kind but in a quieter strain in more recent times,
when impressive pleas appeared in the press for mitigating
the deficiencies in housing conditions and for improving the
standards of nutrition among the poorer classes. The lively

[1] A. D. Lindsay, *The Essentials of Democracy*, pp. 39–40.

reaction of public opinion due to these disclosures was effective in stimulating the Government to take remedial action.

On some few outstanding occasions the press has organized campaigns so as to reveal inefficiencies in war administration or defence measures and to call for redress. Delane's disclosures in *The Times* regarding our inadequate equipment in the Crimean War was the first of these. He succeeded in producing considerable indignation throughout the country which led to the resignation of the Aberdeen Ministry and to the substitution of a more energetic Prime Minister in Palmerston. There was also a public inquiry.

Similar disclosures were made by Lord Northcliffe in *The Times* and the *Daily Mail* in 1915 in regard to the munitions being supplied to our troops in France in World War I. This was followed later by a demand for a Ministry of Munitions. Here again an aroused public opinion induced the Government to take steps to rectify the deficiencies. W. T. Stead of the *Pall Mall Gazette* had a share in effecting an improvement in the state of our defences in 1884 by his articles entitled 'The Truth about the Navy', the influence of which, coupled with the activity of public opinion, caused the Government to strengthen our naval forces.

Incidents of this kind have been spasmodic in the history of public opinion, because they have been largely dependent on the energy and insight of pre-eminent journalists of dominant position. But social reforms have also been influenced through articles and editorials in the press, where the method has been temperate and scientific, and without any evidence of personal direction. This more restrained style is doubtless more suitable to the improved education of the present day.

CHAPTER V

PARTIES AND THE PEOPLE

§ 1. *The growth of parties*

(a) *Under the Stuarts*

PROFESSOR LOWELL has defined 'the essential function of parties and the true reason for their existence' as 'the bringing of public opinion to a focus and the framing of issues for popular verdict'. There are some who scoff at the practicability of these ideals being realized. But it can hardly be denied that, without parties, the people would have taken an even smaller part than they have in determining political issues during the last hundred years. Although some incidents in the history of the development of parties encourage the student to condemn the system roundly as dictated by selfish and sectional interests, it would be a mistake to disparage the party system, because it has had in many respects a disreputable record, and because it has shown itself capable of abuse. Democratic government, in this country at least, is dependent on its maintenance, a consideration which critics are inclined to overlook.

It was a long time before the fundamental justification of the system, namely the promotion of democratic government, came to be recognized. At first, sides were taken merely in order to overcome adversaries and to capture the spoils of office, often with little or no regard for the wishes of the people at large. They were opponents in the sense of antagonists, imbued with animosity. The same tendencies had previously expressed themselves in the blood feud and the private war. But, in modern times, party divisions have in the main subserved the general interest, so that parties now stand in opposition to each other in a more enlightened sense of that term. They represent policies which can be put alternatively to the electorate; and in consequence the electorate is placed in a more favourable position to make its choice effective.

Even in the beginnings of their history, parties in Parliament had their counterparts in the people; but the people were not in a position to decide which party should furnish the Ministry, much less to decide what the Ministry should do. Parliamentary or majority government was not to be operative for many years to come. The Sovereign still remained, as it were, the head of the Ministry; and the role of members of Parliament was not to support one Ministry or prospective Ministry in opposition to another, but, even in Stuart times, was largely confined to carrying out the King's requirements and providing him with funds.

Speculations regarding the precise date at which parties may be said definitely to have emerged are unessential for the present purpose. The period leading up to the Commonwealth and the later years of Charles II have both been taken as the approximate starting-point of organized divisions in Parliament; at neither of these times was there a difference of principle between parties in the sense which is understood today. At these early periods the issue was one between Royalists and Parliamentarians, or between the Court and the Country parties; it was, that is to say, a question rather between King and Parliament than between two equally ranked groups of members.[1] This may be gathered from the use of expressions 'Court' and 'Country', which imply that the relations of the parties were unlike those of the present day. The one had all the influence of the head of the State behind it and relied on that advantage more than on an appeal to the people; the other looked to some extent towards the people for support.

Soon after 1675, when controversy on ecclesiastical matters began to make clearer the division into two parties, which were to be known as Tories and Whigs, there were, indeed, some differences of principle apparent. But the reactionary attitude of Charles II, and, later, the sheer despotism of James II, caused these principles to be obscured by the pressing and universal topic of constitutional government and the freedom of the subject. The problem of the King's prerogative largely monopolized the political stage. It is true that the elections of 1679 and 1681 were remarkable for a sudden manifestation of party electioneering activity; but the political issues were largely concerned with the maintenance of a free constitution.

[1] Cf. David Hume, *Essays, Moral, Political, and Literary* (ed. T. H. Green and T. H. Grose), vol. i, p. 141. 'But 'tis almost impossible, that the attachment of the Court party to monarchy should not degenerate into an attachment to the monarch; there being so close a connexion between them, and the latter being so much more the natural object.'

The Country party applied the most effective sanctions that were available to it in order to defeat Charles II's autocratic exploits. He was threatened that, unless he promised his assent to the Exclusion Bill, to the independence of judges and to other concessions, the people would not be encouraged to contribute to his service. The Court party paid but slight attention to the people. No general effort was made on behalf of the King to capture constituencies. The second Earl of Clarendon wrote, for instance, during the election of 1681, that several gentlemen in the County of Hants were anxious to serve the King 'if they knew which way to do it, but they knew not from whom to take their aim. They expected (I know not why) a declaration from the King and then other members would be sent to Parliament'.[1] In fact, the question of religion cut across political issues; and the threat of the introduction of Roman Catholicism as the established religion led many of the normal supporters of the Court to remain neutral.

Doubtless the Court party was unable altogether to neglect to cultivate popular support as a means of maintaining its position. When, at the end of 1679, the Country party encouraged petitions from the people for the due assembling of Parliament, the King's friends endeavoured to neutralize the effect of these petitions by obtaining addresses expressing 'abhorrence' of the action of the petitioners. The famous Petitioners and Abhorrers have been pointed out as marking a stage in the formation of parties among the people; but, in so far as their own action was spontaneous, they were rather expressive of a division between the supporters of the King's prerogative and the upholders of the rights of Parliament than of the differences between two alternative parties in Parliament.

The high-handed policy of James II still more effectively put party divisions in abeyance. He succeeded in alienating the sympathies of the incipient Tory party and in ranging it, as well as the Country party, against him. As soon as he left the throne the two parties resumed to some extent the opposition to each other which had begun to be a trait of political life. The accession of William III, however, while removing the fear of unduly autocratic government, did much to disorganize the pre-existing political professions. Convulsions in politics have frequently caused a disintegration of parties

[1] *Calendar of State Papers, Domestic, 1680–1*, p. 165.

into groups; and the Revolution was an instance of this
process.[1] It

had shattered the old Tory basis, and largely destroyed the
rationale of the Whigs. The first were drawn by their political
reason to support the Crown, but by their sentiment to hate
usurpation and Dutch wars. The Whigs, if they were to be true
to their past, would be jealous of a kingly rule, but they dared not
overturn the saviour of Whig society. Purely religious scruples
were losing their strength and being absorbed in factious political
systems, but these scruples, too, in so far as they operated at all,
diverted each party from the natural course of their affections.[2]

Thus it was that for some years many politicians did not find
a congenial home in either of the old camps; and this situation persisted into the reign of Queen Anne, during which
many eminent statesmen passed gradually from one side in
politics to the other. Groups formed and reformed themselves
into loosely constructed parties. Professor Trevelyan quotes
a contemporary observer, who, in 1702, divided members of
Parliament as follows: 'Churchmen, High-Churchmen, Low
Church, Non-Conformists, Courtiers, and Sneakers.'[3] Again,
a pamphleteer, writing in 1712, described the parties at that
date as 'Whig, Tory, Old Ministry, New Ministry, Hot
Whigs, High Fliers, October Club, Moderate Men, Old
Whigs, Modern Whigs, and such like'.[4] It is obvious that,
if these descriptions are at all near the truth, the process of
reassortment must have precluded the possibility of popular
issues being elucidated by the action of parties.

Even in so far as members were divided into the two ranks
of Whigs and Tories, party discipline was largely non-
existent in the House of Commons. In the reign of William III
many Whigs maintained an independent attitude and did not
feel themselves bound to support those in office who went
under the same description as themselves. In the early part
of the reign of Queen Anne the High Tories displayed a
detached attitude towards the so-called Tory Ministry. In
both reigns the presence of the leading Ministers in the
House of Lords encouraged in the Lower House a disposition
towards freedom of action, partly because of the absence of

[1] The Parliament which met in Mar. 1690 was described to Harley as
divided into Tories, Whigs, Court Whigs, and Tory Whigs. *Hist. MSS. Comm.
14th Report*, Appendix, Part II, MSS. of Duke of Portland, vol. iii, p. 446.
[2] K. Feiling, *History of the Tory Party*, p. 275.
[3] G. M. Trevelyan, *England under Queen Anne*, vol. i, p. 213.
[4] *The Conduct of Parties in England*, &c., 1712.

control and partly because of the feeling of jealousy which still prevailed between the two Houses.

The first instinct of William III on coming to the throne was to employ one or two Tory Ministers, as well as Whigs, so as to secure the united support of Parliament in his struggle against France. He saw a House of Commons which had gained for itself a decisive position in the government of the country; and he may well have thought that a body of Ministers reflecting the various political leanings of the House would best secure its support. But, in the middle period of his reign, William III, acting under the influence of Sunderland, experimented with a one-party Ministry. For many months before the 1695 election the Ministry was made more and more Whig; and the 'jingo' election of 1695 may be regarded as an early example of an appeal to the people on party lines, an appeal which met with the desired response, namely, the return of a Whig majority. Shortly afterwards, the tide of popular opinion turned in the Tory direction; and William was not prepared to do more than conciliate the Tories. There was a reversion to the system of mixed Ministries, which continued until Queen Anne had been reigning four or five years.

A homogeneous Ministry was again in office near the year 1708. On this occasion it was not the consequence of an experiment on the part of the Sovereign, but of the machinations of the Whigs. Queen Anne acted, when free to exercise her own predilections, under the conviction that mixed Ministries were preferable to those chosen from one side or the other in politics. She was constantly apprehensive of being enslaved by party.[1] As a result of pressure applied by Godolphin and Marlborough, and of the stratagems of the Whigs, she was induced to replace Tory Ministers by Whigs, so as to produce a Ministry of Whig persuasion. In 1710 the Sacheverell incident came as a godsend to the Queen, and she was able to free herself from the domination of the Whigs. Though not yet wholly converted to the wisdom of party government, the Queen must be taken, by her attitude at the

---

[1] 'All I desire', she said, 'is my liberty in encouraging and employing all . . . that concur faithfully in my service, whether they are called Whigs or Tories, not to be tied to one or the other, for if I should be so unfortunate as to fall into the hands of either, I shall look upon myself, though I have the name of Queen, to be in reality but their slave, which, as it will be my personal ruin, so it will be the destroying of all government, for instead of putting an end to faction it will lay a lasting foundation for it.' (*Hist. MSS. Comm. 9th Report*, Appendix, pp. 471–2.)

elections of 1713, to have shown a definite preference for a Tory régime.

Towards the end of her reign, there were signs of the party system assuming the outlines of its modern shape. The Whig Junto provided an example of a close-knit political organization; and, by 1711, the Whig party, with Walpole as its leader in the House of Commons, began to develop into something similar to a modern Opposition. At the beginning of 1714 Queen Anne was induced by Bolingbroke, who played upon her feelings by suggesting that the Whigs were anxiously awaiting her demise, openly to reject the policy of enlisting both parties at the same time in the service of the Crown. Even if the Hanoverian accession had not involved the employment of a Ministry comprised of adherents of one political party, it is probable that the experiences of the reign of Queen Anne would have led to this arrangement proving inevitable. The coalitions of which she had been so fond in principle proved both ineffective and troublesome. Indeed, the period of the later Stuarts is largely notable, in the constitutional sphere, as one in which unsuccessful experiments were made in checking the development of the party system towards its logical outcome.

The employment of mixed Ministries by the Sovereign necessarily delayed the development of the party system. The electorate, in so far as it could be regarded as having any kind of alternative before it which was likely to enable it to make its influence felt, was limited to that of supporting or rejecting Ministers chosen by the Crown, whether they, as a body, represented any party or policy or not. But, in fact, the opportunity of supporting or rejecting the Ministers was hardly existent. There was a considerable body of members of Parliament (perhaps about a fifth part) who were the paid servants of the Crown and therefore the assured adherents of the Ministry of the day, irrespective of the composition of that Ministry. The 'tied' character of these votes restricted the representatives of the people in their freedom to have their views reflected in the formation of the Government. The existence of a body of King's or Queen's 'friends' or 'servants' in the first place obscured, and in the second place limited, the real usefulness of the nascent party divisions. 'I take it for granted', wrote Harley to Godolphin in 1705, 'that no party in the House can carry it for themselves without the Queen's servants join with them; that the foundation is: persons or parties are to come to the Queen, and not the Queen to them.'[1]

(b) Under the Hanoverians

The Court party remained a powerful factor in politics during the reign of George I.[2] Moreover, after his accession, the complete ascendancy of the Whig party effectively set back the progress towards majority government. There could be no alternative choice with but one party in the position to assume office. It was necessary to wait until Walpole had alienated the sympathies of a section of his followers, and until he had quarrelled with Pulteney in 1725, before there appeared any body which could fairly be regarded as an Opposition.[3] A few years earlier, William Shippen, the leader of the Jacobite squires, although having some claim to being a pioneer of parliamentary opposition, was handicapped by the smallness of his forces and the forlorn nature of his cause from ever showing any promise of providing an alternative Ministry. But the contest between Walpole's party and that of his opponents had little relation to the ideal party system. Public spirit was at a low ebb; faction was rife; and there were no permanent principles to which the main antagonists adhered. Indeed, Chesterfield, in advocating an administration embracing opposing parties, hardly exaggerated when he alleged that there was no distinction in principle between them.[4]

And yet there were some rudiments of parliamentary government recognizable at the end of Walpole's Ministry. Walpole had more than once enunciated the principle of the corporate responsibility of the Ministry. It was advanced by him as early as 1733, when he experienced insubordination among his colleagues in connexion with the Excise Scheme. Although the principle was not accepted in its entirety for some years to come, not until the last years of the century, the realization of even the beginnings of the principle was a definite step in the direction of an ideal relation between parties and people.

[1] *Hist. MSS. Comm., MSS. of Marquis of Bath,* vol. i, p. 74.

[2] See, for instance, *Hist. MSS. Comm., Stuart Papers,* vols. v and vi, *passim.*

[3] An interesting account of the beginning and development of the opposition against Walpole, written by Arthur Onslow, Speaker of the House of Commons, is to be found in *Hist. MSS. Comm., 14th Report,* Appendix, Part IX, pp. 458 ff.

[4] *Old England, or the Constitutional Journal,* No. 3; see also an article entitled 'The Rise, Progress, and Decline of the Political Opposition', in the *London Journal* for 2 Oct. 1731.

The Opposition to Walpole had no real cohesion. At the time of the election of 1741 and the period which immediately followed it the Opposition, which had drawn together fairly steadily during the previous ten or fifteen years under the influence of men like Chesterfield, Argyll, and Bolingbroke, proved to be by no means a homogeneous body. A few days before Walpole's resignation in February 1742, it was felt that some sections of the Opposition were ready to make terms with him.

It is generally agreed [said an observer] that Sir Robert will never give up, nor bring anybody in, if he can possibly avoid it; that the Tories would come into any terms; and that the patriots being sensible of that, are so afraid of being left in the lurch, that they only wait for the first good offer . . . Pulteney's terms seem to be a peerage and a place in the cabinet council, if he can get it.[1]

Walpole's loss of office was caused as much by defections from his own ranks as by the organized efforts of the Opposition. Jealousy and a craving for official emoluments were largely responsible for the fall of the great Minister. The new administration consisted partly of members of the so-called Opposition and partly of the old Ministers. No appreciable share was taken by the people in effecting the change.[2]

Nor was the régime of intrigue and venality which existed under the Pelhams and the Whig families productive of party principles. In 1751 Horace Walpole said that

all was faction, and splitting into little factions. . . . The Prince's Court, composed of the refuse of every party, was divided into twenty small ones . . . Opposition . . . and even the distinction of parties having in a manner ceased at this period! . . . All were now sunk in a dull mercenary subjection to two brothers.[3]

Opposition was spasmodic, personal, and ineffective; and, by the end of the reign of George II, the Whig oligarchy had managed so to entrench themselves that the King was no longer free to choose his Ministers at will. George II, although not imbued with such ambitious notions as his successor in regard to the personal ascendancy of the Sovereign, did not, as has sometimes been supposed, fail to take a lively interest

---

[1] Letter of Sir Robert Wilmot to the Duke of Devonshire, 12 Jan. 1742, printed in Coxe, *Memoirs of Sir Robert Walpole*, vol. iii, p. 587.

[2] See pp. 116, 160, below; and see article entitled 'Reasons for a steady Opposition', in the *Westminster Journal*, 26 Mar. 1743.

[3] Horace Walpole, *Memoirs of the Reign of Geogre II* (ed. Holland), vol. i, pp. 47, 228.

in election campaigns. He watched their progress closely; and he exercised a constant influence over the choice of candidates and the expenditure of money. He did not, however, avoid painful reminders of the limitations which had come to surround the position of the Crown since the beginning of the new dynasty. It had been Lord Granville's maxim: 'give any man the Crown on his side and he can defy everything';[1] and in reliance on this principle he advised the King so to treat his Ministry in February 1746 that they resigned in a body and forced the King to recall them, much to his embarrassment, two days later. The Whigs had secured the Hanoverian dynasty, but at the cost to that dynasty of the realities of power.

Immediately on his accession George III set himself to regain the independence of the Crown; and, for this purpose, he attempted to procure the aid of Tory puppets. Thus there arose a semblance of a standing difference of principles between the two parties. On the Whig side, it was said that the Ministry should depend on the majority in the House of Commons; and the Whigs lost no opportunity, however unscrupulous, of securing that majority. On the Court side, it was said that the King should have freedom to direct the government of the country. But there were still many members on both sides who were imbued with the idea that it was due to the King to support his efforts to carry on the business of the nation; and support of the King's Ministers, regardless of party, was considered to be 'a duty while an honest man could support it'.[2] It was not until parties became more adequately organized that the traditional obligation to support the King's Government, as such, fell into decay. Even as late as the early nineteenth century there were many members of Parliament who thought that it was not their province to question the King's choice of his advisers. They held that at least a fair trial should be given to any Ministry before supporting a vote of non-confidence.

George III did not imagine that he could govern in permanent opposition to a parliamentary majority; but he did all he could to interfere with the development of the party system. The elder Pitt, without realizing that he was so doing, to some extent played into the King's hands by his

[1] *Letters of Horace Walpole* (ed. Toynbee), vol. ii, p. 59.
[2] Lord Barrington to A. Mitchell, 13 Dec. 1762; Brit. Mus., Add. MSS. 6834, f. 42, quoted by L. B. Namier, *England in the Age of the American Revolution*, vol. i, p. 58.

refusal to countenance party connexions and by his preference of 'measures' to 'men'. This attitude is evidenced by his
repeated refusals to join the Rockingham Ministry and by
his welcome by the King, in 1766, as the Minister who would
disembarrass him from the shackles of party.[1] If Chatham
did not, as Wilkes asserted to the younger Pitt several years
later, 'annihilate' party, he at least did a great deal to check
its beneficial development. Horace Walpole mentioned 'his
known desire of uniting, that was breaking, all parties'.[2]

It was to a large extent due to the personal efforts and
contrivances of George III that the Crown servants and
adherents were sufficiently large in numbers in the House
of Commons to assist him in turning a working majority in
his favour.[3] After some ignominious experiences of Whig
domination, he succeeded, by skilful management and by
the assistance of the younger Pitt, in freeing himself from the
control of the Whig oligarchs and in gaining some measure
of the independence for which he had striven. The notable
defeat, however, of the Whig families as a result of the
election of 1784 was not secured by party issues being laid
before the electorate. The victory of Pitt was due more to
the dislike of the Fox–North coalition Ministry and the
machinations of the agents of the Crown than to the attitude
of the people respecting any question of policy, though the
alarm raised over Fox's East India Bill provided something
of a standard by which the political situation could be
judged. Nor must it be supposed that the average voter in
1784 had any clear notion of voting for or against the freedom of the Crown to direct the course of government.[4]

There followed, after the year 1784, the long period of
Pitt's administration, during which the pre-eminence and
ascendancy of the Minister and the alternate factiousness
and disunity of the Opposition left little room for the development of the better features of the party system. During
the years leading up to the Reform Bill of 1832, the looming
of big problems caused a shuffling of groups from one party
to another. The chief causes of the disintegration apparent in
1822 were, first, the divisions of opinion on both Catholic
Emancipation and Parliamentary Reform and, secondly, the

[1] *Chatham Correspondence*, vol. iii, p. 21.
[2] Walpole, *Memoirs of George III*, vol. i, p. 15.
[3] *Hist. MSS. Comm., 15th Report*, Appendix, Part VI (Carlisle MSS.), pp. 538,
633, Selwyn to Lord Carlisle, Nov. 1781 and July 1782.
[4] See pp. 194–6 below.

distrust of Canning as a leader by a section of the Tories. In the spring of 1827 Canning's Government included Liberal Tories, such as Palmerston, as well as a few Whigs. The two great parties were each divided into two. It was not until 1830, when the Liberal Tories, with the exception of Peel, joined the reformers, that a return was made to a two-party system if, indeed, it can be said to have previously existed. It may, perhaps, be contended that party principles were for the first time laid alternatively before the people in 1831. The great triumph of the election of that year was the acquisition by the people of the power to decide upon issues advanced by organized parties, or, rather, by parties which were beginning to be organized for the purpose of 'framing of issues for popular verdict'.

The way in which the development of party organization, after 1831, influenced the constitutional position of the people is discussed in the next chapter. That development was, however, delayed for thirty or forty years, at first, by a failure to appreciate fully the tenet secured by the events connected with the passing of the great Reform Bill and, later, by interruptions in the working of the two-party system. The Conservative party was disunited, as a result of Peel's conversion to the abolition of the Corn Laws. For some few years following 1846 such issues as were recognizable were personal rather than party ones. Greville hardly exaggerated when, writing in 1854, he said that there was 'a total dissolution of party ties and obligations';[1] and Morley, when discussing the defeat of the second Derby Government of 1859, described the situation as being one of 'desperate confusion among leaders, parties, and groups'.[2] The period of rivalry, however, between Disraeli and Gladstone was not only one in which the two-party system operated with some degree of usefulness, but was also one in which the improvement of party organization began to influence the definition of issues.[3]

§ 2. *Some hindrances to the development of the party system*

(a) *Faction, real or supposed*

The most cursory sketch of the relation of parties to the framing of issues should include mention of the views which

---

[1] *Journal of Reign of Queen Victoria* (1852–60), vol. i, pp. 180–1.
[2] *Life of Gladstone*, vol. i, p. 621.   [3] See Chapter VI, § 2.

have been held regarding degeneration of party into faction. For many years after the beginning of the activities of parties, it was frequently alleged by those out of office that the administration was based on party for the purpose of advancing private interests; and, by those in office, that opposition was carried on for opposition's sake.

'Tis a miserable circumstance, and the general ruin of prosperous states [remarked a writer of a tract of the time of William III], when parties out of separate interests and passions pursue different ends of their own, without regard to the public, although the chief interest of each; but it is a circumstance beyond common misery, a propensity to ruin more than natural and a fatality in mankind, greater than has been ever observed perhaps in any country or set of men, that they should be divided into parties from the public interest, when there is not so much as any real particular interest in effect, carrying on in any of those different parties. . . .[1]

It is to be noted that, in discussions relating to party government before the nineteenth century, the term 'party' is often used as synonymous with 'connexion' or 'interest'. It had, that is to say, a narrower connotation than it has today. Frequently, writers of the eighteenth century refer to the Tory and Whig 'interest' as alternative to 'party'. The usage is significant.

Bolingbroke's advocacy of a truce to party government at the time of Walpole's ascendancy was in itself obviously based on personal interest; but he showed precocity in his insistence on the necessity of principle as the justification of party government. He maintained that, during the reign of George II, principles were in abeyance; he pointed to the practical settlement of the question of the succession to the throne; and he argued that Walpole was organizing his party merely as a pretext for monopolizing office.

On the other hand, it must not be forgotten that, during a large part of the eighteenth century, any form of organized opposition was suspected and discredited as being factious. Ministers frequently characterized those who opposed them as 'the Faction'. In 1757 Newcastle made proposals to Hardwicke with the object of arranging for the organization of an Opposition. But Hardwicke expressed himself as shocked at the notion of a 'formed general opposition'; and Newcastle

[1] *The State of Parties and of the Public (State Tracts published during the reign of William III,* vol. ii, p. 208).

felt bound to withdraw his suggestion and to fall into agreement with Hardwicke's views.

At an early stage in his career the elder Pitt evinced an
aversion to party. The reasoning which appealed to him was
positive as well as negative. He saw the advantage of a
national and unified Government, comprising all the available talent, and he also realized the dangers and disadvantages of faction. He failed, for many years at least, to see that
the defect of the parties of his time was not that they played
too large a part, but that they did not play their part in an
enlightened way; that, if parties could offer alternative party
principles or programmes, the people would have greater
freedom and more efficient government than they would
under a system which involved competition between the
King and the Whig families.

The views of Pitt on this one subject coincided, as has been
remarked, with those of George III, who aimed at autocratic
rule and desired to be untrammelled by majority government. When he appointed Pitt to office in 1766, he told him
that he relied on his giving 'his aid towards destroying all
party distinctions'. Pitt did not see that

the evil to be feared was not the usurpation of oligarchy, but the
restoration of the personal power of the Crown. Without the
organization which the party system alone could give, the unreformed House of Commons lay at the mercy of the occupant of
the throne.[1]

The critical situation regarding popular liberties which
arose in 1770 induced Chatham, it seems, to modify his interpretation of the value of party government and to realize
that any gain in the competence of the Ministry secured by
non-party government was outweighed by the impairment
of the free choice of the people. The 'state of the nation'
required new remedies; and Chatham showed some signs of
wishing to form an alliance with the Rockingham Whigs in
opposition to the Ministry which had brought the country
to a serious pass. It required, however, the insight of Burke to
affirm that 'party divisions, whether on the whole operating
for good or evil, are things inseparable from free government'.
In his *Thoughts on the Present Discontents*, which appeared
at the time of Chatham's hesitation respecting the advisability of party government, Burke, while admitting 'the

---

[1] Winstanley, *Lord Chatham and the Whig Opposition*, pp. 31–32.

narrow, bigoted, and proscriptive spirit' and other dangers of the system, argued that it was incumbent on politicians to adopt the course that was essential to freedom and not to fly from it because of 'the evils attendant upon it'. He repudiated the notion, which he said had been inculcated by unconstitutional statesmen, that party and faction were 'equivalent terms', and he asserted that adherents to party, while not slavishly following their leaders in every particular circumstance, would be able to subscribe to the 'great leading general principles' of their party 'at nine times out of ten'.

Chatham was not by any means the last notable politician who failed to see party as the instrument of democracy. No one was more enthusiastic than Brougham for the acquisition by the people of a share in government; and he devoted much energy to the diffusion of information among them with this end in view. Yet he held the curious opinion that the party system represented but a stage—and an undesirable one—in the development of a democracy, which should be unhampered by selfishness and faction. He, like Chatham, had observed the perversion of party by the Whig families, and had concluded that faction and party were necessarily inseparable.

It is sometimes alleged that, under the party system as at present in vogue, no influence is allowed to the people and that they are at the mercy of the arbitrary schemes of professional politicians. To this it may be answered that electors, who have issues placed before them by a limited number of public-spirited parties, are much more able to express a decisive opinion on the choice of Ministers and policy than under forms of government in which there are elaborate arrangements for popular intervention in politics. In the United States, the party system has suffered for long periods from absence of settled principles. Bryce, in his *American Commonwealth*, contrasted the position of the United States with that of this country. He regarded the absence of faction as a notable feature of the working of the party system in England. The principle of the maintenance of law and order and existing institutions, on the one hand, and the principle of freedom and progress, on the other, have, in the opinion of Bryce, been steadily brought into operation by the issues raised, so that they have predominated on the whole over the selfish element which is liable to creep into party politics.[1]

[1] 3rd, American, edition, 1909, vol. ii, p. 22.

This is, perhaps, a somewhat optimistic judgement, especially if it is meant to cover the period prior, say, to Victorian times. The opposite view has been strongly expressed by Treitschke. 'The conflict between the two great English political parties', he said, 'has never been one of principles, as Macaulay thought it, but always turned upon who should hold the chief power in the State.'[1] Whatever the truth may be, there is surely the consolation that, if the two great parties had given way altogether to a system of groups, self-interest and intrigue would undoubtedly have played even a larger part than they did.

At various stages in the nineteenth century and also in recent times, there has been displayed an absence, on many sides, of appreciation of the advantages of the maintenance of the two-party system. The fluctuations in the opinions of Queen Victoria on this subject are typical of those of many of her subjects. She wrote, for instance, to her uncle at the time of the break-up of parties in the middle of the nineteenth century: 'One thing is pretty certain—that out of the present state of confusion and discordance, a sound state of parties will be obtained, and two parties, as of old, will again exist, without which it is impossible to have a strong government.'[2] On the other hand, she wrote on 7 October 1884, when the two parties were at a deadlock regarding the Reform Bill: 'I do wish there was some patriotism instead of Party, Party, in all this painful question. I long for the moderates of both sides to form a third party which would be a check to both the others and prevent this mischief the violents are making.'[3]

Difficulty in distinguishing issues, owing to the rapid development of a third party, was experienced in the early twentieth century. Fortunately, there has remained evident a steady propensity to return to two-party government. It has been found that there are generally two conspicuous sides to a question of policy rather than three or more. Disintegration into groups has proved but temporary; and, after a period of dislocation, during which the people have been handicapped in exercising a discrimination between policies,

[1] Heinrich von Treitschke, *Politics* (trans. 1916), vol. i, p. 145. Cf. David Hume, *Essays, Moral, Political, and Literary* (ed. Green and Grose), vol. i, p. 130, where he speaks of parties from principle as 'known only to modern times' and 'the most extraordinary and unaccountable phaenomenon that has yet appeared in human affairs'. [2] *Letters of Queen Victoria*, 1st Series, vol. ii, p. 464. [3] Ibid., 2nd Series, vol. iii, p. 547.

two parties have reappeared and the system has recovered its main capacity for usefulness.

(b) Lack of party discipline

Until some few years after 1832 there was always a considerable interspersion of loosely attached members whose votes could not be counted on by either party; and there was a still larger number of members whose loyalty could not be relied upon in unexpected emergencies. The absence of party solidarity naturally hindered Ministers from maintaining a steady course of policy. Sir Robert Walpole found, on more than one occasion, that the approach of a general election shook the dependability of his majority owing to members' fears of offending their electors by supporting measures which were likely to prove unpopular.[1] This kind of embarrassment was not confined to the last stages of a Parliament. It has been remarked earlier in this chapter that the turning of the balance of votes against Walpole, prior to his retirement at the beginning of 1742, was due to desertions rather than defeats in the constituencies. Many of his supporters bided their time and abstained from voting until it became clear whether or not the tactics of the Opposition were going to prove successful. Horace Walpole wrote to Horace Mann on 16 December 1741: 'It was a day of much expectation, and both sides had raked together all probabilities: I except near twenty, who are in town, but stay to vote on a second question, when the majority may be decided to either party.' And again on 24 December 1741 he wrote: 'We had forty-one more members in town, who would not, or could not come down.'[2]

National affairs were never, perhaps, more agitated and critical, and consequently the people never more alarmed and sensitive, than in 1756, when the elder Pitt first obtained control of the national fortunes, and in 1780, at the time of the disasters in America towards the end of Lord North's Ministry. Both these periods were typical of the stages in the eighteenth century when majorities were specially capricious. In the years leading up to 1780, Lord North possessed a majority which seemed to be proof against annihilation. But during the months which preceded the general election

---

[1] *Hist. MSS. Comm., 15th Report*, Appendix, Part VI (Carlisle MSS.), p. 82; Lord Hervey, *Memoirs of the Court of George II* (ed. Sedgwick), vol. i, pp. 167-8.
[2] *Letters of Horace Walpole* (ed. Toynbee), vol. i, pp. 141, 147.

of that year his majority on more than one occasion fell away. The agitation for measures of reform and for dealing with the scandal of corruption led members, who were shortly to become candidates, to vote against the Government.[1] In 1782, when Shelburne had become Prime Minister, a report was made to him by John Robinson, the Treasury expert in party management, regarding the composition of parties at that time.

Nothing can be more difficult [the report said] than to form a state of the political sentiments of the House of Commons in the present juncture. In a stable, permanent government to whom gentlemen have professed friendship, with whom they have in general acted, and from whom they have received favors, conjectures may be formed with tolerable certainty of the opinions which gentlemen will entertain on particular questions, but, in a state so rent as this has lately been, torn by intestine divisions, and split into different parties, . . . it is the hardest task that can be to class them.[2]

Another observer, who ventured upon an estimate in the following year, 1783, calculated that the Government could count on 140 votes, Lord North upon 120, and Fox upon 90, the balance of votes being uncertain.[3] Even after the striking success of the younger Pitt in the elections of 1784, he sustained occasional defeats. The Westminster Scrutiny, Parliamentary Reform, and the Fortification Scheme are examples. He did not regard the Parliament elected in 1784 as providing him with a reliable majority. 'It was', he said, 'composed of men who think, or at least act, so much for themselves that we are hardly sure from day to day what impression they may receive.'[4] Papers which have been found among those of one of the private secretaries of the younger Pitt give an estimate of the number of members who were 'independent or unconnected' as 108 in 1788, that is to say, four years after he had assumed office. As late as 1806 Canning wrote:

I am particularly glad to receive such accounts as have been sent to me by some of our friends skilled in such mystical matters, of the numerical effect of the new elections. From one quarter I hear the gain of new strength to the Government is no more than 29—and that to Opposition 22—that 5 more are to be considered hopeful for us and 14 as doubtful. . . .[5]

[1] Fitzmaurice, *Life of Shelburne*, 1st ed., vol. iii, pp. 74, 81.
[2] *Parliamentary Papers of John Robinson, 1774–84* (Camden Society), p. 42.
[3] Gibbon, *Miscellaneous Works*, 1814 ed., vol. ii, p. 262.
[4] Rosebery, *Life of Pitt*, pp. 76, 78.
[5] *Hist. MSS. Comm.*, *13th Report*, Appendix, Part VII (Lonsdale MSS.), p. 223.

The constitutional changes consequent on the passing of
the great Reform Bill did not, as might be assumed, immediately bring in their train a stiffening of party discipline.
On the contrary, the large majority in favour of reform
proved unwieldy and vacillating. The democratization of
the constituencies weakened or removed such rudiments of
discipline as had existed under the old corrupt pocket-
borough system; and, for a time, no party organization was
adequate to take their place. Members were even more apt
than before to act independently of the leaders of the party
to which they generally adhered. Peel wrote to Croker in
1833, 'there is no steadiness in the House, . . . the force of
party connexions, by which alone a government can pursue
a consistent course, is quite paralysed'.[1] After some thirty or
forty years, however, the party leaders began to see that
entirely new methods were requisite if the favour of the
increasing electorate was to be secured. As a result of the
development of the organization of parties, a rigid party
discipline was imposed on members; and it has generally been
possible for the best part of a century to estimate fairly closely
the majority on which a Ministry could rely for all normal
purposes at any particular time. There were in the nineteenth
century, and there still are, a few members whose independence of outlook prevents their accepting full disciplinary
control. John Bright was an example. He once explained to
his constituents that he could never forget his own character
and long-held principles and what he believed to be the true
interests of the country 'to abandon all these, and vote as the
necessities of party may require, at the crack of the party
whip'.[2]

(c) Ignorance of constituents regarding composition of parties

Many candidates in seventeenth- and eighteenth-century
elections stood on the ground of their personal and local
reputations as honest, intelligent, and influential citizens.
Their constituencies knew little of their political opinions, if
any, or of the records of their past action in Parliament; and
the voters were, therefore, disabled from casting their votes
with the object of turning the scale in favour of one or other
of the parties vying for supremacy.

Party organizers saw that advantage might be gained by

---

[1] J. R. Thursfield, *Peel*, pp. 125–6.
[2] G. M. Trevelyan, *Life of John Bright*, p. 192.

disseminating information regarding the political records of parliamentary candidates, especially those of candidates of the other side in the campaign. Election addresses to constituencies with a narrow franchise were almost unknown; and such addresses as were published scarcely ever contained any undertakings in regard to policy. Their general use, in anything but a formal shape, is a comparatively modern refinement; and often, no doubt, a candidate who had voted for a measure which proved unpopular trusted that his constituents knew nothing of the matter. Lists of members of preceding Parliaments, marked so as to show how they had voted on important questions, were freely used as electioneering literature. They played an important part in constitutional development. For not only did they provide party managers with a means of denouncing their opponents, but they drew attention to issues in their alternative aspect and thus prepared the way for the later progress towards the submission of political questions for decision by the people.

Even as early as the Commonwealth period there were instances of the publication of division lists at times other than election time. One of the first lists of members divided into two classes, published with the object of influencing voting in a general election, was one circulated prior to the election of 1660. It was entitled *The Grand Memorandum, or a true and perfect catalogue of the Secluded Members of the House of Commons, sitting 16th March, 1659 [1660], being the day of their Dissolution. Also a perfect Catalogue of the Rumpers, some of them sitting with the Secluded Members the same day; Together with the Names of such as were the King's Judges, and condemned Him to death under their Hands and Seals, marked with an ☞*. This broadsheet was expressed to be published

to prevent mistakes, and that the people of this Nation may see and know who have been their Oppressors, and the fatal Betrayers of their Liberties, by erecting High Courts of Justice, and acting many other enormities, &c. And that they may be the better guided in their FUTURE ELECTIONS.[1]

In 1681 a writer of a tract in the Whig interest advised the electors to reject 124 listed members of the late Parliament who had displayed Roman Catholic proclivities.[2] Again, in 1690, the Whigs circulated a paper containing a list of 150 Tories who had voted against the abdication of James II;

[1] Brit. Mus., 669, f. 24 (37).
[2] *Calendar of State Papers, Domestic, 1680–1*, p. 675.

and the Tories replied by circulating a list of those who had voted for the Corporation Bill, as 'Republicans, Fanatics, Latitudinarians, or Atheists'.

There is no reason to think that the distribution of these lists in the early stages of the development of the party system did much more than affect individual election fights in constituencies. Moral and social attributes were in many, if not most, quarters considered to be just as important as political ones.[1] But, in the first years of the eighteenth century, the distribution of division lists seems to have played a considerable part in election campaigns. At the beginning of the reign of Queen Anne the Whigs issued a 'black list' of 167 Tory members of the late Parliament, whom they denounced as the friends of France. The Tories retorted with a list of those who had voted for a standing army; and both sides published defences of their previous conduct. A Tory tract advised electors to pay due attention to records of voting in the preceding House of Commons.[2] Similar party propaganda was used in the 1705 election in connexion with the Bill to prevent occasional conformity, and, in the 1710 election, respecting the impeachment of Sacheverell.[3]

In spite of the hindrances to the working of the party system in the reigns of George I and George II, owing to the prevalence of faction, there were issues of a sufficiently provocative nature to cause a continuance of the practice of distributing division lists with the intention of influencing voters at elections. In 1722 the passing of the Septennial Act remained a scandal in the view of many opponents of the Ministry. Lists of those who had voted for and against this measure were published in the press and in political tracts.[4] The Excise Scheme, too, was still a bogy in the election of 1734 and prompted the issue of division lists with the object, so it was alleged, and doubtless with truth, of securing the removal of Walpole from power. It need not be supposed that the electors regarded themselves as in a position to

[1] See *Some Cautions offered to the Consideration of those who are to chuse Members, &c.* (1695) [by George Savile, Marquis of Halifax], where, among a large number of moral qualifications and disqualifications, voting against the Triennial Bill was the only criterion of a public character.

[2] *Some necessary Considerations relating to all future elections, &c.* (1702).

[3] *Somer's Tracts*, 2nd ed. by W. Scott, vol. xii, p. 474; *An Exact List of the members . . . who, in some or other of the Questions upon the Impeachment of Dr. Henry Sacheverell, &c.* (1710). See also *Chandler's Debates*, vol. v, Appendix, pp. 110–35.

[4] *Weekly Journal*, 17 and 24 Mar. 1722; *A Guide to the Electors of Great Britain, being lists of all those members, &c.* (1722); *An Exact List of the Knights, &c.* (1722).

decide whether Walpole should remain in office; still, it is
interesting to see that it should have occurred, even to a few
persons, that the distribution of division lists was an in-
citement, not merely to reject particular candidates, but to
determine whether the composition of the Ministry should
be changed.

As information on the course of business in Parliament
became more generally available to the public and division
lists began to be published in the press, political tracts of the
class which has been mentioned became less frequent. Nevertheless, these tracts continued down to the time of the younger
Pitt.[1] Towards the end of the eighteenth century reports of
parliamentary proceedings were easily available in several
periodicals. It was not, however, until 1836 that division lists
were officially published as part of the record of the proceedings of the House of Commons. But, by that time, nearly
every candidate found it necessary to declare to his electors
the party to which he belonged, and the publication of lists
was no longer necessary as an aid to enlightening the electors
on the political allegiance of candidates.[2]

(d) Difficulties in computing party strength after general elections

Until comparatively modern times the uncertain character
of party allegiances prevented the possibility of any positive
result emerging from general elections, beyond the mere
election of members. There were many cries and much
turmoil; but no one could say at the end of the election:
'Such and such a party will now take or continue in office
and carry out such and such a policy.'

Recognized tests were, however, applied after the conclusion of general elections, in order to obtain indications of
the comparative strength of parties. The voting on the election of the Speaker and on the question of contested election
returns—both treated in a partisan spirit—were taken as
giving a fair idea of the disposition of party forces. Godolphin
wrote to Robert Harley in December 1701: 'The choice of a
Speaker will be a very decisive stroke in the ensuing Parlia-

---

[1] One of Burke's cures for the *Present Discontents* was the use of 'frequent
and correct lists of the voters in all important questions'.

[2] As late as 1822 a tract was published entitled *The Elector's Remembrancer; or
Guide to the Votes of each member of the House of Commons for the first two sessions
of the Present Parliament*. It gave particulars of the votes of every member on the
main questions of the day. But the composition of parties was in a confused
state in 1822.

ment.' In October 1705 the choice of Smith, a Whig and anti-tacker, was interpreted as denoting that the Whigs had won the victory at the polls. In the following March Godolphin wrote a letter to Robert Harley which shows that, after several months, the balance of parties was far from plain.

I think as you do [he said], that the Tories are more numerous in this Parliament than the Whigs, and the Queen's servants much the least part of the three. My computation runs thus: of the 450 that chose the Speaker, Tories 190, Whigs 160, Queen's Servants 100; of the last about 15 perhaps joined with Tories in that vote of the Speaker, by which they mounted to 205, and so afterwards more or less, in almost every vote.[1]

The last two general elections in which Walpole figured, namely, those of 1734 and 1741, both of considerable interest, left the composition of the parties indefinite at their conclusion. A writer, reviewing the course of the former election in a periodical of 1734, disapproved of a list which had appeared, 'wherein the members are distinguished according to their supposed parties'. He alleged that such lists could not be reliable, since there was not sufficient evidence on which to base them. He criticized published estimates in which the neutral men were all given to the Court 'as if impartial, independent Whiggs must of course vote with the Administration'; the 205 who voted against the Excise were marked as 'standing votes' against the measures of the Ministry, though perhaps it was the only measure they ever opposed.[2] The *Gentleman's Magazine* for 1734 gave lists of members returned, distinguishing them, not by parties, but by reference to their support or opposition to the Excise Bill, to the Septennial Bill, or to both.[3] Sir Thomas Robinson, writing to Lord Carlisle at the end of 1734, said that he had made the best inquiry he could regarding the strength of the contending parties in the newly elected House of Commons, that it was difficult to obtain reliable information, and that the Court claimed a majority of 100, while the Opposition hoped that the majority would be no more than 50.[4]

So also in 1741. *The Craftsman* regarded as a novelty the

---

[1] *Hist. MSS. Comm.*, *15th Report*, Appendix, Part IV (Portland MSS.), vol. iv, pp. 28, 291.
[2] *The Free Briton*, 4 July 1734.
[3] See the numbers for April and May.
[4] *Hist. MSS. Comm.*, *15th Report*, Appendix, Part VI (Carlisle MSS.), p. 143.

publication of a list of the newly chosen Parliament 'wherein those supposed to be in the Court interest are distinguished by being printed in italick characters, from those supposed to be in the Country interest, as it is called, who are printed in Roman characters'. *The Craftsman* also published a dialogue with a 'Mr. Grub' in order to illustrate the editorial opinions on the matter.

Yes, Sir, I have already had a cursory view of several lists; but it is impossible to make any exact calculation of the number, either on one side or the other, till the Parliament is assembled in form. There are many new members chosen, of whom we have not yet had any experience; and how can anybody answer for their sentiments or conduct before they are try'd? Besides, Mr. Grub, can you pretend to be ignorant that several gentlemen of both parties have altered their opinions since the last general election; and how can we judge of their future behaviour? Have not some, who were formerly favourites, been turned out of place? Have not others, who were at the same time treated as malcontents and incendiaries, been since restored to favour, though not to their former places?[1]

The *Gentleman's Magazine* for 1741 published a list of members returned in the election of that year marked in a complicated but significant manner.[2] Some members were described, for instance, as 'said to be in the Country interest', others 'inclined to the Court', others 'thought to be neutral or doubtful', and others, with less uncertainty, 'places under the Crown'.

This indefiniteness persisted throughout the eighteenth century. At the end of the general election of 1761 Newcastle, who had a larger opportunity than most to estimate the result, admitted that he did not know the political leanings of as many as two-thirds of the new members.[3] A few lists purporting to distinguish Court and Country appeared in the press; but they were conjectural. Estimates were produced for special purposes, divided into so many 'pro', so many 'con', and so many 'doubtful'. There was no definite information on which reliance could be placed. Candidates did not often label themselves as being attached to one party or another; and, even if they admitted a preference, they did

---

[1] *The Craftsman*, No. 781, 20 June 1741; No. 786, 25 June 1741.
[2] p. 311.
[3] Sir Lewis Namier has dealt exhaustively with this subject in his work on *England in the Age of the American Revolution*, vol. i, pp. 197–233.

not pretend that the preference would necessarily be permanent.

After the Reform Bill election of 1831 fairly dependable lists appeared, dividing returned members into those for and against the Bill; but the division was not, in terms, based on party distinction. In 1835 even *The Times* did not venture to publish lists of returned members divided according to parties, though it quoted from other periodicals estimates of Radical and Conservative gains. A book of reference, like *Dod's Parliamentary Companion*, did not mark members according to their parties in lists of the new Parliament. But, in biographical notes respecting members, there were descriptions of 'Conservatives', 'of Whig principles', 'Reformers', 'Radicals', or inclined in one of these directions. From 1837 onwards the press gave the numerical result of the choice of the people between the parties and provided lists of returned members plainly showing their allegiances.

The disintegration of parties, following upon the repeal of the Corn Laws, made a division of members into categories a matter of temporary difficulty. At the time of the election of 1857, for instance, *The Times*, in view of the personal nature of the issues, at first gave lists which distinguished members into 'Ministerialist' and 'Opposition', according to the declared opinions upon the attitude of Palmerston regarding Chinese hostilities. After some days, when it became clear that there was a decided majority for Palmerston, members were 'arranged according to their general political opinions'; and they were classed either as Liberals or Conservatives, though some of them could not have fallen very easily into either of these descriptions. The habit of candidates offering themselves as adherents of one side or another in politics has in recent years become so firmly rooted that it may be assumed that any increase in the number of parties will not involve a reversion to the old obscurities.

Attention has been paid in the preceding paragraphs to circumstances which impeded the development of the party system in the direction of its full usefulness and to the manner in which these circumstances changed. The imperfect information available to the people at large in the eighteenth century, first, regarding the political views of parliamentary candidates, secondly, regarding the way in which members had cast their votes in Parliament on important questions, and, thirdly, regarding the balance of party strength at the conclusion of general elections, naturally acted as a serious handicap both to the people's ability to appreciate the political issues of the day and to their votes being interpreted as a declaration in favour of any line of policy. When, as is now the practice, most candidates stand as acknowledged supporters of one of two parties and are pledged to forward its programme, the results of general elections are generally capable of being interpreted as decisions by the people in favour of one Ministry rather than another, or one programme rather than another.

§ 3. *Coalitions*

Several different types of temporary alliances between parties, groups, or even individuals have been described as coalitions. In some of the circumstances of these alliances, the working of the party system and the role of the Opposition in Parliament have not been seriously interfered with. In others, the result of the alliances has been to suspend, or at least to dislocate, the operation of the party system and to restrict the exercise of the functions of the Opposition. It is obvious that the latter class is apt to endanger the immediate, and possibly the ultimate, prospects of democratic government. When the machinery of government is put out of gear, even with the intention of its being reinstated after a period, it may not prove easy, when the time comes, for the pre-existing conditions to be resumed.

There can be no objection either to a reassortment of parties or groups, if based on principle and not merely on self-interest, or to the formation of a new party on a permanent basis, as a result of the emergence of an issue that cuts across prevailing party principles. The Ministries formed in 1806 and 1827 exemplify regrouping of parties, into which it may be said that questions of principle to some extent entered. And Lord Grey's Ministry of 1830, in which Whigs and Canningites joined forces, described by Professor Trevelyan as 'first and foremost a coalition to carry reform',[1] had among other justifications the establishment of the Liberal party.

Up to the time of the younger Pitt, the party system was still so undeveloped that the coalescence of groups, whose political views were not too disparate, was not as a rule

[1] G. M. Trevelyan, *Lord Grey of the Reform Bill*, p. 250.

regarded as being open to question. When, however, force of circumstances drove the elder Pitt into combination with Newcastle in 1757, there were many who regarded as indecorous Pitt's association with one whom he had only just ceased to abuse and deride. And there is no doubt that the people in general would have preferred to have seen him acting independently of the Court faction.

The 'unholy alliance' of Fox and North in 1783 seemed so obviously to be founded on 'interest', rather than on principle, that the general disgust which it produced rendered any proposal of coalition for years afterwards open to suspicion. The Ministry of the younger Pitt, which was formed at the end of 1783, although frequently classified as 'Tory', was not without an infusion of Whig blood. Yet it could hardly be described as a coalition. Few Ministries have been strictly homogeneous. But it is difficult to understand how it was that the younger Pitt contemplated a coalition with Fox in 1784. This would have involved a junction of two extremes. There may have been more excuse for the proposal of a similar coalition in 1792;[1] and there was, perhaps, still more reason for his endeavour to deal with the national emergency of 1804 by again proposing that Fox should join him in the formation of a Ministry.

How far the divisions caused by the issue of free trade rendered inevitable the formation of the Whig and Peelite coalition in 1852 may be open to doubt. Although the permanent affiliations to which the coalition led may give it some justification, it is certain that the members of the Ministry had few political principles in common. The views of some of them were divergent, especially those of Aberdeen and Palmerston. Derby and Disraeli agreed that the basis of the coalition was largely hatred of the latter. It was at this time that Disraeli, who was fond of saying that there could be no parliamentary government if there were no party government, told the House of Commons that 'England does not love coalitions'.[2] But only a politician with exceptionally rigid principles could resist the inducements of coalition in an unstable and deranged condition of parties such as that prevailing in 1852. Indeed, in so far as coalitions tend towards the permanent absorption of groups into parties, they

---

[1] Holland, *Memoirs of the Whig Party*, vol. i, p. 30; *Hist. MSS. Comm., 15th Report*, Appendix, Part VI (Carlisle MSS.), p. 696, Charles James Fox to Lord Carlisle, 25 July 1792.   [2] 123 *Parl. Deb.*, 3 s., 1665-6.

have something to recommend them. Curiously enough, it is now known that, a few hours before denouncing the formation of the Aberdeen coalition, Disraeli had himself been contemplating the possibility of a Radical–Tory coalition, in which Cobden and Bright might share places with his own friends.[1]

In more recent years, coalitions have been promoted on the occasion of large crises, such as war or economic upheaval, in which the safety or stability of the State has been involved, with the object not only of securing the largest possible measure of unanimity in the House of Commons and of mustering the best intellect and energy available regardless of party distinctions, but also of displaying in the international sphere a Ministry with a formidable personnel and united front. It has been asserted that all parties should be represented in Ministries of this special kind and that the normal attitude of the Opposition should be in abeyance. It is to be remarked that coalitions so formed have not been rendered inevitable owing to the reassortment of groups. The intention has been to deal with a particular situation by a temporary modification of the methods of government.

After World War I had been in progress some nine months, signs of weakness and disunity in administration led to a demand, in the press particularly, for a national Government. It was contended that all opposition between parties should cease and that a Ministry made up of politicians of all parties should be formed so that the efforts of the nation should be concentrated on the winning of the war. A Ministry was accordingly formed in May 1915, which comprised twelve Liberals, eight Conservatives, and one member of the Labour party. The leaders of both the Liberal and the Conservative parties asserted that the coalition was formed for the sole purpose of pursuing the war and would not involve any compromise of principles. G. E. Buckle, the joint biographer of Disraeli, wrote to *The Times* pointing out that Disraeli never denounced a national Government such as that under formation; and he drew a distinction between an honourable association of statesmen, undertaken so as to pursue a policy on which they are united, and a sacrifice of convictions for the sake of place and revenge. But there were many who felt later that the advantages that were derived from the formation of this coalition Ministry, which con-

[1] Monypenny and Buckle, *Life of Disraeli* (new edition), vol. i, p. 1255.

tinued, after reconstruction by Lloyd George, until 1922, were largely outweighed by its disadvantages. The loss involved, by the absence of opposition between parties, had to be set off against the gain secured by the concentration of intellectual ability and by apparent unanimity.

Lloyd George's eagerness to continue the War Coalition Ministry after the end of World War I is paralleled to some extent by Churchill's wish that his War Coalition Ministry should continue after the end of World War II so as to enable him to grapple with post-war problems with the maximum of support. Evidently the recollection of the disadvantages of Lloyd George's extended Coalition Ministry persisted until 1945, with the result that Churchill found that it was the resolute intention of the Labour party to require an immediate return to normal party politics. (There were also, of course, other reasons for the attitude of the Labour party at that juncture.) Post-war problems are doubtless highly daunting; and their solution is of critical importance to the national welfare; but coalitions which involve the discontinuance of the party system are surely only justified, if justified at all, by a war in which the nation is struggling for sheer survival.

There is much to be said for the view that the rationale of the party system is equally applicable in times of crises as it is in ordinary times. The suspension of the party system gives an impression that it amounts to a species of competition in politics in which the country can afford to indulge when no serious mischief is likely to result, but which must be dropped when arduous and critical business is in hand.

No doubt standing party differences sink into insignificance in the presence of a war which engages the whole strength of a nation; and anything which has the least savour of faction is specially reprehensible, and must be more rigorously excluded than in times of peace. Possibly all parties may be in broad agreement regarding the necessity of war and even regarding its general conduct; but there still remains the need for the watchfulness and the criticism, which a sensible and high-principled Opposition alone can supply. Moreover, there are always to be apprehended, in connexion with coalitions, the lobbying and accommodations behind the scenes, which the association of members of different parties is almost bound to involve.

Finally, parties in a coalition continue to be so described, though not properly effective as such. This tends to obscure the fact that a coalition is in essence tantamount to a one-party system, in which democracy is at best only faintly discernible. As a permanent arrangement it would be perilous for freedom, since the electorate could no longer choose their Ministries, nor could they have any effective part in deciding policy, because those abilities are dependent on the predominance of the two-party system.

The circumstances of the Joint Ministry of 1931, which was formed to deal with the severe economic crisis of that year, were peculiar, and require some separate remarks. Although the Government was at first described by the Prime Minister as a national Government, he qualified this description by insisting that it was not a coalition Government in the usual sense, but was a Government 'of co-operation', 'of individuals'. It was impossible to describe it as a national Ministry, in the sense of one which represents the whole House of Commons and against which no Opposition is ranged. The Prime Minister further stated that the Ministry was not a coalition of parties, since party principles were to be retained in their integrity. It is difficult, nevertheless, to see how there can be a coalition of individuals in a Ministry without involving a coalition of their followers in Parliament, and consequently in some degree a coalition of parties or groups.

The Ministry of 1931, like that of 1915, was stated by the Prime Minister to be formed to deal with a particular emergency, and it was said to be limited as regards its period by the needs of that emergency. 'When that purpose is achieved', said Ramsay MacDonald, 'the political parties will resume their respective positions'. In fact, the Ministry became increasingly Conservative. Its original members failed to agree on the question of the imposition of tariffs; and disintegration slowly set in.

Presumably the established convention, that, after the resignation of a Ministry, an appeal should be made to the people by the newly appointed successors, ought to apply to the occasion of the formation of a coalition Ministry. Its application was not practicable in 1915 or 1939; but a general election was held soon after the formation of the joint Ministry of 1931. There is not sufficient experience to show whether, in practice, submissions to the people, by joint or coalition Ministries, formed for emergency purposes, are likely to be less definite than submissions during the normal working of the party system; but it would seem that they are. Where a coalition is one of individuals as much as of parties, the tendency must surely be for personal issues to eclipse issues of policy. In the 1931 election the joint Ministry asked for a 'doctor's mandate' to undertake whatever should prove necessary to stabilize the national finances. Nothing could have been vaguer.

CHAPTER VI

PARTY ORGANIZATION AND POLICY

§ 1. *Party allegiance*

BEFORE parties possessed central organizations, the chief method of keeping a party together and of ensuring some degree of collaboration in Parliament was by meetings of members outside the House of Commons, for the purpose of discussion and the stimulation of united action. 'Private meetings' of members were held as early as 1640.[1] In the course of the eighteenth century there grew up a practice of Ministers summoning their adherents to meet together prior to the opening of sessions of Parliament.

It is clear that, in the early history of parties, considerable suspicion rested on any organization by virtue of which members met outside the House and pledged themselves to vote together in a consistent manner. A Whig tract of 1701 entitled *A List of One Unanimous Club of Members of the late Parliament, November 11th, 1701, that met in the Vine Tavern in Long Acre, who ought to be opposed in the ensuing elections* illustrates such an attitude. This tract asserted the impropriety of the co-operation by the members, whose names were given, in voting against the abdication of James II and against recognizing William III.[2] Tory tracts appeared in answer to the Whig imputations and justified the party meetings. 'It has been customary, as well as thought necessary, in all reigns, for members of Parliament to associate at what places they thought convenient, and never till now thought a crime'; and 'as to a club of such members, mentioned in the scandalous pamphlet . . . there was no such club, except in the Parliament House, where they met for the nation's interest and preservation and to stand by His Majesty against the exorbitant greatness of France'.[3]

As early as 1690 the Tory members dined together, to the number of one hundred and fifty, for the purpose of con-

---

[1] *Journals of D'Ewes*, ed. Notestein, p. 22 (note).

[2] Protests against this kind of co-operation may have been made some few years earlier. Cf. *A List of one Unanimous Club of Voters in the Long Parliament Dissolved in 1678, &c.* (published in 1715).

[3] *An Answer to an infamous libel entituled a List, &c.* (1701). *An Answer to the Black List or the Vine-Tavern Queries* (1701).

certing measures before undertaking the general election campaign; and probably similar meetings were held by the Whigs during the elections of 1679–81, since they were more advanced than their opponents in the arts of party management.

Some few years before Walpole was First Minister there were regular party meetings of the members of Parliament who supported the Ministry. These meetings were summoned at the beginning of sessions. Their formal object was to hear a statement of the policy of the Ministry; but it is evident that some discussion ensued; and it may be assumed that the meetings were intended to encourage party loyalty. An entry in the diary of the first Earl of Egmont for 14 January 1734 is informative respecting this kind of party organization. He wrote:

> This day I had two letters, one to be at Sir Robert Walpole's to-morrow at seven at night, the other to be at the Cockpit on Wednesday at the same hour; but I intend to be at neither. The business is to be made acquainted with the King's Speech for Thursday next; the meeting for to-morrow is of a select number, at the other meeting all who please may come.[1]

The Opposition also held meetings of members in Walpole's time. Old Horatio Walpole wrote in 1740:

> The opponents, flushed with their not being beat by a greater majority than 16, have met, Lords and Commons, to the number of 13 of the first and about 60 of the last at a tavern, and exhorted one another to steadiness and unanimity, and continuance in town to lay hold of occasion for the service of the public. . . .[2]

There is reported a numerous meeting of the members of Parliament 'in the British interest' at the Fountain Tavern in the Strand in March 1743, 'who solemnly engaged to give and promote an early and constant attendance in the next session, to support the Constitution and true interest of His Majesty's British dominions'.[3] In 1751 the principal members of the Opposition met at Egmont's house with the object

[1] *Hist. MSS. Comm.*, vol. ii, p. 7; cf. a meeting mentioned in *Lord Hervey's Memoirs* (ed. Sedgwick), vol. i, pp. 179 ff. See also *Hist. MSS. Comm., 8th Report*, Appendix, p. 223, 7 Dec. 1756, H. Digby to Lord Digby; W. Coxe, *Memoirs of Sir R. Walpole*, vol. ii, p. 201; W. Michael, *Englische Geschichte im Achtzehnten Jahrhundert*, vol. ii, p. 585; and an article in 44 *E.H.R.*, pp. 588 ff., by L. B. Namier, entitled, 'The Circular Letters'.
[2] *Hist. MSS. Comm., 14th Report*, Appendix, Part IX, Buckingham, &c., MSS., p. 39; *Letters of Horace Walpole* (ed. Toynbee), vol. i, p. 173.
[3] 13 *Gentleman's Magazine* (1743), p. 161.

of forming plans for the future; and in 1755 sixty-two Tories
met at the 'Horn', 'where they agreed to secrecy, though they
observed it not; and determined to vote according to their
several engagements on previous questions'.[1] In 1762 the
Duke of Grafton and other young men tried to co-ordinate the
efforts of the Opposition by means of meetings of supporters.
George Onslow was one of these and, on his information,
Newcastle wrote to Hardwicke: 'Our friends in the House of
Commons are desirous of collecting themselves together, that
they may know one another; for that purpose they wish to
have a meeting; they are sure they shall be 180 at least. This
deserves consideration. . . .'[2] In 1769 Burke recorded an
Opposition meeting. 'All the minority', he said, '(however
composed) dines together at the Thatched House.'[3] Several
of the clubs of the late eighteenth century, both those which
were exclusively political, like the Whig Club, and those
which were mainly social, like Brooks's, must have helped
from time to time to hold together the members of the
Opposition.

Occasional references such as those given above provide
the chief evidence there is of party meetings in the eighteenth
century whose object was the inducement of unity of action.
But the independent manner in which many members voted
indicates that the meetings that were held were either attended
by an inconsiderable number or were insufficiently unanimous to secure any steady adherence to party.

In the first half of the nineteenth century there was, it
seems, more frequent use of these gatherings, especially in
the few years following the passing of the Reform Bill of
1832, a time at which efforts to obtain unity were particularly
required. The foundation of the great social-political clubs
of the Victorian period, the Carlton Club in 1832 and the
Reform Club in 1836, served to promote unanimity. But the
elaboration of party organization, which began in the middle
of the nineteenth century, soon made the earlier methods
appear primitive. Though meetings of members of Parliament are still held for particular purposes, they are no longer
used to maintain allegiance; and, with rare exceptions, the

[1] Horace Walpole, *Memoirs of the Reign of George II* (ed. Holland), vol. i,
pp. 80–81, vol. ii, p. 13.
[2] C. P. Yorke, *Life of Hardwicke*, vol. iii, p. 438.
[3] *Hist. MSS. Comm.*, *12th Report*, Appendix, Part X (Charlemont MSS.),
vol. i, pp. 293–4. See also *Hist. MSS. Comm.*, *15th Report*, Appendix, Part VI
(Carlisle MSS.), p. 536, Anthony Storer to Lord Carlisle, 26 Nov. 1781.

questions of policy with which they deal are special rather than general.

As regards the organization of discipline within the walls of Parliament, the Patronage Secretary (now the Parliamentary Secretary of the Treasury), who was first appointed early in the eighteenth century, probably exercised, soon after the institution of his office, many of the functions of a Government Whip and, it may be assumed, had an occasional counterpart on the Opposition side.[1] Prior to 1832, no doubt, these officials must have been concerned to influence elections as much as the voting in the House of Commons. But as the necessity for stringent party discipline in the House became more and more apparent during the nineteenth century, the number of Whips was increased and their importance became enhanced. In recent years, although the Whips find it requisite, in the normal state of parties, rather to rally their troops than to prevent their going over to the enemy, the marshalling of the forces to be led into the lobbies continues to hold an important place in the working of the party system.

Various factors have contributed in recent years to party solidarity. Nearly all members of Parliament are now beholden to the party organization or to trade union funds for the payment of their expenses at general elections. It is naturally difficult for these members to break away from their party allegiance. Moreover the more responsible and prudent M.P.s of the party in power have no wish, either from a party or a personal point of view, to precipitate a general election with all the risks that an election due to a defeat in the House would involve. And M.P.s belonging to the party in opposition are likely to be at a personal disadvantage if they are disloyal to their leaders.

Loose loyalties, combined with a notable degree of individualism, are, however, occasionally responsible for breakdowns in party solidarity. Some instances have occurred in the Labour ranks in recent years. On several occasions rebel groups consisting largely of the 'extreme left' have disregarded the instructions of the party whips. In November 1946 about 100 Labour members abstained from voting on a division regarding foreign policy, thus emphasizing their dissatisfaction at a tendency alleged to be pro-American. In

[1] Cf. *Hist. MSS. Comm., 15th Report*, Appendix, Part VI (Carlisle MSS.), p. 547, Storer to Lord Carlisle, 11 Dec. 1781.

March 1947 a mild revolt of some 80 Labour back-benchers induced the Labour Government to shorten the period of National Service, but only temporarily as it proved. From 1951 onwards there were a succession of revolts of 'left-wing' Labour members on questions of defence and of foreign policy. Aneurin Bevan was concerned in these, sometimes as ringleader.

It certainly seems that, in regard to domestic politics, rebellions within the parties in the House of Commons will be infrequent. But issues of defence and foreign policy arouse instincts and emotions that either cut across or are stronger than party allegiance; and it is in this aspect of parliamentary activity that problems of breach of party discipline will probably continue to embarrass party leaders from time to time.

§ 2. *Central and local organization*

From the time of Shaftesbury's pioneer work as an election organizer in 1679 down to the middle of the nineteenth century, some rudimentary central party organizations intermittently influenced the character of the issues raised in the constituencies. The model instructions to newly elected members, which seem to have been circulated by Shaftesbury's Green Ribbon Club in 1681, provide the earliest instance of any widespread attempt by a party headquarters to dictate a party programme.[1] Wharton, in the time of Queen Anne, was the next politician to show a lively appreciation of the value of organizing a general election campaign. He possessed influence in several counties and was tireless in scouring the country in order to secure the return of Whig members. Walpole and the Pelhams, in the elections of 1722, 1734, 1741, and 1747, extended the method and the period of electioneering by arranging speech-making campaigns in the constituences prior to the dissolution of Parliament. The Opposition soon followed suit. Pelham evidently viewed the new methods with repugnance. He wrote to Lord Essex that he had been involved in much trouble and expense and 'most disagreeable conversation throughout the whole country'. He had talked until he was hoarse, but hoped the results would be satisfactory.[2] An Opposition tract of 1741 sneered at Walpole's attempts to control the course of the general election in the country.

[1] See Appendix II and pp. 13, 75 above.
[2] MS. Letter of 15 Oct. 1733, quoted in Torrens, *History of Cabinets*, vol. i, p. 433.

You must know [it said] that when the septennial wars [i.e. the elections at the end of the seven-years' Parliament] draw near, the Commander-in-Chief sits down at his desk, draws the plan of operation for the campaign, and appoints his officers, without any distinction whether they are veterans or raw inexperienced boys, provided they are well recommended, and promise to obey command. He then sends them to their particular posts, with proper ammunition, whilst he generally continues at his head-quarters; and his aides des camps are continually passing backwards and forwards, to bring him an account of the success of every battle.[1]

In 1747 the Duke of Newcastle organized a tour of the counties of Kent and Surrey, so as to influence the constituencies in thos parts; but efforts of this character were more directed towards ensuring that family influence was fully exploited than towards comprehensive election management.

During the second half of the eighteenth century some of the Whig magnates employed men of organizing ability to forward the interests of the groups which they led. Rockingham expected his secretary, Burke, to do more than act as his personal assistant. Burke, indeed, has been described as having 'suggested policies, drafted petitions, arranged for meetings, looked after elections, arranged everything and goaded everybody'.[2] In general, however, party organization on a large scale must necessarily have diminished during the reign of George III, at least so far as the Whigs were concerned; and it is probable that it was not until the period immediately following the death of the younger Pitt that there were signs of the resumption of any effective central organization in the Whig party. Lord Holland records that, in the election of 1807, the Whigs raised some few hundred pounds for the management of the press and the distribution of hand-bills.[3] The Whigs appear, moreover, to have had at this time a central fund, which was used to assist approved candidates in securing seats. The development was probably a fresh one.[4]

Each Reform measure of the nineteenth century, as it provided for further enlargement of the franchise, made it increasingly clear that success in election campaigns would depend on comprehensive arrangements, by which the local organizations in constituencies were linked up with a central

[1] *A Review of a late Motion, &c.* (1741).
[2] Ernest Barker, *Burke and Bristol*, p. 50.
[3] Holland, *Memoirs of the Whig Party*, vol. ii, p. 227.
[4] *Memoirs of Sir Samuel Romilly*, vol. ii, p. 237.

party organization. Development on these lines had important effects on the relation of the electorate to the party
system. The passing of the Reform Act of 1832 soon led to
a quickening of interest in the possibilities of centralizing the
conduct of election campaigns. Even prior to 1832, large
sums were subscribed in London in the Whig interest and
were dispensed by a responsible body, so as to assist needy
candidates who supported Reform.[1] And a short-lived
organization known as 'The Parliamentary Candidate
Society', having its office at the Whig headquarters, the
Crown and Anchor Tavern in the Strand, was instituted to
co-ordinate information, with the object of recommending
Whig candidates to constituencies. Large subscriptions were
raised by Conservatives in preparation for the election of
1834, when a rudimentary central fund was initiated and a
considerable organization of party activities was undertaken
on Peel's behalf by Lord Granville Somerset.

By 1835 the Conservatives had formed local organizations;
local registration societies had been instituted; and, after the
Reform Bill of 1867 was passed, some local working-men's
Conservative associations had come into being.

Until 1850 the party Whips did much of the work suitable to a central organization. Improvement on this crude
arrangement was largely attributable to Disraeli. Soon after
the defeat of the Conservatives in 1852 he employed Philip
Rose, a solicitor, and later one of Rose's partners, to undertake a revision of party organization in the country; and,
in 1867, largely owing to Disraeli's enthusiasm, the National
Union of Conservative and Constitutional Associations was
established. For some years, however, the activities of this
federation were not extensive, its conferences only being
attended by a small proportion of the representatives of local
associations. Disraeli, perceiving that the defeats of the
Conservatives in 1865 and 1868 were due to lack of efficient
organization, proceeded to set up a Conservative Central
Office under John Gorst, who also became honorary secretary of the National Union.

The Liberals instituted a Registration Association in 1861;
and, in 1877, Joseph Chamberlain founded the National
Liberal Federation, which revolutionized the relations between central and local associations. He called a meeting
of delegates of local Liberal associations; and a plan was

[1] Roebuck, *History of the Whig Ministry of 1830*, vol. ii, p. 161.

outlined, which gave the party machine new features and possibilities. He emphasized the right of the people to have initiative in the selection of candidates and the framing of issues. The new organization, the 'caucus' as it came to be called, immediately proved that, as an electioneering expedient, it was extremely effective. From 1880 onwards, many Liberal local associations chose candidates on condition that they adopted the party programme; and any Liberal candidate who offered himself in opposition to a nominee of the association was treated as a traitor to the cause. The procedure which had previously been used was entirely different. Many candidates had offered themselves for election without formal adoption by a local body, though a few had been recommended by the headquarters of the party; and there had been no arrangement by which candidates had become pledged to a uniform party programme.

The periodical meetings of the Federation soon became concerned with the 'planks' of the party 'platform', and the influence of the Federation in this respect was very considerable in the years between 1883 and 1895. In 1883, 2,500 delegates from 500 associations passed resolutions in favour of the extension of household suffrage to the counties and the admission of women to the franchise. A meeting of the Federation in 1886 decided on a programme which included Home Rule, reform of the land laws, a popular system of county government, local option, and free schools; and, in the following year, the Federation passed a set of resolutions known as 'the Nottingham programme', which included Home Rule, one man one vote, free education, reform of the land laws, disestablishment of the Church in Wales, and labourers' allotments. The leaders of the party tried discreetly to protest against these resolutions being treated as a party programme.

Francis Schnadhorst, the capable organizer chosen by Chamberlain to develop his scheme, was the first secretary of the National Liberal Federation. In 1887 he also became honorary secretary of the Central Liberal Association. The virtual fusion of the Federation staff with the Central Office of the party, which thus took place, seriously limited the capacity of the Federation to control the policy of the party. The Central Office ensured that the Federation did not press any proposals of which the party leaders did not approve. In 1891, for instance, the Federation was anxious to have the question of an eight-hour day brought forward; but they were discouraged by the Central Office, since the leaders did not wish to show their hands on this subject.

It began to be obvious that, if the influence of the Federation was to be kept within the limits desired by the party leaders, it would be necessary that the arrangements for the meetings of the Federation should be carefully prepared by the officials of the Central Association. It was pointed out by Schnadhorst, at the time of the historic meeting at Newcastle in 1891, as well as on subsequent occasions, that delegates attended, not to express opinions, but to hear what measures the leaders of the party could adopt with a reasonable hope of maintaining a united party. As Schnadhorst remarked, it would be impossible for three thousand delegates to enter upon a discussion of fresh principles.

At this meeting at Newcastle (which culminated in a speech by Gladstone), the 'Newcastle programme' was adopted, comprising such diverse points as Home Rule, the disestablishment of the Welsh and Scottish churches, local veto on sale of intoxicants, one man one vote, parish councils, and employers' liability. This catalogue—a typical product of popular influence on the construction of a party programme —was a heavy burden round the neck of the Liberal party for some years to come. It was too extreme in one direction for some, and in another direction for others. The result was division of interest and consequent failure of unity and enthusiasm. The Ministry, which accepted the heads of the programme in general terms, made some show of introducing legislation to fulfil the pledge; but little progress was made; and it was found necessary to throw the blame of obstruction on the House of Lords in order to quiet criticism from the local associations. The history of the Newcastle programme has had the effect of discouraging a repetition of this feature in the decentralization of party management. After the further lessons which were learnt in the election of 1895, the Liberal Central Office was given larger authority; and the power of the local associations diminished in corresponding degree.

In more recent years the Liberal party organization was subjected to revision. The National Liberal Federation acted as a useful co-ordinator of the activities of the local associations; but the shaping of party policy and the big schemes for propaganda were in the hands of the Central

Office, or, more accurately speaking, in the hands of the Organization Committee.

It was soon discovered by the Conservatives that the intensive methods invented by Chamberlain were so effective that no party could afford to neglect them. The Conservative local associations were reorganized, and the Federation of Conservative Associations adopted many of the devices of the so-called caucus. In the Conservative party also, the development of the influence of these associations through their Federation was restrained by the close connexion between the Federation and the Central Office. The appointment of Gorst, as both honorary secretary of the National Union and as head of the Central Office, started a precedent which proved no less prejudicial to the activities of the Conservative Federation than the conjunction of the two offices in one person did for the Liberals. The delegates of the local Conservative associations were, in effect, prevented by the officials of the Central Office, which was under the control of the party leaders, from embarking on proposals likely to prove embarrassing. But it was not so necessary for the Central Office to prepare the ground for the Conservative Federation meetings as for those of the Liberals, since the resolutions passed were not regarded as having a close connexion with the construction of the official party programme.

In practice the composition of the Conservative party programme was, and still is, decided by the Leader of the party, generally after full consultation with his colleagues and with the Central Office. The annual party conference often discusses the items which it considers should be included in the next general election programme. Its resolutions have only an advisory quality and are not binding on the Central Office or the Leader of the party. But, for some years now, slowly increasing respect has been paid to the views of the conference on such subjects. The Chairman of the party organization and the Leader of the party have seen the wisdom of treating the conference as having a practical influence on the party's destinies. In 1925, and to a less extent in 1926, the Conservative Party Conference showed itself restive and dissatisfied at the lethargic way in which Baldwin was confronting national problems. Its protests goaded Baldwin into an attempted justification but not into any immediate action. The Conservative Party Conference in 1929 passed a resolution on the subject of Empire trade. Baldwin, at the concluding meeting, said: 'You have today at your great conference passed a resolution on that subject. On behalf of my colleagues and myself I accept that resolution.' This was a diplomatic gesture.

Since World War II, more hopeful encouragement has been given to the representatives of the rank and file of the party. They have been treated as deserving a genuine opportunity of influencing the choice of the party objectives. R. A. Butler told the conference of 1948 that it was helping to make its own contribution to the formation of policy. At the conference preceding the 1950 election a resolution was passed calling for a policy of building 300,000 new houses a year. This item was accepted by the party chairman and later by Churchill, the Leader of the party. It was adopted as an item in the election programme and proved to be an exceptionally valuable one, especially as the undertaking was fully honoured.

The written constitution of the Labour party gives the impression that the party conference has the main responsibility for the formulation of the party's policy and programme. In fact, the status of the Labour Party Conference is much the same as that of the Conservatives. Their resolutions have a great deal of influence; but they are in no sense obligatory on the Leader of the party. There has been, however, and still remains, a strong feeling among the rank and file of the party that the conference should have the preponderant say in the determination of the party programme. This attitude is largely to be explained by the party's history. Unlike the Conservative party which originated in Parliament and later organized its supporters in the country, the Labour party started outside Parliament and had some ground for expecting that it should control its parliamentary representatives.

In effect the Labour party's programme is decided jointly by the Party Executive and the Parliamentary Labour Party, being finally authorized by the Leader of the party. Respectful attention is paid to the resolutions on the subject passed by the party conference; but the Leader of the party does not regard himself as being bound by them. During several years before World War II the Labour Party Conference passed resolutions demanding the abolition of the 'tied cottage'; but Labour leaders when they came into power took no action, and had to explain that the abolition was much more difficult than the conference supposed.

The negotiations between the Labour Party Conference and the party leaders before the general election of 1929 well illustrated the then-existing divergence in their attitudes. Ramsay MacDonald and his colleagues wished to be free to choose their programme in accordance with the political situation as it developed. The conference wanted to prescribe an elaborate programme of socialistic projects. MacDonald pointed out that a large delegate assembly was unsuited to draft a party programme partly because it was unable to assess what was practicable having regard to problems of administration and problems of parliamentary management. When it came to the point, the Labour party programme for the 1929 election was chosen by the party leaders quite untrammelled by any dictation by the party conference. The leaders published a programme of moderate social reform, with only a slight socialist flavour.

Not only in regard to the party programme but in general the position of the Leader of the party and his colleagues has recently been strengthened in relation to the National Executive Committee of the party (the administrative body which is responsible for managing business and general policy as opposed to the parliamentary side of the party's activities). This committee has a considerable proportion of non-parliamentary members; and about half the members represent trade unions. There has been some risk that this body might arrogate to itself the right to dictate to the parliamentary leaders the way in which they should conduct affairs in Parliament and elsewhere. In 1945 Professor H. J. Laski, as chairman of this committee, took it upon himself to tell Attlee, the Leader of the party, how he should comport himself at an international conference. Attlee did not remonstrate with Laski, but he made it clear to Churchill, then Prime Minister, in a spirited correspondence, that he was not subject to instructions from the National Executive Committee. In his autobiography Attlee wrote: 'He [Laski] issued this statement as Chairman of the Executive although he had no authority to do so. The Chairman of the Executive does not make authoritative pronouncements of this kind.' Since this incident the Central Office of the Labour party has issued a statement establishing that although provision is made in the party constitution for consultation between

Labour M.P.s and the National Executive Committee, the latter has no authority over the actions of Labour Ministers or M.P.s when exercising parliamentary duties. This is a valuable point to make plain because the subordination of a Labour Government to a non-Parliamentary body like the National Executive Committee would be subversive of parliamentary democracy.

It is interesting to notice that, in spite of the differences in their historical antecedents, the Conservative and Labour party organizations are tending towards similarity. Their increasing resemblance is due on the one hand to the recognition by the Conservatives that improved education in the electorate calls for a more genuine respect for suggestions emanating from the representatives of the constituencies, and on the other hand to the recognition by the Labour party that it must be guided in essentials by its leaders, who must not be subject to detailed dictation from delegate bodies or non-parliamentary committees.

Labour members, when elected, are required by the Constitution to subject themselves to party discipline. These provisions are more explicit than any adopted by the Conservatives; but the practice of the latter is in fact not much less exacting than that of the Labour party.[1]

As a result of the growth of party organizations, both central and local, during the last century, each party now possesses a machine of vast potentiality. In the first stages of this development in the Conservative and Liberal parties, the vigour of local associations was more notable than the increase in the power of the Central Offices. Latterly, the opposite has been the case. Yet at no stage has there been any real prospect that the extension of local party organization would give the constituencies a commensurate accession of power. The party machinery has provided efficient channels of communication between headquarters and the country; but the traffic in these channels has been chiefly from the centre to the circumference. They have been much more utilized for the exertion of the influence of the central organization and the party leaders than as a means for the communication of the ideas of the local associations to headquarters. The influence of the constituencies, the rank and

[1] The Conservative party has recently tightened its hold by insisting on candidates' election expenses being paid by the local associations.

file, on the Central Offices has been singularly small. It might have been anticipated that federations of local associations would have enabled them to enforce their views on the leaders, if not in respect of party administration, at least in respect of election issues. But, owing largely to the absence of independence of the federation staffs and to the tendency towards concentration of power in the hands of the Leader of the party, his colleagues, and his officers at the Central Office, the local associations have been deprived of much of their possible range of influence.

It does not follow, however, that this course of development has been detrimental to the real interests of the people. The provision of means of communication between the Central Offices and the constituencies, with the ability of the Central Offices to dictate election programmes to candidates, has led to the official definition, and thus to the uniformity of the questions to be put to the electorate. It has been possible for one question or set of questions to be put, instead of a confusing variety of questions. The history of the Newcastle programme is sufficient illustration of the disadvantages of undue initiative on the part of local associations. The people's voice has spoken with less freedom than it would if greater control over the party organizations had been obtained by them; but it has spoken with less ambiguity.

It is, of course, permissible to argue that it would be better for the people to give a doubtful answer to questions of their own asking than a clear answer to questions in which their interest has not been consulted. There is an obvious temptation to politicians to select issues from the point of view of expediency. They can force issues to the front which they anticipate will bring them into power, regardless of their intrinsic worth. They can shelve issues that require decision and action, if they appear to involve exclusion from office. It is sometimes alleged that important measures of reform, although probably favoured by a large majority of voters, are left in the hands of private members because no party finds them worth undertaking. Party managers are afraid that the inclusion in the party programme of proposals which cut across party divisions may endanger existing allegiances. This is certainly true; but it seems to be one of the inevitable drawbacks to the working of the party system as understood to-day. Nevertheless, non-party measures do from time to time receive the consideration of Parliament; and, on these occasions, the Whips allow members to vote in accordance with their independent opinions. One of the most notable instances of an important measure of reform being left for introduction to the energy and enterprise of a private member was Sir Alan Herbert's Matrimonial Causes Act, 1937.

Objections to the strict discipline imposed by all parties on their members in the House of Commons are obvious; but it must be remembered that, the surer the solidarity of a party, the better it is able to carry out its pledges. Undertakings can be given to the people at general elections with a greater sense of responsibility and are capable of being performed with a greater fidelity if the leaders know that their supposed adherents will stand by them. It is only with a large measure of collaboration between members within their parties that parties can be instruments of democratic government.

§ 3. *Party educational departments*

Since the beginning of this century party organizations have included branches devoted to political education. Doubtless, adherents of one party talk slightingly of the 'party propaganda' of their rivals. In recent years, however, much of the work of the educational departments of all parties has been primarily educative and only incidentally effective as training for party campaigners. No party organization would pretend that its political education is impartial. Indeed, impartiality and party activities are inconsistent.

The Liberal party made an early start in this kind of undertaking, with considerable activity in the issue of literature and periodicals from 1887. At first its publications were directed mainly at electioneering, but later the base was broadened.

After their defeat in the election of 1945, the Conservative party's educational department was developed into the Conservative Political Centre, and a good deal of energy and enterprise was put into the project. It aims high, having the express intention of stimulating people to think about politics and not merely to tell them what to think. It eschews propaganda in the bad sense and avoids mass emotional appeal. A 'two-way movement of ideas' is encouraged, whereby the views of headquarters offered to the constituencies are balanced by the transmission of the views of the constituencies to headquarters. The Conservative Political Centre adopts all the standard means of political education, such as conferences, lectures, discussion groups, books, pamphlets, and periodicals.

The Labour party also made considerable strides in the matter of political education during the period following World War II. The quality of party literature was improved; and the party periodicals were brightened and given a wider usefulness. Particular attention is paid to the promotion of discussion groups.

It is much to be hoped that political parties will remain active in this field, and continue to emphasize the need for the formation of opinion by discussion and the qualification for discussion by the exercise of independent thought. In this way we may hope to have a nation of politicians whose political notions are based on enlightenment rather than indoctrination.

CHAPTER VII

THE CHOICE OF MINISTRIES

§ 1. *Ministries dependent on the Crown*

As late as the reign of William III the King not only retained a considerable freedom in the choice of his Ministers, but, in certain respects, he directed their work. William III acted as his own efficient Secretary of State, at least as regards foreign affairs, and, to a less extent, as regards matters of finance. The preference which he displayed for Ministries comprised of members of both parties was doubtless based, in some degree, on a desire to secure financial support from a House of Commons which undeniably occupied a position of enhanced importance. But the selection of Ministers depended chiefly on the King's views regarding the skill, influence, and compliance of the politicians of the day. Such inclinations of the people towards one party or another as were to be gathered from the results of elections of members of Parliament had, at the most, a remote influence on the choice of the King's advisers; and it was, as a rule, only indirectly that the attitude of the House of Commons influenced the composition of the Ministry. Indeed, the King's choice of his advisers was sometimes a determining factor in the membership of the House of Commons. The Whig victory in the elections of 1695 was doubtless largely due to the substitution of Whig for Tory Ministers, which had been proceeding in 1694. Again, in February 1701, the improvement in the position of the Tories in the House of Commons was to some extent attributable to the introduction of Tory Ministers into the Government prior to the election.

As Professor Trevelyan has shown, Queen Anne's chief contribution to the constitutional history of her period was the assertion of her right to choose her Ministers independently of party and of Parliament; and, in her reign too, the composition of the Ministry often had a considerable influence on the membership of the House of Commons rather than the opposite. In 1702 and 1710 her choice (made shortly before general elections) helped to produce Tory majorities. Her habit of arranging alterations in the personnel of her Ministries prior to general elections provides a complete contrast to the principles of the present day.

Although Queen Anne maintained a persistent attitude in regard to the appointment of mixed Ministries, her reign marks the beginning of a dissociation between the Sovereign and the Ministry. The separation between the two led inevitably to a decrease in the initiative of the Sovereign. In fairness to the Queen it must be allowed that the decline in the importance of the position of the Sovereign in her reign was not primarily due to any marked incapacity on her part, except, perhaps, in matters of finance. It is now generally recognized that her obtuseness and stolidity have been overdrawn by many of the older historians. But the accession to the throne of a woman of only moderate gifts at a time when the aspect of foreign politics demanded the highest capacity and statesmanship tended to give the Ministry an identity of its own through its exercise of increased powers.

The times were ripe for a differentiation between the head of the State and the body responsible for its government. Separation between the Sovereign and the Ministry became inevitable during the reigns of the first two Georges, who were unfitted by reason of their foreign origin to direct the Government, though this very reason caused them to insist on being kept informed of the conduct of foreign policy. During periods of stress, such as that of the Spanish War of 1739 and 1740 and the Seven Years War, the need for firm direction and vigorous action resulted in a closer association and a more definite integration of the Ministerial body. Under George II the King's free choice of Ministers was seriously undermined, and he was humiliated by the independent attitude of his later Ministries. In particular, the Pelhams found the way to force themselves upon him and to prevent his keeping Carteret as his Minister.

George III was able to re-establish the supreme position of the Sovereign to a limited extent; but, in spite of his determination to 'be a King', he had to submit to a considerable measure of dictation by the Whig families. He always regarded the acceptance of Ministries that were not of his own choice as involving inroads on his prerogative; and he took the earliest opportunity to devise means to turn them out of office. Many politicians still maintained that it was unconstitutional for the King to have a Ministry forced upon him.[1]

[1] See, for instance *Hist. MSS. Comm., 15th Report*, Appendix, Part VI

The large majority obtained by the younger Pitt in the election of 1784 represented not only a personal triumph for the young Minister, but also a triumph for the King in his assertion of the right to choose his own Ministers; and although this confirmation of the King's choice of Pitt did not imply that in the future the King was to have absolute discretion in respect of the composition of the Cabinet—it was in fact clear that a powerful Minister like Pitt was capable of maintaining himself against the Crown—it meant that, until the era of the great Reform Bill, the Crown retained the power of nominating the Prime Minister and thereby determining in a great measure the composition of the Cabinet. Prior to 1832 the ability of the King to obtain a majority in favour of the Ministry of his choice was a potent factor in enabling him to exercise that choice freely.

In the early years of the nineteenth century George III and George IV (the latter both as Regent and as King) insisted with success on their right to choose their Ministers; and more than one attempt at Cabinet making failed because the views of George IV had been overlooked. It must be borne in mind, however, that the 'group system', into which party government had degenerated in the early nineteenth century, afforded peculiar facilities for the retention of rights which were in fact obsolescent. If there had been two clearly divided parties under George IV, it is doubtful whether he would have been able to sustain his view of the prerogative.

By the end of 1830 it was obvious that the country would insist on an early treatment of the subject of Reform. Canningites and moderate reformers placed themselves under Grey, who, with their concurrence, took his place as leader of the Opposition immediately the new Parliament met in October 1830. When, therefore, Wellington resigned on being defeated in the House of Commons in the following month, the King had no alternative but to appoint Grey as Prime Minister. On this historic occasion his freedom of choice was non-existent; and, in this respect, as in others, it was evident that a new era had set in. As Sir Robert Peel complained in a debate on the Reform Bill:

How could the King hereafter change a Ministry? How could he make a partial change in the administration, in times of public excitement, with any prospect that the Ministers of his choice,

(Carlisle MSS.), pp. 581, 594, Selwyn to Lord Carlisle, 19 Feb. and 16 Mar. 1782.

unpopular perhaps from the strict performance of necessary duties, would be returned to Parliament?[1]

Nevertheless, William IV, oblivious of the implications arising out of the passing of the Reform Act, took it upon himself, in 1834, so to encourage the resignation of the Melbourne Ministry as almost to amount to a signification of dismissal. He did this in the hope that his appointment of a new Prime Minister would lead, as it had in the past, to an assured majority for the Minister of his choice in a new Parliament. The failure of Peel (Melbourne's successor) to secure such a majority meant a death-blow to the power of the King to nominate his Ministers, and would have involved him in considerably greater embarrassment than it did, if the discussion of the constitutional question in the House of Commons had not led to a reaffirmation of the principle of the impersonal aspect of the King's actions of a political character.

Peel's assumption of Ministerial responsibility for the King's intervention can only have emphasized that this phase of monarchical government had come to a definite end; for it must have been apparent that not even the most ambitious Opposition leader could undertake to advise the King to dismiss his existing Prime Minister and to appoint himself.

Even at the present day, the Sovereign, although normally bound to appoint as Prime Minister the acknowledged leader of the party approved by the people, may in peculiar circumstances, such as those which prevailed in 1923, when Baldwin and Curzon were both possible appointees to the premiership, still have to choose between leaders who are qualified for the post. Queen Victoria, on one occasion, passed over the person who was generally regarded as entitled to the appointment. On the final retirement of Gladstone in 1894 it might have been expected that the Chancellor of the Exchequer, Sir William Harcourt, who had in point of service undeniable claims, would have been chosen as Prime Minister. Gladstone had some reason, based on the manner in which constitutional usage had developed, to expect that his advice as retiring Prime Minister would be taken. He had intended, if consulted, to advise the Queen to send for Lord Spencer. But the Queen, on her own responsibility and without consulting the retiring Prime Minister, as has been usual in doubtful cases, sent for Lord Rosebery, the Secretary for Foreign

[1] 11 *Parl. Deb.*, 3 s., 757.
[2] 26 *Parl. Deb.*, 3 s., 76, 83, 89, 215–20, 257.

Affairs, and entrusted him with the formation of the new Ministry. Earlier in her reign, in 1859, she had endeavoured to pass over the person who had the most obvious claim to the office of Prime Minister, Palmerston, and to appoint Granville, a more amenable person. But the failure of the latter to construct a Ministry forced her to entrust the Government to the former. This discrimination between politicians of the same party is of a very different character to the removal of a Ministry, when in possession of a majority in Parliament, such as took place in 1834.

It must be borne in mind that, if it should happen that the two-party system should be superseded by a system of groups, the Sovereign's obligation to select a Prime Minister not only may become more frequent, but may involve a much wider discretion than that exercised for the last hundred years.

There may be occasions, too, when the coalition of parties will impose on the Sovereign the choice of a Prime Minister. If the coalition is one of individuals rather than of parties the extension of the royal powers may prove to be a very serious one, since the Sovereign in these circumstances has not merely to choose one of the leaders of the party approved by the majority of the constituencies, but to choose an individual in his or her own discretion.

King George V had a very difficult problem to settle in 1931, when the Labour party Prime Minister, Ramsay MacDonald, whose administration was caught up in an economic blizzard, resigned owing to dissensions among his colleagues. The natural course for the King to take would have been to send for Baldwin, the Leader of the next largest party, and to charge him with the formation of a Ministry. Alternatively, it was open to him to ask for MacDonald's advice or Baldwin's advice on how to proceed. MacDonald had had only brief experiences as a Prime Minister, and Baldwin was not available for some hours. The situation was urgent. The King, therefore, sought the advice of Samuel, the acting leader of the third party (the Liberals), who impressed the King with his arguments in favour of an all-party government under MacDonald's leadership. This solution of the problem appealed to the King; and, after further negotiations between the party leaders, he commissioned MacDonald to form a Ministry. In this episode the King was undoubtedly placed in a position requiring considerable skill in the interpretation of constitutional conventions.

§ 2. *Ministries dependent on the House of Commons*

The change in the political centre of gravity, from the King towards the House of Commons, which was, in spite of occasional checks, a marked feature of the constitutional history of the eighteenth century, can be largely attributed to Walpole. Not only was he a thorough 'House of Commons man', but he was also the earliest effective exponent of the doctrine of cabinet solidarity and collective responsibility. Even his resignation in 1742, on the defeat of his Ministry in the House of Commons, pointed a way by which the House could extend its power over the life of the Ministry. Competition between the King and the aristocracy, however, prevented these principles from being steadily developed. It is true that the whole Pelham Ministry resigned in 1746, so as to force the King to accept its views; but the resignation savoured rather of stratagem than of recognition of a point of principle.

It was in the interest of the Whig families, in their endeavour to replace a monarchy by an aristocracy, to maintain the dependence of the Ministry on a majority in the House of Commons; but the middle of the eighteenth century was not a period favourable to the liberalization of the Constitution. Half of the reign of George III passed before Lord Chancellor Thurlow's insubordination was checked by the younger Pitt, and the joint and several responsibility of members of the Ministry became a recognized and settled factor. Before that stage was reached Ministers frequently acted in opposition to their own colleagues. Chatham's second Ministry, which George III hoped to be devoid of party colour and entirely dependent on himself, was an instance of the extent to which reaction could go. This Ministry was an administration 'by departments', after the old model which had prevailed just a hundred years before. Chatham had formed the Ministry on the King's prescription of avoiding all party ties; the result was that the members of the Ministry did not loyally pursue any common policy; and some of them acted in open revolt against their chief. Conway, for instance, in 1766, insisted on adopting an attitude of independence from his colleagues and frequently voted against them; and, in the same year, Townshend intrigued against his chief and even went to the length of maintaining, in direct opposition to the Ministerial view,

THE CHOICE OF MINISTRIES

the propriety of taxing the American colonies. This kind of indiscipline was regarded, even contemporaneously, as improper. Chatham, however, had himself assailed the measures of his colleagues in 1755, so that he was hardly in a position to complain.

At the time of the Fox–North Coalition of 1783 Fox urged upon North that the King should not be allowed to act as his own Minister. North replied:

> If you mean there should not be a government by depart-ments, I agree with you. I think it a very bad system. There should be one man or a Cabinet to govern and direct every measure. Government by departments was not brought in by me. I found it so, and had not the vigour or resolution to put an end to it.[1]

It is obvious that, until corporate responsibility became established, Ministries did not regard themselves as dependent on a majority in the House of Commons. Although the King could usually contrive to have a majority for the Ministers of his choice, they occasionally suffered defeat on matters of importance without feeling it incumbent on them to resign, and sometimes even without the Opposition expecting or suggesting that they should do so. A notable instance of this attitude is, naturally enough, found in the course of the second Ministry of Chatham, to which reference has just been made. The Ministers in their budget proposals of 1767 fixed the land-tax at the high figure of four shillings in the pound. The Opposition proposed to reduce the tax to three shillings; and this amendment was carried with the support of some members of the Ministry. Although the Government was thus defeated on a financial measure of importance, the Ministers did not resign. A few years later, between 1780 and 1782, Lord North's Ministry, which was kept in office by the combined prayers and threats of George III, was defeated on several occasions without yielding up office. On one of these occasions, the strangeness of the circumstance of defeat, but not of the absence of resignation, was remarked upon by the younger Pitt, at the age of twenty in a letter to his mother. He described it as a 'great phenomenon'.[2]

It may well be imagined that the King would have treated

---

[1] *Memorials and Correspondence of C. J. Fox*, vol. ii, p. 38. By the phrase 'government by departments' he implied that the head of the Ministry acted as little more than the chief agent of the Sovereign

[2] Stanhope, *Life of Pitt* (1861 ed.), vol. i, p. 38.

with scorn any suggestion that his Ministers' position should regularly depend on the votes of the House of Commons, even in respect of vital questions. There was still current the old principle that it was the duty of members of Parliament in general to support the King's Ministry. In so far as legislative measures were concerned, a party programme was unessential, so that defeats in regard to proposals for legislation were not of so much consequence as they are today, when a positive policy is the very backbone of a Government's existence. No example can, in fact, be found prior to 1830 of a Ministry retiring because it was beaten cn a question of legislation or even of taxation.

The relations of the Ministry to the Crown, the House of Commons, and the people were fully discussed in the early months of 1784, that is to say immediately after the younger Pitt had been given office, although in a minority in the House of Commons. Charles James Fox was the chief exponent of the view that a Ministry in a minority could not continue to hold office, but should resign. Pitt replied that he believed that his Ministry, although not at the moment commanding a majority in the House of Commons, was possessed of the confidence of the nation. But he did not say that he was prepared at that moment to put his belief to the test by advising a dissolution. On the contrary, he soon gave a somewhat ambiguous assurance, on being pressed by the Opposition, which wanted resignation and not dissolution, that he had no intention of obtaining an early dissolution. It is a matter of general agreement that his retention of office, though capable of being vindicated on very broad grounds, cannot be reconciled with constitutional principles. Perhaps the best justifications of Pitt's retention of office in a minority were, first, that he was making a sustained effort to gain a majority and was displaying evidence of his improved prospects, and, secondly, that he was not only entitled, but to some extent bound, to complete the business of the session before advising a dissolution.

In a further debate on 1 March 1784 Fox reiterated his arguments with the object of demonstrating that the House of Commons, 'stationed as sentinels by the people', had power to insist on the resignation of the Ministry; and, on this occasion, he, in his turn, gave consideration to popular arguments and contended that it was the interest of the people which was at the root of the attitude of the Opposition. 'We wish', he insisted, 'to increase the weight of the people in the Constitution; your object [turning to the Ministry] is to lessen their weight.'

In answer to these contentions, Pitt adopted expedients which were as specious as Fox's were disingenuous. He claimed that a Ministry was not bound to resign after a vote of general non-confidence, but that it was necessary for the House to specify particular charges. A Ministry, he said, should not be capriciously condemned until its incapacity had been proved.[1] When Pitt felt the time was ripe—towards the end of March 1784—he advised a dissolution. For the first time a Minister chosen by the Crown, who had not a majority in Parliament, appealed to the people in a manner which implied that the decision rested with them. But the claims of the King to the free choice of his Ministers, and the denial by the Whigs of the right of Pitt to advise what Burke described as a 'penal dissolution', tended to confuse the character of the development in constitutional usage. In some respects even the results of the incidents of 1784 were reactionary, since the House of Commons was flouted and the king's claims sustained at the expense of those of the Whigs.

For a short further period the notion still prevailed that Ministers chosen by the Sovereign should not be opposed by members of Parliament immediately after their appointment on merely personal or general grounds, and that they should be given a fair opportunity of proving whether their administration was acceptable to the House or not. After a few years Pitt's view was proved to be untenable, and the House of Commons was to secure an unqualified right to withhold its confidence from Ministers.[2]

The principle of the dependence of the Ministry on the representatives of the people, although having its roots extending well back into the eighteenth century, was not fully recognized for some years after the passing of the first Reform Act. The earliest vote of censure, which took the form of the modern vote of non-confidence, seems to have been proposed at the end of North's Ministry in 1782. And, as has been remarked, there was no plain example of a

[1] 24 Parl. Hist. 364, 365, 432, 433, 483, 690, 709, 710.
[2] Cf. Lecky, History of England in the Eighteenth Century, vol. v, p. 251.

Ministry resigning because it was defeated in the House of Commons prior to 1830. Walpole's resignation in 1742, which is mentioned elsewhere in this book,[1] is, owing to the personal nature of the attack on the Minister and from other circumstances, such as the incomplete change in the composition of the new Ministry, unsuitable to be regarded as a precedent. Again, it is hardly useful to draw any conclusions from the resignation of Shelburne in 1783, an event in which lack of support from his colleagues had much to do. Even Wellington's resignation, in 1830, followed an unimportant defeat, which was seized upon by the Ministers themselves as an expedient for leaving office on some subject other than Reform.

After the passing of the Reform Act of 1832, however, the question of the importance to the Ministry of maintaining a majority in the House of Commons became a very real one. When, in 1834, Peel was appointed Prime Minister in succession to Melbourne, in circumstances which have already been mentioned, he immediately dissolved Parliament and gained some accession of strength in the House of Commons, but not sufficient to provide him with a majority. He remained in office for some weeks, suffering several defeats in the House. It was at this time that he made his famous appeal for a 'fair trial'; and he had, perhaps, some ground for complaint that he was continually being threatened with votes of non-confidence, which were never brought forward. His opponents preferred to resort to more indirect expedients and pretended to abstain from votes of censure, in order to enable the Ministry to introduce its programme of legislation. Nevertheless, Lord John Russell, who led the Opposition in the House of Commons, characterized Peel's retention of office as 'extraordinary', a charge which led Peel to assert that the adverse votes were, so to speak, accidental and did not imply lack of confidence.[2]

Peel, however, soon realized that it was unconstitutional to continue, for more than a short time, to conduct the Government with a minority in the House of Commons. 'Nothing can, in my opinion,' he said in a memorandum addressed to his colleagues, 'justify the administration in persevering against a majority, but a rational and well-founded hope of acquiring additional support and converting

---

[1] See pp. 108, 116 above and p. 160 below.
[2] 26 *Parl. Deb.*, 3 s., 471, 474.

a minority into a majority.' Unlike Pitt in 1784, he saw no ground for entertaining such a hope. Moreover, Pitt had continued in a minority while waiting for the suitable moment for a dissolution; whereas Peel had gone to the country immediately after his appointment. After some seven weeks' struggle he decided that it would be improper to disregard any longer the steady opposition of the House of Commons, and he resigned.

A situation which was in some respects similar arose in 1841. The tables were then turned. The Melbourne Ministry, for which Russell was leader in the House of Commons, suffered a series of defeats without resigning; and Peel finally moved a vote of non-confidence. The considerable length of the debate and the energy expended, in discussing whether the defeats already suffered were vital to the Ministry or not, are to be explained by the incomplete recognition of the dependence of the Ministry on the House of Commons up to that time.

Peel reviewed, in support of his motion, the circumstances of the reverses of the Liberal Ministry; and he asserted that its continuance in office without the confidence of the House, which he denied to be possessed by the Ministry, was 'at variance with the principles and spirit of the Constitution'. He quoted, in support of his argument, the resignation of Walpole in 1742, of North in 1782, and of himself in 1835, the last after carrying on 'for a short time an unequal contest in opposition to the power leagued against me'. It may be remarked, parenthetically, that the instances of 1742 and 1782 do not carry much weight. The former has already been noticed, and, in the latter, North had for a long time been trying vainly to persuade the King to liberate him; and, when the vote on the motion of non-confidence was taken in 1782, North retained a small majority. In reply to Peel the supporters of the Melbourne Ministry adduced many examples of previous Ministries remaining in office after defeats in the House of Commons, several of them inapposite owing to their remoteness in time, if for no other reason.

It was, however, obvious that a defence could not be made to rest solely on precedents for the entire disregard of adverse votes in the House of Commons. A distinction was, therefore, drawn between the confidence of the House of Commons in general administration and in proposals for legislation. It was contended by Macaulay that a Ministry was not bound to resign because it could not obtain a majority for its legislative projects, unless such a failure involved an inability to carry on the public service.

A similar justification for disregarding the voting in the House of Commons as a determining factor in the life of a Ministry was advanced with much insistence at a later stage in the debate by Lord John Russell. He pointed out that, in the time of Walpole, Chatham, Pitt, and Fox, very little legislation was undertaken and that the function of a Ministry was largely confined to administration. There had been no obligation to introduce legislative changes until after the passing of the Reform Bill. It was unreasonable, he argued, that a Government should possess 'the same general uniform support which was required when Ministries had merely acts of administration to perform'.

The contentions of Macaulay and Russell were effectively dealt with by Peel in the reply which closed the debate. Peel protested that it was not fair for a Ministry to have the power of excluding any legislative measures it liked from those on which an adverse vote would imply a lack of confidence. This was a power which should reside in the House of Commons only. Macaulay's doctrine, that it was the main duty of a Ministry to administer the law and that in this way it could claim the right to show itself indifferent to defeats on legislative proposals, was 'so unconstitutional, so dangerous a doctrine' as he ever heard maintained. Peel strongly repudiated the suggestion that the confidence of the House was based on the record of administration rather than that of legislation. In the first place, the two were 'so interwoven' as 'to render it utterly impossible to draw a line of distinction between them'. And, further, Peel said, 'the character of an Administration and their claim upon public confidence is infinitely stronger on account of their legislative measures, than on account of their administrative acts'. And he pointed to the way in which recent politics had been overshadowed by the importance of such legislation as that respecting Roman Catholic Relief, Parliamentary Reform, and the Poor Law.[1]

Peel's view of the constitutional position was the modern one. And, as regards the distinction between administrative and legislative functions, the claim that a Ministry depends more on its legislative than on its administrative policy is, in

[1] 58 *Parl. Deb.*, 3 s., 803 ff., 881, 885, 1195, 1222–4.

so far as the two can be distinguished, more forcible nowadays than it was at the period of Peel and Russell. Few great administrative changes or reforms can now be carried through without legislative action.

A cardinal principle was secured as a result of the debate on Peel's motion of non-confidence in 1841. In subsequent years discussions have taken place, when no motion of non-confidence was before the House, whether or not a particular defeat was fatal to the life of the Ministry; but it has never again been necessary, in debating a motion of censure, to attempt to establish, with so large a reference to precedent as that made in 1841, that defeats in respect of legislative proposals may raise the implication of a lack of confidence. In discussions subsequent to 1841 hardly any real doubt has been thrown on the principle of the dependence of a Ministry on a majority in the House of Commons.[1]

There has been, in the past, some discussion regarding the ability of the House of Commons to ensure that no Ministry shall remain in office against the will of the House by means of refusal to grant Supplies or to pass the Mutiny Act. This 'ultimate legal sanction' is unlikely ever again to come within the sphere of practical politics. Now that it is fully admitted that a Ministry cannot continue its career in disregard of a clear intimation that it no longer possesses the confidence of the House of Commons, the application of this sanction, crude and clumsy as it is, seems to be unnecessary. It has, in fact, become well understood that a Ministry ought not to be coerced by threats of a refusal to provide requisite funds for carrying on the government. The threat of Fox in 1784 ended ignominiously; and more recent insinuations, made in the nineteenth century, that, unless the Ministry yielded, Supplies might be stopped, did not reflect credit on their authors.

§ 3. Ministries dependent on the people

For a considerable period after the Sovereign ceased to have unfettered ability to choose Ministers, and before the people gained the power to choose between rival Ministries,

---

[1] An elaborate review of the difficulties that face a Ministry, in determining whether a particular defeat is of a kind requiring resignation or dissolution, was provided by Balfour in a statement to the House after the defeat of his Ministry on a vote upon the estimates in 1905. See 150 *Parl. Deb.*, 4 s., 49 ff.

the change of government often depended on the voting in the House of Commons. This period was one in which party loyalties were loose, and consequently Ministries were often uncertain of maintaining their majorities in the House. But, since the time when party solidarity became habitual in the late nineteenth century, governments have not been subject to defeat in the House of Commons unless they have lost the support of a third party. From this stage onwards the choice of Ministries has been in effect in the hands of the electorate. But we must go back over the years and clear the ground.

One or two writers have regarded the circumstances of the election of 1741 as expressive of an advance towards democratic government. It has been said, for instance, that this election was 'the first upon which it was distinctly understood that the fate of an administration depended'.[1] But the motion for the removal of Walpole, which was signally defeated only a few weeks before his reverses in the election of 1741, was not intended by its supporters to be an attack on the whole administration, though Walpole alleged in his defence that, if there had been faults of policy, they were those of the Council or even of Parliament as a whole. It is certainly true that there was considerable talk in the course of the speeches of the supporters of the motion regarding the anxiety of the people to show their disapproval of the 'First Minister'; and charges of maladministration undoubtedly coloured the election campaign, with the result that there arose a popular issue of unusually vivid interest. The issue, however, was rather that of confidence or non-confidence in Walpole than that of confidence or non-confidence in the Ministry; and even the personal issue cannot be said to have been plainly decided as a result of the election.

Evidence for the absence of any effective decision on the merits of the administration, at the election of 1741, can be found in the incomplete changes which were made in the composition of the Ministry after Walpole's retirement and the maintenance of, or at least the eventual acquiescence in, many of his principles of home government. The attack of the Opposition was centred on Walpole himself, who, by his self-sufficient attitude and by his long period of power, had aroused a peculiarly keen animosity against him in a group of ambitious politicians. Many years were to pass before cleaner

[1] Blauvelt, *Development of Cabinet Government in England*, p. 208; and see pp. 108, 116 above. With regard to the election of 1734, see p. 237 (note 1) below.

politics, greater enlightenment, and a more straightforward working of the party system were to enable the people to have any direct and recognized influence on the fate of Ministries.

The few occasions in the eighteenth century when the change of Ministries can in any way be attributed to the influence of the people were those when public opinion, aroused by serious situations in politics, displayed a strong antagonism to particular Ministers at times other than those of general elections. The artificial majorities of the reigns of George II and George III were not always sufficient to impose on the people Ministers of whom they did not approve. The majority in the House of Commons might be unshaken; but there was felt to be an Opposition outside the House which could not be neglected. In 1756 Newcastle, and in 1763 Bute, resigned, chiefly it may be presumed, because they were unable to face the clamour of the people; and North finally secured his freedom from office in similar circumstances in 1782.[1]

It was not until much later that the preference of a majority of the constituencies for one party or the other decided which set of politicians should take office. From the middle of the nineteenth century the people exercised an increasing ability to decide the character of the Ministry to hold office by means of their voting at general elections. In such a period, say, as that between 1870 and 1910, during which the two-party system was to a considerable extent effective, it sometimes happened that a Ministry which obtained a large majority at a general election managed to survive the whole period of a Parliament without suffering serious defeats. The increase in the closeness of party discipline had assisted this development. In these circumstances, the dependence of the Ministry on the House of Commons diminished; and the function of the House became rather that of keeping Ministers in office than of watching to turn them out. As a result, the life of the Ministry has grown more and more dependent on the outcome of the people's voting at general elections, it being understood that Ministries should resign immediately it has become clear that their majority has been lost.

The circumstances surrounding the election of 1841 mark an intermediate stage in the development. Prior to that

---

[1] L. B. Namier, *England in the Age of the American Revolution*, vol. i, pp. 179–80. For the inferences to be drawn from the circumstances of the election of 1784, see p. 110 above, and pp. 194–6 below.

time the Ministry depended, as has been observed, on the
King or only mediately on the people through the House
of Commons. But, from 1841 onwards, the people's verdict
in a general election came to be talked of as the determining
factor in the choice of the Ministry. In and after 1868 that
verdict was, in all clear cases, absolute.

Melbourne's advice to Queen Victoria in 1841 and the
attitude adopted by her as a result of that advice demonstrate
a failure, almost rivalling that of William IV, to understand
the current movement towards democratic control of government. Melbourne told the Queen that the return of a
majority in favour of the Opposition would be 'an affront
to the Crown'; and the Queen so completely accepted this
view of the function of a general election that, in writing to
Lord John Russell five years later, she mentioned the dissolution of Parliament as a valuable instrument in the hands of
the Crown, which should only be used 'with a certainty of
success'. The letter proceeds: 'The Queen strongly feels that
she made a mistake in allowing the dissolution in 1841; the
result has been a majority returned against her of nearly
one hundred votes.'[1] Neither the Queen nor Melbourne
seems to have interpreted the events connected with the
passing of the Reform Bill as pointing towards the ability of
the people to choose between alternative Ministries without
any regard to the views of the Sovereign.

The elections of 1841 resulted in the return of a large
majority opposed to Melbourne. He determined to meet
Parliament for the reason that the opinion of members could
not constitutionally be inferred, save as a result of voting
in the House of Commons. When Parliament met and an
amendment was moved in the House of Lords to the effect
that the Ministry had not the confidence of the House of
Commons and of the country, Lord Melbourne remarked:

The meaning of this motion in plain English is, 'we [the
Opposition] have now a majority in the House of Commons'. To
judge by some of the declarations at the hustings, I suppose there
is such a majority. At the same time it must be recollected that
members are sent *ad consultandum de rebus arduis regni*. We are not,
therefore, to judge what the conduct of members may be by their
declarations on the hustings.[2]

The amendment to the Address in the House of Commons

[1] *Letters of Queen Victoria*, 1st Series, vol. ii, pp. 107–8.
[2] 59 *Parl. Deb.*, 3 s., 71.

was carried against the Melbourne Ministry by a majority of over ninety. Disraeli, when speaking in this debate, argued that Melbourne's proper course should have been to have resigned after the vote of lack of confidence recorded in the last Parliament and, in particular, after the country had confirmed the judgement of Parliament by their votes in the elections. The Liberals pointed to Peel's retention of office for some weeks in 1835; but Disraeli distinguished that occasion on the ground that Peel had not been subjected to a vote of non-confidence. It was evident that Disraeli was nearly, if not quite, alone in his advanced interpretation of constitutional usage. Lord Broughton observed, in his *Recollections of a Long Life*,[1] that both Graham and Stanley, on Disraeli's side, gave a negative shake of the head when Disraeli made his point.

In 1866 the Conservatives, although in a minority, came into office in the course of a Parliament in which the Liberals, divided on the question of Reform, had been bound to resign after a few months of power. But the Conservatives did not, in accordance with the convention of the present day, at once advise a dissolution and appeal to the people. They remained in office for more than two years and secured the passing of the Reform Act of 1867. In 1868 they advised a dissolution; and, on suffering a clear defeat in the election, they immediately resigned without waiting to meet Parliament. This resignation has been described as 'a mark in the constitutional history of the country'. As Spencer Walpole observed:

It is the first open recognition in history that the House of Commons itself was of less importance than the electors. . . . The first election in which all borough householders were entitled to take part was the first election whose decision, without any parliamentary confirmation, decided the fate of a Ministry.[2]

The Queen, instead of clinging as long as possible to her Ministers, saw that it would be more dignified and less painful both to her and to Disraeli to assent to immediate resignation. In her letter to Gladstone, in which she charged him with the formation of a Ministry, she said:

Mr. Disraeli has tendered his resignation to the Queen. The result of the appeal to the country is too evident to require its

[1] Vol. vi, p. 40.
[2] *History of Twenty-five Years*, vol. ii, p. 347. See also the views of Freeman, quoted in A. Todd, *Parliamentary Government*, vol. i, p. 244.

being proved by a vote in Parliament, and the Queen entirely agrees with Mr. Disraeli and his colleagues in thinking that the most dignified course for them to pursue, as also the best for the public interests, is immediate resignation.[1]

The precedent set in 1868 has been followed by both parties on every occasion in which the two-party system has been in plain operation. But some few years elapsed before it was freely admitted that it was the decision of the people, and not merely convenience, which dictated this course.

In 1885 and in 1892 Salisbury did not immediately resign, although in each case he was clearly in a minority as the result of the general election. But on these occasions, as in the more recent instance of Baldwin in 1923, the Opposition was not composed of a single party; and it was only reasonable that any doubts, dependent on the reassortment of groups or parties, should be left to the determination of the voting in Parliament.

Beaconsfield's resignation immediately after the election of 1880 was an obvious sequel to the precedent of 1868; but the circumstances surrounding the similar resignation of Gladstone in 1874 indicate that both the Queen and Gladstone had a very imperfect conception of the true inferences to be drawn from the change in practice.

The explanation given by Gladstone in the House of Commons of the reasons for his resignation in 1874 without meeting Parliament throws some light on his attitude. He was, he said, actuated by motives of convenience. If he had decided to retain office and meet the House of Commons, the business of the House would have been very considerably delayed, and, in consequence, the legislative programme of the Session seriously impeded. He gave no indication that any broader considerations had affected his decision.[2]

His determination, in 1886, to resign immediately after the election did not display any fuller appreciation of the significance of constitutional developments. The reasons given by him for the action taken on that occasion were concerned with an interest for the best welfare of Ireland, with the reunion of the Liberal party, but not with the decisive element in the voting of the electorate.[3]

The old principle by which voting in the House of Commons determined which party had won a general election

---

[1] Morley, *Life of Gladstone*, vol. ii, p. 252.   [2] 218 *Parl. Deb.*, 3 s., 128-9.
[3] Morley, op. cit., vol. iii, p. 346.

died hard. Even as late as the election of 1923 King George V wrote: 'The Sovereign ought not to accept the verdict of the polls, except as expressed by the representatives of the electorate across the floor of the House of Commons.' There was, however, a special justification for the decision being left to the House of Commons on this occasion, because the situation was complicated by the Labour party, the Conservatives, and the Liberals being all returned in considerable strength. The three-party system was at its height. The Labour party (who were in the event to take office) were not the largest party. Would they obtain the support of the Liberals and so obtain a working majority? It was appropriate that this question should be decided by the House of Commons.

After the 1929 election King George V recognized that the factors had changed, and he agreed that Baldwin (the defeated Leader) should accept the verdict of the polls without delay. As a result of the voting at this election the Labour party was the largest of the three parties, and thus the verdict at the polls was clearer than in 1923.

The growth of democratic control is not the only explanation of the acceptance of the election result as the determining factor. To some extent the practice of not waiting for the decision of Parliament may be attributed to the sensible attitude of a combatant, who, seeing himself beaten, wishes out of regard for his reputation to admit the fact without further ado. There is little doubt that this consideration was a factor in determining Disraeli to create the precedent of 1868.

The failure of the Conservative Ministry, in 1866, to advise a dissolution and to appeal to the people, immediately after the resignation of the Liberals, has been mentioned above as a late example of the practice of the old régime, under which a change of Ministry did not involve a general election. Nowadays, whenever the two-party system is in operation, the decision of the people is invoked not only when a Minister who is outvoted in the House of Commons anticipates that he retains a majority in the constituencies, but also when a defeated Minister voluntarily gives up office without advising a dissolution. The new Minister takes the earliest opportunity of submitting a choice of Ministries to the electorate; and this is an additional evidence of the enlarged powers of the people and a corresponding decline in the powers of the

House of Commons. The resignation of a Minister may be
due to a particular defeat in the House of Commons; but
convention does not allow his successors to rest their title
on the votes of the House. The people's opinion must be
consulted at the earliest moment which is consistent with the
disposal of outstanding business.

When it is said that the people choose between two alternative Ministries it must be understood to mean a choice
between two Ministries to be nominated by the leaders of the
parties concerned. It is primarily a choice between two
leaders. Normally the leader of a party is, at the present day,
placed in that position as a result of the vote of a party
meeting. But, if the two-party system is to cease to be operative, the capacity of the people to make their choice will be
considerably reduced, since in these circumstances they cannot indicate by their votes the class of members of which it is
desired that the Ministry shall consist. And, as has already
been mentioned, such a reduction in the capacity of the
people would necessarily involve an enlargement in the
capacity of the Sovereign.

This chapter, which is concerned with the dependence
of Ministries upon the Sovereign, the representatives of the
people, and the people themselves, is designed so as to demonstrate that, although the three kinds of control have followed
one another in historical sequence, the phases overlap, and
that, even at the present day, all three are to some extent
effective. The Sovereign still retains power to select Prime
Ministers when the normal system is dislocated. The House
of Commons, although it has suffered during recent years a
decline in its influence, may in the event of an increase in the
number of parties regain the full degree of its negative control
over Ministries. And the last of the controls, that of the
people, depends so intimately on the present working of the
party system that it might, perhaps, once again become subordinate to that of the Sovereign and the House of Commons.
The people would then be left with the bare function of
selecting representatives. But, if the Sovereign's power became enlarged, it would not presumably be exercised with
the same detachment from the people's views as it was in the
days of royal autocracy. It may be assumed that it would be
exercised in a manner best calculated to interpret the wishes
of the people.

CHAPTER VIII

PRELUDE TO THE MANDATE

§ 1. *Royal influence as handicap*

(a) *Procurement of subservient M.P.s*

THE influence of the Sovereign over the course of elections during parts of the seventeenth and eighteenth centuries was often active in individual constituencies. Majorities were secured for candidates whose attitude was ascertained to be loyal by means of promises of appointments and the use of patronage.

It is unnecessary for the present purpose to look back further than the period of the later Stuarts—prior, that is to say, to a time when a steady popular interest in politics is discernible—so as to remark on the extent to which local elections were interfered with on the Crown's behalf. In that period and in the reigns of the first three Georges this interference seems to have been habitual, except, perhaps, in the reign of William III.

Although much of the organization of placemen after the Restoration may well have been arranged without obstructing the free use of votes in constituencies, there is no doubt that Charles II occasionally endeavoured to secure the return of particular candidates who were favourable to his views. In 1679, for instance, Danby told the Duke of Newcastle that the King 'desires you will promote as much as you can the choice of good members in those places which are influenced by your Grace'.[1] James II was equally, if not more, active in this way. His Secretary of State (Sunderland) took steps, immediately after his accession, to see that 'persons of approved loyalty and affection to Government be chosen' at the elections in Leicestershire.[2] This instance is but typical. Similar precautions were taken in 1687.

It is probable that interference with local elections diminished during the reign of Willam III, in spite of the fact that the royal corruption of members of Parliament by

---

[1] *Hist. MSS. Comm., 13th Report,* Appendix, Part II, MSS. of Duke of Portland, vol. ii, p. 153.

[2] *Hist. MSS. Comm., 12th Report,* Appendix, Part V, p. 86. See E. Porritt, *The Unreformed House of Commons,* vol. i, pp. 395–420.

baits of pensions and places continued. As a foreigner, he
was unlikely to wish to concern himself with the details of
electioneering. But in the following reign the management
of constituencies was, it seems, extensive. Very soon after
her accession and immediately before her first general election Queen Anne caused the powerful Duke of Newcastle to
be informed that she 'relied entirely upon your good inclinations and intentions to promote her service as you might do
upon her being ready and desirous to give you any mark of
her favour that can be agreeable in your circumstances'.[1]
She certainly lost no time in establishing relations with a
prominent election manager. There is some evidence that
Crown influence was felt in the constituencies during the
election of 1705.[2]

It would be particularly interesting to know to what extent
the influence of the Court diminished the free expression of
the people's votes in the election of 1710, since the change
in the representation due to that election was considerable.
On the one hand, Swift asserted that 'the Court was so far from
interposing its credit, that there was no change in the Ad-
miralty, not above one or two in the Lieutenancy, nor any
other methods used to influence elections'.[3] It is unlikely that
this was his real opinion, since he was engaged in justifying
the position of the Tories. He observed, in a private letter
in 1711, that the Queen might obtain any kind of majority
she liked after a dissolution 'by managing elections'.[4] On the
other hand, it is certain that several offers of the exercise
of influence in constituencies were made to Harley shortly
before the election, coupled with suggestions that the assistance so given should be rewarded by appointments under
the Crown,[5] and that some Crown appointments were contemplated or made with the object of securing the return of
members favourable to the Tories.[6] Harley, it seems, had let

[1] *Hist. MSS. Comm., 13th Report*, Appendix, Part II, MSS. of Duke of Portland, vol. ii, p. 183.
[2] *Hist. MSS. Comm., 15th Report*, Appendix, Part IV, MSS. of Duke of Portland, vol. iv, pp. 189–90, 30 May 1705. See also *A Collection from Dyer's Letters
concerning the Elections of the Present Parliament* (1706), pp. 3, 10.
[3] *The Examiner*, No. 25, 11–18 Jan. 1711. This assertion was repeated later
by him in *Memoirs relating to that change which happened in the Queen's Ministry of
1710* and in *An Enquiry into the Behaviour of the Queen's Last Ministry*.
[4] *Journal to Stella*, 9 Dec. 1711.
[5] *Hist. MSS. Comm., 15th Report*, Appendix, Part IV, MSS. of the Duke of
Portland, vol. iv, pp. 561, 565, 570.
[6] Ibid., pp. 576, 590, 608, 615. *Hist. MSS. Comm., 11th Report*, Appendix,
Part V, MSS. of Earl of Dartmouth, vol. i, p. 297.

it be known that he desired to have as many supporters in
the ensuing Parliament as he could possibly procure;[1] and
this object was not to be attained by honest electioneering.
A note, written by him during the period of the election,
mentioned the desirability that the 'bent and disposition of
the people should be guided and directed for the Queen's
service and the public good, and not to be at the disposal
of particular persons'. This could be done, he said, 'by steady
management'; and he remarked on the effect of appointments which had been and might be made.[2]

The Whig politicians took advantage of the alien interests
of the first two Georges to annex to the Ministry of the day
much of the royal patronage. But George II struggled to
retain control of the management of local elections. He was
helped by the offers of local magnates to influence returns,
so as to obtain support for the Ministers chosen by him.[3]

George III made a determined effort to maintain a predominance of royal influence over elections. He lost no time
in insisting on his rights. In the year following that of
his accession he saw to it that the boroughs attached to
the Duchy of Cornwall, which had been allowed to fall into the
hands of the Ministry, were once more at the disposal of the
Sovereign; but he was not able, it seems, upon this occasion
to regain the more general Crown influence which had been
appropriated by the Duke of Newcastle.[4] Between his accession and the resignation of Lord North, in 1782, George III
continued to be extremely active in mastering and practising
the art of election management.[5] After that date, either his
interest declined or his opportunities were limited.

The two sovereigns who succeeded George III lacked
either the pertinacity or the opportunity to influence particular returns on the eighteenth-century scale. Elections came
to be managed almost exclusively by the Treasury without

[1] Hist. MSS. Comm., 15th Report, Appendix, Part IV, MSS. of Duke of Portland, vol. iv, p. 598.
[2] Hardwicke, Miscellaneous State Papers, vol. ii, pp. 485 ff. A list of appointments, made prior to the election, is given in a tract entitled The Right of the
Sovereign in the Choice of his Servants (1714).
[3] Hist. MSS. Comm., 15th Report, Appendix, Part VI (Carlisle MSS.), p. 52.
See also Hist. MSS. Comm., Report on MSS. of Mrs. Stopford-Sackville, vol. i,
pp. 151–2. The results of the profound researches of Sir Lewis Namier may be
found in the first volume of his work on England in the Age of the American Revolution, pp. 123–34.
[4] Dodington's Diary, 2 Feb. 1761.
[5] See L. B. Namier, England in the Age of the American Revolution, vol. i, pp.
153–78.

any noticeable interference on behalf of the Crown. For some years of the reign of George III the Treasury had done a large amount of business in the buying of seats in Parliament: and there was considerable truth in the statement made by Creevy, in 1809, that 'it was perfectly well known that a dissolution of Parliament was not an appeal to the people, but to the Treasury'.[1] The terms of a letter, written by Hawkesbury to the King in 1806, imply that the members attached to the Government of the day might still be instrumental in turning the balance.[2] But a Statute which was passed in 1809 to prevent traffic in seats seems to have had some effect, for Lord Liverpool, as Prime Minister, stated confidentially, in 1812, that he had then only one Treasury seat in his disposal.[3] After 1832 the influence of Government money ceased to be exercised in election contests; and the business of management of elections was thenceforward in the hands of party organizations.

Emphasis has been laid on the interference with the returns of members by the Crown as a factor in the prevention of unconstrained voting, not only because it has a bearing on the more general management of elections, which is mentioned in the following paragraphs, but because Crown influence at most times exceeded any other kind of political influence. It is obvious, however, that corruption or intimidation of voters limited the free expression of the people's opinions, whatever the source from which the interference came. The extent of election management undertaken by different groups of Whigs during the eighteenth century is still the subject of investigation; but the buying of seats by the Pelhams alone must have been sufficient virtually to disenfranchise thousands of electors among a confined electorate.

(b) Assured results of general elections

The peculiar circumstances surrounding most of the general elections of the reigns of William III and Anne make it difficult to determine the extent to which the votes of the electors affected the policy of government. The fact that the sympathies, and even the wishes, of the Sovereign were

---

[1] 14 *Parl. Deb.*, 1 s., 116. See also *Hist. MSS. Comm.*, MSS. of J. B. Fortescue Esq., vol. viii, pp. 394, 396, 397, 398, 414.
[2] C. D. Yonge, *Life of the Earl of Liverpool*, vol. i, p. 219.
[3] Ibid., p. 444.

generally made plain prior to general elections greatly diminished the value of the results of the returns as indications of the views of the people. If, as happened on several occasions, the Sovereign reconstituted the Ministry shortly before the election of a new Parliament, it was certain that there would be a majority for the favoured party. Not only was there an overwhelming tradition for support of the Ministers of the Crown, but many influential persons in the constituencies were either induced or were anxious to ensure that candidates approved by the Sovereign should be elected.

There was under William III and Anne a fairly constant relation between the results of general elections and the attitude of public opinion. The Sovereign was conscious of the desirability of maintaining agreement between his policy and the views of his subjects. Public opinion occasionally influenced the Sovereign's choice of Ministers. But it cannot be said that the return of a majority for one party rather than the other cast an obligation on the Sovereign or the Ministry to pursue a particular course of action.

The ability of William III to secure Parliaments which were either in agreement with his apparent predilections or favourable to his purposes was illustrated in the 'jingo' election of 1695, and also in the two elections of 1701. After the Whig element in the Ministry had been steadily strengthened, the return of a Whig majority in 1695 enabled the King vigorously to pursue his war policy. During 1700 he found himself impressed with the necessity of including in his Ministry some Tory politicians; and he accordingly gave offices to Godolphin and Rochester. Public opinion seemed to call for such a step; and 'to sweeten the humours and measures of the new Parliament the King was willing to oblige these men who were . . . distinguished by the name of the Church Party [i.e. Tories], who had thought themselves neglected'.[1] This change having been effected, the question of the succession to the throne and the conditions of foreign policy led the King to dissolve Parliament. He expressed the need of having 'the more immediate sense of the Kingdom in so great a conjecture'.[2] The strengthening of the Tory position in the Ministry was followed by the return of a Tory majority in the House of Commons.

But in the autumn of 1701, when the people had changed

[1] White Kennett, *History of England*, vol. iii, p. 793.
[2] 5 *Parl. Hist.*, 1233.

their outlook and were in agitation against the Tory attitude towards France, Somers, one of the most sagacious and disinterested of statesmen among the Whigs, was anxious that the King should place himself in a strong position to carry out his war policy. For this purpose Somers regarded dissolution as requisite. He accordingly proposed to the King that he should either change his Ministers or else display an intention to do so. He assured him that success was certain.

No Hazard, [he said] for let the majority fall as it will, the present temper will force them to do what the King will desire. But the majority will be sure, if it be considered upon what foot it was understood the last Parliament was chosen; and yet how small a majority and how obtained. . . . But, to set himself and his people at ease, he must trust those whom the body of the people do not distrust.[1]

Somers evidently thought that, if the publicly acknowledged views of the Sovereign were shown to be in accord with the trend of opinion in the country, the usual tendency for a proportion of members of Parliament to support the Ministry of the day would be increased. Such was the disposition of parties in relation to political differences, that he expected a majority in a new Parliament to be in favour of the King's policy, even though a large number of old members was returned. This advice proved to be reliable.

The Proclamation issued at the dissolution of Parliament in November 1701 disclosed a novel attitude towards the electors by suggesting that they should choose their representatives with a view to a particular policy being supported. No previous communication of the kind had admitted so intimate a connexion between the people and the course of policy. The terms of the Proclamation are worth quoting at some length. It ran thus:

Whereas Our loving subjects have universally by their loyall addresses, expressed their resentment of the injustice and indignity offered to us and our People, by the late proceedings of the French King, in taking upon him to own and declare the pretended Prince of Wales to be King of England, Scotland and Ireland; and have thereby also in the most dutiful manner, expressed their affection to our Person and Government, and their steady resolution at this time to do all things which can be desired from good Englishmen and Protestants, We have received the same with great satisfaction and have thought it

[1] Hardwicke, *Miscellaneous State Papers*, vol. ii, pp. 453-5.

reasonable in this extraordinary juncture to give Our subjects the opportunity of choosing such persons to represent them in Parliament as they may judge most likely to bring to effect their just and pious purposes and in order thereto to dissolve this present Parliament. . . .[1]

It was observed, at the time the Proclamation was issued, that its phraseology implied a new distribution of political power. Defoe hailed it as 'a glorious recognition' and 'an unexampled testimony of the just rights of the People'.[2] An opponent, who expressed his apprehension at the increase of the people's power, wrote that 'to appeal from their representatives to the multitude is setting the axe to the very root of the Constitution'.[3] Defoe, however, insisted that the terms of the Proclamation provided proof that 'the people are in some measure judges of the actions and management of their representatives'.[4]

The royal invitation to the electors to choose representatives to carry out 'their just and pious purposes' can hardly have meant that the policy of government would be made dependent on the way in which the people cast their votes. And the fact that the source of the appeal was the King himself, and not merely a party leader, restricted the free choice of representatives. The incident was an isolated one; and it does not seem to have led to further developments.

Results of general elections in the reign of Queen Anne always confirmed any plainly shown preferences of the Sovereign for the policy of one party rather than the other. It may be assumed that these preferences were not made apparent without some regard to the movements of public opinion. But their expression, prior to general elections, limited the significance of the people's part in the proceedings. The reconstitution of the Ministry shortly before the dissolution of Parliament may be described, in the words of Professor Trevelyan, as 'the cause, not the effect, of the electoral decision'.[5]

Although the Queen made no direct appeal for the support

[1] Public Record Office, *Chancery Warrants*, Series 2, File 2808; British Museum, 21 h. 3 (221).
[2] *The Original Power of the Collective Body of the People of England, Examined and Asserted.*
[3] Charles Davenant, *The Danger of Appealing to the People from their Representatives in Parliament* (reprinted in *Political and Commercial Works* (1771 ed.), vol. iv, pp. 267 ff.).
[4] *Some Remarks on the First Chapter in Dr. Davenant's Essays.*
[5] *England under the Stuarts*, p. 485.

of the Tories in the election of 1702, she made it sufficiently clear that her sympathies were with the Tory party to ensure that it obtained a majority. 'My own principles', she said in her Speech, 'must always keep me entirely firm to the interests and religion of the Church of England and will incline me to countenance those who have the truest zeal to support it.' The election of 1710 may be cited as the outstanding example of the Queen's choice of a time for change in the composition of her Ministry which corresponded with a change in the views of her subjects. It also well illustrates the meaningless character of an election which was immediately preceded by a decision by the Sovereign to undertake a fresh course of policy.

The reaction of public feeling against the Whigs in 1710, engendered by the Sacheverell trial and dissatisfaction with the continuance of the war, was sufficient to encourage the Queen to conform to it. 'Her Majesty,' Swift said, 'following her own inclinations and those of her people, resolved to make some changes in the Ministry and take Mr. Harley into her councils.' He described the new appointments which were made prior to the election as happily in consonance with public opinion rather than due to it; but he also remarked that 'it was the most prudent course imaginable to the Queen, to lay hold of the disposition of the people for changing the Parliament and Ministry'.[1]

If the constitutional standards of today were to be applied, any display of the personal predilections of the Sovereign in politics would be regarded as irregular. But, after making allowance for the position in which the Sovereign stood in the early eighteenth century, the undue use by George I of his influence, so as to secure support for the Whigs in general elections, appears to be unjustifiable. It is impossible to defend it on the ground that attention was being paid to the prevailing tendency of public opinion.

Soon after the new King's arrival in England Lord Cowper wrote a paper for his information which was naïvely entitled *An Impartial History of Parties*. In this paper it was pointed out

that the parties are so near an equality, and the generality of the world so much in love with the advantages a King of Great Britain has to bestow . . ., that 'tis wholly in Your Majesty's power,

[1] *An Enquiry into the Behaviour of the Queen's Last Ministry; The Examiner*, Nos. 14 and 25.

by showing your favour in due time (before the elections) to one or other of them, to give which of them you please a clear majority in all succeeding parliaments.

George I adopted this advice whole-heartedly, and replaced the Tory Ministry with one consisting of Whigs. This action was taken prior to his first general election.

In the concluding paragraph of the Proclamation preceding this election, the King announced that he did not doubt that 'our loving subjects' would, in choosing their representatives, 'have a particular regard to such as shewed a firmness to the protestant succession when it was in danger'.[1] As Lecky observed: 'In the face of such a proclamation, emanating from the Sovereign himself, a Tory Parliament would have been a direct incentive to civil war.'[2] The result of the election was the return of a large Whig majority. The Proclamation was vigorously criticized by the Tories; and Sir William Wyndham was reprimanded by the Speaker for saying in the House of Commons that certain expressions in the Proclamation were not only unprecedented, but also of dangerous consequence to the very being of Parliament.[3]

The sole excuse for the undisguised attachment of George I to the Whigs in 1715 was the peculiar situation created by the change of dynasty. A repetition, therefore, of this display of personal preference in the election of 1722 was still less justifiable. An appeal of a markedly partisan character was then made by George I in the Speech announcing the dissolution of Parliament, in which it was stated that he was 'firmly determined to continue to countenance such as have manifested their zeal for the present establishment'.[4] There was again, of course, a large Whig majority as a result of the election. Sir J. Vanbrugh wrote to Lord Carlisle that 'my Lord Townshend and his near friends seem to think it chiefly owing to the firm declaration in the King's Speech who[m] he would trust and stand by'.[5]

In the circumstances which have been described in the foregoing paragraphs, the people had but little freedom or opportunity to make decisions on political issues. Although some faint notions of the ability of the electors to decide

[1] 7 Parl. Hist. 24.
[2] Lecky, History of England in the Eighteenth Century, vol. i, p. 211.
[3] 7 Parl. Hist. 51.
[4] 7 Parl. Hist. 982.
[5] Hist. MSS. Comm., 15th Report, Appendix, Part VI (Carlisle MSS.), p. 37.

issues began to be current at the time of William III and
Anne, the leading part still played by the Sovereign in
politics was largely responsible for the delay in the development of democratic principles. It must be recognized, however, that contemporary accounts of election contests, about
that period and even earlier, point to considerable popular
interest in the public questions which were debated at
election times. The variety and violence of party cries may
be cited in support of this appraisement. How, then, it may
be asked, could the interest have been so well sustained, if the
actual influence of the electors was so slight?

It is true that some of the cries represented a keen desire
on the part of the people for the execution of certain policies.
The demand for 'no standing army', which became articulate
immediately after the Restoration and was a prevalent election catch-phrase in the elections of 1681 and 1698, and the
cries of 'exclusion' in 1681 and 'no Dutchmen' in 1698, which
were to some extent spontaneous, are instances of this. But
such cries as were not the result of party intrigue were merely
an outlet for pent-up feelings; and it was not seriously expected that the elections would bring about the results for
which clamour was raised. A people whose political existence
was just beginning to be recognized was very naturally ready
to avail itself of the opportunities of general elections to
ventilate repugnance for opponents and to indulge in the
pleasures of obloquy. Calling adversaries 'Tackers' and
'Sneakers' was a new game which appealed to the simple
intelligences of the time. The very word 'excise' aroused a
blind antagonism throughout a large part of the eighteenth
century. Chesterfield said that it would have to 'change its
name by Act of Parliament before it will go down with the
people, who know names better than things'.[1] And the history
of the use of the slogan, 'the Church in danger', during the
seventeenth, eighteenth, and nineteenth centuries, would
provide the basis of an interesting exposition of the methods
of fomenting the prejudices of the people for party ends.

§ 2. *Early mentions of elections in connexion with policy*

Although there may not have been any real capacity in the
people to determine issues by voting at elections in the reigns
of William III and Anne, many of the political broadsheets

---

[1] *Lord Chesterfield's Letters* (1845 edition), vol. iv, p. 461.

and tracts of the later part of the seventeenth and earlier part of the eighteenth century provide evidence that the notion of such a capacity was beginning to be propagated. From about 1680 onwards scarcely a general election took place without the country being flooded with tracts or sheets entitled 'Cautions to Electors', 'Advice to Freeholders', or 'An Address to the People of England', in which disquisitions on the personal qualifications of candidates developed into discussions of matters of policy. They appeared occasionally before the Restoration.

At first the choice of members by the electors was frequently described as a likely reflection of the views and characteristics of the nation at large, either from an international or from a domestic point of view. As early as the reign of Charles I, George Wither, the poet and pamphleteer, wrote in an election tract:

I will offer to your consideration that which I conceive to be the best measures . . . for replenishing the House of Commons with such members as shall be likely . . . to become instruments of removing our present mischief, and by establishing a happy peace among us for the future; if we be not grown so corrupt a body that we will not be represented by good and discreet men; which it seems . . . made us choose a representative body in corruptions and failings, like unto ourselves.

> The butterflies produce not bees;
> Good-fruits grow not on evill-trees.

. . . And what good can be had, or what benefit can be looked for from such a choice? Or what better choice can be made unless you seriously, prudently and conscionably manage your elections?

> When wolves are by the flock for guardians chose,
> Who marvailes, if their skins and lives they lose.[1]

It was said in 1681, to take a later example, that

they whom you chuse will represent your qualities, as well as your persons; and if you send us up a false glass, it will represent you with an ugly face. . . . You have formerly had the character of a sober temperate nation; but, if you chuse drunkards to represent you, they will conclude that you are all drunk.[2]

A similar strain of argument is found again during the election of 1702:

What do you think our Allies thought of our Parliament, when

---

[1] *Letters of Advice touching the choice of Knights and Burgesses for the Parliament* (1646).   [2] *The Certain Way to save England, &c.* (1681).

instead of raising money to carry on a vigorous war against France, they clog'd the funds with idle pretences of religion? Bad enough to be sure. But what do you imagine they thought of us that chose 'em? Much worse without doubt. They could do no other than believe 'em to be the true representative of the English nation, for the thing representing ought to resemble the thing it represents both in its nature and qualifications, and so foreigners could conclude no other, than a mad people chose a mad Parliament.[1]

Occasionally anti-papist tracts of as early date as 1679–81 made some suggestion that the right choice of Parliament-men would result in the adoption of policies salutary to the nation. In a tract of better quality than many of its period it was asserted that 'a good Parliament' (a wisely chosen Parliament, that is to say) might, among other advantageous steps, 'advise his Majesty to such things as shall fortify the Protestant interest and terrify the French tyrant into a greater moderation towards the disconsolate Hugonots'.[2]

Sometimes political periodicals or pamphlets described general elections as displaying the 'sense' or the 'disposition' of the nation, without positively suggesting that there was an obligation on Parliament to give effect to any particular policy. For instance: 'The general choice of the same members in the last Parliament, that had served in the two former, sufficiently shews the sense of the nation.'[3] Or:

If elections of members to serve in Parliament be the best standard to judge the disposition of the Kingdom by, it is not so long since we had an opportunity of feeling the pulse of the nation; but that we may reasonably conclude that, all other things remaining as they did, the temper and complexion of the generality of the people is also much the same.[4]

Or: 'Your choice now will be the best standard by which to judge the present disposition of the Kingdom.'[5]

The stage was past in which merely the personal characteristics most suitable to candidates were discussed by pamphleteers. The policies which would be undertaken were

---

[1] *The Observator*, vol. iii, No. 100.
[2] *An Address to the Honourable City of London and all other Cities, Shires and Corporations, concerning their choice of a new Parliament* (1681). Cf. *England's Great Interest in the Choice of this new Parliament* (1679).
[3] *The Impartial Protestant Mercury*, 12 May 1681.
[4] *An Impartial Account of the Nature and Tendency of the late Addresses, &c.* (1681).
[5] *The Best Choice of Parliament Men, &c.* (1701).

defined.[1] But there was, so far, little suggestion that the decision in regard to those policies rested with the electors.

Matters were carried a stage farther when policies were described as possible or impossible according to the way in which a general election went. For example:

If the Parliament, which will now be chosen [November, 1701], should consist of the same persons, or of men of the same temper with the former Parliament, it will be impossible to perfect or support that alliance which is forming for the security of England and Europe against the power of France.[2]

Or:

Wherefore, it greatly behoves all electors at the next choice, to take especial care that they do not put any, who did not appear for that Bill [the Occasional Conformity Bill], into a capacity to bring the like mischief upon this nation hereafter.[3]

A famous Tory election tract, entitled *English Advice to the Freeholders of England*, written by Bishop Atterbury and issued at the time of the election following the death of Queen Anne, concluded with lists of 'merits' or alternative policies in parallel columns. On the one hand, for instance, there was: 'No new war, no new taxes'; and, on the other: 'A new war, six shillings in the pound, a general excise and a poll-tax.' At the foot were the words: 'Choose which you please.' The Whigs countered by producing a tract in similar form. Among the alternatives were: 'King George and the illustrious House of Hanover' and 'The Pretender, Mass and wooden shoes.'[4]

The preceding examples of the unofficial portrayal of the people in a responsible guise are, with the exception of the last mentioned, taken from the period of the later Stuarts. Yet further progress, in the reigns of George I and George II, is apparent in the attempt to make specific legislative proposals issues in elections, after the manner in which they are made at the present day. *The Freeholder's Journal* and *The Weekly Journal or Saturday's Post* tried to make the Septennial Act an issue in the election of 1722. Again, in 1734 *The*

---

[1] A particularly graphic example of this stage is to be found in the *Harley Papers* (Hist. MSS. Comm. (Portland MSS.)), vol. viii, p. 54.

[2] *A Letter sent to a Gentleman, &c.* (1701).

[3] *Advice to all Freeholders and other Electors for the ensuing Parliament.* See also *Advice to the Electors of Great Britain, occasioned by the Intended Invasion from France* (1708).

[4] *Somers' Tracts*, 3rd Collection, vol. iv, pp. 353, 379.

Craftsman[1] argued that the result of the election proved a general opposition to the Excise Scheme, while the periodicals supported by the Ministry challenged this inference.

Agitation for the passing of a Bill to reduce the number of placemen in Parliament in 1739 and 1740 encouraged the Opposition to claim for the people power to prove their insistence on this legislation by means of the exercise of the franchise. Pulteney, in his *Address to the Electors . . . Occasioned by the late Secession*, pointed out that, by pledging or instructing candidates on the subject of a Place Bill, 'it will be possible, if it should appear to be your general sentiments, to compose a majority of the next Parliament of such gentlemen as are honest enough not to acknowledge the necessity of this law, but also to exert their utmost endeavours actually to obtain it'. Another tract told the electors that 'you will shortly . . . have it in your power to make the most effectual law against filling the House of Commons with place-men, by making independence in your candidates the rule of your choice'.[2]

These instances form a link with the subject-matter of Chapter II of this book, which deals with the influence of constituents on members. The development of the power of the people as a whole cannot be fully appreciated without regarding its preparatory local development in separate constituencies. It was a simple extension of ideas for constituents, who had obtained a measure of control over their particular representatives, to conclude that a wider control would be exercised over Parliament in general, provided that the interests of the majority of the electors in the whole country were focused on the same point.

During the reign of George II, not only were politicians talking of the capacity of the people to decide issues, but there were some signs of official admissions of this capacity. It has been seen that the terms of the Proclamation announcing the dissolution of Parliament in the autumn of 1701 suggested that the people's choice of their representatives might affect the course of politics; but in 1735 the Speech delivered before the Session contained statements which implied some recognition of the determinant capacity of the people to be exercised through the process of voting.

The sense of the nation [the Speech ran] is best learned by the choice of their representatives; and I am persuaded that the

[1] 25 May 1734.   [2] *A Serious Exhortation* (1740).

behaviour and conduct of my faithful Commons will demonstrate to all the world the unshaken fidelity and attachment of my good subjects to my person and government.

It was beginning to be seen that it was worth the while of those in authority to credit the electors with enlarged political powers, even though there was no intention that those powers should be admitted in practice.[1]

§ 3. *The attitude of the people in the eighteenth century*

Not only during the period of the later Stuarts, but during a large part of the eighteenth century, such election addresses as were issued by candidates seldom contained any reference to current politics. They were confined, as a rule, after requests for votes and 'interest', to assurances of the good intention of the candidates towards advancement of the concerns of the country in general and of the constituency in particular. They contained such vague expressions as 'the preservation of our glorious Constitution', 'the rights and liberties of the people', 'the steady pursuit of the public good', or 'concurrence in every measure which shall be deemed necessary for vindicating the rights and honour of this nation'.[2] On rare occasions only was there included a pledge to support the introduction or the repeal of legislation. A candidate for one of the apple-growing constituencies, for instance, told his electors, in 1763, that he would contribute, as much as was in his power, to the repeal of the tax lately imposed on makers of cider.[3] But this particular pledge can be explained by the strong resentment which was aroused in the areas affected by the imposition of the tax.

The terms of the addresses of the rival candidates at the election for the County of Norfolk in the important election of 1784 illustrate respectively the old style and that which was to become prevalent at a later period. The Whig candidates issued a joint letter simply stating that, in the event of their election, it would be their 'mutual determination to discharge the important trust reposed in us with fidelity and independence; and to support to the best of our judgment the interests of this country and the principles of our glorious constitution, as established at the Revolution'. On the other

[1] See § 5 of this Chapter.
[2] Cf. an address drafted by Dr. Johnson in 1780, Boswell, *Life of Johnson* (Everyman ed.), vol. ii, p. 313.
[3] *St. James Chronicle*, 1 Nov. 1763.

hand, the Tory candidate wrote: 'I stand forth to give the County of Norfolk an opportunity of . . . sending to Parliament two members who agree in condemning the violent and arbitrary resolutions of the last House of Commons.'[1]

Apart from a few special instances of popular issues which aroused excitement among the masses, some of them fomented by political agents, there was an almost continuous condition of lethargy and lack of interest during the reigns of the first three Georges. Several causes contributed to this situation. At one stage the overwhelming predominance of the Whigs, at another the absence of any difference in party principles, and, all the time, the flagrant inequity of the state of representation and, still more, the scandal of placemen and corruption, sometimes exaggerated, but sufficient to discourage the most optimistic—all these tended to render the average citizen indifferent or disgusted. Even in what appear to have been critical times, the amount of concern in elections was meagre; and the number of contests never reached more than a small proportion of the possible number. Although the rowdyism usual in constituencies with the wider franchise gave an impression of political excitement and enthusiasm, 'interest' in the sinister sense excluded interest in the more reputable meaning of that term.

Contemporary comments on the apathy of the public can be found at stages when the country's destiny might well have aroused general anxiety. It was complained by a promoter of a political periodical in 1753 that 'of the various points which have been agitated for some years passed, only the French players and the Jews Act had made any manifest impression on the minds of the people'.[2] And in 1764 Charles Townshend wrote of the subdued state of the national temper and the habitual and general indifference and distrust.[3] There were, it is true, a few years of widespread agitation in the metropolis regarding Wilkes and the Middlesex election (1768–71); and, a few years later, the subject of the independence of the American colonies aroused strong feelings among limited sections of the public. But in 1774, a year

[1] *Journal of the Proceedings of the Election of Two Knights of the Shire to represent the County of Norfolk in Parliament* (1784), pp. 24–28. See also *Election Magazine* (Norfolk) (1784), pp. 13, 39.
[2] *The Protester*, Nov. 1753.
[3] *Hist. MSS. Comm., 11th Report*, Appendix, Part IV, MSS. of Marquis of Townshend, p. 136.

of great consequence for the nation, Burke wrote to Rocking-ham: 'Your Lordship remarks very rightly on the supineness of the public. Any remarkable highway robbery at Hounslow-heath would make more conversation than all the distur-bances in America.' Again, in 1775 Burke wrote:

I am satisfied that within a few years there has been a great change in national character. We seem no longer that eager, inquisitive, jealous, fiery people, which we have been formerly, and which we have been a very short time ago. . . . No man com-mends the measures which have been pursued or expects any good from those which are in preparation; but it is a cold languid opinion, like what men discover in affairs that do not concern them.[1]

The only doubt which this account suggests is that Burke made too great a contrast between 1775 and the period a few years earlier. The despondency among the people seems to have recurred over a course of years; and, as each tentative movement towards reform proved to be abortive, this de-spondency became accentuated. Fox wrote to Grey in 1801 that, until he saw that the public had some dislike, letting indignation alone, to absolute power, he saw no use in stating in the House of Commons the principles of liberty and jus-tice.[2]

The inability of Parliament itself to take any effective share in many aspects of government during the eighteenth century may provide some explanation of the persistent apathy. Not only during the earlier part of the century, but even during the later part, there was a frequent absence of any real or large issues before Parliament. Dr. Johnson maintained in 1777 that, with the exception of America, 'there was hardly ever any question of great importance before Parliament, any question in which a man might not well vote upon one side or the other'.[3]

There were, however, three occasions in the eighteenth century (1701, 1710, and 1768–71) when sections of the people not only exhibited a marked desire that the evils of ineffective or perverse government should be set right, but also took particularly drastic steps towards effecting the change in policy which they regarded as requisite. Petitions for the

[1] Burke's *Correspondence*, vol. i, p. 453; vol. ii, p. 48.
[2] *Memoirs and Correspondence of C. J. Fox* (ed. Russell), vol. iii, p. 340.
[3] Boswell, *Life of Johnson* (Everyman ed.), vol. ii, p. 149.

dissolution of Parliament were organized, so that the people might display by their votes their disapproval of the conduct of the Ministry of the day.

In the earlier instances of 1701 and 1710 the petitions seem to have been used by the party to which the Sovereign was about to give a large measure of favour as a device to attest the support of public opinion; and, for this reason, the dissolution of Parliament swiftly followed after the petitions. In the middle of 1701, while the anti-popery and anti-French feeling ran very high, many petitions were presented to the King praying him to dissolve Parliament. Again, in 1710, the reaction against the Whigs which followed the Sacheverell trial led the Tories to organize similar petitions, which alleged that Parliament no longer represented the sentiments of the people. The protests which were raised against the constitutional impropriety of this kind of petition naturally came, in 1701 and 1710, from the party which was not in possession of the favour of the Sovereign.[1] It is not surprising to find that, after the petitions of 1701 had been followed by a general election which produced a majority for an anti-French policy, the House of Commons passed a resolution to the effect that it was the right of the people to petition for the calling, sitting, or dissolving of Parliaments, as well as for the redressing of grievances.[2]

It was under different circumstances that, during the years 1768 to 1771, the agitation respecting Wilkes and the Middlesex election led, among other methods of demonstration, to petitions from several counties, as well as cities and boroughs, begging for the dissolution of Parliament. The County of Somerset, for instance, prayed the King to remove his Ministers and to dissolve 'that Parliament, in which your people can no longer place a confidence'.[3] The petition of the City of Westminster was described by Horace Walpole as 'a step not only absurd, but of most dangerous precedent'.[4] He considered it ridiculous that it should be thought likely that the King, who had an obsequious House of Commons, should expose himself to the risks of an unnecessary general election. It was true enough that Ministers would, from a

---

[1] It is not at all certain that the Sovereign approved this method of expression of popular protest: cf. White Kennett, *History of England*, vol. iii, p. 828, where quotations are given from petitions for dissolution in 1701.

[2] *Journals of the House of Commons*, 26 Feb. 1702, vol. xiii, p. 767.

[3] *Lloyd's Evening Post*, November and December, 1769.

[4] *Memoirs of George III*, vol. iii, pp. 381–2.

self-interested point of view, have committed an act of amazing folly in taking the risks that a general election would have involved in the enraged state of large numbers of the public. It was useless for petitioners to maintain, as did the Yorkshire petitioners, that they sought 'an opportunity of demonstrating their zeal for the Constitution by a choice of men who will guard the honour of the Crown and support the rights of the people'.[1] Similarly, it was ingenuous of the City of London, whose petition had been ungraciously answered, to send a formal remonstrance to the King in which the remonstrants assured themselves that the King would 'restore the constitutional government and quiet of your people by dissolving this Parliament and removing those evil Ministers for ever from your councils'. It is no wonder that the King returned an answer in which he referred to the remonstrance as 'disrespectful to me, injurious in my Parliament, and irreconcilable to the principles of the Constitution'.[2] In contrast to the outcome of the petitions of 1701 and 1710, no dissolution followed the petitions of 1769, since their organizers were acting in opposition to a Ministry chosen and approved by the King; a Ministry, that is to say, which the King had every intention of maintaining.

Few Ministers in 1769, however, deemed it politic to deny the right of citizens to present petitions for dissolution. Lord North is reported as having characterized them as unconstitutional; but, on being reminded of the very general scope of the right to petition, he qualified his remarks.[3] Lord Egmont was bold enough to declare in the House of Lords that these petitions were 'highly censurable and treasonable'.[4]

The critical situation in which the country was placed in the years around 1770 led Lord Chatham to make two motions in the House of Lords for a humble address to his Majesty to dissolve Parliament. This expedient was doubtless suggested to his mind by the petitions which had been reaching the King from many constituencies. Both the motions were negatived; but their terms are suggestive of a greater power in the people than was currently acknowledged, and they mark an interesting stage in the development of the

---

[1] 39 *Gentleman's Magazine*, 1769, p. 526. This petition was said to have been drafted by Wedderburn, who in his early days supported Wilkes. See *Grenville Papers*, vol. iv, p. 442 n.
[2] *Cavendish Debates*, vol. i, 15 Mar. 1770; 16 *Parl. Hist.* 894.
[3] 16 *Parl. Hist.* 578; Lecky, *History of England in the Eighteenth Century*, vol. iii, p. 346.   [4] *Chatham Correspondence*, vol. iii, p. 419.

notion of drawing inferences from the results of general elections.

On the first occasion Lord Chatham proposed that his Majesty should 'take the recent and genuine sense of his people, by dissolving this present Parliament and calling, with all convenient despatch, a new Parliament'. A proposal of this kind, though not novel, was significant, coming as it did from the most notable statesman of the day. On the second occasion he used similar language, including the expression 'recur to the recent sense of his people'. Its use provides an interesting link between the elder and the younger Pitt. The latter aroused some comment in 1784, when he advised the employment of almost the same words in the Speech from the Throne prior to the dissolution of Parliament in that year.

At the times when petitions for the dissolution of Parliament were prevalent public petitions in general were numerous. But there is an important distinction between the particular class of petition which has just been discussed and petitions of other kinds. Petitions for dissolution did not merely, like other petitions, pray that a certain policy should or should not be carried out; but they prayed, in effect, that the petitioners might, with the rest of the electorate, demonstrate that a particular course should be adopted as a result of the balance of voting. It is this distinction, doubtless, which provided the chief argument for those who contended that these petitions were unconstitutional; and it is the suggestion of a determinant element which makes them of particular interest in tracing the history of the development of the principle of the mandate.

§ 4. *Defective representation*[1]

As early as the reign of Charles II the reproach of the inadequate representation of the people in Parliament was the subject of comment among the more discerning. The Earl of Shaftesbury described the position as notorious, since boroughs with a handful of voters sent two representatives to Parliament, while boroughs of considerable size were unrepresented. It soon came to be understood that the real attitude of the electorate could only be ascertained from the composition of the House of Commons (if, indeed, it could

---

[1] It is unnecessary to trace the history of the representation in this place, because, among other reasons, that work has been adequately done in books devoted to the subject.

be ascertained at all) by excluding from consideration all the nominated members or by paying attention only to the character of the returns for popular constituencies. It became customary thus to scrutinize and analyse election results so as to raise inferences regarding the 'sense of the people'.

This practice was occasionally adopted only a few years after the defects in representation began to be generally recognized. The results of the elections of members for the City of London, of Westminster, and the County of Middlesex were regarded as providing a significant clue to the attitude of the whole of the inhabitants of the country, since these constituencies were situated at the centre of the political life of the kingdom and enjoyed a wide franchise. In the City of London and the City of Westminster, every male inhabitant householder had a right to vote; and in the County of Middlesex, as in the counties generally, the suffrage was in the forty-shilling freeholders.

County elections generally were cited, from the early eighteenth century, as providing a fair criterion of the true views of the whole body of persons with similar qualifications to the county voters. It was obvious that 'the sense of the people' could not be collected from the results of the elections as a whole, including those of the 'pocket' boroughs; but an analysis of the votes of the county freeholders or of the numbers of members returned by counties was a useful guide for the assessment of the situation. By virtue of a law of 1430, anyone who owned freeholds to the value of forty shillings could vote at a county election. This was not, according to modern standards, a very wide franchise, since only a small proportion of the inhabitants were owners of land; but it was wide according to standards of the eighteenth century; and it must be remembered that, as the value of money altered, the county franchise became automatically enlarged.

Swift, writing in *The Examiner* in 1711, remarked that 'the truest way of judging the dispositions of the people in the choice of their representatives is by computing the county elections'.[1] And there was, at the conclusion of the election of 1734, a spirited controversy between *The Craftsman* (the famous Opposition periodical) and *The Free Briton* (the Walpole periodical) with regard to the efficacy of the county election results as a standard by which to judge 'the sense of the people'. *The Craftsman* denied that the borough elections

[1] *The Examiner*, No. 25, 11–18 Jan. 1711.

provided any indication of the view taken by the people on the state of politics. The writer alleged that, if the Ministerial supporters, 'who boast so much of their success, will be pleased to look over the list of the knights of the shire, I believe that they will find at least three to one chosen against them'.[1] *The Free Briton* was forced merely to insist 'that the sense of the people hath declared itself on the side of the present establishment is clear from the majority of the new Parliament'.[2]

These methods of surmounting the defects of an ineffective system of representation continued to be utilized down to the time of the Reform Bill of 1832. They were even adopted by Peel in 1829, who was hard put to it to justify his change of front respecting the relief of Roman Catholic disabilities, when, in one of the most canvassed incidents of his career, he made the sudden decision to propose relief legislation after having declared himself a determined opponent of any such concession.

In making his speech in the House of Commons proposing this enactment, Peel thought it desirable to establish that there was no popular opposition to it displayed at the preceding election of 1826. He pointed out that the fifteen largest counties and the twenty most populous towns returned members who were in favour of relief legislation. 'This', he said, 'is a practical and constitutional method of determining the sense of the people.'[3] It was, indeed, a curious argument to be used by one who was shortly to prove an inveterate opponent of any large measure of reform.

Peel had an unlucky way of involving himself in the creation of precedents of a democratic tendency and of later finding reason to regret his precipitancy in so doing. Another instance of this feature in his career will be mentioned shortly. He certainly lived to regret having contended that the wishes of the people could not only satisfactorily but properly be ascertained by an analysis of the votes of members for popular constituencies. Two years later, during the Reform Bill debates of 1831, Lord John Russell, in remarking how fond Peel was of quoting the earlier speeches of his opponents, proceeded to quote the ill-considered arguments of Peel in 1829, and added that he proposed to adopt the same course

---

[1] *The Craftsman*, 25 May 1734.   [2] *The Free Briton*, 20 June 1734.
[3] 20 *Parl. Deb.*, 2 s., 737.

in reference to Reform, namely to analyse the county results in the preceding election. He took the members for seventeen counties, who voted on the Reform Bill at its second reading, and found that there were twenty-seven of those members in favour of the Bill and only nine against it.[1] Later in the year Earl Grey treated Peel in the same unsparing manner, quoting the passage which had been used by Lord John Russell. It would have been legitimate to have asked Peel why, if he was satisfied with the state of the representation, he found it necessary to adopt an analysis of votes of members of popular constituencies only.[2]

No doubt any method which provided a reasonable opportunity of estimating the real judgement of the people was better than none; but the value of the examination of the results of county elections and the votes of county members prior to 1832 must not be exaggerated. In the first place, the proportion of contested to uncontested county elections was always small—less than half. Sometimes there were fewer contests than ten. In the second place, the county franchise was not always exercised freely and without corruption. The influence of the aristocratic families was very powerful in some counties: several counties were for long periods the preserves of Whigs or Tories; or the membership was even shared between them by arrangement.

There was a comforting, but dangerous theory, deserving of passing notice, which possibly eased the consciences of some few in the pre-Reform days who were afraid of Reform, namely the theory of virtual representation. Mansfield asserted in 1766, in opposition to the repeal of the Stamp Act, that the American colonists were 'virtually represented'. At the time when the discussion of the legality of the taxation of the American colonies was at its height, Burke regarded it as absurd to suppose that a kind of representation, which had proved insufficient for Wales and the Palatine counties, could be satisfactory for a far greater and far more distant part of our territories.[3] But some years later, in *A Letter to Sir Hercules Langrishe* (1792), he discussed virtual representation in what seem to be very unconvincing terms. At that time he regarded virtual representation as possibly superior to actual representation, though he admitted that virtual

---

[1] 3 *Parl. Deb.*, 3 s., 1511.　　　　[2] 7 *Parl. Deb.*, 3 s., 959–63.
[3] Cobbam, *Edmund Burke*, p. 62.

representation could not exist independently of actual representation. The general inference to be drawn from his
elaborate disquisition is that he was searching for a justification of inaction in the matter of Parliamentary Reform.

Pitt adopted the same theory in 1783, when, in speaking
on a motion for reform in the representation, he wished to
find a basis for discountenancing any proposal for a wide
extension of the franchise. Members of Parliament, he said,
genuinely represented the people at large and not merely
those who had elected them.[1] This view was freely adopted
shortly before and during the debates on the Reform Bill of
1832. Peel, in opposing the principle of universal suffrage,
asserted that there existed a 'general representation' of the
people in the House of Commons.[2] But Sir James Scarlett
(afterwards Lord Abinger), although he had started his
career as a Whig and mild reformer, seems to have surpassed
all others in a perverse interpretation of the theory of virtual representation. In 1831 he told the House of Commons
that he considered reform unnecessary, since public opinion
found its way sufficiently into the House, 'first, by means of
the number of members returned for popular places; and,
secondly, from the very fact of the great numbers of the
House'.[3]

The futility of arguing that the virtual representation of
persons for whom rights were claimed provided an adequate
excuse for opposing the reform of the franchise and of the
distribution of seats was exposed by Macaulay in an indisputable manner.

> A virtual representative [he said] is, I presume, a man who acts
> as a direct representative would act: for surely it would be absurd
> to say that a man virtually represents the people of Manchester,
> who is in the habit of saying No, when a man directly representing
> the people of Manchester would say Ay. The utmost that can be
> expected from virtual representation is that it may be as good as
> direct representation. If so, why not grant direct representation
> to places which, as everybody allows, ought, by some process or
> other, to be represented.[4]

[1] 23 *Parl. Hist.* 831. W. Paley in his *Principles of Moral and Political Philosophy*
(1785), Book VI, chapter vii, maintained that, 'by annexing the right of voting
for members of the house of commons to different qualifications in different
places, each order and profession of men in the community become virtually
represented'. This was in the true Whig tradition.
[2] 24 *Parl. Deb.*, 2 s., 1243.
[3] 7 *Parl. Deb.*, 3 s., 158.
[4] 2 *Parl. Deb.*, 3 s., 1197.

§ 5. *Alleged submissions to the people*

Although it is unlikely that anyone will be misled into concluding that at any time during the eighteenth century the people were in a position to exercise effective political power, other than of a most crude and indefinite character, it is possible to find occasions in which it suited politicians, as a matter of prudence, to act as if the sense of the people were systematically followed. They sought the moral support of the electorate in situations which demanded every reinforcement that could be made available. The few occasions on which the people were mentioned by those in authority as possessing an influence on the government of the country were those of emergency, when the usual disrespect for popular opinions dissolved before the tide of popular frenzy. This attention to the people's voice had sometimes at its back the fear of their ultimate physical preponderance, which is recognizable from time to time during the century.

It is, of course, a truism that politicians pay compliments to electors at election time and attribute to them many virtues and capacities which, when the election is over, are rapidly forgotten. It is necessary, therefore, to examine the circumstances of any allegation respecting the extent of the people's powers which is made at election time, with the object of ascertaining the motive behind it. But, whatever the circumstances, it is difficult to believe that a Minister of the eighteenth century would have troubled himself to look for any expression of the inclination of the people that might be disclosed through the voting at a general election and to adjust his policy accordingly.

In 1774, when the seriousness of the situation regarding the American colonies was growing extreme, Lord North wrote to the King, informing him that he advised the dissolution of Parliament 'lest popular dissatisfaction, arising from untoward events, should break the chain of those public measures necessary to reduce the colonies to obedience'.[1] It does not seem necessary to infer from these words that Lord North was prepared to follow the dictates of the electorate. Presumably he merely thought that the result of the election, which was almost a foregone conclusion, might enable him to point to a fresh Ministerial majority so as to

---

[1] *Correspondence between George III and Lord North*, vol. i, p. 219. Cf. the attitude of Lord North in 1780, p. 193 below.

strengthen his position abroad. The circumstances of the election of 1784, shortly to be mentioned, also illustrate a superficial recognition of the people's political capacity.

Again, it is very probable that Grenville dissolved Parliament in 1806 as a matter of party convenience and expediency; but, upon the opening of the new session, he defended himself against criticisms regarding the sudden dissolution by ascribing his action to solicitude for a pronouncement by the people on the question of the prosecution of the war. He said that 'it was surely a wise measure in His Majesty to appeal to the sense of his people, to refer to them the conduct of his servants, and thereby to call upon them to pronounce, in the eyes of the world, their sense as to the further prosecution of the contest'.[1] Considerable justification was required, at the time of this dissolution, for ending the period of Parliament before six or seven years had run; and if, as may be assumed, the real object of the dissolution was no more than an attempt to secure a large majority, some laudable intention had to be expressed so as to avoid the criticisms of the censorious.

Speeches by Pitt and Fox in the debate on Grey's motion for Reform in 1797 throw light on the conflicting opinions which were held regarding the value of inferences to be drawn from the results of general elections. Pitt, in attempting to justify the existing state of the representation, asserted that it could be shown from recent examples that there was a close connexion between the return of members and the sentiments of the people.[2] This was, perhaps, the inevitable attitude of a Minister in Pitt's position; but it must have been difficult for him to have convinced himself that 'circumstances attendant on general elections' could provide any useful guide to the pulse of the public.

Fox, however, breathing the unconstrained air of opposition, was able to expose the almost transparent speciousness of the arguments which implied that the votes of the people had any but the most remote influence on the course of public affairs.

It is a notable argument [he observed] that because we do not find, at the general election, very material changes in the representation, the sentiments of the people continue the same, in favour of war, and in favour of his Majesty's Ministers. The very ground of the present discussion gives the answer to this argument.

[1] 8 *Parl. Deb.*, 1 s., 27.   [2] 33 *Parl. Hist.* 677.

Why do we agitate the question of parliamentary reform? Why, because a general election does not afford the people the means of expressing their voices; because this House is not a sufficient representative of the people. Gentlemen are fond of arguing in this circle. When we contend that Ministers have not the confidence of the people, they tell us that Parliament is the faithful representative of the sense of the country. When we assert that the representation is defective, and shew, from the petitions to the throne, that the House does not speak the voice of the people, they turn to the general election, and say that at this period they had an opportunity of choosing faithful organs of their opinion; because very little or no change has taken place in the representation, the sense of the people must be the same. Sir, it is in vain for gentlemen to shelter themselves by this mode of reasoning. We assert that, under the present form and practice of elections, we cannot expect to see any remarkable change produced by a general election. We must argue from experience. Let us look back to the period of the American War. It will not be denied by the right honourable gentleman that, towards the end of that war, it became extremely unpopular, and that the King's Ministers lost the confidence of the nation. In the year 1780 a dissolution took place, and then it was naturally imagined by superficial observers, who did not examine the real state of representation, that the people would have returned a Parliament that would have unequivocally spoken their sentiments on the occasion. What was the case? I am able to speak with considerable precision. . . . I can take upon me to say that the change was very small indeed: not more than three or four persons were added to the number of those who had from the beginning opposed the disastrous career of the Ministers in that war. I remember that, upon that occasion, Lord North made use of precisely the same argument as is now brought forward: 'What,' said he, 'can you contend the war is unpopular, after the declaration in its favour that the people have made by their choice of representatives? The general election is proof that the war continues to be the war of the people of England.'[1]

Perhaps the most ludicrous instance of the type of argument thus impugned by Fox is to be found in the debates leading up to the passing of the Reform Bill of 1832, when it was suggested that, if, as was asserted by reformers, the sense of the people had been adequately shown in the preceding general election, the state of the representation must have been satisfactory as it stood.

The divergency between Pitt and Fox at the time of the

[1] 33 Parl. Hist. 709-11.

debate which included the above-quoted speeches was not
merely limited to facts, but was also concerned with principles. They took different views of the people's proper place
in the Constitution. Pitt had by the end of the century been
forced by weight of responsibility, accompanied by changed
circumstances, into a position widely different from that of
his younger days. He probably spoke his considered opinion
when, three years later than the delivery of the speech which
has just been noticed, he observed with regard to Ireland:
'There may be occasions, but they will ever be few, when an
appeal to the people is the just mode of proceeding on important subjects.'[1] Fox, on the other hand, tended steadily
in a democratic direction; and his withdrawal from Parliament at the end of the Session was, perhaps, a proof of his
real conviction that the defects in the representation rendered
the whole parliamentary system a calamitous farce.

§ 6. *The election of 1784*

The election of 1784, at which the younger Pitt routed
the Fox–North coalition, holds a singular position among
eighteenth-century elections and demands separate remarks.
Its influence in the development of the principle of the mandate was not, it seems, as large as writers on political history
have, until the last few years, implied. Although the words
of the King's Speech prior to the dissolution of Parliament—
that His Majesty felt it a duty to 'recur to the sense of his
people' by calling a new Parliament—were quoted on more
than one occasion in the nineteenth century in order to justify
appeals to the people of a more authentic character, recent
historical research has proved that even the narrow electorate
of 1784 did not have the opportunity, in any genuine sense,
of pronouncing judgement on the question of the King versus
the Whig families, the Indian question, or, indeed, any other
question. It was convenient for Pitt to frame the Speech on
behalf of the King, and to address the House, as if the people
were to determine the course of politics; and to speak after
the election as if it had been open to the people to declare
their views on the situation. Doubtless, expressions such as
these led to the notion that the people had at last been able
to revolt against the state of dependence and repression
under which the Whig régime had placed them for several

---

[1] 35 *Parl. Hist.* 83–84.

decades. As a fact, the result of the election of 1784 was due
to a complex variety of causes, of which the voting of the
electors was only one. The marshalling of a strong body of
members, who were interested in defeating the steps by which
it was thought that the Fox–North coalition was attempting
to gain a party advantage out of the revision of the constitution of East India, was probably as important an element in
the victory as any turnover in the votes of the electorate.

The King had, say, a hundred 'Friends' in Parliament;
and Pitt, though having but some fifty adherents, seems to
have discovered that the mishandling of the India Bill by the
Fox–North Ministry, in the autumn of 1783, would give him,
if reinforced by the support of the Crown, an opportunity,
which had not existed earlier in the year, to enlarge his
forces. There was warrant for an attempt to oust those who
had presumed to dictate to the Sovereign. It might be possible, he reckoned, by attaching to himself those concerned
with the East India Company, as well as those who were
likely to follow the chances of royal favour, to organize a
majority in the House of Commons. In other words, it is
tolerably clear that what has been described as a great victory
was a victory in management only and did not represent
any signal advance in the power of the people.

The various circumstances, mentioned in this chapter as
proof of the inability of the people in the eighteenth century
to act as a decisive factor in politics, are nearly all present in
the election of 1784. There was no straightforward division
into parties which could enable issues to be framed and
submitted. Apart from the ambiguities following from the
unprincipled alliance between Fox and North, the scanty
party loyalties of the period had been disturbed by the recent
reassortment of groups in Parliament, which made any
attempt by party agents to estimate the strength of parties
an almost impossible task. The investigation which has been
made into the preparations, calculations, and attitude of
John Robinson, the great party organizer enlisted on Pitt's
behalf, proves that little, if any, consideration was given to
the effect which the views of the electors on any of the public
questions of the day might have on the election results.
'Interest' was of much greater importance.

The form of election addresses prepared for constituencies
with popular franchise in 1784 does not seem to suggest that
candidates offered alternative programmes to their electors

more generally in this election than in any other eighteenth-century election.[1] The addresses of Fox and his opponents in the famous Westminster contest of 1784 contain the usual empty verbiage characteristic of the election addresses of the time. Those of Lord Hood and Sir Cecil Wray contained no reference to the political situation, but merely such expressions as 'high and important trust', 'zeal and fidelity', and 'conformity to your wishes and sentiments'; while the only reference in those of Fox (there was more than one address) to public matters was concerned with the absence of justification for dissolution and with his intention to oppose 'that secret influence by which the present Administration was created'.[2]

But the small number of contests which took place in the election is the most convincing evidence that the people were not in fact in a position to decide anything by their votes. Only about a third of the members returned were under the necessity of going to the poll. It is absurd, therefore, to suppose that this election did much more than provide a nominal precedent for any extension of the powers of the people.

[1] Cf. remarks on the election for the County of Norfolk, p. 181 above.
[2] *History of the Westminster Election*, 1784, 2nd ed., pp. 87, 131, 187; and on the election generally see *The Parliamentary Papers of John Robinson, 1774–84* (Camden Society), Introduction, pp. viii–x; also 31 *E.H.R.*, pp. 224 ff., being an article on 'Public Opinion and the General Election of 1784', by W. T. Laprade.

CHAPTER IX

THE PEOPLE AND POLICY

§ 1. *The great Reform Bill*

INCIDENTS in politics, during the years just preceding the introduction of the great Reform Bill, prepared the public mind for the recognition of new constitutional principles. The necessity of obtaining the authority of the people for an important change of policy came under discussion in connexion with proposals for the relief of Roman Catholic disabilities. The Duke of Wellington and Sir Robert Peel had introduced and carried a measure of Roman Catholic Emancipation in 1829, though indisputably pledged, in a general sense, to the opposite policy.

It was argued, even in 1829, that a politician in the position of Peel should not suddenly change his publicly acknowledged attitude to a great national question without giving the electorate an opportunity to declare upon it. Peel, in introducing the measure for Roman Catholic relief, endeavoured to vindicate his change of front by challenging the contention that the people were opposed to concession. For this purpose he referred back, as has been seen, to the circumstances of the last preceding general election, that of 1826. He said that the general election was the time for public opinion to declare itself, that public opinion should be gathered by the exercise of the elective franchise and not merely at public meetings: strong admissions for a statesman who was shortly to bemoan, in debates on the Reform Bill, the prospect of the enlargement of the powers of the people and of the diminution of the preponderance of the Legislature. He proceeded to the analysis of the election results of the county and large city constituencies, to which reference has been made in the foregoing chapter.[1] By his endeavour, then, to avoid the criticism which was levelled against him on the ground of his breach of pledge Peel involved himself in the acceptance of the principle that policy should follow the declaration of public opinion expressed by the votes of the electorate.

[1] 20 *Parl. Deb.*, 2 s., 737, and pp. 188–9 above.

There were many signs during the two or three years before the fight over the great Reform Bill that there was a quickening of interest in the subject of Reform. The middle classes were beginning to follow the lead of the working-men in pressing for representation. The subject, which had from time to time been raised in Parliament during the preceding half-century, was once more brought forward in the House of Commons in the early part of 1830. Although the 'glorious days of July' in the Paris revolution served to intensify the atmosphere in the latter part of the general election of 1830 in England, Reform can hardly be said to have been an issue in that election;[1] but, even before the French influence took effect, the question of Reform had been much in the air, as a result particularly of the agitation of local Political Unions. Between the dissolution of Parliament in July and its meeting in October strikes and revolts in various parts of the country proved that the masses were intent upon some improvement in their political, as well as their economic, position. It was the realization that at last the middle classes had been aroused from their state of lethargy and were no longer willing to be left without effective part in the business of government that induced Lord Grey to resume his place as a leader of the Reform movement. Immediately on the re-assembly of Parliament, the Duke of Wellington raised a storm of indignation by his cavalier treatment of a comment on the absence of any measure of Reform from the King's Speech; and, as an indirect result, Lord Grey within a few days succeeded him in office.

The extent to which Lord Grey's earlier attitude in the matter cast an obligation on him and his Ministry to endeavour to introduce legislation was mentioned by him shortly after the Reform Bill was introduced on 1 March 1831. The new Prime Minister said that he gathered from the preceding speech of the Duke of Wellington that it was admitted that a strong desire among the people to procure revision of the franchise had been manifested at the general election, and that it was impossible for the Government to avoid giving that subject its earliest consideration. For his own part, he regarded parliamentary reform as a condition of his acceptance of office: he considered himself 'pledged to it when out of office, and still more when in office, from a

[1] Cf. the arguments of Gladstone and of Asquith on this subject later in the century; 304 *Parl. Deb.*, 3 s., 1547; 29 *H.C. Deb.*, 5 s., 813.

sense of public duty'.[1] Lord Grey felt that he was not only
justified in bringing in a measure for Reform, but that he was
even under an obligation to do so, although the question had
not been specifically placed before the people at an election.
He had, for many years, held himself out as a keen exponent
of democratic principles; and, since there were obvious indications that public opinion was moving rapidly in favour of
legislation, he felt himself bound to put his professions into
practice. As matters turned out, a general election became
necessary in 1831, at which an express mandate was given
for the passing of the Reform Bill. The King's Speech prior
to the dissolution of April 1831 stated in the most un-
ambiguous terms that there was to be referred to the people,
not merely the question of the support of the Ministry, but
the question whether or not a Reform Bill was to be passed.
It was hardly necessary that the issue should be defined in the
formal Speech. It was blazed abroad and adopted in every
constituency in which there was a contest. Lord John Russell,
speaking two days after the dissolution, in support of the
Reform candidate at Southwark, thus interpreted the King's
Speech to the electors:

> On this occasion the electors had more than a common duty
> to perform, for they were called upon not merely to select men
> the best fitted to defend their rights and interests, but to answer
> by their conduct this question put to the electors of the empire
> by His Majesty in dissolving Parliament: 'Do you approve—ay or
> no—of the principle of a reform in the representation?'[2]

The distinction between the appeal to the people in 1784
and that of 1831 lies chiefly in the clear submission, in the
latter instance, of a question of policy. It was even contended
that matters had gone a stage farther and that the people
were asked to determine upon the form in which the measure
should be enacted. The Duke of Wellington observed that
in 1784 the people were not called upon to deliberate on any
measure, but were appealed to in favour of the men whom
the King had named as his Ministers. But he alleged, truly
enough, that, in the case of 1831, the reference was 'not
whether the King was to be supported in naming his Ministers—not whether Parliament was to be reformed, because,
upon the principle of reform, there was a majority in the late
House of Commons, but upon a particular plan of reform
which was accordingly discussed throughout the country'.

[1] 3 *Parl. Deb.*, 3 s., 1075-9.   [2] *The Times*, 26 Apr. 1831.

He charged the Ministry with having been the cause of the unconstitutional practice, hitherto unknown, of electing delegates for a particular purpose rather than 'to deliberate upon matters of common concern, and to decide according to the best of their judgment, after such deliberation and debate'.[1] Similar views were also expressed in the House of Commons.

Peel did not display, in connexion with the Reform Bill, the same anxiety to comply with the people's views as he had in 1829. In his speech in the House of Commons on the introduction of the Bill in March 1831 he showed himself far from ready for the reference to the people which was to set the seal on their capacity to determine the main lines of the policy of government. He preferred 'the reason and calm judgment of this House' to 'some intrinsic and higher authority—the feelings and wishes of the people'.[2]

When it became increasingly clear, as the country grew more and more insistent, that a considerable extension of the franchise would have to be enacted by one side or the other, he became resigned to the necessity of Parliament following the will of the people expressed by their votes on a great national issue. By so doing he accepted a principle which was more important than the contents of the Bill.[3]

Although Home Secretary in the Ministry of Lord Grey, Lord Melbourne, as is well known, was not an enthusiastic supporter of Reform. His axiom of 'Why not leave it alone?' truly epitomized his attitude towards any advanced proposals. During the autumn debates, however, on the second reading of the Bill in the House of Lords, after maintaining in a characteristic passage the propriety of resisting the will of the people, he suddenly and with dramatic force asserted that Parliament had sufficiently resisted the pressure for Reform and that the sustained demand for legislation, authentically expressed, must be met.[4]

It is unnecessary to recount the various shifts and expedients by which the Opposition tried to maintain a hopeless rearguard action. During the winter and spring of 1831–2 Lord Harrowby, Lord Wharncliffe, and others (known as 'the waverers') tried to arrange an accommodation. And by the critical stage of April 1832 several of the Tory peers were willing to admit their agreement with Lord Harrowby,

---

[1] 7 *Parl. Deb.*, 3 s., 1193.
[3] 7 *Parl. Deb.*, 3 s., 458.
[2] 2 *Parl. Deb.*, 3 s., 1339.
[4] 7 *Parl. Deb.*, 3 s., 1177–8.

who was bold enough to declare in debate that the Opposition in the House of Lords could no longer hope to resist the measure, 'which the House of Commons had sanctioned for a second time by a large majority, and in favour of which the people of England had expressed a decided opinion'.[1]

As a result of the passing of the Act of 1832 the principle of the extension of the franchise was secured. It was put into effective practice by the Act of 1867; and later Reform Acts have carried the principle, it may be assumed, near the limit of its application. But another principle of capital importance was, as has been remarked, secured at the time of the passing of the first Reform Bill. It was indisputably established that the people could decide questions of policy by their votes at general elections. The full effect of this principle was not realized for some years, although a few shrewd observers seem quickly to have appreciated what had happened. Among these was Cobbett, who pointed out, in his trenchant articles in *The Political Register* in the summer of 1832, that the taking of pledges had assumed a new complexion with new possibilities. 'We all know', he said, 'that, if the House of Commons had not been pledged, we should have no Reform Bill.' He did not speak merely of single members being pledged, but of the House of Commons.

It is fairly certain that few of the Ministers responsible for the passing of the great Reform Bill saw the prospects of the new era as clearly as Cobbett. Indeed, many of them regarded, or affected to regard, that measure as a final settlement of the problem of democratic government.[2] But, although an incomplete understanding of what is, perhaps, now generally regarded as an essential object of general elections (the choice, that is to say, of Ministries or policies) was to persist for some time, nevertheless the period of the Bill of 1832 must be looked back on as the most critical in the history of the development of the people's part in government.

Details respecting the degree in which the franchise was extended by the Reform Act of 1832 do not directly concern the present topic. It is enough to observe that the Act deposited electoral power in the hands of considerably less than

---

[1] 12 *Parl. Deb.*, 3 s., 150.
[2] Although Peel adopted this view, he had, in the early debates on the Bill, criticized the proposed changes on the ground that they were bound to lead to more extensive concessions; see 2 *Parl. Deb.*, 3 s., 1345-6.

one million voters in a population of twenty-four millions, and that the lower middle classes soon exhibited their active discontent at a measure which has since been described as having promoted the 'undue predominance of the bourgeoisie'.[1] It must be remembered, however, that, at the time, the redistribution of seats was regarded as just as important a feature in the Act as the increase in the number of voters. Even the progress which was attained by the enlargement of the electorate was to a great extent neutralized by various forms of corruption and chicanery which grew up under the new régime. Bribery had, of course, flourished before the Act in those constituencies where the number of voters was so large that seats could not be purchased outright. But, under the new arrangements, the bribery of voters in a greater number of constituencies than before reduced to a considerable extent the benefits attributable to a smaller trade in seats. Moreover, the introduction for the first time of a system of registration or official listing of voters, under the provisions of the Act of 1832, gave unscrupulous party agents opportunities to influence the casting of votes in an improper manner.

Some ineffective attempts were made prior to 1832 to check corrupt practices. As early as 1695 a statute, 7 & 8 William III, c. 4, aimed at reducing bribery by candidates; and another statute, 2 George II, c. 24, made an almost equally fruitless attempt at preventing voters from accepting bribes. But the Acts of 1854 and 1883 both had beneficial results in checking the abuses of corruption, as also did the introduction of an enlightened system of trying election petitions in 1868. Nevertheless, it is true that, throughout a large part of the nineteenth century, the working of incipient democracy was hindered by a degree of corruption not much less than that of the preceding century, though of a different kind. Between 1832 and 1872 a vast amount of intimidation was practised; and in some respects the benefits of the wider franchise were discounted more by intimidation than by corruption. This serious interference with the free exercise of the franchise was largely removed by the introduction of the ballot in 1872.[2] Although, then, in theory political power

[1] Monypenny and Buckle, *Life of Disraeli* (new ed.), vol. ii, p. 1515.
[2] The comparative effects of corruption and intimidation were considered by Macaulay in the opening passages of his speech to his electors at Edinburgh on 29 May 1839. *Writings and Speeches* (1882 ed.), p. 574.

passed, in 1832, from the upper to the middle classes, there
were still, for many years, stumbling-blocks in the way of a
genuine transfer.

§ 2. *Peel and the publication of programmes*

A subject so compelling in importance as that of Reform
was not to force its way as an issue into every general election.
But if issues, even of less concern, were to be explicitly and
adequately submitted to the people at elections, it would be
necessary to adopt a practice by which they should be published and explained in programmes put forward by party
leaders. Such a practice was initiated, oddly enough, by
Peel; and, as happened with him on more than one occasion
when he was actuated by opportunism, he repented at leisure
of his precipitancy.

Upon his unexpected appointment as Prime Minister, after
the dismissal of Melbourne in 1834 and while Parliament was
not sitting, he saw that he could have no hope of obtaining
a majority unless he found some means of laying his policy
before the country. He could not explain his programme in
Parliament; and he and his colleagues decided that the best
way of effecting a similar result was to outline the policy of
the Ministry in a manifesto nominally addressed by him to
his own constituents at Tamworth, but actually addressed to
the electorate at large. He drafted this address, obtained the
approval of the Cabinet to it, and sent copies to the London
daily press.

Peel's address at once became famous under the title of
the Tamworth Manifesto. As Greville remarked, it made a
'prodigious sensation';[1] and well it might.

When before did a Prime Minister think it expedient to
announce to the people, not only his acceptance of office, but the
principles and even the details of the measures which he intended
to produce, and to solicit—not from Parliament, but from the
people—that they would so far maintain the prerogative of the
King as to give the Ministers of his choice not indeed an implicit
confidence, but a fair trial. In former times such a proceeding
would have been thought derogatory and impugned as unconstitutional, and would have been both; but the new circumstances in which the Reform Bill has placed the Crown, by making
its choice of Ministers immediately and absolutely dependent on
the choice of the several constituencies, and, in the first instance,

[1] *Journal of Reigns of George IV and William IV*, vol. iii, p. 178.

quite independent of the concurrence of the assembled parliament, have rendered such a course not merely expedient, but inevitable.[1]

Thus spoke the oracle of Conservatism, *The Quarterly Review*. It is true that the article which thus disclosed the novelty of the proceeding was written in defence of Peel's conduct (almost certainly by Croker); but the writer did not refrain from emphasizing the significance of the departure.

Cobbett, who, as has been seen, had a very broad conception of the effects of the passing of the Reform Bill, could not resist twitting Peel on his method of appealing to the people. Why were the people of Tamworth entitled to a full declaration of Peel's principles? It was proper for him to make such a declaration in his capacity as member of Parliament; but what was the reason for 'selecting them as a channel, through which to make this general manifesto?'[2]

Peel stated in his manifesto that he felt it incumbent upon him to enter into a declaration of his views of public policy, and that he availed himself of what he regarded as a legitimate opportunity of communicating to the public at large 'that frank exposition of general principles and views which appears to be anxiously expected and which it ought not to be the inclination, and cannot be the interest of a Minister of this country to withhold'. The Reform Bill, he explained, constituted a new era; and it was the duty of a Minister to declare explicitly, first whether he would maintain the Bill itself, and, secondly, whether he would act upon the spirit in which it was conceived. He expressed himself as prepared to maintain the Bill as 'a final and irrevocable settlement of a great constitutional question'; and, if willingness to adopt the spirit of the Bill did not involve more than a fair review of existing institutions and redress of abuses and grievances without infringing on established rights, he and his colleagues were prepared to subscribe to those principles.[3]

The chances of Peel's Ministry at the polls were undoubtedly improved as a result of the publication of the manifesto, though a clear majority was not obtained. But Peel himself soon came to recognize that the exigencies of his sudden appointment and of the peculiar political situation had driven him to undertake a course which might prove a

[1] 53 *Quarterly Review*, p. 265 (Apr. 1835).
[2] *Cobbett's Political Register*, vol. lxxxvi, p. 771.
[3] *Memoirs*, vol. ii, pp. 58 ff.

troublesome precedent. In writing to his friend Croker in 1835, he admitted that the Tamworth Manifesto 'too much referred to necessities imposed by the Reform Bill'; and he expressed the view that 'the necessities rather arose from the abruptness of the change in the Government, and, to say the truth, from the policy of aiding our friends at the election'.[1] This was certainly so. In his desire to obtain support from the enlarged electorate, Peel had committed himself to more advanced views than those which he afterwards cared to maintain.

Much assistance was obtained by the Whigs, in the election of 1834, from a tract written by Edward Lytton Bulwer (as he then was) entitled *A Letter to a Late Cabinet Minister on the Present Crisis*. This tract had an immediate and immense popularity and a circulation in excess of any similar publication. It not only insisted on a maintenance of the policy of Reform, but it also recognized the new effect which was to be given to general elections. 'Remember', he said, 'that you are . . . now fighting for things, not men—*for the real consequences of your reform.*' This tract was not in any way an official product of the Whig party; but its widespread influence on the course of the election ensured that votes were given for 'things' as well as for 'men'. It was, therefore, due to the attitude of both sides that the election of 1834 marked an advance towards democratic government.

Expediency has, somewhat naturally, influenced politicians, either consciously or unconsciously, in their views of the admissibility of the mandate. An alternation in their attitude can often be distinguished. When faced with the immediate prospect of a general election, they have found it convenient to produce an attractive policy and to appeal to the people upon it, in the hope of securing a majority. When confronted in the House of Commons with the prospect of a dissolution in circumstances which suggested that a general election would not bring about a result favourable to them, they have contended that the occasion was not an appropriate one for an appeal to the people. If in power, they have seen no reason why an important measure should not be passed without 'going to the country'; but if in opposition, with the tide turning in their favour, they have expressed themselves as shocked at the prospect of some new principle of legislation

[1] *Croker Papers*, vol. ii, p. 256.

being undertaken without its being submitted to the electorate.

The incidents leading up to the dissolution of Parliament in
1841 illustrated not only a change in the attitude of Peel from
that implied by the Tamworth Manifesto, but also a strange
failure to apprehend the new function of dissolutions of Parliament, which the events of 1831 and 1832 had entailed.
The Melbourne Ministry, growing in popular discredit without realizing it, owing largely to its failure to cope with the
difficulties produced by the financial depression, were defeated on a question of finance, but remained in office.
Many of the Whig Ministers, as well as the Whigs generally,
were keen to have a dissolution; but Melbourne was steadily
opposed to it. He held the old-fashioned view, which was
also shared by Peel, that the Crown ought never to make an
appeal to the people unless it was fairly certain that the Ministry would obtain a majority, however much the political
situation might call for an expression of the people's views.
Melbourne's Ministry did not decide, as a Ministry might
today, that, having been defeated on an important question, it should give the electors an opportunity of choosing
between it and an alternative Ministry, but decided that the
state of public opinion should be sounded and a dissolution resorted to only if there were found to be a strong
probability of the Ministry securing a majority at an election.[1]
Sir John Hobhouse was one of the few politicians on either
side who had a clear and progressive conception of the proper
function of a general election. He protested, in the Cabinet,
against the question of dissolution being made to depend on
the likelihood of obtaining a majority in the new Parliament,
and he asserted that an appeal to the country was for the
purpose of ascertaining its opinion. This seems to be self-
evident today; but it was very far from being so in 1841.[2]

Within a few days of the defeat of the Melbourne Ministry
Peel proposed a motion of want of confidence, at the same
time contending that, if his motion proved successful, the
occasion was not a proper one for Melbourne to advise a
dissolution. It was dangerous, he said, to admit any other
recognized organ of public opinion than the House of Commons; and he added that, if the Ministry considered that it

[1] Greville, *Journal of the Reign of Queen Victoria, 1837–52*, vol. ii, pp. 1–2;
Lord Broughton, *Recollections of a Long Life*, vol. vi, pp. 26–28.
[2] Ibid., p. 20.

was appropriate to refer the situation to the opinion of the constituencies, the indications of recent by-elections clearly suggested that a majority of the constituencies were opposed to the Ministry. In the event of a general election he would not submit a policy to the people. According to the standards of the present day Peel would have felt bound, on carrying his motion and on succeeding Melbourne in office, to take the earliest opportunity of submitting himself to the electors; and the fact that he estimated that the general feeling in the country was opposed to the Whigs should, it might be supposed, have encouraged him to advise a dissolution.

Sir John Hobhouse, on behalf of the Ministry, replied to Peel that he could not see why the time was inopportune for an appeal to the people. Why should not they, if defeated in the House of Commons, lay their policy and principles before the country? He furthermore charged Peel with inconsistency in respect of his attitude towards the issue of election programmes.

The right honourable Baronet has said . . . that he shall not make any particular exposition of his principles. But, when the right honourable Baronet came into office in 1834, he thought differently. He then thought it right to make an exposition of his political principles in his famous Tamworth Manifesto. . . . He did not then deem it improper to make an appeal to the country.

The precedent of 1831, for referring questions of policy to the people at general elections, was expressly adopted by Lord John Russell, the leader of the Liberals in the House of Commons. After discussing the alternative between resignation and advising an appeal to the country, he said:

On a subject of so much importance to the people [as the fiscal question] I feel that it is our bounden duty to offer such advice to her Majesty as we may think will ensure the decision of it by the electors of the realm, duly consulted upon the question.[1]

Much against Melbourne's better judgement, and to the subsequent regret of the Queen herself, the Ministry, after having been defeated on Peel's motion by one vote, advised a dissolution rather than resignation. The Queen's Speech prior to the dissolution exhibited a democratic strain. The general election was to take place so as to provide an opportunity of ascertaining 'the sense of my people upon matters

[1] 58 Parl. Deb., 3 s., 817–18, 850–1, 1212 ff.

which so deeply concern their welfare'. In this formal way, therefore, the people were asked to demonstrate by their votes how they were disposed towards alternative financial policies.

The Duke of Wellington's mistrust of the increase in the powers of the people was awakened by the form of the Queen's Speech, just as it was in 1831. He criticized the character of the appeal to the people as going farther in a democratic direction than any earlier instance. Melbourne justified the terms of the Speech by reference to the precedent of 1784; and he said that the later Speech seemed to him the milder of the two. The Duke, however, insisted that the circumstances of 1784 were entirely different, since, in that instance, the dispute was essentially one between prerogative and privilege and was 'exclusively a question in the House of Commons'.[1] The distinction between the election of 1784 and that of 1831 has already been discussed; and the same principles of distinction apply to a large extent between the elections of 1784 and 1841. Melbourne would, perhaps, have been on safer ground if he had justified the form of the Queen's Speech by referring to the circumstances of the election of 1831; but he may not have had sufficient time to produce the most effective reply, or he may not have taken very seriously the rigid and reactionary views of the venerable statesman.

Peel's vacillation in the matter of the appropriateness of appeals to the people, as well as his conservative understanding of the true purpose of a dissolution, is again illustrated in the period between his repeal of the Corn Laws and his resignation in 1846. He undoubtedly regretted the failure of the Liberals to form a Ministry in 1845, since he would thus have been saved the approbrium of introducing a policy which was in direct opposition to the principles which he had upheld during the whole of his preceding political career and particularly at the last general election, that of 1841. But at the time of preparing for the introduction of the repeal of the Corn Laws he refused to appeal to the constituencies, for the reason that the question was one arousing too keen an interest to be so determined. It might surely have been thought that a question of sufficient importance to be raised as an issue in every constituency should be settled by a

[1] 59 *Parl. Deb.*, 3 s., 77, 81.

general election. This, however, was not the way in which the
problem presented itself to Peel, whose views on it seem to
suggest consideration for every other aspect of the situation
but that which concerned the rights of the people.[1]

He was well aware that he would be severely criticized for
his change of front regarding the Corn Laws; but he cannot
have suspected the asperity and the virulence with which
Disraeli was to denounce his apostasy. In January 1846 the
measure for abolishing the Corn Laws was introduced; and
Disraeli lost no time in charging Peel with having neglected
to obtain the opinion of the people on proposed legislation
diametrically opposed in tenor to the principles embraced
by the Ministry at the last general election. At the outset
Disraeli seized upon Peel's vindication on his retention of
office, on the ground that no Liberal Ministry could be
formed, as incapable of being sustained. In his first important
speech on this topic, he complained that it was not

a legitimate trial of the principles of free trade against the principles of protection, if a Parliament, the majority of which are
elected to support protection, be gained over to free trade by the
arts of the very individual whom they were elected to support in
an opposite career.[2]

As soon as Peel had secured the passage of his free trade
legislation the defeat of his Ministry in the House of Commons
forced him to decide whether to resign or to advise a dissolution of Parliament. He did not find this decision very easy.
The Conservative party was split in two: free trade had been
carried chiefly, of course, by Liberal votes. It seemed impossible for him to obtain a working majority. There is to be
found in his *Memoirs* a memorandum, prepared for Cabinet
use a day or two before he decided to resign, in which he
reviewed the possible questions on which an effective appeal
could be made to the electors in the event of a dissolution.
He reiterated his firmly rooted notion that a Minister ought
never to advise a dissolution without having a conviction
that a victory at the polls is morally certain. It is curious that
it did not appear to have occurred to him that a Minister
might be under an obligation to the people to give them an
opportunity of deciding a question of policy, regardless of
what the probable result of that election might be. He re-

[1] *Sir Robert Peel's Memoirs*, vol. ii, pp. 163, 166, 167.
[2] 83 *Parl. Deb.*, 3 s., 122; see also his speech in a later debate (83 *Parl. Deb.*, 3 s., 1320).

mained an ardent supporter of a view of the Crown's position which was becoming—or, indeed, had become—obsolete. No one would say now, as Peel said then, that 'unsuccessful dissolutions are, generally speaking, injurious to the authority of the Crown' and that the prerogative of dissolution is 'a great instrument to the Crown for its protection'. But these views were widely held and were, naturally enough, approved by Queen Victoria. Peel expressed the opinion that the dissolution of 1841 was unjustifiable and concluded that the proposed dissolution, if likely to have the same result, would be equally unjustifiable.[1]

Within almost a few hours of Peel's deliberations on this subject it became obvious that his party had no prospect whatever of success at the polls; and he announced to Parliament his immediate resignation of office. He did not tell the House that resignation had been chosen because the alternative was impossible, in the sense that it would prove unsuccessful for the Ministry. He preferred to explain that, owing to the abolition of the Corn Laws having been carried, dissolution had become unnecessary. His explanation is in some respects puzzling. It emphasizes the fact that he did not regard dissolution from the people's point of view. He considered the Crown, he considered his party; but he evidently found it difficult to regard himself as under obligations to the people.

We have advised her Majesty [Peel informed the House of Commons] to accept our resignation at once, without adopting that alternative to which we might have resorted—namely, recommended to the Crown the exercise of its prerogative, and the dissolution of the present Parliament. I do not hesitate to avow, speaking with a frankness that I trust will offend no one, that if her Majesty's Government had failed in carrying, in all their integrity, the main measures of commercial policy which it was my duty to recommend, that there is no exertion that I would not have made—no sacrifice that I would not have incurred—in order to ensure the ultimate success of those measures, or at any rate to give the country an opportunity of pronouncing its opinion on the subject. For such a purpose I should have felt justified in advising dissolution, because I think the continuance of doubt and uncertainty on such important matters would have been a greater evil than the resort to a constitutional mode of ascertaining the opinion of the nation. But there has been for-

[1] *Letters of Queen Victoria* (1st series), vol. ii, pp. 95, 107–8; *Sir Robert Peel's Memoirs*, vol. ii, pp. 292 ff.

tunately no necessity for a dissolution of Parliament upon that ground.[1]

Peel's supposition that, although he found it unnecessary to appeal to the people before he succeeded in repealing the Corn Laws, he might have had to appeal to them after he had failed, was certainly not disingenuous; but it is characteristic of his outlook in regard to this aspect of constitutional practice. The passage quoted above is full of points which arouse criticism. One of the most obvious is the inference that 'the resort to a constitutional mode of ascertaining the opinion of the nation' was an evil to be suffered. It is not fair, however, to examine too closely the words of a speech in Parliament, even though it is one for which the occasion demanded careful preparation.

In 1847, the year following that in which the Corn Laws were abolished, the Liberals dissolved Parliament; and Peel, although he had found cause to regret the Tamworth Manifesto of 1834, rushed ardently into the general election struggle and issued another manifesto to his constituency, which was generally described as such, and which was expressed in terms that proved it to be intended for the whole electorate. It was enthusiastically accepted by his followers as the programme of the 'Peelites'. In this manifesto he reviewed, and attempted a justification of, his policy towards the Roman Catholics and his repeal of the Corn Laws. And he stated that it was his earnest hope that his constituents would make their choice of a representative exclusively on public grounds—that they would not permit the consideration of mere personal regard to influence their judgement.[2]

The precedent of the Tamworth Manifesto of 1834 proved itself to be firmly established at the election of 1847. It was followed by all parties. The Protectionists, led by Lord George Bentinck, regarded his manifesto-letter to his constituency at King's Lynn as descriptive of their official policy; and the Liberal party accepted the main speech of Lord John Russell in support of his candidature in the City of London as signifying its programme. Henceforward it was a matter of routine for each party to have a common plan to present to the people; and in this way the submission of issues for the decision of the electorate was greatly facilitated.

[1] 87 *Parl. Deb.*, 3 s., 1042.
[2] C. Taylor and C. Mackay, *Life and Times of Sir Robert Peel*, vol. iv, pp. 194, 195, 222.

§ 3. *Disraeli and Gladstone; occasions for reference to the people*

The vicissitudes of politics scarcely allow politicians to maintain an undeviating course of principle. It is repeatedly found that the axioms expounded by them in opposition sometimes have to be forgotten amid the pressure and problems of office. Disraeli's caustic criticisms of Peel's volte-face over the repeal of the Corn Laws were to a modified extent applicable to his own record in connexion with the passing of the Reform Act of 1867. His party, in 1865, was nearly as heavily pledged to some measure of Reform as was that of the Liberals. With the help of renegades from the Liberal ranks, he succeeded in defeating Gladstone's Reform Bill of 1866 on no other ground than that it was too extreme a measure. On coming into office, on the resignation of the Liberals, Disraeli was faced with a critical situation in the country, which seemed to be moving from unrest in the direction of rebellion; and conciliatory steps were clearly required in order to ensure the national welfare. By a leadership, which has been described as 'a masterpiece of unscrupulous adroitness',[1] he secured successive amendments to the Reform Bill which he introduced, and so rendered it, in effect, more extreme than that of the Liberals.

It may be contended that the state of the country not only forbade an appeal to the people, but also dictated a bolder measure than that proposed by the Liberals. And it is hardly necessary to read Disraeli's *Coningsby* and his *Sybil* to ensure the conviction that the terms of his Bill were in consonance with his genuine political tenets. Nevertheless, he plainly transgressed the principles of the relation of public opinion to party which he had upheld at the time of Peel's apostasy in 1846. A party which had succeeded to office as a result of adopting a particular policy, namely moderation in Reform, had been responsible for legislation involving an entirely different policy, without any submission to the people. The incident provides a close analogy to Peel's conversion to the necessity of meeting the Roman Catholic claims in 1829.

It is, perhaps, fair to observe that, owing to the increase in the extent of popular agitation in the second half of 1866, it would have been easier for Russell to have advised dissolu-

[1] W. E. H. Lecky, *The Map of Life*, pp. 138 ff.

tion instead of resignation immediately after his defeat on Reform in June 1866, than for Disraeli to have appealed to the people soon after accession to office. Judged according to the standards of the present day, Russell's insistence on resignation was not justifiable. But, even at that time, there were many who thought that dissolution was the proper course for the Liberals to choose. Gladstone told Russell that the objections to dissolution were superficial, that the temporary loss of supporters and the inconvenience of a quickly repeated general election were of less importance than the maintenance of the principles of the Constitution, which, in his view, required dissolution.[1] Russell's chief reason for resignation was a peculiar one. He was apparently of the opinion that there was a general apathy in the south of England on the subject of Reform, an estimate which was soon to prove fallacious.[2]

No one suggested that, on Russell's failure to dissolve, Disraeli should have appealed to the people, simply because he was under an obligation to obtain a new lease of authority. The convention which required a dissolution at the time of a change of Ministries was not yet settled. It subsequently became almost an invariable rule that there should be an appeal to the people as soon as practicable after the change from a Ministry of one party to that of another.

The dissensions raised by the question of Reform soon yielded place in the field of politics to Gladstone's sudden and sensational proposals in regard to the disestablishment of the Irish Church. On being defeated by a large majority on a vote respecting this question, Disraeli, acting fully in pursuance of the constitutional convention as recognized today, determined not to resign but to advise a dissolution so as to obtain the ruling of the people. One of the reasons given by him in the House of Commons for regarding dissolution as the proper course to adopt was the absence of any previous opportunity for the people to declare upon the question at issue in a general election.

Gladstone, however, did not want a general election; and he argued that, where a Minister was defeated by any majority of more than a very small number, he should resign and should not have the privilege of appealing to the people.

[1] *The Later Correspondence of Lord John Russell*, vol. ii, p. 351.
[2] *Letters of Queen Victoria*, 2nd series, vol. i, p. 335.

He cited in his favour the defeat of Peel in 1846, when Peel did not dissolve but resigned—an uninstructive example, as has already been observed.[1] And he mentioned as inapplicable Melbourne's dissolution on being defeated merely by one vote in 1841.[2]

The necessity of submitting to the people a new political proposal of very general interest before it was introduced in Parliament was debated in the House of Lords. The Conservative Lord Chancellor (Cairns) emphasized the constitutional importance of Gladstone's new proposal and the fact that it had never been referred to the constituencies; and he asserted that the earliest occasion should be taken of obtaining the views of the people. On the Liberal side, Earl Grey used the argument, which was heard at the time of the debates on the first Reform Bill and which was again to be adopted in the later part of the nineteenth and the early part of the twentieth centuries, to the effect that the reference of projected legislation to the electorate would turn Parliament into an assembly of delegates.[3] This argument is obviously based on too extreme a view; and it is easy to reply that only proposals of particular or of constitutional importance should, if opportunity and the safety of the State permit, be submitted to the people. It may be freely admitted that, in regard to ordinary legislation, Parliament should be left to use its discretion, provided that a Ministry does not act in a manner that is inconsistent with the principles under which office was assumed.

As a result of the dissolution, the people declared with no uncertain voice for the disestablishment of the Irish Church. The reasons for the victory of Gladstone at this election are not relevant to the present subject; but it is worth remarking that the people were in this instance provided with an unusually straightforward issue. Investigation into the practicability of inferring decisions by the people at elections proves that these decisions have only been plainly given on few occasions. In 1868 the issue of the disestablishment of the Irish Church was peculiar, since it was, to all intents, the sole issue before the people; and it was, moreover, an issue in respect of which the people of England could obtain no direct benefit, so that self-interest and partiality were eliminated in an exceptional degree.

[1] See pp. 210–11 above.   [2] 191 *Parl. Deb.*, 3 s., 1710 ff.
[3] 191 *Parl. Deb.*, 3 s., 1688–9.

The views of Melbourne and Peel, expressed in 1841 and 1846 respectively, that dissolutions should only be advised by a Ministry if likely to be successful, did not survive in the later Victorian period in the same simple form. The dignity of the Crown ceased to be regarded as being involved in appeals to the people. But, even then, appeals to the people were hardly regarded from the people's point of view. The party leaders, in considering the advisability of a dissolution, were inclined, at that time as in more recent times, to dwell on party prospects rather than on the problem whether the welfare of the nation required a submission to the arbitrament of the people.

A very remarkable instance of this frame of mind is provided by the controversy in which Disraeli and Gladstone were engaged in 1873. Gladstone, on being defeated in the House of Commons at the second reading of the Irish University Bill, resigned. The Queen sent for Disraeli, who told her that, as he had no stable majority, he was not prepared to take office, and that he could not advise a dissolution. The latter statement was evidently to be explained by his realization that the turn of his party would be better served by allowing Gladstone's already discredited Ministry to become further discredited. But this explanation naturally could not be expressed. Overtly, his contention was that he should not be forced to form a Government in the last months of an expiring Parliament, and that it would be difficult for a newly appointed Minister to frame issues at short notice and without the advantage of being in possession of official information.[1]

A well-sustained correspondence was addressed to the Queen by the two statesmen, Gladstone alleging that it was incumbent on Disraeli to accept office, and Disraeli maintaining his refusal. Finally, Gladstone was forced to resume the position of Prime Minister. But what seems nowadays the oddest aspect of this controversy is the failure of both Gladstone and Disraeli to take a public-spirited view of the situation. 'That the continuance in office of a weakened and discredited Ministry was a grave evil, which only an appeal to the country could cure, does not seem to have impressed the mind either of Mr. Gladstone or of Mr. Disraeli.'[2]

[1] Salisbury accepted such a position in 1885; and his party suffered considerably as a result; but Campbell-Bannerman was highly successful in 1906, after having taken office at the end of the Parliament of 1900-5.

[2] Paul, *A History of Modern England*, vol. iii, pp. 310 ff.

The controversy between Gladstone and Salisbury in 1885, on the defeat of the former in a division on an amendment at the second reading of the Budget, had some few similarities to that of Gladstone and Disraeli in 1873; but some of the circumstances and the outcome were different. Gladstone's defeat in the House of Commons in 1885 was the result of an amendment by the official Opposition, although not on a very vital point. He then retained, it seems, a majority for his general policy. The natural course for Salisbury to adopt, after Gladstone's resignation and his appointment to office, would have been to dissolve Parliament. But, in this instance, that course was impossible for some months owing to the redistribution of seats (the result of the Reform Act) being in process. Consequently Salisbury cannot be blamed for not at once appealing to the people. And his claim to receive from Gladstone pledges to facilitate the transaction of public business while he remained in a minority was entirely justified, though he only secured from Gladstone some rather vague assurances.[1]

There are to be found in debates in Parliament, soon after the Reform Act of 1867 was passed, occasional arguments to the effect that legislation of primary importance must be referred to the people before enactment. Evidently the widening of the franchise was having the effect of encouraging democratic tendencies. Lord Salisbury was specially notable for the expression of these advanced views. In the debate on the proposals for the introduction of the ballot, in 1872, he asked the House of Lords to reject the Bill on the ground that the question had never been an election issue, and that the electorate had never had 'a fair opportunity of considering whether it likes the ballot or not'. He admitted that there was no rigid provision for reference to the people as there was in the United States of America or in Switzerland; but he thought that this absence of provision was a reason why the House of Lords should ensure, on the people's behalf, that the House of Commons, 'in thus tampering with the laws under which it was itself elected, had not transgressed the mandate it received'.[2]

[1] See 298 *Parl. Deb.*, 3 s., 1623 ff.
[2] 211 *Parl. Deb.*, 3 s., 1494–5. Lord Salisbury remarked on this occasion that the conception of the House of Commons as 'the expression of the opinion of the Nation' involved 'a constitutional fiction which it is convenient for practical purposes to respect; but which is only literally true on certain occasions and on certain subjects'.

Lord Salisbury's call to the House of Lords to maintain the mandate principle was repeated a few years later. The Reform Bill of 1884, which was introduced by Gladstone, was to confer the franchise on householders and lodgers in the counties in the same way that the Act of 1867 had conferred it on the same classes in the towns. About two million electors were to be added—that is to say, approximately the same number as that added by the Acts of 1832 and 1867 together. The Conservatives did not choose to fight this Reform Bill; but they attempted to delay it by an amendment in the House of Lords, as they were of opinion that it should be passed at the same time as a Bill for the redistribution of seats.

It is doubtful whether the claim of the House of Lords to act as guardian of the people's liberties has ever aroused much answering enthusiasm. In this instance the House of Lords, on adopting this role, became conscious that its solicitude evoked the opposite of approval in the country. Lord Salisbury, in his speech in the House, gave vent to democratic views which must have struck the older Liberals as in marked contrast to the old Tory outlook of 1831 and 1832. But perhaps the feature of his speech which is most interesting is the stress laid on the importance of consultation with the people where large constitutional changes were in contemplation.

As a mere party matter, [he said] we have no desire to force a dissolution; but we do, with reference to this great revolution in the machinery for electing the members of the House of Commons—we do urge upon the Government, not only the prudence but the justice of consulting the people. We do urge upon them that they have no right to make these vast constitutional changes without formally consulting the opinions of those by whose authority they really, in the long run, make them, and whose interests will be specially affected. . . . In the presence of such vast proposals we appeal to the people.[1]

The Conservative plan was immediately interpreted by Gladstone to the people as an insidious claim on the part of the House of Lords to force a dissolution. Further consideration of the situation led Lord Salisbury to regard the prospects of his plan as doubtful; and, within a short time, he agreed to confer with Gladstone on the deadlock between the two

[1] 290 *Parl. Deb.*, 3 s., 468-9.

Houses. An accommodation was quickly reached, much to the subsequent indignation of some members of the Conservative party. The provisions of a Redistribution Bill were settled, on the understanding that the House of Lords would pass the Reform Bill without forcing an appeal to the people. It thus became unnecessary for Lord Salisbury's protests on behalf of an outraged electorate to be pressed any farther.

Claims such as those which were made by Lord Salisbury in 1872 and 1884, that the House of Lords should exercise a guardianship on behalf of the people, helped to familiarize politicians with the principle of the mandate. The part played by the House of Lords in more recent years, between 1909 and 1911, raised questions in connexion with the application of that principle in a much more acute form. These questions will be noticed in § 6 of the present chapter.

§ 4. *Home Rule (1885–6)*

Shortly after the extension of the franchise effected by the Act of 1884 another great issue provided what is one of the best-known illustrations of the problem, how far important constitutional changes can be undertaken without reference to the people.

Prior to the election of 1885 projects for the self-government of Ireland had been cautiously ventilated by both parties. The Liberals knew as well as the Conservatives that to adopt Home Rule as a definite proposal would mean a break-up of party unity. They were anxious to avoid coercion; but they were highly apprehensive of imperilling their party prospects. As a result of this hesitant policy the leaders entered on the election campaign of 1885 with programmes which either did not include any references to Ireland or which contained only oblique references. Gladstone himself used non-committal phraseology. He contended that Ireland should have as much self-government as was consistent with the integrity of the 'United Kingdom'. During the election campaign, but too late to affect it, it was rumoured that he accepted the principle of a national legislature for Ireland. The main heads of his election address covered subjects of a domestic nature, such as local government and registration; and the majority of the Liberals took this programme as their election guide. Gladstone, displaying his more democratic mood, concluded his address: 'The work is ready, the workmen are ready, and only await the mandate of the constituencies to proceed with it.' He did not, however, as far as anyone could tell, mean that the work of granting Home Rule for Ireland was ready. The section of his election address which dealt with Ireland did not suggest that he had anything more in his mind than improvements in the arrangements of local government.[1] The central passage in this section ran as follows:

To maintain the supremacy of the Crown, the unity of the Empire, and all the authority of Parliament necessary for the conservation of that unity, is the first duty of every representative of the people. Subject to this governing principle, every grant to portions of the country of enlarged powers for the management of their own affairs is, in my view, not a source of danger, but a means of averting it, and is in the nature of a new guarantee for increased cohesion, happiness, and strength.

It will be noticed that he merely mentioned the grant of enlarged powers to 'portions of the country'.

The election of 1885 was, so far as England and Scotland were concerned, fought in many constituencies on the rival programmes of social amelioration; Lord Randolph Churchill's Conservative democracy, Joseph Chamberlain's Radical proposals, and Jesse Collings's 'three acres and a cow', specially designed for the new rural electorate, all played a considerable part in the campaign. In some quarters the old cry of 'Church *versus* Dissent' also occupied a prominent place. But the voice of Gladstone was undoubtedly heard more clearly than any other.

By the time Gladstone had become Prime Minister, a few days after the reassembly of Parliament, his conversion to the necessity of Home Rule had become generally known; and, as a consequence, Lord Hartington, among other Liberals, refused to join his Ministry. As soon as Gladstone brought his Home Rule proposals before the House of Commons Lord Hartington charged him with fighting the recent election under false pretences, of having gained seats which would have been lost if Home Rule had been included in the programme, and, finally, of proposing to introduce a measure of the first importance without informing the electorate.

[1] Gladstone, in the following year, published a denial that the only indication given by him of proposed changes was in respect of local government. See W. E. Gladstone, *The Irish Question*, p. 20.

In regard to the last of these counts, Lord Hartington thus addressed the House of Commons:

I am perfectly aware that there exists in our Constitution no principle of the mandate. I know that the mandate of the constituencies is as unknown to our Constitution as the distinction between fundamental laws and laws which are of inferior sanction. But, although no principle of mandate may exist, I maintain that there are certain limits which Parliament is morally bound to observe, and beyond which Parliament has morally not got the right to go in its relations with the constituents. The constituents of Great Britain are the source of power, at all events in this branch of Parliament; and I maintain that, in the presence of an emergency which could not have been foreseen, the House of Commons has no more right to initiate legislation, especially immediately upon its first meeting, of which the constituencies were not informed, and as to which, if they had been so informed, there is, at all events, the very greatest doubt as to what their decision might be.[1]

Lord Hartington was naturally averse to admitting a principle by name, like that of mandate, which, besides having a flavour of continental republicanism, was contrary to the traditional tenets of most Liberals. But it would be difficult to find any other single term by which to describe the obligations which he mentioned as being due to the electorate.[2] As time went on and the contest over Home Rule developed, his views seem to have become more advanced. In 1893, as the Duke of Devonshire, he contended, in the debate on the second reading of the Government of Ireland Bill, that not merely the general issue of Home Rule, but also the form of the measure should be submitted to the people. He denied that the House of Commons had received 'any mandate upon Home Rule', and he asserted that the proposed measure should be submitted to the people for their approval before being passed into law.[3]

The reply which Gladstone made to Lord Hartington's strictures after the election of 1885 was extremely skilful in its combination of adherence to parliamentary authority with moderate recognition of democratic principles. He expressed himself as not being quite certain whether Lord Hartington meant that the Irish question should not be brought forward because it had not been referred to the people at the general

---

[1] 304 *Parl. Deb.*, 3 s., 1241–4.   [2] See p. 9 (n. 1) above.
[3] 17 *Parl. Deb.*, 4 s., 30–31.

election. 'It seems to me', he said, 'that this is an extraordinary doctrine. I want to know where it is laid down by
any constitutional authority.' He proceeded to contend that,
as there had been no mandate for a policy of Irish coercion,
no mandate was needed for the grant of self-government.

> If [he argued] you do not want a mandate for the measures
> of force and repression, intended to maintain the law, much less
> do you want a mandate for measures intended to maintain and
> strengthen the law by laying hold of the hearts of the people, and
> which aim at no force and no repression, but at a union far closer
> and more durable than that which now exists on the Statute
> Book.

This argument amounted to a repudiation of the necessity
of obtaining the concurrence of the people to proposals which
were admittedly of constitutional importance. It could hardly
be a plea, such as had been raised on some earlier occasions,
that so great urgency prevailed that an appeal to the people
was inopportune.

In several speeches of about this time Gladstone resorted
to the citation of precedent—an expedient of doubtful
validity in periods in which new constitutional conventions
are rapidly developing. The instance with which he chose
on this occasion to enforce his denial of the necessity for a
mandate was not a very convincing one. He pointed out that,
in spite of the fact that Reform was not an issue in the election
of 1830, Lord Grey's Ministry introduced its Reform Bill a
few months after taking office, when, as Gladstone said, it
was realized that the country was demanding Reform. It
must have been a moving spectacle to watch the aged statesman recalling, as he did, the circumstances of an election
which had taken place fifty-six years before. But he seems to
have failed to measure the contrast between the circumstances
of the autumn of 1830, when the whole country was roused
to a pitch of extreme excitement over its demands for Reform, and those of the spring of 1886, when it could not be
pretended that the people of England and Scotland were
overwhelmingly enthusiastic for the cause of Home Rule.
Moreover, as has already been remarked, it was not until the
year 1831 that the principle of the mandate became definitely
established. It was hardly pertinent, therefore, for Gladstone
to argue by reference to events which occurred before that
date.

His arguments do not strike the reader of the present day

as persuasive; nor were the principles which he expounded those of a whole-hearted democratic leader. But he wisely included an observation, to the effect that the members of his Ministry would be the last persons who would object to referring the question of Home Rule to the people.[1] It was a true instinct that prompted this remark, since, two months later, his Home Rule Bill was defeated in the House of Commons by a majority of thirty.

When Gladstone dissolved—for he regarded resignation as 'showing the white feather'—he did not display the least hesitation respecting the propriety of referring the issue to the people. Indeed, it was only natural that, when the election had become inevitable, he should view the electorate from a different angle to that of a Minister with a hopeful majority in Parliament. He described the dissolution as 'the people's dissolution' on the analogy of the description of the battle of Inkerman as the soldiers' battle. In a speech at Edinburgh, in the course of the new election campaign, he asked what was the true issue which the people were called upon to decide. And he told his hearers that the question which they were to decide in the affirmative or in the negative was the proposition for the establishment of a legislative body in Ireland for the management of exclusively Irish affairs.[2] Once again expediency made history.

§ 5. *Tariff reform* (*1903–6*)

Although it may be said that, at the early part of the twentieth century, the Conservatives were more disposed to magnify the power of the people in regard to policy than the Liberals, circumstances continued to conspire to make it difficult for politicians of both parties to maintain a consistent attitude in respect of the principle of mandate. Whereas the 'khaki' election of 1900 was alleged by the Liberal Opposition to have had but a single result, namely to authorize the Conservatives to take the necessary steps to conclude the South African War, the Conservatives repudiated this allegation. When the Ministry proceeded to pass the Education Act of 1902 the Liberals contended that its mandate had been exceeded. In May of the next year Joseph Chamberlain electrified the country by suddenly announcing his proposals for

---

[1] 304 *Parl. Deb.*, 3 s., 1547.
[2] *Speeches of W. E. Gladstone*, vol. ix (1886–8), pp. 128, 133, 134. See also the terms of the dissolution Speech, quoted on p. 287 below.

colonial preference. Balfour, the Prime Minister, wished to give mild, but non-committal, support to the newly raised project, and at the same time to keep it in suspense, since he saw that precipitate action was bound to imperil the prospects of his party by causing serious divisions of opinion. Nevertheless, Chamberlain, although he remained friendly to the Government, resigned in September 1903; and a few Conservative free-traders, apprehensive of the maintenance of their principles, adopted the same course.

During the next two and a half years, those, that is to say, between the announcement of Chamberlain's policy and the resignation of the Conservative Ministry, Balfour used every possible device to avoid the forcing of the issue. The Liberals, on the other hand, scenting the prospects of a Conservative defeat in a cry of 'dearer food', did all they could to press Balfour not only to formulate definite proposals for tariff reform, but even to undertake a measure. They conveniently forgot their earlier protests about the limited character of the mandate which had been obtained by the Conservatives at the last election.

Chamberlain, in making his famous Birmingham speech on 15 May 1903, in which he announced his new proposals, observed that the people would have to be consulted before such a momentous change in fiscal policy could be introduced. 'I think', he confidently stated, 'that our opponents may, perhaps, find that the issues which they propose to raise are not the issues on which we shall take the opinion of the country.' On 28 May 1903 the new fiscal question was first discussed in the House of Commons. Balfour found it impossible to declare that the people were ready to accept a tax on food; and, when pressed by Lloyd George, he undertook that his Ministry would not deal with the question without first putting it to the country at a general election. In the same debate Chamberlain plainly declared that there would have to be 'a new mandate given to the Government, if the suggestions which I have thrown out are to be carried into practical effect'; and he added that he would do everything in his power to bring the question in all its bearings before the people.[1]

In March 1904, Balfour, acting consistently with his earlier attitude, denied that the fiscal question would be dealt with in the current Parliament. The Liberals tried to manœuvre

[1] 123 Parl. Deb., 4 s., 178.

so that Chamberlain's proposals should be introduced in Parliament; and Balfour maintained that he could not proceed with them because, among other reasons, he had no mandate from the people to do so. He agreed with Asquith that 'as a legal proposition' it was not necessary to submit legislative measures to the electorate; but he did not agree that it would be within 'the limits of constitutional propriety, as distinguished from constitutional law', to introduce 'a great and fundamental change' such as that involved in the policy dealing with 'dumping' without previously submitting it as an issue at a general election.[1]

Later in 1904 Balfour announced that he proposed that the fiscal question should be discussed at a future date in conference with the Colonies, but only after a dissolution had first taken place. He further proposed that the fiscal reforms should not be introduced, even if the conference should prove that they were desirable, until after the holding of a second general election. The Liberals began to see that the prospect of the question being fought out in Parliament was remote; and they pressed for its submission to the people. At the beginning of the session of 1905 Campbell-Bannerman said that the country was waiting with impatience for an opportunity of expressing its judgement; and Asquith formally proposed that, 'the various aspects of the fiscal question having been now fully discussed in the country for nearly two years, the time has come for submitting the issue to the people without further delay'. Austen Chamberlain indignantly denied that, when a question had been sufficiently discussed, it was necessary to take the immediate decision of the country. This, he said, was a doctrine which would only be developed by an Opposition; and Joseph Chamberlain did not then press for an immediate election, though he had stated, shortly before, that the sooner the matter was referred to the people the better he would be pleased.[2]

Towards the end of 1905 Joseph Chamberlain's loyal restraint broke loose; and he demanded dissolution at the earliest possible moment. Balfour's difficulties became irresistible. They would have brought matters to a crisis long before in the person of a less resourceful and, perhaps, more resolute and far-seeing politician. The period of Parliament was running out; and he resigned, leaving to the Liberals

---

[1] 131 *Parl. Deb.*, 4 s., 678–9.
[2] 141 *Parl. Deb.*, 4 s., 121–2, 190, 194, 338.

the chief burden of framing the issues for reference to the electorate.

In this protracted episode the principle of mandate was largely accepted by both parties. The Liberals felt encouraged to support the principle, because they considered that the raising of an issue of 'dearer food' would bring them into power. The Conservatives had good reason to accept the principle, because they had no desire to precipitate the issue; and they were able to delay a dissolution for a considerable time. On both sides, however, it was, for the most part, genuinely admitted that a fiscal change of such a cardinal character, and one so closely affecting the lives of the people as that suggested by Joseph Chamberlain, could not be undertaken without the clear approval of the sovereign electorate.

After the overwhelming Liberal victory of 1906 the question of free trade versus protection was soon laid on one side. The election left no doubt on that score. But, before proceeding to their legislative programme, the Liberals carried a motion in the House of Commons by the huge majority of 474 to 98 to the effect

that this House, recognizing that in the recent general election the people of the United Kingdom have demonstrated their unqualified fidelity to the principle and practice of Free Trade, deems it right to record its determination to resist any proposal ... to create in this country a system of Protection.

In this way the fiscal problem passed out of the arena of politics for several years, not without having elicited a valedictory affirmation of the principle of the mandate.

§ 6. *The conflict regarding the powers of the House of Lords (1907–11)*

The lines of development of the people's part in politics took quite a different turn as a result of the election of 1906. The Liberals had, indeed, a very large majority in the House of Commons; but in the House of Lords they were in a proportionately small minority. Several of their important legislative measures were thrown out by the House of Lords; and they were placed in the ignominious position of being told that, as guardians of the rights of the people, the members of the Upper House must give the people an opportunity of pronouncing upon legislation, which, in their view, was inconsistent with public opinion. This was not an altogether new experience for the Liberals. The House of Lords had adopted a similar attitude on earlier occasions, when the Conservatives had been out of office. Lord Salisbury had, as has been seen, taken the view in 1872 that the House of Lords was entitled to maintain its objection to Bills passed by the House of Commons until 'the judgment of the nation has been challenged at the polls and decidedly expressed';[1] and he had also asserted the duty of the House of Lords to act as the people's guardian in 1884.

After the rejection by the House of Lords of the Education Bill and the Plural Voting Bill, the Liberal Prime Minister (Sir H. Campbell-Bannerman) moved in the House of Commons, in June 1907,

> that, in order to give effect to the will of the people as expressed by their elected representatives, it is necessary that the power of the other House to alter or reject Bills passed by this House should be so restricted by law as to secure that, within the limits of a single Parliament, the final decision of the Commons shall prevail.

The debate on this motion respecting the relations between the Houses threw considerable light on current views regarding the relations between Parliament and the electorate. On the one hand, the Liberals contended that the House of Commons was given for the period of a Parliament a general mandate to enact such legislation as it chose. On the other hand, the Conservatives held that, if the House of Lords was not satisfied that an important measure had the support of the electorate, it was entitled to reject it. Very little was said of the intermediate view that a Ministry received, as a result of a general election, a mandate to enact any legislation which was consistent with the voting on such issues as were raised at that election or which was not both new in character and of constitutional importance.

The terms of the speech of Sir H. Campbell-Bannerman on this occasion illustrate the divergency between the views of the two parties.

> The supremacy of the people in legislation implies, [he said] in this country at any rate, the authority of the Commons. The party for which I speak has never swerved from that position, and, unless you are going to fall back on some foreign method, such as the referendum or the mandate or the plebiscite, or some

1 Lady Gwendolen Cecil, *Life of Marquess of Salisbury*, vol. ii, p. 26.

other way of getting behind the backs of the elected to the electors themselves, such as was advised by both the first and third Napoleon . . ., then there is no course open but to recognize ungrudgingly the authority which resides in this House, and to accept the views of the nation as represented in its great interests within these walls.

If the Prime Minister had claimed somewhat less, if he had not claimed so extensive a competence during the period of Parliament, his contentions would have been difficult to refute. He would, it seems, have done better to have confined himself to an allegation that, in the particular instance under discussion, the authority obtained at the preceding election was sufficiently wide to cover the legislation which the House of Lords had rejected. If he intended to allege, as seems likely, that it is not possible or proper to refer a particular issue to the electorate, this view conflicts strangely with his clamorous insistence in 1905 for giving the people 'an opportunity of expressing judgment on the fiscal question'.

Most of Campbell-Bannerman's opponents contented themselves with reinforcing the demand that there should be an appeal to the people. But a great constitutionalist in the Conservative ranks, Sir William Anson, seized upon the weak point in the Prime Minister's argument. He emphasized the implication of the Liberal proposition, namely that, when once elected, the House of Commons could do whatever it liked, and that the people should be powerless for the whole of a period of a Parliament, however unexpected and egregious might be the policy which a Ministry was about to undertake.[1]

It is fair to observe that Campbell-Bannerman, like Morley and one or two other Liberals of the old school, maintained fairly consistently that there was no such doctrine as that of mandate. When the Conservatives declared in 1900 that a dissolution was necessary in order to obtain the mandate of the people for the bringing of the South African War to a conclusion, he characterized their explanation as a mere excuse and stated his mistrust of special mandates, which he described as alien to the British Constitution.[2]

The same kind of deadlock occurred in 1909 over the

[1] 176 *Parl. Deb.*, 4 s., 911, 918–20, 1002.
[2] Address to the electors of Stirling Burghs, Sept. 1900; see *The Times*, 22 Sept. 1900.

Budget, which certainly contained provisions that gave Conservative members of the House of Lords some ground for distinguishing it from the normal Finance Bill. It was contended that, although there was considerable evidence to support the view that legislation imposing taxation should not be amended or even simply rejected by the Upper House, the Finance Bill of 1909 contained, under cover of financial provisions, general legislation of a new and fundamental character. It was thought, therefore, that a favourable opportunity had arisen to express a solicitude for the rights and interests of the electorate by rejecting the Bill. The Marquess of Lansdowne, on behalf of the Conservative party in the House of Lords, moved an amendment to the motion that the Bill be read a second time, to the effect 'that this House is not justified in giving its consent to this Bill until it has been submitted to the judgment of the country'. This amendment was adopted by a large majority in the House of Lords.

The arguments of the mover were simple and straightforward. The Bill, he said, with its important provisions had 'never been before the people of this country'. He did not think that the House of Lords should undertake the responsibility of giving its concurrence until it was satisfied that the people desired that the Bill should become law. The Upper House should, he contended, adopt the position of guardian of the people's constitutional right to be consulted when fundamental political changes were demanded by the Government of the day. Lord Morley, on behalf of the Government, maintained the precise converse of the attitude of Sir William Anson in the debate of 1907. Whereas Anson had complained that the Liberals were claiming full power for the House of Commons during the period of a Parliament, Morley complained that a Conservative House of Lords was attempting to cut down the normal period of Parliament, which should continue without interruption for another two or three years. He entirely neglected the question, whether or not new proposals of constitutional importance justified a break in the normal period of Parliament in order that such proposals might be submitted to the people.

The debate produced an interesting difference of opinion between Lord Curzon and Lord Courtney of Penwith respecting the distinction between the right of the House of Lords merely to reject Bills and the right to force an appeal

to the people. Lord Curzon took the view that it was 'inherent in the rights of any Second Chamber' to 'compel a
reference to the polls' in a case where the Government of
the day introduced a measure which was either 'in flagrant
conflict with the expressed will of the nation' or had never
been submitted to and approved by the people. Lord
Courtney, who had a considerable reputation as a constitutional authority, held on the contrary that, although the
House of Lords had the right to reject Bills, it had not the
right to force a dissolution and reference to the country.

> You may, for example, [he said] reject an Education Bill, or an
> Irish Land Bill, and Parliament . . . may go on for two or three
> years . . . but in rejecting the Finance Bill, as you will do, you
> compel at once an appeal to the country, and thus you are acting
> in a manner for which no precedent can be cited, in a manner
> which has never been attempted even by the boldest advocate
> of the rights of your Lordships in past times.

Lord Courtney's reliance on the absence of precedent does
not appear to be convincing, since the responsibilities of the
House of Lords in relation to the people could only be judged
according to standards which had grown up since the mandate principle had become generally acknowledged; and this
period was not extensive enough to permit of the application
of precedents.[1]

Lord Lansdowne's arguments in favour of his motion were
generally approved by the Conservative party at the time
of this debate; but, in the retrospect of after-years, many
members of the party felt that the disaster, as it seemed to
them, of the passing of the Parliament Act, 1911 (which
limited the powers of the House of Lords), was mainly attributable to the rejection of the Finance Bill in 1909. It is easy
to advance broad principles regarding the necessity for
popular approval of novel and important proposals; but it
is a delicate matter for a hereditary House to determine
which proposals fall within these principles.

The deadlock between the two Houses, arising out of the
rejection of the Finance Bill in 1909, was chiefly responsible
for the necessity of two general elections in 1910; and a considerable amount of argument ensued regarding the nature
and extent of the mandate which was obtained on these
occasions. Most of the discussion in Parliament centred

[1] 4 *H.L. Deb.*, 5 s., 731 ff., 1139, 1260, 1266, 1345.

round the question whether the people had given a mandate for the passing of the Parliament Bill of 1911. The subject of Lords versus People was one of those raised in the election of January 1910; and, prior to the election of December 1910, the Ministry issued the terms of its proposed Parliament Bill, limiting the powers of the House of Lords to reject legislation. Proposals for constitutional reform had already been mooted by the Conservatives; but there had been no debate on the Liberals' concrete proposals prior to the dissolution in November 1910. The result of this second election was much the same as that of the first, namely to give the Liberals a majority consisting of little more than the Irish members, who supported the Liberals in the hope of securing a measure enacting Home Rule.

When the Parliament Bill came to be debated in both Houses in the first half of 1911, there was, as might be expected, a complete disagreement between the parties on the question whether the second election of 1910 had given the Liberals a mandate to pass the Bill in the terms made public prior to the election. Asquith, the Prime Minister, asserted that his Ministry had a mandate to pass the Bill more or less in the form which had been published. And the Lord Chancellor (Loreburn) maintained that the Bill was made 'the main and crucial point . . . at the general election by both sides'. So also Lord Haldane, who said that there had been as true a referendum as any one could wish to see, since the propositions of the Bill had been specifically submitted to the country; 'line for line they were made the predominant feature at the last election'. On this occasion, it is to be noted, all the Liberals admitted the existence of the mandate principle.

On the other side, the Conservatives denied the existence of anything like a definite mandate for the Bill. Balfour allowed that, in December 1910, the people had shown themselves desirous of dealing 'with what is called the constitutional question'. But that 'they actually gave the Government a mandate for this particular way of dealing with it, I do not believe in the least'. They merely, he said, were resolved that there should be some amendment of the relations between the two Houses; and he characterized as absurd the suggestion that they could be in a position to form an opinion on the terms of the Bill, in the absence of a previous discussion of them in the House of Commons. He contended that any allegation 'that the people had clearly this issue and in the main only this issue before them, is a complete and absolute travesty of the notorious facts of the situation'. Both Lord Curzon and Sir William Anson also argued that the people had not a sufficient opportunity of considering the terms of the Bill, that the Conservatives had not had time before the election to criticize it, and that the issues of December 1910 were far from plain and straightforward. These contentions almost amount to the requirement of two general elections before an authentic mandate can be obtained from the people. At the first general election the principle underlying the proposed legislation must be approved. At the second general election the terms of the proposed legislation must be submitted after the principle of it had been debated and discussed. To expect this procedure is to render the principle of mandate, if not absurd, at least impracticable.[1]

No better illustration than the debates of 1911 could be found of unqualified admissions by both parties of the principle of mandate and, at the same time, a complete disagreement regarding its effect. It should, however, be added that the Conservatives, although basing their arguments to a certain extent on the nature of the issues, were also able to allege with some force that, if the voting strength of the Irish members had been eliminated, the Liberals would have obtained no real majority at the elections of 1910, so as to justify a claim for a mandate of any kind.

The ability and responsibility of the House of Lords to act as guardians of the people's interests, although limited as a result of the provisions of the Parliament Act of 1911, continued to be operative until further curtailed in 1949. The Bryce Report on the Reform of the Second Chamber (1918) assumed that one of the chief functions of the House of Lords after 1911 was to enable the opinion of the people to be taken on subjects which were considered to be of fundamental importance and which had not been previously submitted to them. But the fact that the House exercised this function with a high degree of restraint may be attributable in part to its experiences in the years 1909 to 1911.

§ 7. *Politicians' proneness to opportunism*

The difficulty of tracing obvious lines of development in the history of the mandate principle during the last century

[1] 8 *H.L. Deb.*, 5 s., 678, 762; 9 *H.L. Deb.*, 5 s., 442, 573, 820, 1005; 24 *H.C. Deb.*, 5 s., 1055, 1056, 1089, 1111; 25 *H.C. Deb.*, 5 s., 1693, 1701–2.

has been seen to be largely due to the influence of political expediency. On occasion a statesman like Peel, who was constitutionally indisposed to encourage the intervention of the people in matters of government, was forced, as in 1834, to admit the people's ability to decide on the choice of Ministries or the adoption of policies. And a statesman like Gladstone, who had many of the qualities of a democrat, was unable, in some of the many circumstances which he had to face, to admit the people to the fullest capacity which was claimed for them. Throughout the last hundred years, however, the succeeding measures for widening the franchise tended more and more to induce politicians to accept the principle of popular mandate; and at the present day universal, or virtually universal, suffrage has made the attitude of the old Liberals like Morley impossible, or at least inadvisable, to maintain. No Minister who is charged in Parliament with being unfortified with the mandate of the people would dare nowadays to assert that Parliament is competent to pass whatever legislation it pleases, regardless of the necessity of obtaining popular approval.

Since the stage when expediency was apt to determine whether the principle of the mandate should be admitted or not, opportunism has too often influenced both the occasions on which the principle has been applied and the results of its application. Circumstances, which were to some extent avoidable, have prevented several of the elections of the twentieth century from having as much of the effect of the referendum as they might have had. The character of the issues and the times at which they have been raised have frequently been affected by a narrow party outlook; and issues have been emphasized or ignored from this point of view rather than from that of public interest.

The main or at least the final responsibility for the definition of election issues must obviously rest primarily on the Leader of the party in office. He has information from Government Departments and other official sources which is not available to the Leader of the Opposition party. It is of essential importance to the beneficial working of the mandate principle that the Prime Minister shall disclose the real issues to the electorate, and, if they are urgent ones, that he shall disclose them promptly regardless of considerations of party advantage.

It was in this respect that Baldwin grievously failed to perform his duty to the State in 1933 and 1934. He knew that a vigorous policy of rearmament was necessary in view of the information he had of Germany's rapid increase in her armed forces. But he failed to seek prompt authority from the people to take essential defensive measures because he considered that there was a widespread feeling in the country opposed to any rearmament. He knew that the people were ignorant of the facts; and if he had had the courage and the inspiration of a genuine political leader, he would have disclosed the whole situation to them and called on them to support him in the policy which he realized was the right one and the urgent one for the country's safety. G. M. Young, in his biography of Baldwin (p. 204), pointed out that, even at a later stage, he had an admirable opportunity shortly before the 1935 election to prepare the way for a patriotic policy with the leaders of the trade union movement, but he failed to take advantage of it, through, it would seem, the lethargy which frequently disabled him from energetic action. When the next general election came in 1935, while including in the party programme the need for filling 'gaps in our defences', he did not give rearmament the most predominant place among the issues, as his colleague, Neville Chamberlain, wished.

Speaking in the House of Commons in November 1936, Baldwin excused himself from telling the people the facts in 1933 or 1934 on the ground that there was a strong pacifist feeling running through the country. 'Supposing', he said, 'I had gone to the country and said that Germany was rearming and we must re-arm, does anybody think that this pacific democracy would have rallied to that cry at that moment? I cannot think of anything that would have made the loss of the election from my point of view more certain.' He remarked in his speech that he put these views before the House 'with an appalling frankness.'[1] His frankness was more appalling than he realized. If, in 1933 or 1934, he had aroused the people's patriotism with the facts about the rate of rearming in Germany, he might well have won an election then on the rearmament issue, and thus have been able to provide the country with adequate protection. If he had failed to secure a majority, he would at least have done his duty and have placed the responsibility where it properly

[1] 317 *H.C. Deb.*, 5 s. 1144.

belonged. This deplorable episode should remind us that the mandate principle can be a source of national peril. Without any such principle, Baldwin could have gone ahead with rearmament with parliamentary authority alone. As it was, the need for the people's authority for a large pro- gramme of rearmament had the effect of paralysing him, because he thought too much in terms of electoral gains or losses and too little in terms of leadership and the nation's urgent need.

CHAPTER X

THE ISSUES

§ 1. *Verdicts on the past*

THE preceding chapter has comprised a sketch of a few outstanding incidents in the progress of the political capacity of the people. Some light may be thrown on the problems raised by the application of the principle of mandate by a more analytical treatment of the subject. It is proposed, therefore, to pay attention in this and the following chapter to the various classes of issues which have been raised at general elections, the proper occasions for raising them, and the manner in which they have been raised.

Perhaps the most obvious division of the kinds of issues which can be submitted to the people is that which separates them into those that relate to the past rather than the future and those that relate to the future rather than to the past. And yet, in some sense, all issues must look to the future. When it is said that the people give verdicts on the past, it is meant that the choice of Ministers is based more on the records of past administration than on proposals for the future. In the early history of the people's part in government, political discussions at election time tended to turn on past administration. Nowadays the electors are less confined than they were to personal considerations; and they are commonly given the opportunity of declaring their views upon the future policies as well as on the past records of the parties.

As has already been remarked, some rudimentary notions of a decision by the people on future policy were spread abroad as early as the reigns of William III and Anne, although it was not then seriously expected that the people's preferences would necessarily be adopted. The habitual submission of prospective issues naturally came later than that of issues dealing with the past. An excellent reason for the lack of control over future activities was the absence of any recognized obligation on the part of Ministries to produce legislative programmes. The ascertained future policy of a Ministry was chiefly confined to such matters as war and diplomacy. The anti-French policy of William III, which was the central feature of the election of 1701, provides an example of this type of issue: but such examples were isolated; and it was not until after 1832 that prospective issues became general, as a result of the acceptance of the obligation to produce party programmes.

Nor was there, at the time of William III and Anne, anything more than a vague foreshadowing of the ability of the electorate to give judgement on the past record of the Ministry in office. Reflections on the character and efficiency of Ministers were intended to influence particular contests; but no determinative effect from the total results of the returns was anticipated, since the unfettered power of the Sovereign to settle the constitution of Ministries was still unquestioned. The Tories, for instance, in the first election of the reign of Anne were feverishly anxious to regain the ground which they had lost to the Whigs in the anti-French election of the previous year. 'The electors were asked to reflect who had voted for a standing army, who had obstructed the commissioners for public accounts, who "signed treaties for the dishonour of England", who delivered up the right of impeachment, and who had put fortunes in their pockets.'[1] But the turn-over of votes in favour of the Tories which occurred at the election did not involve the appointment of an all-Tory Ministry. The indictment of the last Ministry of William III in the election campaign was not expected to do much more than ensure that the electors should recognize the candidates who had been involved in the alleged delinquencies.

So also in the elections of 1713 and 1715; although the Commercial Treaty and the Treaty of Utrecht respectively were criticized by the Whigs, it was rather the Parliament than the Ministry which was denounced. Inquiry was promoted regarding those responsible for alleged maladministration; but it would have been premature to have maintained that the Tory Ministry stood condemned as the result of the voting at the general election of 1715.

The unequal condition of the parties and the growth of corruption in politics after the accession of the Hanoverians left the submission of issues at a standstill. The Tories attempted, with but small effect, to make the enactment of the Septennial Act of 1715 an issue in the election of 1722. They charged the Whigs with the intention of constituting

[1] K. Feiling, *History of the Tory Party*, p. 365.

themselves into a 'Long Parliament', and they revived the
name of 'Rump', so as to awaken the sentiments of the preceding century. But the hopelessness of their endeavour
materially to strengthen their position in Parliament left
little room for the possibility of a declaration by the people on
the merits of the Act. The situation was only a little more
hopeful when the Opposition attempted the disparagement
of Walpole's Excise Scheme in the election of 1734, though
the idea of the election being a 'trial' of the Ministry was
beginning to be understood.[1]

Some signs of a judgement on the past became noticeable
when Walpole's resignation was forced upon him shortly
after the election of 1741;[2] but it was not until considerably
later that any approach to retrospective issues in the modern
sense was recognizable. After 1832 it was frequently the practice to submit to the judgement of the people the propriety
of past policy. Peel, for instance, in the election of 1847,
endeavoured to justify to the electorate his financial policy
of the preceding year.

The most natural time for the predominance of retrospective issues is that subsequent to a period of considerable
legislative activity. The Labour Ministry of 1945–50 was
such a period. It was then that the Ministry secured the
enactment of many measures of vast consequence to the
nation, including nationalization on a large scale. Consequently the general elections of 1950 and 1951 were notable
for their emphasis on verdicts on past policy. The Labour
party was ready to rest on its oars. Further measures of
nationalization were mentioned by its leaders with restraint.
The party's chief emphasis in appealing to the electorate was
in regard to their recent achievements, not so much those of
nationalization which was having 'teething' troubles, but more
generally in regard to 'fair shares' and full employment. The
Conservatives even more clearly wanted the country to have
a rest from radical legislative activity. They were content to
select as a main election issue the assertion that the nation's
anxieties were attributable to the allegedly mistaken policies
of the Labour party during 1945–50. The positive proposals
of the Conservatives, such as a large increase in the housing
programme, were not preponderant issues. The extent and

---

[1] *Hist. MSS. Comm., 15th Report*, Appendix, Part VI (Carlisle MSS.), p. 125,
Sir Thomas Robinson to Lord Carlisle, 8 Dec. 1733.
[2] See pp. 104, 105 above.

the far-reaching character of the socialist legislation of 1945–50 were exceptional; and those circumstances presumably explain the concentration of both parties on the past. They may also explain the unusual situation in which the Labour party, lately in power, pointed proudly to its record, and in which the Conservatives with equal assurance pointed to that record as one disastrous to the national interest.

The recurrent financial crises which are perhaps an inevitable feature of present-day national politics will undoubtedly be treated as tests of governmental efficiency; and in so far as they coincide with, or precipitate, general elections they will tend to attract increasing attention to retrospective issues. There have already been indications of this tendency in the elections of 1931 and 1951, each of which followed closely on a financial crisis.

§ 2. *Men and measures*

The catch-phrases 'not men but measures' and 'men, not measures' have had a long history; but it is only during the last century that they have indicated partialities for issues regarding the future and issues regarding the past respectively. Before that period they were used in support of alternative principles on which Ministries might be formed. 'Measures' were preferred to 'men' in the eighteenth century chiefly owing to a distrust or dislike of party methods and sectional interests. This was the feeling which led the elder Pitt to consider that Ministers should be selected for their ability to carry out a policy rather than for their party connexions. Burke, when he described 'the cant of not men, but measures' as 'a sort of charm by which many people get loose from every honourable engagement', obviously had Pitt in mind.

'Men, not measures', interpreted in more modern sense, applied, that is to say, to election issues, epitomized the attitude of Tories like the Duke of Wellington when they saw the policy of Reform being submitted to the people in 1831. The Duke had no objection to the people choosing between rival Ministries; but for them to take a part in the determination of legislative policy appeared to him to endanger the stability of the Constitution. Like many others, he thought that the people, while able to judge of the suitability of their rulers, were neither able nor should be allowed to judge of the effect of prospective measures. In a debate in the House of Lords in October 1831 he drew a distinction between the personal character of the issues in the election of 1784 and the political ones in 1831.[1]

On two or three occasions in the middle of the nineteenth century there were reversions to the notion, then becoming obsolete, that the mandate of the people was exclusively a personal one and had no relation to policy, And this was so, in spite of the fact that the business of government had undergone a vast change from that of a hundred years before. The contrast between the task of Ministers and the activities of Parliament in 1750 and in 1850 is evidenced by the contents of the statute-book. A volume of the statutes at the earlier period contains a high proportion of legislation of a local and almost trivial character. But the Ministers of the Victorian period had large programmes of legislation to carry through, affecting the life of the nation in many different aspects.

The circumstances in which the discredited Liberals insisted on clinging to office in the spring of 1841, after they had been defeated on an important financial question, throw light on the hesitation with which any control of policy by the people came to be recognized. Peel argued that there were no precedents which would support the Liberals' retention of office, and that Pitt's refusal to resign or dissolve Parliament in 1784 was not a parallel case. In reply to these contentions, Lord John Russell quoted precedents going back to Queen Anne's reign for a defeated Ministry retaining office. He alleged that the Ministry needed merely to retain confidence in its administrative ability, and not necessarily confidence in respect of legislation; and he pointed out that, up to the time of Pitt, the Ministry was not expected to bring forward legislative measures.[2]

Peel himself, in 1846, displayed uncertainty regarding the admissibility of issues other than personal ones, when deliberating on the nature of the issue which he should place before the country at the ensuing election. 'On what ground shall we appeal to the country?' he asked. 'Surely not on the mere personal one, were we justified in proposing the Corn Bill? We must appeal to it on some principle. The

[1] 7 Parl. Deb., 3 s., 1192; cf. pp. 199, 200 above.
[2] Cf. pp. 158, 159 above.

natural one seems to be "Free Trade and the destruction of Protection".[1] The Duke of Wellington, at Peel's request, considered these alternatives and recommended that the issue should be simply the one, whether Peel should continue to be Prime Minister or not.

When party ties are temporarily broken, the absence of agreed party programmes leaves personal issues as the only issues before the people. In the middle of the nineteenth century there was not only a derangement of party allegiances which was chiefly attributable to the separation of the Peelites from the Conservatives on the question of free trade, but the personal note was emphasized by the presence of a popular figure, Palmerston, who was capable both of holding Ministers together and of attracting a following in the country. It naturally happened that the question of his support tended to exclude all other issues.

After Palmerston had been defeated in the House of Commons in 1857, on a motion to the effect that his management of British affairs in China had been too rigorous, Disraeli challenged him to stand by the Chinese issue and by a negation of the principle of further Reform. Although the challenge was accepted, the real issue in the ensuing election, as was appreciated by the people, was one of confidence in Palmerston, with the endorsement of the policy of the Crimean War in the background. Gladstone, who was at the time occupying an independent position in politics, accurately described the situation as follows:

This was not an election like that of 1784, when Pitt appealed on the question whether the Crown should be the slave of an oligarchic faction; nor like that of 1831, when Grey sought a judgment on reform; nor like that of 1852, when the issue was the expiring controversy of protection. The country was to decide not upon the Canton River [i.e. the Chinese question], but whether it would or would not have Palmerston for Prime Minister.[2]

At the time of the defeat of the Derby–Disraeli Ministry on the question of Reform in 1859 the Conservative party was disunited. In view of the confused state of politics the Ministry felt justified in obtaining a dissolution, although the Parliament had only lasted two years. It did not desire to submit the question of Reform as an issue in the election.

[1] *Sir Robert Peel's Memoirs*, vol. ii, p. 295.
[2] J. Morley, *Life of Gladstone*, vol. i, p. 564.

Other questions of policy, such as those respecting China, India, and Italy, were either settled or no longer in dispute. The issue proved to be a personal one between Palmerston and Russell on the one hand and Derby and Disraeli on the other. Derby, the Prime Minister, took pains to confine the contest to personal grounds in his statement in the House of Lords prior to the election. No appeal, he said, was made to the country on the subject of Parliamentary Reform. The question to be submitted was that of confidence or lack of confidence in Ministers. Disraeli, too, described the dissolution as involving an 'appeal to the country on our personal position'.[1]

The Liberal party disapproved the unwillingness of the Conservatives to stand by the subject of their defeat or even to state what it was pleased to describe as the 'forensic issue'. On the assembly of the new Parliament Palmerston expressed this disapproval; and he thus defined the issues in the election:

We have had an appeal to the country. It was not upon the Reform Bill; it was not upon one measure or another, it was simply an appeal to the country to determine whether the present Government does or does not possess the confidence of Parliament or of the people.[2]

It is interesting to remark that, immediately after Disraeli's announcement in the House of Commons of the impending dissolution, Palmerston had insisted that Reform would be the issue in the election in spite of anything which Disraeli might say to the contrary. His subsequent change of view, by which he described the issue as a personal one, is an illustration of the predominance of Ministries over Oppositions in regard to the submission of issues. It would not, perhaps, be so easy today for a Ministry to evade issues of policy and to deny that an important measure on which it was defeated, a measure proposed by it, was an issue in an election immediately following that defeat. A measure in respect of which a Ministry suffers a defeat, if a vital one, will, it may be supposed, generally become one of the main issues in an election precipitated by the failure to pass that measure.

By 1865 Palmerston had become an idol of a large section of the community, and almost a national institution. When, therefore, he appealed to the people in that year, at the end

[1] 153 *Parl. Deb.*, 3 s., 1289–91, 1307.   [2] 154 *Parl. Deb.*, 3 s., 182.

of a Parliament which had lasted nearly its full period, he was not afraid of claiming a renewal of confidence in his administration without raising any particular positive policy. The man counted more than any question of measures. Even Bright's enthusiasm for Reform did not bring that subject into the position of an issue, though it was widely discussed in the constituencies. It was fully realized that the aged statesman ought not to be, indeed could not be, frustrated.

An even more obvious example of the ability of a politician with a forceful character to reduce issues to personal factors is that of Gladstone. His unfailing capacity, in his prime, to hold the political stage and monopolize the attention of the electorate aroused such a lively antagonism as almost to suggest that he was aiming at the role of dictator. Randolph Churchill criticized Gladstone's part in the election of 1886 in a bitter tirade; but a recollection of the ways of Palmerston renders a charge of novelty in this respect against Gladstone untenable, for Palmerston concentrated an interest in and appealed for confidence in himself as much as he did for confidence in his Ministry or his policy. Gladstone, wrote Randolph Churchill in his most trenchant manner,

demands a vote of confidence from the constituencies. Confidence in what? In the Liberal party? No! The Liberal party, as we know it, exists no longer. In his Irish project? No! It is dead; to be resuscitated or not, either wholly or in part, just as may suit the personal convenience of the author. In his Government? No! They are a mere collection of 'items', whom he does not condescend to consult. In himself? Yes! This is the latest and most perilous innovation into constitutional practices. A pure unadulterated personal plebiscite, that is the demand; a political expedient borrowed from the last and worst days of the second Empire.[1]

Exaggerated as is this description of Gladstone's attitude in the election of 1886, it has in it a certain element of truth. Emphasis on personal factors has been the frequent result, as well as the cause of the disorganization of party allegiances. Just as questions of policy were eclipsed in the Palmerston period, largely as a result of the derangement of the party system, so, to a less extent, were they under Gladstone after the Liberal party had been split in two through the introduction of proposals for Home Rule.

[1] Winston Churchill, *Life of Lord Randolph Churchill*, vol. ii, p. 495.

Obvious examples of statesmen who have in recent years gained the intense loyalty of millions of electors are Stanley Baldwin and Winston Churchill. Baldwin ended by being widely disparaged as lacking in the essential qualities of leadership. But, until about 1936, he was regarded by the rank and file of the Conservative party as the embodiment of reliability. He was pictured as the straightforward type of statesman with an understandable attachment to his pipe. In the 1929 election he was proclaimed by the Central Office as the 'safe' man, with 'safety first' as his watchword. This proved not to be quite the effective key-note; and he lost the election. But, in 1935, he was represented as the leader to be trusted in an awkward situation. 'You can trust him', the party posters said. And, this time, the 'man' outranked the 'measures'; and the Conservatives were returned with a large majority.

After World War II the Conservatives tried to adopt similar tactics and to make the election of 1945 turn on the nationwide popularity and immense prestige of Winston Churchill. He was the man who had saved the country and could continue to do so. The Labour party on the other hand, who had a leader of retiring disposition, offered a bold socialist policy for the country's post-war reconstruction. In spite of the people's abundant gratitude to Churchill for his inspired and inspiring leadership, the electors seemed at that moment to have been more impressed by the legislative proposals of the Labour party than by the offer of Churchill's continued leadership. The 1945 election was *par excellence* an example of the alternative of 'man' or 'measures'; and no completely convincing explanation has yet been given of the choice that the people then made. At the very time when it might be supposed that the man to whom the nation owed everything would eclipse all other claims to attention, the electors left him in a minority.

In the 1950 and 1951 elections, Attlee, though still modest and retiring, began to catch the imagination of the people. The statesman who appears to the elector as a man very like himself in his habits and manners has a wide appeal. Attlee toured the country in the 1950 election campaign in a smallish pre-war car driven by his wife. He was a leader who could be easily understood.

By 1955 Attlee had grown in statesmanlike stature, and the Labour Party Central Office decided that his personality could be exploited much in the same way as had those of great parliamentary figures in the past. Posters inscribed 'You can trust Mr. Attlee' and 'Top Level Talks—send Attlee' were widely circulated. But this plan did not succeed in making the election turn on a competition between the qualities of the two party leaders, Eden and Attlee.

There are times when the electors prefer the ordinary man as a leader rather than the brilliant one. Bonar Law and Baldwin are examples of this preference. However that may be, personal issues, whether based on a statesman's capability or character, undoubtedly conduce to the exploitation of factors which divert the attention of electors from the essential consideration of policy; and for this reason are generally ill advised. They should be discouraged by all concerned, except in peculiar circumstances. During normal party government in England, 'measures' generally arouse a larger interest among the people than 'men'; and it is only when the party system breaks down or where a politician of exceptional personal authority occupies the political arena (or a combination of both situations) that issues of 'men' become of greater importance than those of 'measures'.

§ 3. *Mixed issues and party tactics*

The passing of the great Reform Bill not only led to an increased capacity in the people to deal with election issues, but also, for that very reason, to a reorganization of parties and to new methods of conducting general election campaigns. It became the normal course for both parties to raise issues, a procedure which was capable of producing complications and ambiguity. The Ministry might rely on its own past record and appeal to the people on that score; it might raise the issue of proposed legislation; or it might do both. The Opposition might raise the issue of the Ministry's past record or of proposed legislation or both.

When several issues have been raised by both sides, the circumstances or the qualities of leading politicians have sometimes determined which of the issues should be the effective one. But there has been no certain means of ensuring that any particular issue was isolated and voted upon. Frequently politicians and others have discussed, after an election was over, what was the prevailing issue; and on occasion only a very dubious conclusion has been reached.

It is but seldom that the situation has been clearly defined at the opening of an election campaign.

A few illustrations will prove how uncertain and bewildering were the attitudes of parties at many elections. In that of 1837 the Liberal Ministry chiefly relied on its past record as promoters of the great Reform Bill, while the Conservative Opposition, not desiring to produce a positive programme of its own, tried to make the election turn on the dangers of the alleged possible legislation of a radical and subversive nature, which, it was suggested, might be undertaken if the Liberals obtained a majority. In 1841 a very different course was adopted. The Liberals, after a period of growing discredit, had been defeated in Parliament and were anxious to avoid raising the issue of their past administration. They preferred to emphasize the danger of the monopoly or protectionist proposals which they ascribed to the Conservative party. The Conservatives, on the other hand, maintained that the question for the people to try was not the merits of protection, but the question whether the Liberal Ministry, as a result of its past record, deserved the confidence of the people; and they published a catalogue of alleged examples of Ministerial mismanagement.

These two elections, of 1837 and 1841, provide a notable contrast. The former is an instance of a Ministry relying on its past record and the Opposition on the Ministry's supposed future measures; and the latter an instance of a Ministry avoiding its past record by bringing the anticipated projects of the Opposition into the limelight of the contest, while the Opposition insisted that the past record of the Ministry constituted the real issue. In the former instance the Ministry had the greater favour with the people and the effective issue seems to have been that chosen by it rather than that chosen by the Opposition; and in the latter instance the Opposition gained the people's ear, and the issue which it selected seems to have predominated.

As has been seen, the 'group' politics of the middle of the nineteenth century do not provide normal examples of election issues;[1] it is well, therefore, to pass over that period. In the election of 1874 similar tactics were practised to those just described. A Liberal Ministry, thoroughly descredited with the people, attempted, as it had done in 1841, to deflect attention from a judgement on its past administration by

[1] See p. 240 above.

adverting to the future. On this occasion, however, Gladstone did not, and indeed hardly could, bring to the front any alleged inexpedient projects of the Conservatives, since the Conservatives were careful not to advance any very definite proposals. But he produced some tempting benefits which might be secured by future legislation, such as the repeal of the income-tax and reform of local taxation. Once again the Conservatives tried to exploit the discredit of the Liberals to the fullest extent. They were determined that the past record of the Ministry should be kept in prominence; and this proved to be the leading issue. Disraeli discoursed upon Gladstone's 'career of plundering and blundering', 'incessant and harassing legislation', and neglect of foreign policy. His own programme for the future was hazily outlined and not pressed forward. It consisted merely of general sentiments regarding the improvement of the condition of the people.

Other elections in the later part of the nineteenth century, while presenting some different features to those already portrayed, further illustrate the large part which party tactics have played in the discrimination between prospective and retrospective issues and in the direction given to election campaigns. Certain changes in method, which became apparent on the revival of the two-party system, are to a large extent attributable to the eager, active mind and forceful qualities of Gladstone, as exemplified in his advocacy of the disestablishment of the Irish Church and of Home Rule for Ireland.

When, in 1868, Disraeli had suffered the unusual experience of defeat on a legislative proposal brought forward by the leader of the Opposition (Gladstone), he was naturally desirous of avoiding the concentration of the electors' attention on that issue and of making the most of his own past policy. He spoke, in his address to his constituents, of the success achieved by the passing of the Reform Act of 1867, of his foreign policy, and his provisions for national defence. But he was unable to avoid the prospective issue of the disestablishment of the Irish Church, which the Liberals succeeded in forcing into the foreground. While Gladstone asserted that his proposals provided the solution of an urgent problem, Disraeli had to be content to adopt an attitude of negation, of 'uncompromising resistance' and alarm respecting the outcome of the policy, if adopted.

On several occasions the election tactics of the Conservatives consisted either in criticisms of the proposals or of the past record of the Liberals or in simple reliance on their own past record. Expediency often restrained them from producing a positive programme. Disraeli himself seemed studiously to avoid explicit positive proposals in his election addresses. On the other hand, it was a necessary consequence of the Liberal creed for that party to be more constructive in its treatment of issues; and, once it had accepted Home Rule as part of its programme, this prospective issue inevitably dominated every other issue in a series of election contests.

In 1880 Home Rule had not yet been adopted as a 'plank' in the Liberal 'platform'; and the election of that year displayed characteristics which give it a singular place in the development of the submission of issues. The Liberals decided that, with the help of Gladstone's Midlothian orations, they could gain more by emphasizing the past delinquencies of the Beaconsfield Ministry than by producing positive proposals of their own. But the Conservatives, after a period of more than six years in office, feared the swing of the pendulum; and, at the instance of Beaconsfield, they endeavoured to make the trial between the parties depend on the supposed intentions of the Liberals regarding Home Rule.

The document which amounted to the election manifesto of Beaconsfield described Home Rule or the 'disintegration of the United Kingdom' as a 'destructive doctrine', and as 'a danger, in its ultimate results, scarcely less disastrous than pestilence and famine'. It did not contain any reference to proposals of the Conservatives, and it only included incidental justifications of the Ministry's past policy regarding Ireland and foreign affairs.

Gladstone, on the other hand, made a violent attack on the record of the Beaconsfield Ministry. Some months before the election he stated, in his first Midlothian speech at Edinburgh, that the past record of the Ministry would be the issue which the people would have to try at the ensuing election. He arraigned the administration in the following highly coloured phraseology:

If faith has been broken, if blood has been needlessly shed, if the name of England has been discredited and lowered from that lofty standard which it ought to exhibit to the whole world, if the

country has been needlessly distressed, if finance has been thrown
into confusion, if the foundations of the Indian Empire have been
impaired, all these things as yet are the work of an Administration
and a Parliament; but the day is coming, and is near at hand,
when that event will take place which will lead the historian to
declare whether or not they are the work, not of an Administration and not of a Parliament, but the work of a great and free
people. If this great and free and powerful people is disposed to
associate itself with such transactions, if it is disposed to assume
upon itself what some of us would call the guilt, and many of us
must declare to be the heavy burden, of all those events that have
been passing before our eyes, it rests with them to do it. . . .
Gentlemen, this is the issue which the people of this country will
have to try.[1]

Nearly all Gladstone's efforts were devoted to arousing a
revulsion of feeling against Conservative imperialism and an
adventurous foreign policy. He did not make any considerable proposals for legislation, beyond one for the enlargement
of the franchise in the counties, upon which his supporters
were not at all enthusiastic.

It soon became clear to the Liberals that Beaconsfield did
not intend to accept Gladstone's statement of the issues, but
meant to avoid as far as possible all references to the past.
Gladstone wrote, at the end of 1879, to Lord Granville:
'For several reasons I should believe that they intend sailing
on the quiet tack. Having proved their spirit they will now
prove their moderation. In other words, they want all the
past proceedings to be, in the main, "stale fish" at the election.' When, however, he had read Beaconsfield's election
manifesto, he saw that it was not merely proposed to avoid
the past, but to avoid it by the novel process of laying
emphasis on the presumed future policy of the Opposition.
He immediately, in his fourth Midlothian speech at Edinburgh, objected, with much justification, to the stratagem
of Beaconsfield. It was, he asserted, an entirely new departure
to make the issue to be tried at a general election the merits
of the Opposition rather than the merits of the Government.
It had always been considered that it was the Government
that should be exposed to criticism.[2]

Gladstone was able, in 1880, to assert with a clear conscience that neither he nor his party had officially adopted
the principle of Home Rule; and the same can be said with

[1] *Speeches in Scotland by W. E. Gladstone*, vol. i, pp. 57–58.
[2] Ibid., vol. ii, pp. 21–22.

almost equal correctness of the election of 1885. But, immediately after the latter election and in the elections of 1886 and 1892, Home Rule was definitely the main issue advanced by Gladstone and his supporters. When, therefore, the Conservative Ministry appealed to the people in 1892, the Liberals had no ground for complaining that the appeal was based, first, on the Conservatives' resistance to the Liberal Opposition's proposal for Home Rule, and, secondly, on their own record of work done. So long as an issue retains its hold upon the interest of the people, neither party can complain if its opponents make it the primary one for decision at the next general election. Gladstone himself did not complain. He kept Home Rule sternly in the forefront, and advanced the heterogeneous items of the Newcastle programme, which was dictated to him by the party convention, as issues of the second rank.

It has frequently happened that a Ministry has preferred to screen its inglorious exploits or absence of achievements behind its promises or projects for the future, or that an Opposition has felt more sanguine in relying on the unpopularity of a Ministry than in the proposal of new measures, the approbation of which by the people appeared to be questionable. In such ways as these the people have been deprived of necessary opportunities both of giving judgement on past administration and of expressing opinion on future policy.

In quite recent years opportunism has hindered party leaders from raising urgent issues at general elections because these issues would probably involve loss of votes. It requires a heroic brand of statesman to tell the electorate that they must face temporary inconvenience for ultimate benefit. In the 1955 election neither side was willing to advance policies for tackling the two most critical problems of the day, namely progressive inflation and the inability of trade unions to check unofficial strikes.

Expediency can induce political parties not merely to ignore essential issues in the interest of electoral victory, but also to undermine the electors' ability to judge on the merits of election issues. As we have seen, some not very reputable party tactics have from time to time been aimed at exploiting the alleged risk that the nation will suffer from the surmised policy of the opposing party. The temptation to raise apprehensions in the minds of electors by alarmist methods persists to the present day. Conservative candidates have occasionally been involved in these methods. In 1924, the 'Zinoviev Letter' was published in the middle of the general election campaign. The inference which some people drew from it was that the Labour Ministry had been discreditably subservient to Communist influences. There were insufficient facts to substantiate this inference. Nevertheless a number of Conservative candidates did not hesitate to imply that the Labour party was allied to communism; and this charge was undoubtedly a powerful factor in the defeat of the Labour party at this election. In 1931, when a general election was requisite so as to obtain the authority of the electorate to deal with the highly critical economic situation, some Conservative candidates represented the Labour party as being likely to use the savings of the poor (in the Post Office Savings Bank) in order to make the Budget balance. Here again an election scare contributed to the heavy losses suffered by the Labour party in the election.

Nor have the Labour party been exempt from this undesirable feature in the periodical battles for power, for in the 1951 election some of their leaders and candidates tried to influence votes by suggesting that war would be more likely under a Conservative régime than under a Labour one; and a few of these candidates went so far as to characterize Churchill as addicted to war. These unworthy insinuations were repeated in modified form in the 1955 election, when Herbert Morrison, in his election broadcast on behalf of the Labour party, remarked that 'some people have doubts about Sir Anthony Eden's desire for peace'. Surely it was obvious that in the nineteen-fifties no British statesman would have failed to do his utmost to avoid war.

The electorate, having had some experience of the election scare, which is, they find, generally fabricated at the last moment for tactical reasons, are beginning to be suspicious of it. This suspicion, combined with a recognition by politicians that the expedient is to say the least an unseemly one, and often fails to succeed in the long run, may tend to its diminution.

§ 4. *Prospective issues*

In recent years there has been a tendency for all parties to include proposals for the future in their manifestoes, to

the comparative exclusion of references to the past record
of the Ministry. This tendency is, doubtless, to some extent
due to a growing realization that there is a greater prospect
of success in raising constructive issues than in justifications
or criticisms of the past. And it is also to be explained as being
the outcome of the increasing temptation, in view of the
widening of the franchise, for all parties to place reliance on
the electioneering value of promises of future benefits to the
people. Even as early as the debates on the Reform Bill in
1831 Peel warned the House of Commons that, as a result
of the increase in the number of voters, there would be an
inclination on the part of members 'to gratify their constituents by popular measures'. This tendency first, perhaps,
became noticeable shortly after the enlargement of the
franchise effected by the Reform Act of 1867; but it was only
after the Act of 1884, and to a still greater extent after the
grant of almost universal suffrage in 1918 and 1929, that it
became general.

When discussing the proposed terms of Disraeli's address
for the election of 1868, Gathorne Hardy ventured to suggest
that it might be well for Disraeli to include some promise of
the introduction of a measure of social amelioration.[1] And
in 1874 Gladstone endeavoured to improve the chances of
his party at the polls by promising to repeal the income-tax,
to diminish local taxation, and to give relief to the general
public in respect of articles of popular consumption. Disraeli
replied that these were 'measures which the Conservative
party have always favoured and which the Prime Minister
and his friends have always opposed'. Moreover, he maintained that the improvement of the condition of the people
had been for many years his constant aim.

After the Liberals came into power in 1906 the amount
of legislation conferring benefits on large sections of the community showed a remarkable increase; and there were not
lacking those who accused the Ministry of bribing the electorate. Lord Rosebery, for instance, at the time when the
extent of the mandate obtained for passing the Parliament
Bill of 1911 was under discussion, alleged that the authority
of the two elections of 1910 was impaired as a result of the
bribe offered to the electorate by the allowance of old-age
pensions.[2]

[1] *Gathorne Hardy, First Earl of Cranbrook, A Memoir*, vol. i, p. 282.
[2] 9 *H.L. Deb.*, 5 s., 1005.

At the end of World War I, and after the passing of the Representation of the People Act, 1918, from which there followed the biggest increase in the suffrage ever made in this country, all parties vied with each other in producing schemes for settling the country into prosperous peace conditions. The situation in 1923 was a little different. Though again all parties had prospective measures to promise, resistance to the main proposal of the Ministry, namely tariff reform, took a leading place in the Liberal and Labour manifestoes. These parties did not offer merely alternative measures to those of the Ministry, for the Ministry's main proposal was of such vital and general concern that it was bound to prevail over any others. The Labour party, however, besides opposing tariff reform, made proposals for a comprehensive scheme of national work, credit facilities for farmers, and a national levy, to be expended presumably on 'social services'. The Liberals adopted nearly every possible alternative. They criticized the Ministry's past record; they opposed the Ministry's proposals for the future, in respect of tariff reform; they opposed the Labour party's proposals for a capital levy; and they had, among other proposals of their own, one for the development of national credit. When three parties had all put forward positive programmes and two of them had criticized the past record of the Government, it was a hard business for the electors to know what were the predominant issues of the election.

As a result of the growth in the size of constituencies, the scale has steadily changed from the stage when political prospects were affected by payments of money to owners of nomination boroughs and when corrupt practice meant personal solicitation, to the stage when candidates of a party repeat their leaders' promises of benefits to those whose votes may turn the balance in their favour.

I sometimes think [said Baldwin in 1931] that the time may come when our enlightened posterity may think it just as inconceivable that men should be returned to Parliament by making promises which they know can never be fulfilled as we regard it as impossible that men should be returned for rotten boroughs.[1]

Dean Inge went so far as to suggest that general elections have become public auctions at which the contending parties bid against one another for votes by each promising a larger

[1] *The Times*, 13 June 1931, p. 9.

share than the other of the plunder of the minority.[1] This, perhaps, is an extreme view. But the willingness, or even eagerness, of both political parties to offer the benefits of the 'welfare State' has certainly led to an undesirable competition in the framing of election programmes. If this competition continues, as is probable, it will certainly moderate from time to time owing either to the disillusionment of the electors or to the practical limitations of finance.

There is a natural inclination for the Labour or Socialist party to appear in the light of idealists, and for the Conservative party to appear in the light of realists. It follows that the idealist party is more likely to have a programme of novel legislation, whereas the realist party may be more concerned to improve administrative efficiency. This latter may be just as valuable to the nation as is legislation; but it cannot be portrayed to the electorate in so attractive a light.

After the end of World War II post-war reconstruction and new social legislation were prominent in the election campaign of 1945, as might be expected after six years of concentration on defeating aggressors. The more specific legislative proposals were advanced by the Labour party, whose programme included ambitious items of nationalization. These proposals captivated a large proportion of the electorate and undoubtedly formed the essential issues of the election.

In 1955 there was no clear-cut question of policy on which the electorate was asked to decide; and the predominant issue amounted in effect to a choice between rival political principles. The Conservatives, who had during three-and-a-half years of office succeeded in improving the standard of living, offered a continuance of a 'welfare State' in which steady progress was linked with the ideas of free enterprise and a property-owning democracy. On the other hand, the Labour party offered a continuance of a 'welfare State' in which 'fair shares' of the profits of industry was emphasized, and in which an increased measure of governmental control was proclaimed as a beneficial feature of policy. The Conservatives epitomized the election issue as a choice between freedom and controls, and the Labour party as a choice between a bountiful socialized State and outworn individualism. Both parties were lavish with promises of social benefits, but none of these attained the proportions of a critical question.

[1] *More Lay Thoughts*, p. 303.

§ 5. *Rules for the submission of issues*

It is no easy matter, in the confusion of election issues which has prevailed in the last hundred years, to discover standards by which to determine the proper rights and obligations of the Ministry and the Opposition respecting the definition of such issues. Is a Ministry always under an obligation to produce a policy? Has a Ministry a right to adopt proposals of the Opposition as issues? Has an Opposition the right to raise prospective issues? Is an Opposition ever under an obligation to state its future policy? It is desirable to attempt to elicit some kind of answers to questions of this nature.

Since social legislation has become a matter of extreme technicality, it is difficult for a party leader to describe his party's future policy with any particularity, unless he has been in recent touch with the specialists in Government Departments. In 1873, after Gladstone had been defeated on the Irish University Bill, Disraeli, the Opposition Leader, was actuated by these considerations, as he himself explained in connexion with his refusal to form a Government. 'There was', he said in Parliament, 'no issue before the country—for I do not suppose that anyone would maintain that the Irish University Bill was a question on which we could dissolve.' He argued that his party could not appeal to the country without having 'a matured and complete policy'.

I would suggest [he added] that it is impossible for those who sit on the Opposition bench suddenly to have a matured policy to present to the people of this country in case Parliament is dissolved. An Opposition, of whatever party it may be formed, is essentially a critical body; it is not a constructive one and it cannot be.

He cited the Central Asian question, the New Rules for International Law, the French Treaty of Commerce, and local taxation as matters on which it would be difficult to give the electorate proper guidance, unless a Minister had been in power and had had recent access to official information.[1] Gathorne Hardy in particular, among Disraeli's followers, was unable to identify himself with this view; but there is little doubt that Disraeli's real object, as mentioned above,[2] was to keep the Gladstone Ministry in office until it had be-

[1] 214 *Parl. Deb.*, 3 s., 1931–4.
[2] See p. 215 above.

come further discredited, a stratagem which proved completely successful.

The contentions of Disraeli have never been repeated in so extreme a form. Perhaps a Ministry, only just in office, may be entitled to some excuse for putting forward its policy somewhat tentatively and in general outline; but on no recent occasions have prospective new Ministries declared themselves incapable of putting a policy before the electorate. In recent years a few leading politicians in Opposition have maintained a closer touch than hitherto, and have even engaged in such regular deliberations as to earn the description of a 'shadow Cabinet'. This kind of organization, assisted by the research departments set up under the Central Offices of parties, has placed Oppositions in a better position to frame constructive programmes than in the days of Disraeli.

Sometimes Ministries have tried to embarrass their successors by resigning rather than dissolving, so that the other side should have to produce a policy and not merely act as critics. When Gladstone's Home Rule Bill was defeated in 1886, some of his colleagues were in favour of resignation rather than dissolution, mainly on the ground that the incoming Government would have to go to the country on a policy of its own. But Gladstone insisted on dissolution. Similar considerations probably affected Rosebery when he decided to resign on a chance vote regarding a minor question in 1895, and also Balfour, who preferred resignation to dissolution in 1905. The occurrence of incidents such as these proves that it is understood to be incumbent on a Ministry, however new, to produce some kind of positive programme.

The question, whether a Ministry is entitled to adopt the proposals of an Opposition as issues, is well illustrated by the incidents connected with Gladstone's policies regarding Ireland. When he suddenly caused consternation in the country, during the Derby–Disraeli Ministry of 1866–8, by proposing the disestablishment of the Irish Church and by his defeat of the Ministry on that subject, he precipitated a situation to which no existing rules applied. As matters proved, the only question for decision was Gladstone's Irish Church proposal, which became the main issue of the 1868 election; and no one thought of blaming Disraeli for not bringing forward a positive policy in competition with that of Gladstone. The situation in 1880 was altogether different. At the election of that year, Beaconsfield, who again raised no positive issue, endeavoured to gain a majority for his party by censuring in the most vigorous terms the policy of Home Rule—a policy which the Opposition party had not in fact officially adopted. He may, in some subtle way, have sensed the course which Gladstone was about to take; but there was no justification for his attempt to centre the interest of the electors on an Opposition proposal which had never been formulated.

Whether or not the Opposition is, as a matter of general practice, entitled to dictate that its own prospective policy shall dominate as an issue over one raised by the Ministry is not a question capable of receiving a straightforward answer. If there are circumstances, such as those of 1868, where a Ministry is defeated on an important proposal raised by the Opposition, the policy of that proposal will almost of necessity become the leading issue in the ensuing election. But in ordinary circumstances, if an Opposition leader is a man of sufficient force of character to secure the attention of the people, there can be no more objection to the trial of a positive issue raised by the Opposition than to the trial of one raised by the Ministry. In the election of 1929, Lloyd George, by reason of his compelling personality, was in a large degree successful in rendering the issue of unemployment the ruling issue of the election.

No one would suggest that the Opposition party is under an obligation to produce, in preparation for a general election, a detailed programme of legislative projects. Gladstone was, it seems, justified in replying to Parnell's attempts to persuade him, in 1885, to formulate with precision his proposals with regard to Ireland, that he was not in office, and that it did not lie with him to make proposals. He also stated, in a memorandum addressed to Lord Rosebery, that it was not 'the province of the person leading the party in opposition to frame and produce before the public detailed schemes' such as those for Home Rule. 'The plan for Ireland', he told his son, Herbert Gladstone, 'ought to be produced by the Government of the day. Principles may be laid down by others, but not the detailed interpretation of them in a measure.'[1]

But if the Opposition has, when in office at an earlier time, made abortive attempts to pass an important measure, it may be fair for the Ministry to ask the Opposition to state

[1] Morley, *Life of Gladstone*, vol. iii, pp. 239, 258.

its policy in regard to the further advancement of that measure. Towards the end of the Conservative Ministry which lasted from 1886 to 1892 it became obvious that the main issue in the ensuing election would again be Home Rule, the subject, that is to say, which had been raised by Gladstone in 1886, and which the Conservatives had eluded by introducing an Irish Government Bill—a Bill which represented the lengths to which they were disposed to go. During the final session of the Parliament Joseph Chamberlain, with some show of reason, tried to extract from Gladstone a definite statement regarding the Liberal policy on Home Rule. In February 1892, four months before the dissolution, Chamberlain taunted Gladstone with a shyness in regard to this matter, which was, as every one knew, due to a lack of unanimity among his colleagues.

He [Gladstone] knows my plan now [said Chamberlain]. Will he not tell me something about his? I do not ask for all the details; general lines will be quite sufficient for my purpose. . . . We are all going to an election. . . . We ought to know, it is not too early to ask for, the policy of the Opposition, which is to be their principal object if they go into power. It is not too early to ask that they should put that forward for general discussion, so that the country may pronounce upon it with full knowledge.

In so far as Chamberlain was seeking information in regard to the form which Gladstone's Home Rule policy would take, if he were returned to power, his request was fair; and there is no doubt that this was what he was chiefly seeking. If, however, his words are to be understood as a general inquisition into the positive policy of the Opposition, it is questionable whether Gladstone might not have replied that his chief obligation was to criticize the past record and proposed future policy of the Ministry and that, beyond this, he was not bound to do more than deal with subjects which had already been before Parliament, especially those for the introduction of which he had been responsible.

A similar situation arose in 1905, not long before the end of the Balfour Ministry. Balfour had been harassed by the Liberals for many months to give an explicit statement regarding his attitude towards the projects of tariff reform. He had replied to these applications, but he realized that the issue of tariff reform was in many respects unpromising; it was fraught with many pitfalls. Political tactics, therefore, demanded that the tables should be turned on the Liberals;

and Balfour, having claimed that he had honestly tried to state his policy regarding the fiscal question, invited the Opposition to state its policy in respect of Education, Licensing, and Chinese Labour, among other topics. But the Liberals were far too astute to lay themselves open to attack in this simple fashion. No express response was made to the invitation; and it does not seem that there was any obligation to make any.

The difficulties which an Opposition Leader experiences in producing a detailed programme of legislative projects for a general election campaign are considerable because he must rely a great deal in this respect on the help of the appropriate civil servants. He cannot, moreover, be expected to be explicit about foreign policy if he has not been recently supplied with Foreign Office reports and information. Churchill, when in Opposition, was pressed by the Conservative Party Conference of 1949 to make a declaration of policy. He contended that his party had 'neither the power nor the responsibility to decide the policy or shape the fortunes of the State'. Policies undertaken by parties in Opposition without adequate investigation have sometimes proved embarrassing to them on attaining office.

What, then, may be regarded as the normal procedure of the Ministry and the Opposition respectively in selecting issues for presentation at a general election? A Ministry which has been for some time in office should, it may be assumed, be ready to vindicate its past record, and should also be prepared to produce a considered statement of its proposed policy for the future. If the Opposition has published a programme of future policy, it is open to the Ministry to criticize it, and, if it likes, to treat it with sufficient seriousness to ensure that the Opposition obtains the distinction of raising the predominant issue.

If a Ministry has only succeeded to power a short while before a dissolution, it will be justified in reflecting on the past record of the Opposition and will not be under an obligation to produce a well-matured programme of future policy.

An Opposition party, on the other hand, unless it has recently been in office, can raise the issue of its own future policy to as slight an extent as it likes, subject to the obligation of stating its views with some particularity on subjects which have previously been in controversy in Parliament and which still remain undetermined. It is also open to it to raise the issues of the Ministry's past record and the Ministry's proposals for the future.

If an Opposition party has been in office until shortly before a dissolution, it must justify its own past record instead of questioning that of the Ministry.

Whatever the circumstances of a Ministry may be at the time of an election, there is an onus upon it to make some proposals in regard to the future, even though they be only roughly outlined or extremely tentative, such as those of Bonar Law in 1922.

§ 6. *Influences affecting the submission of issues*

Party leaders do not possess the exclusive capacity of prescribing election issues. There are others who have occasionally exercised a considerable influence on the choice of the subjects to be submitted to the people, of which politicians who are not party leaders and political associations are examples.

The notable development of party organization in the last half-century has enabled the Liberal Party Conference once or twice, and more recently, but to a less extent, the Labour Party Conference, to dictate to leaders the issues to be raised in election campaigns. Even the Conservative Party Conference has occasionally been able to exercise some influence on the selection of issues. As early as 1883 delegates to the number of two thousand five hundred from five hundred Liberal associations met in conference at Leeds and discussed a reform programme which they desired the Liberal Ministry to adopt. And in October 1891 the Liberal Party Conference held its famous meeting at Newcastle and drew up a programme of a most heterogeneous character, which was accepted by Gladstone to stand beside Home Rule among the issues of the election of 1892.[1]

Although the extent of the influence of party conferences on the selection of issues has fluctuated from time to time, party leaders, whatever the party they may have led, while reserving to themselves very considerable freedom, have not been able to afford to display too obvious a neglect of the resolutions of party conferences respecting the composition of programmes.

Political and other associations of many different kinds

[1] Cf. Chapter VI, § 2.

have also been responsible for influencing the framing of issues. The first outstanding examples of this class are provided by the organizations which, early in the nineteenth century, interested themselves in the abolition of the slave trade and of slavery. Prior to the election of 1826, James Stephen, the friend of Wilberforce, endeavoured to make the abolition of the slave trade an issue by publishing an address to the whole electorate, in which he recommended that candidates, having been interrogated whether or not they were West-India merchants or proprietors of slaves, should not be supported if the answer was in the affirmative. And again, prior to the election of 1832, the Anti-Slavery Society presented the Whigs with an ultimatum, which, owing to the high proportion of the abolitionists in the electorate, caused the abolition of slavery to be very generally supported in the Whig party; and the Emancipation Bill of 1833 was passed as a direct result of the agitation of the society. The measures instituting free trade, too, though never before the people as a prospective issue, would hardly have been enacted but for the instigation of the Anti-Corn Law League. And, down to the present day, associations endeavour to use their influence, so that there shall be included among the election issues the proposals in which they are interested. At the election of 1906 manifestoes were issued by the Cobden Club, the United Irish League of Great Britain, and the Free Church Council. The last mentioned dealt with such diverse matters as education, temperance, and Chinese Labour.[1] Support of the League of Nations principles was the outstanding issue in the election of 1935. The prominence of this issue was mainly attributable to the vigorous and nationwide campaign waged by the League of Nations Union in the two or three years preceding the election.

Not only associations, but independent members of Parliament have sometimes been responsible for the submission of election issues. The occasions have, however, been rare. Before 1832 it may be said to have been almost unknown for an ordinary parliamentary candidate to include subjects of controversy in his election addresses, even though they were approved by the leaders of his party. Gladstone, in his first address to his constituents at Newark in 1832, aroused some consternation in a very limited circle by including mention

[1] See pp. 88–95 above.

of such proposed points of policy as the allotment of cottage grounds and a living wage for workmen. It is obvious that the suggestions of this budding Tory politician had no effect whatever on the course of the election as a whole, especially as his constituency was practically a nomination borough; and incidents of this kind were extremely infrequent at that period. After 1832 the growth of party organization soon acted as a restraint on the declarations of candidates of an independent turn of mind.

During the Victorian period, however, two or three private members with outstanding personalities and vigorous views were able to reach the public ear. Bright and Cobden may be recognized as having made their personal influence felt through the Anti-Corn Law League. After the advent of free trade, Bright again influenced the shaping of issues. Palmerston, in the election of 1865, was content merely to seek a renewal of confidence in his Ministry and in himself; but the subject of Parliamentary reform raised considerable interest at the election; and this phase in the campaign was chiefly due to Bright's intervention.

Shortly before interest in the issue of Home Rule extinguished interest in all other issues, there came into the forefront of politics two spirited democrats, the one, Joseph Chamberlain, attached to the Liberal party, and the other, Randolph Churchill, attached to the Conservative party. Both of them having an independent and progressive cast of mind and capable of attracting a wide popularity, they were able to gain an influence in the country which qualified them, if not to submit their own programmes for the people's judgement, at least materially to enlarge the scope of the programmes of the parties to which they were attached.

Chamberlain, who was a member of the Gladstone Ministry of 1880–5, made speeches of a strong Radical persuasion during 1885, which not only caused offence to the Queen, but alarmed his leader, who protested against the 'unauthorized programme', consisting of such projects as free education, improved housing, and the payment of members. Some attempt was made by Gladstone to bring his advanced colleague into line with the official policy; but Chamberlain's proposals, as well as the three acres and a cow of Jesse Collings, played a considerable part in the election of 1885.

The Conservative party had somewhat similar embarrassments to face as a result of the advocacy of Tory democracy by Randolph Churchill. His personal popularity was as large as, if not larger than, that of Chamberlain. And notwithstanding the fact that his Dartford programme of 1886, which included projects for a Land Bill, provision of allotments, and reform of local taxation, cannot, perhaps, be described as unauthorized, it caused considerable perplexity and astonishment in Tory circles. It was thought at least that Churchill was arrogating to himself some of the functions of his leader.

Although Joseph Chamberlain changed his political allegiance and joined the Conservative party, his temperament was such that he could not fit into any party mould. The story of his raising the tariff reform issue in 1903 and of its submission to the electorate in 1906 has already been noticed. It is only necessary, in view of the wide knowledge of the circumstances, to make bare mention of this second outburst of Chamberlain, as the most signal of the instances of the submission of a great issue being influenced by a person who was not a member of the Ministry or a leader of the Opposition. If it be said that the policy was officially adopted by the Conservative party, then it must be admitted that the adoption was attributable to Chamberlain alone. The extent to which he secured support for his plan among the Conservative party appears from a contemporary estimate of the character of the members returned at the election of 1906. It was computed that, of 157 Conservative members elected, 102 were Chamberlain Tariff Reformers, 36 Balfourites, 16 Unionist Free Fooders, and 3 unclassified.[1]

The occasions on which party leaders have failed to ensure that the programmes which they intend to announce at general elections will be accepted by their followers have happily been rare. In 1895 disunion in the ranks of the Liberals was the cause of a variety of issues being prescribed by Liberal ex-Ministers. Rosebery, the late Prime Minister, was not in a sufficiently strong position to insist that the issue on which he wished the election to be fought, namely the reform of the House of Lords, should be the one accepted by his party. Morley, for instance, asserted that Home Rule was the issue; Harcourt chose local option; and many private members stood for the Newcastle programme. It is obvious that, in circumstances such as these, not only is the interpretation of the voting at the election, as a decision on policy,

[1] *Annual Register*, 1906, Part I, p. 12.

impossible, but the prospects of the disunited party are rendered hopeless; and so it proved in 1895.

When the relative importance of issues respecting the future and the past was discussed a few pages back, the growing tendency for promises of prospective benefits to engage the attention of the electorate at the expense of the exercise of judgement on the past administration became noticeable. This tendency is apt to be emphasized when politicians are able to transgress the limits authorized by their leaders and to succeed in having the acceptability of their own projects determined by the people. Although it is not inevitable that issues raised independently of the authority of party leaders will consist of offers of short cuts to Utopia, there is a serious risk of this being so.

An issue is not as a rule submitted to the people without their first showing some evidence of their interest in the subject for treatment, and at least some indication of the probability of their approval. This is, indeed, one of the most elementary principles of political strategy. There have been occasions when party leaders have preferred to allow their parliamentary candidates to raise a particular issue in their constituencies, if pressed to do so, rather than to prescribe that issue as one officially recognized by the party. In other words, they have deemed it wise to wait for evidence of a demand from the people before committing themselves to a policy which might prove their undoing. The Derby Ministry could not make up its mind in 1852, until it was too late to affect the course of the election, whether the issue of protection was one which could prudently be adopted. Consequently individual Conservative candidates were left to raise the standard of protection or not to do so, as they or their constituencies pleased. This was what the Conservative party leaders wanted, namely a means of discovering the current of feeling in the country. As it proved, among a general obscurity of election facts, one point was clear—the people did not want protection. But the decision was not one made after an official submission. If it can be so described, it was inferred from local investigations.

An opposite result occurred, or was alleged to have occurred, in 1866. Gladstone and many others of his party, although they had been in favour of the measures of the Liberal Reform Bill of 1866, admitted that the Liberals did not officially raise the issue of Reform in the election of the preceding year. The Liberal Ministry, Gladstone said, was of opinion that the Reform question should not again be pursued until there had developed such a state of public opinion as might seem to afford a prospect of success. 'We left the country', he explained, 'to pronounce its own impartial judgment; we waited . . . for spontaneous indications of the public mind with regard to the representation of the people in Parliament.' And he concluded that the inference to be drawn from the conduct of the constituencies was that the people desired the introduction of another measure of Reform.[1]

It is a little difficult to understand how it is possible for the electors to raise an issue and, at the same time, to give judgement on it. Presumably the meaning to be attributed to Gladstone's words is this: if sufficient interest in the subject of Reform were taken in the constituencies, candidates would have been forced to raise the issue independently of direction from their party leaders; and, if the returns of members for constituencies in which the issue was raised were examined, it would be seen that, in most cases, the candidates who favoured Reform had been returned.

Incidents of this kind suggest a solicitude for the wishes of the people which can be over-estimated. The hesitation to raise an issue officially has generally been due as much to divisions among party adherents or to doubt regarding the efficacy of the proposal to secure a majority as to a desire not to force the submission on an unwilling electorate. This was particularly clear when, in 1880, the leaders of the Liberals being divided on the question whether Home Rule should be an issue, it was held that this must be left as a matter for individual decision of Liberal candidates.

It has not always been the habit of party leaders to wait for the people to give proof of their desire for the introduction of particular measures of importance. The absence of any general demand did not prevent Gladstone from undertaking the project of the disestablishment of the Irish Church in 1867. This measure was not the result of pressure, or even of any very widespread interest on the part of the people; but the Bill was not formally introduced until after the people had declared in its favour in the election of 1868. Again, Chamberlain's speech in 1903, which comprised the first

[1] 183 Parl. Deb., 3 s., 115.

exposition of his proposed policy of tariff reform, came as a surprise both to his colleagues and to the people at large.

Although it may be said that party leaders generally confine their proposals to subjects which have attracted the attention of the public, it is, perhaps, impossible to point to any great policy which has been made an election issue as a result of its initiation by the people themselves. Those who assert that there can be no such thing as the spontaneous action of public opinion will readily agree with this conclusion. It is necessary for the agitation of politicians or political associations or some other agency to kindle the interest which has been described as the normal condition precedent to the submission of an issue to the people.

The movement for free trade in the early Victorian period has been instanced as one having its origin in the people; and, in so far as this statement implies an origin at the circumference of the political structure rather than at the centre, there is some truth in it. But in fact its advancement, if not its initiation, was, like that of any other policy, due to persons whose identity is discoverable. The Anti-Corn Law League took so large a part in the transaction that it is hardly fair to exclude it from the main share in the credit, or discredit, of securing the passing of the necessary measures.

Another instance of an issue alleged to have had a purely popular origin is that of Chinese Labour in the election of 1906. But examples of this kind suggest another factor, which is easily confused with the influence of the people, namely the influence of the press; and this factor has been so fully discussed in books on the development of democratic government that it seems unnecessary to pursue the subject here.[1]

[1] See, e.g., Bryce, *Modern Democracies*, vol. i, pp. 104 ff.

CHAPTER XI

THE ISSUES *(cont.)*

§ 1. *The time for elections*

(a) *Auspicious moments*

IT has been seen that, from the earliest stage in which the people have had any control over the course of policy, the choice of the subjects for their consideration has not been necessarily confined to the Ministry in power, though the Ministry has obviously been in a peculiarly advantageous position to determine that choice. But the choice of the time for the submissions of issues has, within the limits of the prescribed periods of Parliaments, always been in the hands of the Sovereign or the Ministry. Now that it is an accepted convention of the Constitution that a dissolution will be granted on the advice of the Ministry almost as a matter of course, the Ministry alone controls the very important factor of time. There may, however, have to be some modification of this convention, as is remarked later,[1] if the two-party system is superseded by a three-party system or a system of groups.

The ability of the Ministry to determine the times for dissolutions has upon numerous occasions enabled it to seize upon advantageous situations for appeals to the people. A favourable opportunity for the raising of a cry, the satisfactory outcome of a foreign policy undertaken by the Ministry, and even the unpreparedness of the other side have induced the leaders in power suddenly to fix on a date for dissolution considerably in advance of the time when the current Parliament would normally expire.

Between the passing of the Triennial Act of 1694 and of the Septennial Act in 1715 the three-year period of Parliament was not strictly maintained. On more than one occasion, a dissolution was sought at a time earlier than that which might normally have been expected. The most notable of these occasions was the dissolution of November 1701, when the Parliament had been in existence for less than a year. In the preceding months it had become obvious that

[1] See pp. 273, 281 below.

the attempt of the French King to dictate to England on the subject of the succession to the English throne was arousing a violent popular antagonism to France and, consequently, an enthusiasm for the policy of war, in support of which William III desired a reliable majority in the House of Commons. William III, therefore, seized upon this favourable conjuncture to dissolve Parliament. The device proved successful, since the King obtained an assured majority in favour of his plans.

Another wave of popular sentiment was exploited by the Ministry in 1713, when a dissolution was precipitated so as immediately to follow the public thanksgiving for peace. It was said, in a letter to the Earl of Oxford, that many of his supporters were

impatient for a dissolution, not only for putting an end to expenses, but because they think they can never go to their elections with more advantage than while the impressions made by the rejoicings at the thanksgiving and by the Queen's incomparable speech are fresh in the minds of their electors.[1]

Considerations of the same kind applied just ninety-nine years later, when the unexpected dissolution of 1812 was attributed to the desire of the Government to benefit by the more peaceful conditions and by the occurrence in that year of a plentiful harvest.

For many years after the passing of the Septennial Act of 1715, Parliaments normally lasted nearly their full term of seven years. In 1747, however, after but six years had run, the Government decided that a surprise dissolution would help to consolidate its majority. Discreet preparations were made; and, among other steps, it was arranged that the British troops in the Netherlands should for the moment remain on the defensive, in case the Ministry should lose support owing to a military reverse. The strategem appears to have been entirely justified by the event, and several seats were gained.

It was not until 1774 that a similar experiment was undertaken—this time with a smaller measure of success. The Ministry did not take action under the impression that the occasion was specially propitious. The political outlook could by no means be described as a cheerful one. On the contrary, the position was extremely depressing. Relations with the

---

[1] *Hist. MSS. Comm.* (Portland MSS.), vol. v, p. 308.

American colonies had steadily worsened; and it was feared that they might even become disastrous. Encouraged, however, by an interval of some hopefulness, the Ministry determined to hasten the date of a dissolution, which would have been inevitable in 1775. The intention was rather to face the election campaign before the prospect grew even less bright, than to seize upon a particularly auspicious moment. The King approved, and even initiated, the design. He reckoned that the unexpectedness of the dissolution would assist the country gentry and would frustrate the 'nabobs', whom he expected to be unprepared.[1]

A successful result could only be claimed by the Ministry in so far as it could be said that a débâcle had been avoided. The Ministry suffered from the disadvantage of unpreparedness, which affected it adversely, as well as the Opposition. Although some preparation for the election could be made in secret, secrecy was bound to handicap those who relied on the element of surprise as well as those for whom the surprise was arranged.[2]

This game of catching opponents unawares is altogether unjustifiable and cannot tend towards the proper ends of government. The Grenville Ministry in 1806, although claiming to dissolve Parliament so as to obtain a confirmation by the people of its war policy, had for a main object an improvement in Parliamentary strength. But it soon found that it could suffer from reprisals. The Portland Ministry, which quickly succeeded it, almost immediately followed the precedent of a sudden dissolution and appealed to the people in 1807—a proceeding, in the view of many observers, as unnecessary as that of 1806. The Portland Ministry, as the King's saviours from the bugbear of Roman Catholic Emancipation, succeeded in fostering the old cry of 'No popery'; and it was evident that the Ministers were determined to take advantage of the heats so engendered before they had time to subside. Although the formal issue raised in the King's Speech was the propriety of the conduct of the Sovereign in changing his advisers, the religious question was undoubtedly that which was intended to sway the votes of the electors.[3]

The protest of Hawkesbury (the Opposition leader in

---

[1] Correspondence of George III and Lord North, vol. i, p. 201.
[2] A. von Ruville, William Pitt, Earl of Chatham, vol. iii, p. 285.
[3] 9 Parl. Deb., 1 s., 552.

1806) that there was nothing at issue between the two sides respecting the prosecution of the war is very similar to the protest of Grenville (the leader of the Opposition in 1807) that, as far as his party was concerned, there was no ground for the submission of any issue respecting the Roman Catholic question. Each in turn felt aggrieved, and rightly so, at the opportunism of the other. Hawkesbury said, in 1806, that he could find no cause, except that of convenience, to warrant the dissolution, since 'on no subject which ever engaged the attention of the country had there been such complete unanimity as in regard to the supporting his Majesty in the prosecution of the war'.[1] Likewise Grenville, in 1807, asserted that there was 'no idea entertained of withdrawing public confidence from Ministers. The alarm was, therefore, ill-founded'.[2] There can be little question but that both the dissolutions were determined upon chiefly with the object of securing an enlarged majority.

The only safeguard against abuses of this kind is their ultimate condemnation by public opinion. That Ministries should have the power to choose the time for appeals to the people is, as Peel once said, a principle 'of a delicate nature to meddle with',[3] but that they should indulge in sudden and unexpected appeals for ends of their own and apart from the true interests of the people is indefensible and must lead to the submission of false and not real issues.

These considerations have become more fully realized in modern times, with the result that imputations of mixed motives are rarer. The sudden dissolution of 1900, however, which led to the 'khaki election' was widely criticized as an attempt to make capital out of a passing patriotic fervour. It is certainly difficult to believe that the desire to obtain the authority of the people for the completion of the South African War was the principal motive for the dissolution. But the dissolution could not have been long delayed, as the Parliament was in its sixth year.

Instances may be found in which severe temptations to profit by fortuitous situations have been resisted. In the summer of 1878, Lord Beaconsfield, after returning from his triumphs at the Congress of Berlin, and after receiving a considerable ovation from the London crowds, had to decide whether he would seize what was an almost assured oppor-

[1] 8 *Parl. Deb.*, 1 s., 21.   [2] 9 *Parl. Deb.*, 1 s., 602.
[3] 58 *Parl. Deb.*, 3 s., 819.

tunity of his party obtaining three or four years' extension of office. The question was debated in the Cabinet, which decided that it was not proper to exploit the recent success in foreign policy, and that there was no constitutional ground for obtaining a dissolution, when the Ministry had had consistent and sufficient support in the House of Commons. It has been suggested that the Conservatives would have displayed strategical ability if they had arranged an election immediately after gaining credit from the outcome of the General Strike in 1926. But many persons thought that it would have been unscrupulous to profit by such an opportunity.

A problem much like that which had confronted Lord Beaconsfield in 1878 was discussed in the House of Commons in October 1938 after Neville Chamberlain's agreement with Hitler at Munich. Churchill, who had heard that Chamberlain might quickly arrange a general election so as to take advantage of the popularity that for a short time greeted his diplomacy, asserted that an appeal to the electorate in such circumstances by a Prime Minister with a large working majority would be 'an act of historic, constitutional indecency'. Chamberlain replied that he did not want a general election at that juncture but he would not accept the idea as being 'constitutionally indecent'.[1] A few years later Churchill himself, as Prime Minister in 1953, remarked in the House of Commons, in a discussion on the possible date of a general election, that it was certainly not the wish or intention of the Government to take advantage of any temporary fluctuation in public opinion in the hope of securing an electoral victory.[2]

Churchill resigned in 1955, and Eden, his successor, at once obtained a dissolution of Parliament when its period had only run three and a half years. Some of his political opponents accused him of seizing on an auspicious moment for the Conservatives, because the Labour party was at that juncture lacking in unity. Aneurin Bevan had recently rebelled against party discipline; and he had a considerable following. It is, however, likely that any Prime Minister obtaining a dissolution well in advance of the end of the period of a Parliament will be open to charges of choosing a time when either the Ministry has achieved a recent success or when its opponents are in disarray.

[1] 339 H.C. Deb., 5 s., 371, 548.
[2] 520 H.C. Deb., 5 s., 21.

Just in the same way that Ministries have sometimes seized upon auspicious moments to appeal to the electors so also have they been astute in avoiding inauspicious occasions. It was admitted, after the event, by both Wellington and Peel that Wellington's resignation in November 1830, when defeated on an unimportant vote, was only a pretext for an escape from office and that the real reason was a desire not to 'expose his Majesty and the country to the consequences which might result from the Government going out on the question of parliamentary reform'.[1] Peel saw disadvantages in appealing to the country on an issue of free trade in 1846. Queen Victoria offered Russell a dissolution after his defeat in the House of Commons in February 1852; but the situation was so unpromising that he and his colleagues were unanimous in declining the offer. The circumstances in which Balfour preferred resignation to dissolution in 1905 are mentioned at a later stage in the present chapter. These are but one or two reminders of circumstances in which expediency has restrained Ministries from making appeals to the people. But just as a higher standard, it may be hoped, is prevailing in regard to the choice of time for elections, so too there is, perhaps, less disposition nowadays to shirk submissions to the people on proper occasions, even though they may seem unpropitious.

(b) Change of Ministry

There was in the eighteenth century a common opinion that each Parliament should run its full course of seven years; and that there was no justification for a break in the period, even though a change in the Ministry occurred. After the dismissal of the Fox–North Coalition Ministry in 1783, Fox and his supporters were afraid of a dissolution; and their arguments against the admissibility of Pitt's securing a new Parliament were to some extent based on the notion that a change of Ministry did not justify an appeal to the people. Burke described a dissolution in such circumstances as 'penal'; and it was characterized by Fox as unconstitutional. The opinion of Lord Somers, many decades old, was quoted in support of an assertion that the King had no power to allow a new Minister a new Parliament.

In the course of the mutual recriminations regarding the dissolutions of 1806 and 1807, just mentioned, it was main-

---

[1] A. Todd, *Parliamentary Government*, 2nd ed., vol. i, p. 187.

tained that the dissolution of 1784, after the course of Parliament had run but four years, was altogether unique and unsuited to form a precedent. Hawkesbury then emphasized the fact that, with one exception (demises of the Crown apart), no Parliament had lasted less than six sessions since the passing of the Septennial Act in 1715. If it had been an accepted rule that a change from one Ministry to another not only justified, but usually involved, a new Parliament, the surprise dissolution of 1807 would not have been open to criticism by the Opposition.

Peel's decision, however, to advise a dissolution of Parliament in 1834, when he issued his famous Tamworth Manifesto, was justified by him in Parliament chiefly upon the ground that a change of Ministries was, of itself, sufficient reason for the summoning of a new Parliament. He quoted the dissolutions of 1784, 1806, 1807, and 1831 as instances of dissolutions following upon changes in Ministries. It is doubtful whether this argument carried much weight, since the four occasions of dissolution which he mentioned were not regarded as necessarily required by the appointment of new Ministers.[1] Moreover, it does not appear to be certain that, if Melbourne had resigned, instead of obtaining a dissolution, in 1841, Peel would have then submitted himself to the people immediately after assuming office. His remarks in Parliament prior to the dissolution rather suggest that he would not have done so.

As has been noticed when the influence of the people on the choice of Ministries was discussed in Chapter VII, the defeat of the Government on a vital subject or a change of Government from one party to another did not come to be recognized as involving an appeal to the people until towards the end of the reign of Queen Victoria. When, for instance, the Liberals resigned owing to their difficulties in dealing with the question of Reform in 1866, the Conservatives, who succeeded them, did not consider it necessary to obtain an immediate general election. The same Parliament included Ministries from opposite sides of the House.

At the present day, however, it has become a recognized convention that there shall be a new Parliament for a new Ministry in all ordinary instances: in other words, a change of Ministry requires a fresh reference to the electorate. A dissolution followed immediately after the Bonar Law Ministry

[1] 26 *Parl. Deb.*, 3 s., 226-7.

succeeded the Lloyd George Ministry in 1922. And the difference of opinion which existed regarding the need for a general election in 1931 was doubtless settled largely as a result of the realization that the change from the Labour Ministry to the Coalition or Joint Ministry required, according to modern usage, a fresh mandate from the people. As Ramsay MacDonald said in his manifesto, 'The working of Parliamentary institutions, of democratic responsibility, and of constitutional practice demands it.'[1]

The argument, then, which was in times past used by the Opposition against a dissolution, on the ground that the period of a Parliament should not be interrupted, may be regarded as obsolete, unless a three-party or group system becomes prevalent. In this event, the more frequent changes in the composition of Ministries, incidental to a multiplicity of parties, may cause a revision of the present understanding regarding the suitability of times for appeals to the people.[2]

(c) Absence of tumult

Another argument, favoured both by Ministries and Oppositions, has had as its object the prevention of threatened dissolutions of Parliament. This, like the argument that Parliaments must run their full course, may be regarded as inapplicable to present conditions.

From the beginning of the period when general elections took the form of appeals to the people down to the middle of the nineteenth century, it was frequently contended that questions of policy should not be referred to the people when those questions stimulated passionate excitement. The Septennial Act of 1715 was passed to avoid the turbulence which, it was thought by the Whigs, would be encouraged by a general election at a time when Jacobitism was a real menace. In the event of a genuine apprehension of rebellion, very strenuous steps are doubtless justified; and it was on these grounds that the Septennial Act dealt not merely with the term of future Parliaments but also with that of the current Parliament. It referred, however, to the 'more violent and lasting heats and animosities among the subjects of this realm', which had been occasioned as a result of the institution of triennial elections.

Whether or not the passing of the Septennial Act had the effect of reducing the intensity of 'heats and animosities'

---

[1] *The Times*, 8 Oct. 1931.   [2] See p. 281 below.

seems to have been a matter of controversy. In a debate on a
motion for the repealing of this Act in 1734, the Opposition
maintained that there had been greater ferments since 1715
than there had been before that date. However that may be,
the debate included a bold and, as it was then, an original
observation by Sir William Wyndham, the leader of the Tory
Opposition, in regard to the more general aspect of popular
interest in election campaigns.

As to the elections coming on when the Nation is in a ferment
[he said] it is not so far from being an objection to frequent
elections, that it is, in my opinion, Sir, a strong argument in
favour of them; because it is one of the chief supports of the
freedom of the nation. It is plain that the people seldom or ever
were in a ferment, but when incroachments were made upon
their rights and privileges; and when any such are made, it is
very proper, nay it is even necessary, that the people should be
allowed to proceed to a new election, in order that they may chuse
such representatives as will do them justice, by punishing those
who have been making incroachments upon them. . . .[1]

Sir Robert Walpole, in defending the retention of the Septennial Act, mentioned the fickleness and instability of the
people as a ground for the longer period of Parliaments.

When the periods of Parliaments were reduced by the
provisions of the Parliament Act, 1911, from seven to five
years, no one thought of suggesting that the alteration would
increase the opportunities for 'heats and animosities' among
the people. The clause in question received less than one
hour's consideration in the debate in the House of Commons
—partly as a result, no doubt, of the application of modern
rules of procedure. It seems to have aroused very little
interest, in notable contrast, for instance, to the circumstances
of the debate of 1734.[2]

In the nineteenth century the strongest objections to taking
the judgement of a turbulent people proceeded from Peel.
When the question of Roman Catholic claims was being
debated in 1821, he said that he should deprecate on that,
as he had done on other subjects, an appeal to the excited
passions of the people. 'Against such appeals', he stated,
'I should always set my face; believing, as I do, that the deliberate wisdom of Parliament is better calculated to weigh

[1] 9 *Parl. Hist.* 458. Cf. Hallam, *Constitutional History* (1876 ed.), vol. iii, p. 237.
[2] 25 *H.C. Deb.*, 5 s., 343–54.

maturely the important bearings of any great question, than the general opinion of parties elsewhere.'[1]

Opponents of the great Reform Bill, and Peel in particular, viewed with more than concern the reference of that Bill to the decision of the electorate. Then, if at any time, the people were in a ferment; and it was widely feared that a general election might, in the prevailing circumstances, lead to a state of civil war. The King himself, a short while before the dissolution of April 1831, wrote to Grey, the Prime Minister, stating his firm conviction that, if 'what is called an appeal to the people' were made 'when a spirit of agitation which has been so long in progress has been much increased by the introduction of the Bill and the discussion upon it, this country would be thrown into convulsion from Land's End to John O'Groats House'. The King, at that stage, refused to assent to proposals for a dissolution which might, as he thought, involve disorder and bloodshed.[2]

Peel condemned the idea of a submission to the people in regard to Reform, after as well as before the election of 1831. Even when the election was safely over, he deprecated the taking of the opinion of 'an already excited people, on a question of all others requiring sober and dispassionate enquiry', and predicted that, 'when the steady good sense and reason of the people of England shall return, they will be the first to reproach us with the baseness of having sacrificed the Constitution in the vain hope of conciliating the favour of a temporary burst of popular feeling'.[3] After the House of Lords had thrown out the Bill, in the autumn of 1831, the agitation became more intense than ever; and the opponents of Reform once more deplored the passing of legislation on a matter of such deep concern in times of excitement. At this stage Macaulay disclosed, in a masterly way, the evasion practised by the Tories. When there were but small signs of popular interest in Reform, they placed reliance on the apparent lack of demand. When the whole country was convulsed, they alleged that the time was inappropriate. 'Half the logic of misgovernment', he said, 'lies in this one sophistical dilemma: If the people are turbulent, they are unfit for liberty: if they are quiet, they do not want liberty.'[4]

Although Peel came to accept the result of the Reform Act

[1] 4 Parl. Deb., 2 s., 1003.
[2] Correspondence of King William IV and Earl Grey, vol. i, pp. 179–82.
[3] 4 Parl. Deb., 3 s., 891–2.   [4] 9 Parl. Deb., 3 s., 381–2.

of 1832 as a settlement which had to be respected, he still seemed to retain his belief in the danger of submitting questions to the people which might arouse in them too keen an interest. His view of the political conditions in the spring of 1841 was that Melbourne should resign and leave him to succeed without the necessity of a general election. One of his arguments against Melbourne's threatened dissolution, the technical right to which he did not deny, was the alleged inflammation of the popular mind by the Ministry in regard to 'such a subject as the sustenance of the people'. Although it was not generally known for some years afterwards, Melbourne's personal view (which was in opposition to that of the majority of his colleagues) was that it was undesirable to dissolve Parliament and appeal to the people 'when their passions were raised on any subject, but more especially on such a subject as food'.[1]

Hobhouse and Macaulay both replied to Peel's argument. The former merely disclaimed responsibility for the excited state of the people. 'Surely', he said, 'the agitation, if agitation there is to be, is no fault of ours.' And, after defining the fiscal question which the country would have to determine, he added: 'If the people feel a lively interest in the determination of this question, I cannot help it.' Macaulay, however, went to the root of the matter when he asserted that it was only proper that the people should take the most intense interest in matters closely affecting them.

It has been said reproachfully [he remarked], 'What! dissolve on a popular question, when there is such agitation, such excitement!' But on what suit or popular question should there be a dissolution? On what question appeal to the people, but a question in which they felt interested? As to the agitation which was suggested, there was no agitation but of the most legitimate description; there was no excitement—no agitation—but what was created of and by the people. Surely the right honourable baronet [Peel] did not mean to suggest that the people were not to feel excited, were not to get up an agitation among themselves upon questions which they could not but perceive came home to their pockets, to their best interests and comforts?[2]

[1] Lord Broughton, *Recollections of a Long Life*, vol. 6, pp. 26–28.
[2] 58 *Parl. Deb.*, 3 s., 817–21, 850–1, 887. On another occasion Macaulay observed that 'in this country scarcely any great abuse was ever removed till the public feeling had been roused against it; and that the public feeling has seldom been roused against abuses without exertions to which the name of agitation may be given'. 'The truth is', he added, 'that agitation is inseparable from popular government.' 51 *Parl. Deb.*, 3 s., 821.

In spite, however, of Peel's submissions to the people in his Tamworth Manifestoes on occasions when he badly needed the people's votes, he remained to the end, as has already been pointed out, chary of appealing to them on issues of policy. When the great question of the repeal of the Corn Laws was at its most critical stage, he considered it dangerous to refer it to popular decision. In writing a review of his action at that time, he explained that there seemed to him to be grave objections to inviting an expression of the opinion of the people on a subject which would not only raise the heats and animosities so often apprehended, but would, as a result of the excitement which would be raised in the constituencies, preclude the possibility of a dispassionate consideration in Parliament.[1]

A study of the problems of crowd psychology and of the effects of mass suggestion appears to have emphasized the unsatisfactory quality of decisions made by large numbers of persons who are incapable or, what is important in the present context, are rendered incapable of calm and deliberate judgement. While few politicians would contend nowadays that the people must not be allowed to have matters referred to them which stimulate them to excitement, it is widely realized that any calculated attempt by party or other political organizations unduly to arouse the emotions of electors must stultify the means of democratic government. In several of the incidents which have been described so as to illustrate objections to appeals to the people at times of political excitement, there was a notable failure to recognize this distinction. It was, however, clearly denoted by Macaulay in 1841, when he remarked that the excitement over the issue of the day was legitimate, in that it was 'created of and by the people' and was not provoked by politicians.

In recent years improved general education, the decrease in the practice of holding public meetings at election time, and the growth of the vast influence of broadcasting have tended to a more sober and thoughtful consideration of election issues. Consequently the risks of the electorate being worked up into a state of ferment are nowadays much reduced.

(d) Adverse by-elections

On several occasions during the last century it has been contended that, in the event of a succession of by-election

[1] Sir Robert Peel's *Memoirs*, vol. ii, pp. 163 ff.

results going adversely to the Ministry, the views of the people should be ascertained without delay by means of a general election. This is, of course, an argument which is much more likely to be used by the Opposition than by the Ministry. It is suggestive of the close connexion between the two means of popular expression, namely public opinion and voting.

The circumstances of 1841, to which reference has been made in the preceding pages of this chapter, produced arguments based on the course of by-election results of a different character from those more lately adopted. In that year Peel made a motion of want of confidence in the Melbourne Ministry, and at the same time asserted that the occasion was inopportune for a dissolution, because there was evidence from recent by-elections that the Liberals were in a minority in the country. He alleged that, among some twenty by-elections held during the current Parliament, in which changes in party representation had taken place, sixteen had been adverse to the Liberals and only four in their favour.[1] In the days of Peel it had not yet become recognized that, if there was a clear indication of a trend of public opinion against the Ministry, the people should be given an opportunity of electing a new Parliament. Consequently, the loss by the party in office of more by-elections than they had won was used by the leader of the Opposition as an argument for resignation rather than for an appeal to the people.

After the Reform Act of 1867, a balance of by-election results in favour of the Opposition, if not admitted as a reason for an early general election, was confidently advanced as such on several occasions. While it is probable that Gladstone would not have wished publicly to ascribe in so many words his advice of a dissolution in February 1874 to recent bad fortune in the constituencies, he told the Queen that he had laid before the Cabinet 'a pretty full outline of the case as to the weakness of the Government since the crisis of last March, and the increase of that weakness, especially of late, from the unfavourable character of the local indications'. He also spoke to her of 'the course of local elections' having been unpropitious. A more intimate communication, written to a supporter, Lord Aberdare, disclosed more fully Gladstone's real motives. He wrote: 'The continual loss of elections and the expediency of avoiding being further weakened have

[1] 58 Parl. Deb., 3 s., 817–18.

determined us at once to take the opinion of the country and
to stand or fall by it.'[1]

In 1874 the course of recent by-elections was indirectly
admitted to be a reason for an appeal to the people in
Gladstone's manifesto to his electors, published prior to the
general election. He told his constituency that the Ministry
had been embarrassed by the rejection of its measures by the
House of Lords, a course, he said, which that House would
hardly have taken had 'the isolated and less certain, but still
frequent and fresh indications of public opinion at single
elections continued to be in harmony with the powerful and
authentic, but now more remote judgment of [the general
election of] 1868'.[2] It will be remembered that the crisis of
1873, to which Gladstone referred, had arisen in very peculiar
and unusual circumstances. The Conservatives had avoided
any situation likely to precipitate a dissolution, since they
believed that the longer it was delayed the more marked
would be the swing of the pendulum in their favour. The
Liberal Ministry, on the other hand, would have been glad
to have found some opportunity for an early dissolution,
since it was fully aware that the sooner the campaign took
place the less were its chances of defeat.

The reasons for Gladstone's advice of a dissolution in 1874
were the subject of a heated altercation between Asquith and
Balfour in the House of Commons in 1905, when the Opposition charged the Conservative Ministry with maintaining
itself in office in the face of adverse by-elections. Balfour, the
Prime Minister, argued that, in spite of the terms of Gladstone's advice to the Queen, above quoted, Gladstone had
alleged that it would be improper for a Government to go
out simply because by-elections had gone against it, without
considering other motives, and that

all precedent, all law, all common sense, shows that it is for the
House of Commons, and the House of Commons alone, to determine whether a Government shall receive that measure of support
which will enable it to carry out the duties entrusted to it by the
Sovereign and expected from it by the country.[3]

It may well have been that, although Gladstone had no
objection to telling the Queen that the adverse course of
by-elections was one of the strongest motives for his advice

[1] The letter was quoted some years afterwards in the House of Commons.
150 *Parl. Deb.*, 4 s., 73.   [2] *Annual Register*, 1874, Part I, p. 2.
[3] 141 *Parl. Deb.*, 4 s., 160–2, 181–2.

to her, he would have preferred that it did not become generally known that it had a predominant influence in determining the date of the general election, lest the occasion came to be used as a precedent.

The Conservative Ministry, which resigned at the end of 1905, had been urged by the Liberals as early as the spring of 1904 that its proper course was to dissolve, because a certain number of by-elections had been going against it. Balfour flatly denied this obligation. 'I do not for one instant admit', he said, 'that the by-elections are a test, or ought to be regarded as a test of public feeling. . . . They are not, and they cannot be made, the index and the test of what the feeling of the people of the country is as a whole.'[1]

It is obvious that constitutional law does not recognize an obligation on a Ministry to dissolve Parliament even after a succession of sensational changes in local representation. If enough seats are lost by a Ministry to place it in a minority in the House of Commons, the problem solves itself. If a Ministry, whose majority at the beginning of a new Parliament is so large that it is not turned into a minority by the loss of a considerable number of seats, insists on retaining office after such a loss, it cannot be forced to dissolve. But, surely enough, it will pay a double penalty, in number of casualties, when a dissolution becomes inevitable.

(e) General remarks

The tactics adopted by Balfour at the end of 1905, when he finally resigned rather than advise a dissolution, appear to have violated the proper standards governing the relations between a Ministry and the people. If, as the Balfour Ministry presumably realized, it was questionable whether it retained the confidence of the people, the proper course was a dissolution of Parliament. As it was, Balfour seems to have decided that it would prove a good tactical move, in the interests of his party, to throw the onus of the production of a programme on the Liberals, who, he judged, were ill prepared for such a course. The situation was in many respects similar in 1895, when Rosebery resigned after a defeat in the House of Commons on a minor question, in preference to dissolving Parliament. The weakness of his position was evidently his reason; but Salisbury, who succeeded him, told the Queen that the constitutional course would have been for Rosebery

[1] 132 Parl. Deb., 4 s., 1015–16.

to dissolve; and the Queen seems to have agreed with this view.[1]

It is probable that resignations, like those of 1885, 1895, and 1905, unaccompanied by appeals to the people, will become increasingly rare. Unless, indeed, a Ministry confesses itself to be in so weak and incompetent a condition as to be unable to stand in competition with an alternative Ministry, it will presumably, on being defeated in the House of Commons on an important vote, seek the judgement of the country, as it did, for instance, successfully in 1831 and 1857, and unsuccessfully in 1841, 1859, 1886, and 1924. But, even if this course does not become usual, a Ministry should not shift the onus of dissolution on to the Opposition simply by way of finesse.

Once again, it must be remembered that constitutional conventions may be modified if the two-party system ceases to be operative.

It has been accepted for many years that the·Sovereign can only very exceptionally refuse to dissolve Parliament, when advised so to act by his Ministry. Even as far back as 1806, when it was admitted by the Opposition that the King was entitled to grant a dissolution whenever he chose, it was evident that the King realized that he could not refuse his consent without at the same time requiring the resignation of the Ministry.

This understanding was questioned by Lord Oxford and Asquith in 1923, during the first Labour Ministry, a Ministry which had fewer assured supporters in the House of Commons than the Conservative party, and which could only retain a majority if it continued to be reinforced by the Liberals. Those who differed from Lord Oxford and Asquith maintained that the Labour Ministry might at any time insist on a right to force a dissolution, although it turned on an issue selected by that Ministry, and although the dissolution appeared to its opponents to be arbitrary and unwarranted. As matters turned out, the Labour Ministry obtained a dissolution in 1924, in circumstances which were allowed on every side to be sufficient, so that the question of a right to a dissolution was not put to a trial.

The system in this country, which provides for a maximum

[1] *The Letters of Queen Victoria*, 3rd Series, vol. ii, p. 525.

period for Parliaments, has, it seems, several advantages over those which provide for fixed times for general elections. France (in practice) and the United States of America provide the most obvious examples of the latter. The character of the issues raised in England differ from those which arise under systems with fixed terms. Where it is possible for the supervention of important points of policy to precipitate general elections, it is more likely that issues of policy will predominate rather than issues which concern the choice of rival party leaders. In so far, moreover, as issues of policy enter into the election campaigns in either system, they are more likely to be precise in England than in a country having a legislature with a fixed term, since a question is probably ripe for decision if a Ministry obtains a dissolution on a defeat in regard to it in the House of Commons. Where the electors know that no general election can possibly take place before a certain date, party organization does not maintain a constant efficiency, and interest in politics during the periods between elections is apt to flag, with the result that public opinion fails to carry out its function of preparation for the decisions which the people have the opportunity of making through the casting of their votes. It may well happen, as in France, that a representative chamber with a fixed term obtains great power, at the expense of the Ministry and the people.

But the comparative merits of the two systems are not confined to the difference in the kinds of issues encouraged by them. Fixed times for elections, provided they are sufficiently far apart, have the advantage of enabling a Ministry to look forward to an uninterrupted period in which to work out the policy that it proposes to undertake. Viewed in this light, the comparison becomes one in which the advantages of efficiency in administration must be set against a more intelligent intervention of the people in politics.

§ 2. *Formulation of issues*

(a) *The official Speech*

Until the present century the decision of the people on questions of policy at general elections was not facilitated by any recognized and uniform method of formulating issues. The electorate only became aware of the programmes of party leaders in an indirect or anomalous manner.

During some parts of the eighteenth and nineteenth centuries, the King's and Queen's Speeches to Parliament, leading up to dissolutions, were regarded as the authoritative method of communicating the issues, not only to that assembly, but in some sense through it to the people.[1] Under William III the issues may be said to have been raised by the King himself, since he was in many respects his own chief Minister. But later on the King's Speech was that of the Sovereign only in form: it was drawn up by the Ministry of the day, which was responsible for its terms. The intermediate or transitional stage seems to have occurred in the reign of Queen Anne. Swift observed that it was well known 'that Speeches on these occasions are ever digested by the advice of those who are in the chief confidence, and, consequently, that they are the sentiments of Her Majesty's Ministers, as well as her own'.[2] A further stage in the development of the Speech was commented upon by Wilkes in circumstances which are notorious. In the famous No. 45 of the *North Briton* in 1763, he asserted that, for many years past, the legislature and the public had understood the King's Speech to be that of his Ministers; and there was quoted in support of his assertion the authority of Shippen in 1733, Pulteney in 1739, and Argyle and Carteret in 1740.[3]

Even as late as 1841 the Duke of Wellington criticized the form of the Queen's Speech on the ground that it appealed to the opinion of the people in regard to the fiscal question; and he charged the Ministry with having aggravated the case by permitting the Queen to make such a Speech. It is unlikely that many politicians besides the Duke took this view of the position. The expression of it, however, led the Prime Minister (Melbourne) to explain that 'the Speech was that of her Majesty's Ministers, and did not in any way, as the noble Duke said it would, commit the Sovereign to its sentiments'.[4] True as this statement was, Queen Victoria exercised

[1] Cf. Chapter VIII, § 1, above, which includes several remarks about the King's Speech prior to dissolution of Parliament. The full text of the Speeches is easily available in 'Hansard'.

[2] *The Examiner*, No. 19, 30 Nov. to 9 Dec. 1710.

[3] See *The North Briton, Forty-six Numbers Complete* (1772); 9 *Parl. Hist.* 88, 617, 630. Shippen advanced this view as early as 1717, 7 *Parl. Hist.* 508. See also the statement of Henry Fox in 1761, mentioned in Horace Walpole, *Memoirs of George III* (ed. Barker), vol. i, p. 95. No. 45 of the *North Briton*, having characterized a passage in the Speech from the Throne as 'the most abandoned instance of ministerial effrontery ever attempted to be imposed on mankind', was consigned to the common hangman to be burned as a seditious libel. Cf. p. 49 (n. 1) above.   [4] 59 *Parl. Deb.*, 3 s., 77, 81.

a close supervision over the wording of the Speeches from the Throne; and in 1864 she insisted on the deletion of a paragraph on the ground that it was unduly bellicose in tone and might precipitate a war with Germany.[1] Although this kind of influence has long since ceased to be exercised, the Sovereign is still often supposed by those who are not acquainted with constitutional history to be personally involved in the principles expounded in the Speech from the Throne. The arrangement by which the Sovereign is made the mouthpiece of the views of the Ministry of the day has the merit of perpetuating an interesting tradition; but it is open to the objection that it is apt to be misleading to many citizens.

During the period when the notion of issues being decided by the people was still in a rudimentary state, at the end, that is to say, of the seventeenth century, the arguments in support of party candidates (both of the Ministerial and the other side) could only be disseminated by such means as political tracts and periodical publications. This remained for many years the chief means available to the Opposition for raising issues. But, from the time of the Proclamation leading up to the general election of November 1701, the Speech from the Throne (or Proclamation, as the case might be) became, for more than a century, the formal method of communicating such issues as the Sovereign or the Ministry wished to lay before the people. The communication was not only in form, but largely in fact, confined to Parliament. It was, however, open to candidates to repeat to the constituencies the issues disclosed in the Speech.

It has already been seen that the Proclamation of 1701 marked an interesting stage in the history of the development of the people's ability to decide issues.[2] But, during the greater part of the eighteenth century, the absence of any effective issues meant that the formal communications of the Sovereign seldom contained any matter of concern to the voters at general elections. Not infrequently, in the middle of the century, the King's Speech which preceded the election contained no mention of any question of future policy, either because there was none to mention or because it was not

[1] *Queen Victoria's Letters*, 2nd Series, vol. i, p. 154; Lord E. Fitzmaurice, *Life of Lord Granville*, vol. i, pp. 457–8.
[2] See pp. 172–3 above.

desired to make any submission. In 1768, for instance, the following indefinite language was used: 'In the approaching election of representatives, I doubt not but my people will give me fresh proofs of their attachments to the true interest of their country, which I shall ever receive as the most acceptable mark of their affection to me.' This was no more than to ask for the support of the King's Ministers, because they were the King's Ministers. The omission of any more precise submission was possibly due to the temporary enlargement of royal influence.

Especial interest, however, attaches to the form of the Speeches of 1784 and 1831, since the elections which took place in those years are among the most important landmarks in the progress of popular government. In the former Speech the King was made to say: 'I feel it a duty I owe to the Constitution and to the country, in such a situation, to recur as speedily as possible to the sense of my people by calling a new Parliament.' In the latter:

I have been induced to resort to this measure [the prorogation of Parliament with a view to its dissolution] for the purpose of ascertaining the sense of my people, in the way in which it can be constitutionally and authentically expressed, on the expediency of making such changes in the representation as circumstances may appear to require, and which, founded upon the acknowledged principles of the Constitution, may tend at once to uphold the just rights and prerogatives of the Crown, and to give security to the liberties of the people.

The phraseology of the appeal to the people in the Speech of 1784 implied that they had a new determinant capacity. But, as has already been noticed, modern research has proved that the appeal was more a compliment than a reality, and was less genuine than has sometimes been supposed. The Speech of 1831, however, is distinguishable as containing an explicit reference to a particular subject of future policy.[1] Admittedly, the formal announcement only specified an issue which was, in the peculiar circumstances, in everybody's mouth. Nevertheless, the official recognition of the ability of the people to express 'constitutionally and authentically' their decision on the question of Reform marked not only an advance in the direction of democracy, but also a turning-point in the development of the methods of formulating issues.

[1] See pp. 199–200 above.

(b) Election addresses of party leaders

From the time of Peel's Tamworth Manifesto of 1834 a change began to be noticeable. It was discovered that election campaigns, as a result of the widening of the franchise, required a larger measure of popular management than hitherto. It was not sufficient to talk to the people through the channels of Parliament. Election addresses of political leaders were seen to be more effective than the official Speeches from the Throne. A few quotations from the Speeches themselves, of the middle of the nineteenth century and later, are sufficient to prove that they were no longer the vehicle by which the Ministry's message was conveyed.

It is true that, in the middle of the century, the disintegration of parties made it difficult for the statement of issues to be clearly expressed. But, even when the two-party system again asserted itself, although the Speeches contained a review of the legislation lately accomplished, the real points of controversy regarding future policy were rarely to be found in the formal announcement of the approaching prorogation or dissolution of Parliament.

The following passage, in the Speech of 1852, admirable though its sentiments are, might well have been omitted for the guidance it gave respecting the circumstances of the election: 'It is my earnest prayer that, in the exercise of the high functions which, according to our free Constitution, will devolve upon the several constituencies, they may be directed by an All-wise Providence to the selection of representatives whose wisdom and patriotism may aid me.'

So completely did the formal Speech cease to be important, that the wording of the Speeches of 1865 and 1880 must have led to the expectation that, as far as that part of the Speech dealing with issues was concerned, a stereotyped and meaningless form would be adopted. In 1865 it was said that

the electors of the United Kingdom will soon be called upon again to choose their representatives in Parliament; and Her Majesty fervently prays that the Blessing of Almighty God may attend their proceedings and may guide them towards the attainment of the object of Her Majesty's constant solicitude—the welfare and happiness of Her people.

And in 1880 this form was repeated, almost word for word.

In the election of 1874 no prospective issues of any kind were raised in the Speech. But some rather oblique reference was included, in the Speech of 1868, to the proposal of the disestablishment of the Irish Church, which was clearly understood to be the issue for decision. Mention was made of the expression of the people's opinion 'on those great questions of public policy which have occupied the attention of Parliament and remain undecided'. And since that date there have occasionally been references in the Speeches to real prospective issues to be raised in ensuing elections. In 1886, for instance, the general election was described in the Speech to have been arranged 'in order to ascertain the sense of my people upon the important proposal to establish a legislative body in Ireland for the management of Irish as distinguished from Imperial affairs'. And in 1923, when some degree of protection was proposed by the Conservatives, the Ministry was stated to be convinced that, 'unless measures for the safeguarding and development of the home market are adopted, no permanent improvement in their situation can be expected'. But, generally speaking, the leaders of the party in power prefer to state the issues of the election elsewhere than in the formal Speech. It has become realized that it is more effective to communicate directly with the country than through the channel of Parliament. Opposition parties nowadays find convenient means of notifying their programmes directly to the people; and Ministries are aware that they will be at a disadvantage unless they adopt equally direct methods.

Peel's action in issuing the Tamworth Manifesto in 1834 was a new departure in two respects. It was novel for the Conservatives to submit to the people questions of future policy, and it was likewise novel to use the leader's address to his constituency as the means by which to publish this submission to the electorate as a whole.

It was not long before the new arrangement superseded the old. Election addresses by leaders were soon treated as the recognized means of stating the party programme to the people. When Peel issued his second Tamworth Manifesto in 1847, the leader of the Protectionists also issued a manifesto-letter to his constituency, which was regarded as the statement of the protectionist policy; and, similarly, a published speech of Lord John Russell was accepted by the Liberals as their programme. Disraeli, in referring to the issues raised by the Liberals in 1865, quoted the Prime

Minister's address to his constituents as that 'which in this country is looked upon as the programme or manifesto of a political party'.[1] This phraseology implies the use of a method which, although established, had only become so within a few years. In the election of 1868 it was fully understood that the party programmes were to be looked for in the election addresses of Gladstone and Disraeli.

When party leaders were members of the House of Lords, it became necessary, owing to the impossibility of their using the election address as a manifesto, to devise some other means by which they could communicate with the people. This did not prove a very difficult matter. Lord Beaconsfield, in 1880, wrote an open letter to the Duke of Marlborough, the Lord-Lieutenant of Ireland, which was widely published and which acted as the alternative to an election address. Similar expedients have subsequently been used.

(c) Gladstone and the direct method

Gladstone was the first frankly to admit the necessity of treating the whole country as one great political platform immediately before a general election, but not without a considerable amount of adverse criticism being directed at him for his demagogic tendencies. Political leaders had stumped the country more than a century before Gladstone. Pelham, in 1734, and the Duke of Newcastle, in 1747, for instance, had travelled round many constituencies, so as to influence the course of general elections. But it is unlikely that they entered at all fully into discussions of political prospects and policies; and it is certain that any pronouncements they made did not obtain a wide publicity.

Before the time of Gladstone, and even during his time, it was considered unusual, and even undignified, for leaders to make election speeches outside their own constituencies. Some earlier Ministers, like Canning, had taken the public into their confidence on aspects of politics and had made speeches to large numbers at times other than election times, fully intending their remarks to reach a wider audience through the instrumentality of the press. This kind of activity had little or no connexion with election campaigns or the decision of election issues.

Gladstone's first use of the direct method of appealing to

---

[1] 183 *Parl. Deb.*, 3 s., 76.

the people seems to have been made in 1857. It was thus described by the Duke of Argyll:

He entered upon one of those campaigns of speaking to the electors with which we all became familiar in later years, and which Disraeli cleverly called 'pilgrimages of passion'. I rather think they were novel in our Parliamentary habits. Prominent men, of course, have always made speeches to their own constituents, or elsewhere; but I rather think that Gladstone initiated the practice of setting out on a campaign of oratory, all over the country, for the purpose of influencing its decision. It struck me as very strange, and on the 5th of April I find myself writing to Aberdeen: 'Gladstone has been making a speech in every town— every village—every cottage—everywhere where he had room to stand, and at Liverpool it was an avowed canvas for [Lord] Derby'.[1]

During the years 1862 to 1866 Gladstone was steadily building up and enlarging his popularity among the people. He visited industrial centres and received addresses from working-men. He toured Lancashire, conducting an agitation in favour of his Reform Bill. But these activities were not directly concerned with an election campaign. It was shortly before the election of 1880 that the charge was laid against him of 'bringing in a system of perpetual canvas, and removing the political centre of gravity from Parliament to the platform'.[2]

The words of Gladstone himself, in one of his concluding speeches in the Midlothian Campaign of 1879, are the best evidence of the speaker's own view of the object he had before him. He said that he wished 'to be enabled, in the face of a patriotic people, to make something like a detailed exposition of a difficult and complicated case . . . to be placed with unusual fulness before the people of the country for their consideration and decision'.[3]

This Midlothian Campaign had been fought when Gladstone was in Opposition. When, however, he had to make his great bid for a majority in favour of Home Rule in 1886, he was Prime Minister. But he did not hesitate to undertake a campaign involving a series of speeches in places outside his constituency. The Queen, who had never approved his 'oratorical crusades', felt it necessary to make a protest. The incident is interesting for the explanation it drew from Glad-

---

[1] *Eighth Duke of Argyll: An Autobiography*, vol. ii, p. 75.
[2] *Selborne's Memorials*, Part II, section 1, p. 470.
[3] *Speeches in Scotland by W. E. Gladstone*, vol. i, p. 211.

stone. He told the Queen that, 'since the death of Lord
Beaconsfield, in fact since 1880, the leaders of the Opposition,
Lord Salisbury and Lord Iddesleigh . . . have established a
rule of what may be called popular agitation, by addressing
public meetings from time to time at places where they were
not connected'. This was the reason, he said, why he had
'deviated from his previous and, he believed, uniform practice'. He felt obliged to use all requisite means in order to
place what he thought to be the true issue before the country.[1]

Gladstone's implied tribute to the scrupulous propriety
of Disraeli in these matters was amply justified. The bio-
graphers of Disraeli point out that, with few, if striking, exceptions, it was only in Parliament or in his constituency
that he made political speeches.

I have never in the course of my life [said Disraeli himself]
obtruded myself upon any meeting of my fellow-countrymen
unless I was locally connected with them, or there were peculiar
circumstances which might vindicate me from the imputation of
thrusting myself unnecessarily on their attention.[2]

The fiction by which an address to the electors of a particular constituency has been in fact understood to be addressed to the electors of the whole country is one which
proved convenient at a stage when the idea of submissions
to the people had not become as fully accepted as it is today.
The more straightforward method of making speeches to
large audiences, intended for publication verbatim in the
daily press, has more lately had a considerable vogue; and
even this method has again been largely superseded by the
publication in the press of official party manifestoes or programmes or by broadcast speeches to every elector desirous
of hearing the issues explained by the party leaders. All these
different methods have been used until very recently, though
it seems that the use of a leader's election address to his constituency as a party manifesto has now been discarded.

(d) Modern manifestoes

It was only a short move from Gladstone's practice of addressing the whole people, under the guise of speeches to his
electors in Midlothian, to the elimination of the local aspect.
An early step towards this elimination was taken, surpris-
ingly enough, by Lord Salisbury in the election of 1892. It

---

[1] J. Morley, *Life of Gladstone*, vol. iii, p. 344.
[2] Monypenny and Buckle, *Life of Disraeli* (new ed.), vol. ii, p. 521.

is true that, being a member of the House of Lords, he had no constituency to address; but he did not consider it necessary to adopt the expedient of Lord Beaconsfield in 1880, to which reference has been made, namely of addressing an open letter to a public figure. Lord Salisbury aroused some comment, in 1892, by addressing a manifesto 'to the electors of the United Kingdom'. As Prime Minister, he defined in this manifesto the issues upon which, in his opinion, the election would turn. After claiming credit for the record of the Conservatives in regard to social questions, he turned to the question of Home Rule for Ireland. The election, he said, was of 'terrible importance' to the Irish. 'On your votes', he told the whole body of the electors, 'will depend whether it will be to them a message of hope or a sentence of servitude and ruin. . . . It is for you to determine whether this rash experiment, this dangerous novelty, shall be tried.'

Some few years passed, however, before the direct method of placing issues before the people became general. In 1918 Lloyd George, jointly with Bonar Law, issued a coalition election manifesto addressed to the whole electorate. This manifesto gave direction to the election campaign. It is only proper to remark that the resumption of the direct address to the electorate was largely to be explained by the non-party character of the appeal. But since 1918 there has been an increasing tendency to eliminate the fiction by which addresses to particular constituencies or speeches to particular audiences were understood to be intended for the whole body of voters. Baldwin was one of the last of the party leaders to retain the use of the election address to his constituency as his means of announcing the programme of his party; but in 1929 he published a *Message to Britain*; and in 1931 he again adopted the more modern method and published in the press an election manifesto, addressed 'to the members of the Conservative and Unionist Party'.

Lately the practice in this matter has been settling down to uniformity. The Leader of the Conservative party, in whom great power has always been concentrated, has been in the habit of publishing the party's election programme in the form of a personal statement of his own, though a party manifesto has also been published. The Labour party has adopted a steady practice of issuing a party manifesto. The manifestoes are now always addressed to the whole of the electorate.

It is, then, no longer considered shocking for a political leader to address a manifesto, outlining his party programme, to the country at large. As far back as Disraeli's time it began to be understood that a clear decision of the people at a general election should be accepted directly by the Ministry of the day, without the necessity of awaiting its confirmation in Parliament. It is only sensible, therefore, that, if the answer is given directly, the question should be put in the same way.

It remains to add that no means of publicity has done more to assist uniformity and clearness in the formulation of issues than that of broadcasting. It is reckoned that at every general election three or four of the most prominent of the election broadcasters are listened to by about half the electorate, perhaps some fifteen million voters. Instead of election issues being stated variously in different parts of the country, as used to be the practice, they are nowadays discussed by the party leaders on one national platform. In a brief broadcast talk a wise speaker confines himself to a few points. Consequently the predominance of the radio over other methods of publicity tends to eliminate the more insignificant issues and to concentrate attention on one or two main ones. These will probably be the issues selected by the Prime Minister or the Leader of the Opposition, which will be put before the electorate in their election broadcasts.

It is natural that the party leaders should select issues which appeal to the personal interests of the voters. The atmosphere in which voters listen to the competing claims is a quiet one, that of the home. There is none of the mass-excitement of the big political meetings of earlier generations. Consequently subjects that affect the family in the home, such as the cost of living, better housing, and national defence, are those which are likely to be raised for the people's decision at general elections. Nowadays party leaders, in planning their election broadcasts, consider it worth while to show special sympathy with family anxieties.

In the last few decades there has been a steadily increasing impact of government activity on the lives of ordinary people. This impact inclines voters to think of politics as that which does something to them or for them. It is not surprising, therefore, that this view of politics should influence the attitude both of politicians and of the electorate in regard to election issues.

(e) Particularity

When measures come before the people at election time, the extent to which they are to decide upon the particular terms in which the legislation is to be enacted is often left uncertain. The course of practice has been irregular; and the opinions expressed on the subject have been diverse.

The concern of the Duke of Wellington at the submission to the people, in 1831, not merely of the general question of Reform, but of the particular terms of a measure of Reform, has already been mentioned.[1] It was observed at the time of the controversy on the great Reform Bill that the electors were requested, 'not to choose legislators, but to be legislators themselves'.[2] Although it was certainly the fact that the cry of 'the bill, the whole bill and nothing but the bill' implied that the people insisted on expressing their opinion in favour of a minimum increase in the franchise as well as on a general principle of Reform, it can hardly have been imagined that the electors were capable of forming a critical judgement on the wording of a complicated piece of legislation, containing eighty-two long clauses, some of which dealt with details of procedure.

Home Rule for Ireland, like Parliamentary reform, aroused feelings of such intense interest that it naturally prompted the question whether the submission to the people was in respect of a general policy or of particular terms. Gladstone, embarrassed by the difficulties of carrying such a measure, opposed the idea of particular submission. In a speech before the first general election at which Home Rule was specifically made an issue, he asked the question: 'What is the true issue? Is it . . . a choice between opposite policies in respect of Ireland . . . or is it a choice . . . upon the particulars of a large and complicated Bill?' He then, having expressed the view that the electors were excellent judges of policy, continued: 'It is a policy . . . upon which you are called to vote. It is not a detail, a particular, or even a Bill.'[3]

Gladstone's Home Rule proposals continued to be a source of alarm to his opponents and of discomfort to his supporters. It did not become easier to find a scheme that was not open to searching criticism in an election contest. In the year following the election of 1892, the Government of Ireland

[1] See pp. 199–200 above.
[2] *Annual Register*, 1831 (Part I), p. 151.
[3] *Speeches of W. E. Gladstone*, vol. ix (1886–8), pp. 133–4.

Bill was before the House of Lords; the Duke of Devonshire (the Lord Hartington of the earlier Home Rule contests) did not abate his strenuous opposition; and he was naturally insistent that no Bill should be passed unless it was submitted, in terms, to the electorate. His speech in the House of Lords on the subject not only maintained the opposite opinion to that of Gladstone in regard to the extent of the submission to the people, but it also distinguished between issues that can be put in the form of a simple question and those that cannot be adequately appreciated unless outlined in the form of legislation.[1]

The controversies which arose in regard to the particularity of the submissions for the people's decision in regard to Reform and in regard to Home Rule lead to the conclusion that, where the question is capable of being put in a simple form allowing of a plain 'Yes' or 'No', the submission of the provisions of a legislative proposal may be unnecessary. But where the acceptability of a proposed legislative measure depends on its scope, then it is proper that some particulars of its intended form shall be submitted to the electorate for approval.

At the time when Conservative members of the House of Lords asserted that it was the duty of the Upper House to ensure that the Finance Bill of 1909 was not passed without the express assent of the people, it was argued by Lord Morley and Lord Courtney of Penwith that legislation of so complex a character was unsuitable for submission at a general election. The former remarked, in the debate on the second reading of the Bill in the House of Lords, that, 'if there is any one matter which cannot be usefully or wisely submitted to a plebiscite, it is a Budget. It is one of those things on which you cannot say, Yes or No.'[2] A motion was, however, carried to the effect 'that this House is not justified in giving assent to this Bill until it has been submitted to the judgment of the country'. And, although the issues before the people in the first election of 1910 proved, as was predicted by Liberal peers in the debate in the House of Lords at the end of 1909, to include other questions besides the Finance Bill, the terms of that Bill were among the submissions to the people on that occasion. No one would, however, suggest that the people were able to exercise more than a superficial judgement on the projects of the Bill. It was obvious that many of its

[1] 17 *Parl. Deb.*, 4 s., 30–1.   [2] 4 *H.L. Deb.*, 5 s., 1143.

technicalities were beyond the easy comprehension of the average elector.

Some remarks have already been made on the difference of opinion between the Liberals and the Conservatives, in 1911, in regard to the particularity of the mandate obtained as a result of the submission at the second general election in 1910 on the question of the relations between the two Houses.[1] Soon after the assembly of the new Parliament, the Liberals maintained that, since the draft of the Parliament Bill had been made public prior to the election, and since they had obtained a majority, the people had decided in favour of the particular terms of the measure. Asquith asserted that 'the Bill, Preamble and Clauses' had been submitted to the people. Balfour, on the contrary, refused to admit that the people 'actually gave the Government a mandate for this particular way of dealing with' the constitutional question. He did not believe that, 'if you cross-examined the odd thousands of electors who returned the Government to power, you would find they could tell you exactly what this Bill is'. (This would make the contention of the Liberals dependent on a very high standard.)

When, however, the Parliament Bill was in the Committee stage in the House of Lords, Haldane no longer relied on a particular mandate in respect of its literal terms. He gave the House a disquisition on the working of the representative system in this country, and claimed that the Ministry had a general mandate to enact a statute carrying out the intentions of the people. He claimed that the electors, as a general rule, took a keen interest in the subject-matter of legislation of constitutional importance and that, when they have considered and approved the principles of a Bill proposed by a Ministry, they have done as much as they can be required to do.

A general approval [he said] is given to the principles of the Bill, and the member representing the constituency is left to work out the details with the other representatives and the Government. The constituencies do not want to be consulted on every point that arises in the discussion in the House of Commons, and never express a wish that their representatives should come back and consult them upon details.[2]

[1] See pp. 229–31 above.
[2] 8 *H.L. Deb.*, 5 s., 678, 762; 24 *H.C. Deb.*, 5 s., 1056, 1111; 25 *H.C. Deb.*, 5 s., 1693; 9 *H.L. Deb.*, 5 s., 214–15.

It is obvious that, if the electors wished to take a hand in the detailed enactment of every statute, the process of legislation would become an impossible one. Even if they wished to concern themselves with the details of a large number of statutes, the representative system would become a farce.

CHAPTER XII

CONCLUSIONS AND TENDENCIES

§ 1. *Arguments for and against the referendum*

THE absence of set rules, defining either the form in which submissions to the people should be made or the subjects which require to be submitted, renders difficult any attempt at discovering precise principles regarding the extent of the people's power to take a part in government. One of the advantages claimed for the referendum is the explicit form in which questions can be put. This is highly arguable. In the operation of the referendum it may happen that questions which at first sight seem clear prove in the light of developing circumstances to be ambiguous. Consequently the answers when given are often far from easy to interpret.

There were frequent debates in Parliament on the comparative merits of the general election and the referendum at the period when the relations of the two Houses were under discussion in 1910 and 1911. On one occasion Balfour remarked: 'Whether the referendum be a good thing or a bad thing, at all events it is a decision of the people on a particular thing, but a general election, be it a good thing or a bad thing, is not the decision of the people on a particular measure.'[1] Curzon made the same point when he argued that 'the class of questions which go to the referendum would be much more easily put in a concise and compact shape, admitting of "aye" or "no", than are all the mixed and complicated issues that go before a general election'.[2]

It is easy to find examples of general elections in which a number of confused questions were placed before the people; but it is extremely difficult to find more than one or two elections in which a single issue or one or two clear issues have been raised. Balfour, at the same time that he made the remark quoted above, observed that, in the course of his long political career, he had no experience of an election in which there were not mixed issues. The only one of which he had heard that had one particular issue overriding all others was

[1] 21 *H.C. Deb.*, 5 s., 1752.　　　　[2] 6 *H.L. Deb.*, 5 s., 945.

the election of 1831. He might, perhaps, have added the election of 1868, where the proposal for the disestablishment of the Irish Church was notably predominant.

The elections at the beginning of the present century, one and all, involved mixed issues. The 'khaki' election of 1900 can hardly be said to have had as its sole issue the question of the prosecution of the South African War.[1] In 1906 the questions of the modification of the Education Act of 1902, of a preferential tariff, and of Chinese Labour all played a considerable part. The first election of 1910 turned primarily on the powers of the House of Lords, especially in relation to the rejection of the Lloyd George Budget; but it also turned on the merits of that Budget and on proposed changes in the fiscal system. It would require a miracle, Balfour said, for a verdict of a general election to decide several questions at once, so that

when the constituents choose Mr. X. rather than Mr. Y., or Mr. Y. rather than Mr. Z., they pronounce specifically and precisely upon a large number of utterly disconnected propositions, supported by arguments having no connection with each other, belonging to different departments of policy, and that, when they vote on all these points for Mr. X. or Mr. Y., they give a final and conclusive answer.

Most of the leaders of the Liberal party and of the Labour party have opposed the introduction of the referendum; and, among their objections, they have protested that it is no more possible to isolate issues under a system of referendum than under the system at present in vogue in this country. In order to substantiate their allegations they have had to point to the experiences of foreign countries where the referendum is in use. Asquith, among others, expressed himself as feeling no doubt but that the referendum would fail to disentangle confused issues.

The referendum [he said] might be nominally and ostensibly on some particular point; and everybody knows that the whole machinery of both parties in the State would be brought to bear on the determination of that issue. You would have the turmoil, the tumult, and a large part of the expense of a general election; and, while I have the highest possible respect for the intelligence and political insight of my fellow-countrymen, I do not believe it would be possible for them, under these conditions, completely to segregate the particular issue on which the referendum

[1] Cf. Lord Salisbury, 8 *H.L. Deb.*, 5 s., 783–4; and see p. 302 below.

took place, and entirely to ignore the whole of the rest of the field of politics.[1]

Ramsay MacDonald was able to state, from study of the working of the referendum in Switzerland, that there was no more definiteness under that system than with a general election. 'Our general elections', he remarked, 'have undoubtedly mixed issues, but the referendum has just as mixed issues, and in some cases even more complicated issues than those found at a general election.'[2] It is certainly true that the Swiss authorities on the subject do not seem to be agreed on the practicability of isolating issues under their system.[3]

Although the people are asked at a referendum to vote for or against a definite proposal, and although there is a fair chance of obtaining a clear answer, experience has shown that electorates find the greatest difficulty in dissociating themselves from allegiances to persons and parties. Even when both sides agree to isolate a particular question, it is found that other questions press themselves on the notice of the voters. In 1929 the Ministry in Australia was willing to accept a proposal of the Opposition that the Arbitration Abolition Bill should be submitted to the people at a general election, and that the submission should be treated in the nature of a referendum. When, however, the election came to be held, the fate of the Bill, although the main issue, proved not to be the sole issue on which votes were cast.

In our own country an unofficial referendum, known as the Peace Ballot, which was organized by the League of Nations Union, secured answers from nearly twelve million voters in 1934-5. Several questions were asked with regard to the operation of League of Nations principles. Although it was unofficial and therefore not a referendum in the normal sense, it illustrated the extreme difficulty of obtaining results that are not misleading. Recent experience has indicated that the referendum is widely regarded in this country as un-English and not likely to be welcomed. Churchill, at the conclusion of his Coalition Ministry in 1945, suggested a referendum to authorize the maintenance of the old Parliament until the end of the war against Japan. The suggestion was strongly opposed by Liberal and Labour ex-Ministers.

[1] 15 *H.C. Deb.*, 5 s., 1174-5.
[2] 21 *H.C. Deb.*, 5 s., 1770.
[3] See Felix Bonjour, *La Démocratie suisse*, translated under the title *Real Democracy in Operation*, and also Simon Deploige, *Referendum in Switzerland*.

Attlee even described the referendum as a tyrannical Nazi expedient.

When the Conference on the Reform of the Second Chamber, presided over by Lord Bryce in 1918, considered the referendum as a means of disposing of controversies between the two Houses, one of the reasons for rejecting it was its supposed unsuitability to the conditions of a large country, like the United Kingdom, for different parts of which peculiar legislation is sometimes required. But this objection applies equally to the submission of issues at general elections. It has frequently happened that different sections of the people, local or functional, have each been interested in one in particular of several issues raised at an election. Each section has voted for or against the proposal with which it was specially concerned. In these circumstances, the sum totals of the votes for the different parties give very little indication regarding a decision on any of the issues.

The election of 1892 has been cited as an example of this state of affairs. The Welsh electors were interested primarily in the question of the disestablishment of the Welsh Church; the London electors in Municipal Reform; the agricultural labourers in parish councils; the town artisans in Employers' Liability; and the miners in the Eight Hours Bill. All these questions were raised by the Liberal Ministry; but it would have been a hopeless task for any one to draw any particular conclusions from the Liberal victory at the polls regarding a decision by the people on a question of policy. No single issue had been put; and it could not be convincingly maintained that the people had approved all the proposals, owing to the variety of interests concerned. Some sort of devolution is the best palliative for this kind of embarrassment to the working of the mandate principle.

The referendum as part of the constitutional machinery has the undoubted advantage of enabling a submission to the people to be made upon occasions when it is most required and is most likely to be significant. Issues can be dealt with as they arise and are not so likely to be fabricated for party purposes. On the other hand, the referendum tends to direct attention to issues of policy to the exclusion of personal issues; and there are some who prefer a system which allows both these classes of issues to be determined by the people. If the referendum were introduced into this country, it is probable that the importance of general elections would be considerably diminished. There would be a tendency for the referendum to be regarded as so much superior to the general election for the purpose of submission of prospective issues that the general election would be confined to the determination of issues of a personal and retrospective character.

Whether the introduction of the referendum would diminish the importance of Parliament and the sense of responsibility of members is a question which has been fully discussed in recent years. On this subject, the opinion of constitutional authorities in countries where the referendum is operative is naturally of interest in regard to the effect on the position of their legislatures. M. Felix Bonjour, formerly President of the Swiss National Council, has expressed the clear opinion that the status of the legislature is rather enhanced than lowered.

> Far from diminishing the importance of parliamentary labours, [he has remarked] the referendum obliges members to prepare laws and decrees with the greatest possible care, and by imposing upon them the duty of justifying their work to the people, it helps to make them public men in the widest sense of the term; it adds to, rather than detracts from, the importance of their function.[1]

Decided views have been expressed in this country on both sides of the question. Lord Curzon, in the debates on the relations between the two Houses in 1910, put the alternatives in this way:

> What does the charge [that the referendum would destroy the sense of responsibility of the members of the House of Commons] mean? I suppose it means that members of Parliament would say 'Never mind what we do, never mind what vote we give. The matter will be settled by the people, and therefore we may be indifferent'. . . . It has had in Switzerland, and I believe it would have here, exactly the opposite effect. I myself believe that it would stimulate the sense of responsibility of individual members of Parliament, because they would feel that they might be called to account by a referendum of the people at no short date afterwards.[2]

Asquith, on the other hand, when criticizing the Conservative proposals for the introduction of the referendum at the time of the conflict between the two Houses in 1911, foretold that the referendum would reduce a general election to a 'sham parade' and would 'degrade the House of Commons to the level of a talking club'.[3]

[1] F. Bonjour, *Real Democracy in Operation* (translation), p. 84.
[2] 6 *H.L. Deb.*, 5 s., 946.   [3] 21 *H.C. Del.*, 5 s., 1751.

One of the reasons why the use of the referendum, for adjusting differences between the two Houses, was discarded by the Conference on the Reform of the Second Chamber in 1918 was that its use, when once introduced, 'could not be confined to the cases for which it was in this instance proposed', and 'that it might tend to lower the authority and dignity of Parliament'. And on various occasions, when the merits of the referendum have been debated in Parliament, it has been asserted that its adoption would imperil the principle of representative government. It is noteworthy, however, that few politicians have had the temerity to assert that the development of the referendal element in submissions to the people at general elections has interfered with the representative character of members of Parliament.

§ 2. *The extent of the mandate*

Various opinions are held regarding the proper limits of submissions to the people. On the one side, it is maintained that there can be no effective decision unless a single issue is raised. According to other opinions, it is possible for several issues to be determined at one election. Others, again, hold that general party programmes can be voted upon, so that authority may be given to proceed on the principles outlined by the party leaders. And there are even those who consider that, when a Ministry obtains a majority, it has a general commision to introduce whatever legislation it may deem requisite.

Shortly after the 'khaki' election of 1900 the Conservatives proceeded to introduce, and Parliament passed, legislation dealing with education and licensing. Many Liberals objected that the Conservatives merely had a mandate to finish the South African War and could not deal with other matters. Balfour took exception to the doctrine propounded by Campbell-Bannerman, to the effect that a Parliament which is elected when one subject is before the constituencies is incapable of dealing with other subjects, especially if they are of outstanding importance.[1] 'I believe', he said, 'that doctrine to be utterly wrong and unconstitutional.' In support of his contention, he cited the election of 1880 and stated

---

[1] Campbell-Bannerman had, as a matter of fact, raised the issue of education in his election address in 1900; see *The Times*, 22 Sept. 1900.

that, although Gladstone obtained his majority, in so far as it was obtained on a positive issue, so as to enable him to deal with the question of the treatment of Christians in the Near East, he did not hesitate to deal with the problems of personal liberty in Ireland, which suddenly presented themselves; and that no one criticized the fact that he dealt with those problems, however much they disapproved of the way he acted.[1] The example selected by Balfour does not appear to be a very cogent one, since the election of 1880 was decided almost entirely on retrospective issues, namely the past administration of the Beaconsfield Ministry. Nevertheless, it is true that it would be an excessively stringent principle for a Ministry to be disqualified from introducing more than one important piece of legislation during its whole period of office.

When the extent of the mandate of the people was being discussed in connexion with the Parliament Bill of 1911, Ramsay MacDonald characterized the notion that there could only be a single mandate at an election as a novel one. He understood that 'the whole underlying assumption of representative government is that you can have a series of mandates given at the same time'. 'If', he said, 'it is going to be "one mandate, one general election", then, of course, there should be no general elections at all, because you can never have only one mandate.'[2]

An intermediate view, which is probably that approved by the largest number of those who have concerned themselves with this question, and which certainly appears to have much to commend it, allows a Ministry to proceed to carry out a party programme outlined at an election and does not disable a Ministry from varying or adding to it, provided that no marked change in party principles is involved and no considerable change of a constitutional character undertaken which was not foreshadowed at the time when the last submission was made to the electorate.

The view that a Ministry which has obtained its majority can introduce whatever measures it pleases, whether included in a programme or not, may be described as that of the old Whig school. It was so claimed by Morley. When speaking on the subject of the Finance Bill in 1909, he, after denouncing the principle of mandate, which was then being

[1] 132 *Parl. Deb.*, 4 s., 1014–15; cf. 141 *Parl. Deb.*, 4 s., 160–2, and 8 *H.L. Deb.*, 5 s., 783–4.   [2] 21 *H.C. Deb.*, 5 s., 1767–8.

vigorously promoted by the Conservatives, reminded the House of Lords that, on his Liberal colleagues objecting, in 1902, that the Conservatives had no mandate to pass the Education Bill, he formally dissociated himself from that objection.[1] And in the debate on the Parliament Bill in 1911 he reiterated his opinions. 'I have never', he said, 'assented to the idea that a Parliament is to be confined to a single great issue.' He went so far as to assert that, 'when a general election returned a Parliament, it entrusted power to Ministers to pass whatever Bills they thought fit'. In order to provide an example of a Ministry carrying through important proposals, which were not mentioned at the time of the election of Parliament, without any objection being made to the principle of so doing, he chose the election of 1868 and Gladstone's Ministry of the following years. This example is a particularly pertinent one, because, to all intents, the sole issue of the election was the proposal for the disestablishment of the Irish Church. Nevertheless, as Morley pointed out, the singleness of the issue did not prevent the Gladstone Ministry introducing measures for the reform of land-tenure in Ireland, for the reform of the Army, and the reform of the Civil Service.

These things [he remarked] were not in the minds of the electors. How could they be? Probably they were not even in the minds of the Ministers at the elections, but the electors did what I believe most electors would do. They returned a First Minister . . . to whom they were determined to give a chance of showing his . . . constructive ability, and they left it in his hands and in the hands of his colleagues. That is in my view the right theory of the result of a general election.[2]

When the indefinite language of many of the party programmes of the Victorian period is recollected, especially that of Disraeli,[3] it would seem that the difference between the opinion that a Ministry can do anything that comes within its programme and the opinion that it can do whatever it likes may be a very fine one. But it would certainly not be fair to allow the vagueness of a programme to justify a wide interpretation of the extent of the authority to undertake legislation.

[1] 4 *H.L. Deb.*, 5 s., 1142.
[2] 8 *H.L. Deb.*, 5 s., 700–1.
[3] See, for example, his election address of 1852, quoted in Monypenny and Buckle, *Life of Disraeli* (new ed.), vol. i, p. 1186.

§ 3. *The degree of authority*

Some supporters of the principle, that a Ministry is not confined to measures which have been specifically raised as issues, have been willing to admit that a general mandate given at an election is more authentic in the earlier years of a Parliament's period than in the later; that a new measure of importance is more easily admitted to be within a general mandate when a Ministry is comparatively fresh from the polls than when a Parliament is approaching the end of its term.

Lord Salisbury's objection to the Bill for introducing the Ballot in 1872, to which reference has already been made,[1] is a typical example of the allegation that a Ministry's commission can be so stale that it ought not to undertake important legislation of a fresh character without express authority from the people. Lord Salisbury asserted that, as the Parliament of 1872 was four years old, the issues on which it was elected were obsolete and that, so far from having authority to legislate in regard to the Ballot, the Ministry had, as a body, been opposed to legislation on this subject at the time it was first formed.

The views regarding the extent of the mandate which were taken by the successful parties in the 1931 election and the 1945 election were in complete contrast, showing either that practice may vary widely according to circumstances or that the constitutional conventions in this matter are still unsettled. In 1931, Ramsay MacDonald asked for and obtained (admittedly in a formidable economic crisis) a 'doctor's mandate' to do whatever was found to be necessary to stabilize the affairs of the nation. In 1945, the Labour party asked for a definite mandate to carry out several specific legislative projects; and it considered itself pledged to accomplish its programme in full. Such an attitude as this can prove injudicious because a heavy legislative programme cannot be transformed into Acts of Parliament in less than, perhaps, three or four years, by which time the political and economic situation may have changed to such an extent that so rigid an adhesion to elaborate election-undertakings might be unwise in the national interest. In the heated discussions, in Parliament and in the country, about the Bill for nationalizing the steel industry towards the end of the Parliament

[1] See p. 216 above.

of 1945–50, the allegation that the Ministry's commission was stale was forcibly expressed by Conservative speakers.

Just as a mandate can be considered to be stale in respect of measures introduced late in the period of a Parliament, so, contrariwise, a mandate can be accepted as fresh and authentic in the early stages of a Parliament. The attribution of a higher degree of authority to a mandate which is recent in date was naturally approved by the Liberals in the difficult situation in which they were placed in 1910. Their important legislative proposals had been rejected by the House of Lords; and some means had to be found of avoiding future dead-locks. The Liberals, therefore, proposed to include in the terms of the Parliament Bill a provision that, broadly speaking, any measure passed by the House of Commons within two years of an election should become law, even though rejected by the House of Lords. Asquith told the House of Commons that

there is a strong, nay, almost irresistible presumption that a measure passed by a majority of the House of Commons still fresh, or relatively fresh, from the polls is a measure which is approved in its main principles by the majority of the people, and which, therefore, in accordance with the principle of democratic govern-ment, ought to be allowed to pass into law.[1]

The Conservatives were able to point with some effect to the change in the Liberal attitude from that adopted by them in 1902 to that adopted in 1911. They reminded the Liberals, in the course of the debates on the Parliament Bill, that the Conservative Education Act of 1902, for which the Liberals had alleged there was no mandate, was passed within two years of the general election of 1900. If the Liberals had then held their opinions regarding the efficacy of mandates of recent date, they would not have been able to look askance at the Conservatives for exceeding their authority.

The Bryce Report on the Reform of the Second Chamber (1918) assumed that one of the chief functions of the House of Lords was to enable the opinion of the people to be taken on subjects considered to be of fundamental importance which had not been previously submitted to them.[2] This report was made after the date when the ability of the House of Lords to veto legislation passed by the House of Commons had been modified by the Parliament Act 1911. This modified power was severely curtailed by the Parliament Act 1949,

[1] 15 *H.C. Deb.*, 5 s., 1179.   [2] See p. 231 above.

with the result that the House of Lords has to all intents and purposes been deprived of all functions except that of making suggestions about the form of legislation and of educating the nation by means of its learned debates.

It should be recognized that the Parliament Act 1949 cannot be regarded as altogether of democratic tendency if the House of Lords was properly considered to be a guardian of the determinant capacity of the electorate. The virtual elimination of the delaying power of the House of Lords has the practical effect of enlarging the powers of the Ministry and reducing the opportunities of the electorate to express its views on fundamental issues which have not come before it at general elections.

§ 4. *Illogicalities*

Many important questions of policy are settled without any complaint being raised that the people have not been consulted. How is it, then, that in respect of some measures a mandate is expected, and in respect of others of equal or greater intrinsic importance it is not?

Some consideration has been given in this country to the desirability of defining the classes of measures which require the express mandate of the people before being introduced. Proposals for altering the position of and succession to the Crown were selected, during the debates on the Parliament Bill of 1911, as those which should be included. Steps have been taken in foreign countries to specify in formal Constitutions the matters requiring submission by referendum. Many of these Constitutions have made provisions forbidding any amendment to their terms without a plebiscite.

Measures of importance have frequently been undertaken in this country without any previous reference to the people, where, for example, the safety of the State would have been endangered by publicity or by delay or where the subject was one of too great complexity or technicality to be appreciated by the ordinary voter.

Foreign policy is generally beyond the scope of and unsuitable to popular decision. On more than one occasion Gladstone withstood the pressure even of members of Parliament to be kept conversant with treaty negotiations, on the ground that the ultimate interests of the nation might be prejudiced by disclosure. Lansdowne's important steps in foreign policy between 1902 and 1904, especially in regard to Anglo-Japanese and Anglo-French relations, were taken entirely on the responsibility of the Ministry. England entered World War I without more than an assumption that public opinion was in favour of that course; it was certainly impossible to wait for a formal reference. The peace terms of 1919 were as important to the nation as the entry into the war; but the questions for decision were far too abstruse for the comprehension of the people, as also were undertakings like those comprised in the Treaty of Locarno. (In World War II it was obvious that the people were solidly behind the Government's declaration of war, so that the Ministry could have felt exempt from any anxiety on that score.)

The period following World War I showed quite a remarkable intensification of public interest in foreign politics, and in the policy of the League of Nations in particular. Millions of people had lost relatives in the war or had suffered from it in other ways; and most of these were intent on supporting any plan which might avoid a repetition of widespread slaughter and misery. By 1935 the degree of popular attention to this subject was so considerable that the main issue of the general election of that year was the maintenance of the Covenant of the League of Nations and the doctrine of collective security. The reference to the electorate on this subject was not a success from two points of view. First, the League of Nations, so excellent in theory, was apt to fail in practice chiefly because some member-States did not stand by their undertakings. Secondly, the Baldwin Ministry (and later the Chamberlain Ministry) violated the principles of the League in regard to Italy's aggressive action against Abyssinia, thus rendering the reference to the electorate futile.

Political parties in this country have generally succeeded in maintaining a fair measure of agreement on the subject of foreign policy; and, as a result, it is not often a matter of contention at general elections. In 1945, at a time when foreign politics were of critical importance, the views of the parties on the subject as expressed at the general election were remarkably similar, differing only in emphasis, with both parties strongly supporting the United Nations principles. Many people consider (and surely it cannot be seriously controverted) that every effort should be made to keep foreign politics clear of party strife so that continuity of policy may be facilitated, and consequently the country's diplomacy made more effective.

As regards matters of internal and constitutional interest, radical alterations in the law relating to rating, local government, and poor law have been made without any specific authority from the people, and without any protests respecting the absence of that authority. It is obvious that legislation involving technicalities of administration is inappropriate for framing as an election issue. No circumstances can more easily involve highly technical questions than national economic crises. Even professional economists are perplexed and baffled by them. Consequently it is not surprising that the crucial decisions to abandon the gold standard in 1931 and to devalue the pound in 1949 were made without consulting the electorate. In any case urgency would probably have prevented such consultation. Subjects like these are essentially of a kind upon which the people can give only a retrospective opinion, if any at all.

The Representation of the People Act, 1918, which enacted a larger increase in the franchise than any previously made in England, produced so vast a change in the Constitution that it is difficult to imagine one that could be more vast, unless of a revolutionary character. It may be supposed that no reference was made to the people respecting this matter, because the answer was regarded as being so much a foregone conclusion that it would have been altogether absurd to have put the question.[1] In the earlier instances of extending the franchise, there may have been some doubt concerning the opinions of the electorate. Ministries of the middle of the nineteenth century certainly acted as if this was so. But, nowadays, it seems to be assumed that any offer of supposed benefits or advantages will be snapped at by the voters, who are imagined to be eager to accept all bounties that may be offered to them regardless of their ultimate value.

While the absence of any popular control over the introduction of large classes of legislative and other measures may require explanation, it must be borne in mind that public opinion has a close bearing on the shaping of a considerable proportion of the legislative output. A few remarks on this subject have been made in Chapter III of this book, where

[1] Cf. pp. 3–4 above.

notice has also been given to the steps which are taken nowadays to ensure that the views of interested persons and bodies are obtained and considered, both in respect of Acts of Parliament and also of the rules and regulations made by Government Departments in pursuance of powers conferred on them by statute. As regards the future, there seems to be no reason why means cannot be devised, in suitable instances, for the fuller consideration of legislative proposals at general elections through the official publication of impartial summaries.

§ 5. *Accurate representation or effective decision*

The arrangement by which the results of voting at a general election are interpreted as a decision by the people on questions of policy or, at the least, on the choice of a Ministry, depends to a very large degree on a combination of a straightforward working of the two-party system with single-member constituencies. If one of the two parties obtains a clear majority, there is a possibility of definite decisions by the people being inferred. It is obvious that, under this kind of arrangement, there cannot be an accurate representation of every shade of political opinion. The representation is rough and ready, and the majority for one side or the other is apt to be exaggerated.[1] On the other hand, under a system of groups rather than parties, or a system like that of proportional representation, which is necessarily accompanied by a number of parties representing many shades of political opinion, voters can in all probability select candidates who reflect their own particular views; but that is the limit of their capacity.

It is a question which of the advantages is preferable. A general election may produce a Parliament that accurately mirrors the various shades of opinion prevalent among the electorate. Such an election will not provide any intelligible answer regarding matters of policy or even settle the choice between two alternative Ministries. Contrariwise, a general election that provides some opportunity of inferring decisions by the people as a whole will only produce a Parliament that reflects the opinions of the electorate broadly and approximately.

[1] It is not always realized that an exaggerated majority, due to the use of single-member constituencies, may often prove an aid to stable government, and that it can fairly be regarded as an advantage rather than an anomaly.

The French political system, in which there are many groups, and no very large parties, produces accurate representation (or may be capable of doing so) at the expense of effective decision by the electors. The people may choose between the programmes of different groups; but none of these programmes can be carried out in its entirety. The strongest group is always in a minority; and every Ministry is a coalition Ministry. The result of the voting can involve no more than the adoption of general principles. It cannot lead to the undertaking of a complete party policy.

Even in this country, where the party system, and not the group system, prevails, the result of a general election becomes ambiguous or, at the best, merely negative on the advent of a third party. In spite of there being a predominant issue in an election, it may well prove that a Ministry which takes office without a clear majority over the other two parties is unable to claim a mandate to pursue a particular policy. In the election of 1929, for instance, when 280 Labour, 260 Conservative, and 57 Liberal members were returned, it was not possible to draw any positive conclusions from the voting; and even the negative conclusions were not very evident.

Among the considerable discussions which have been devoted to the characteristics and possibilities of proportional representation and the alternative vote, some attention has been paid to the effect which these systems might have on the people's capacity to make decisions at general elections. A short reference was made to this aspect in the Report of the Royal Commission on Electoral Systems of 1910, in the following terms:

On the question whether the representation of all parties in proportion to their voting strength is in itself desirable, we may point out that it is not a fair argument against the present system that it fails to produce such a result, because it does not profess to do so. A general election is in fact considered by a large portion of the electorate of this country as practically a referendum on the question which of two Governments shall be returned to power. The view may be right or wrong, but it has to be taken account of in any discussion which turns on the composition of the House of Commons.[1]

Systems like that of proportional representation succeed in enabling voters to pick out from a list of candidates one

[1] Cd. 5163 of 1910, para. 126.

who accurately represents their particular shade of political opinion; and they have other advantages as well. But these systems inevitably diminish the influence of the people as a whole on the policy and choice of Governments. The numerous parties or groups which are the usual accompaniment of proportional representation are certain frequently to reassort themselves. New alliances involve new Ministries; and large changes in the composition of Ministries often follow one another without any general election and without the people having any opportunity to indicate the Ministry of their choice or the policy or programme which they prefer.[1]

If it were part of the object of this book to forecast the future, the opinion might be hazarded that there would be a greater likelihood of the introduction of the referendum, if proportional representation or the alternative vote were adopted, than there is under the present arrangements, for there would be a strong current of opinion in favour of the people retaining at least as large a capacity of directly influencing the course of government as they have at present; and they would undoubtedly tend to be worse off in this respect, if proportional representation or the alternative vote were introduced unaccompanied by the referendum.

§ 6. *The capacity of the people*

Some of the remarks made in the preceding sections of this chapter naturally provoke the question—are the people capable of understanding and dealing with more than the simplest problems of government? Nearly three hundred years ago, James Harrington included among his political aphorisms one to the effect that the people cannot see, but can feel. This estimate was accepted by Prince Albert, when he said, following closely Harrington's phraseology, that 'the masses on which popular government rests only feel and do not think'. This remark was perhaps an ill-advised one for a person in Prince Albert's position to make at a time when democracy was beginning to make considerable strides. But a similar distrust of the political capacity of the people has been expressed by distinguished thinkers of as diverse types

[1] In the recurrent controversies in France on the comparative merits of *scrutin d'arrondissement* and *scrutin de liste* the arguments for the former have been comparable with those in support of the present system in this country; and the arguments for the latter correspond to some extent with those in favour of proportional representation.

as Carlyle and J. S. Mill, both of them, nevertheless, having a real sympathy for popular aspirations.

Before the middle of the eighteenth century Montesquieu, in his *Esprit des Lois*,[1] drew a distinction between the ability of the people to judge of past facts and the comparative merits of rulers, on the one hand, and of questions of policy, on the other.

The people [he said] are extremely well qualified for choosing those whom they are to entrust with part of their authority. . . . But are they capable of conducting an intricate affair, of seizing and improving the opportunity and critical moment of action? No; this surpasses their abilities.

And Burke, whose general opinion of the political capacity of the people is well known, followed Montesquieu, in this as in some other respects, by drawing the same distinction. Burke admitted that the English people were capable, not only of judging public men, but also of judging 'whether the main drift of their councils, for any series of years, was wise or foolish, and whether things went well or ill in their hands'.[2] But his speeches and writings yield many instances of his poor opinion of the people in the sphere of constructive politics.

A recent estimate of Dr. A. F. Pollard is strikingly consonant with those of Montesquieu and Burke; and it certainly cannot be said that he adopts a narrow or prejudiced view of the ultimate possibilities of the people's part in government, since he holds that 'the increase of popular education automatically widens the legitimate sphere of popular judgment', and he sees no reason why, when the people are able to understand the conditions of foreign policy, they should not claim its control—a stage the arrival of which seems to be very remote. In spite, however, of these evidences of goodwill towards the extension of democracy, Dr. Pollard's general conclusion on the present capacity of the people is markedly restrained. After observing that 'it is only the crudest of doctrinaires who think that the people can govern themselves in the sense of administering their own complicated affairs', he concludes that

the best the public can do is to judge of the work that is done in its service without attempting to do the work of its servants. It is

[1] Book 2, chapter 2.
[2] *To a Member of the Bell Club at Bristol*, 31 Oct. 1779.

not a bad judge of the effects of legislation and government because it is the public which feels them; and, as Washington said, the people must feel before they can see. They are not, however, good judges of legislative proposals, because to foresee effects requires a natural imagination combined with expert political intelligence.[1]

One of the disabilities sometimes attributed to the people is that of being short-sighted; they are apt to concentrate their attention on the advantages of immediate benefits without weighing the future risks. This imputation has been put in its extreme form by Sidney Smith, who remarked: 'The people are the best judges of their immediate gratifications and the worst judges of what would best conduce to their interests for a series of years.' Similar sentiments were very generally expressed about the time of the debates on the great Reform Bill, especially by Peel, who frequently argued that the precipitate demands of the people should not necessarily be satisfied, and that the people themselves would be the first to blame an ill-considered compliance with their importunity.

As has been noticed in the preceding chapter, it is perfectly true that the people do not and, indeed, cannot themselves produce constructive proposals. These come either from the party leaders or from individuals or associations, who are in a position to bring them into prominence. But the inability of the people to make proposals does not involve their inability to judge of the merits of proposals; and it is undoubtedly arguable that the people are able to form a sound opinion on some of the simpler questions of future policy.

A rash remark by Gladstone, to the effect that the people are 'excellent judges of policy',[2] has already been quoted— a sweeping assertion which few would endorse. But more sober opinions of a liberal trend encourage the hope that there is a sphere, though a limited one, in which the people are capable of judging of the advisability of proposed legislation.

The effectiveness of the people's decisions on simple questions should not be imperilled by attempts to thrust upon them the function of dealing with proposals of future policy, the results of which are beyond their capacity to estimate. At the same time, a strict exclusion of the people from all

---

[1] A. F. Pollard, *The Evolution of Parliament*, 2nd ed., pp. 346–9.
[2] See p. 293 above.

decisions in regard to future policy would make their position approximate to that prescribed by those Chinese constitutionalists who used sardonically to allow the people to share in what was already accomplished, but did not admit them to consultation in any new proposals. It may well be that the system adopted in this country, which includes a principle of mandate of an elastic character, will prove, if wisely developed, to be superior both to the rigid systems under which the referendum may involve the people in detailed questions of legislative policy and to those under which the people are strictly confined to restrospective judgements.

§ 7. *The future*

The principle of the people's mandate has been recognized as operative by statesmen and by constitutional experts for the best part of a century. Its operation was at first tentative and experimental. Now, after many years of trial, it is still indeterminate and its scope controvertible. But there is no reason why it should not settle into a rational and beneficial procedure, provided the two-party system is effective, and provided it is conscientiously and sensibly managed. Unfortunately the people's mandate has often enough been treated by statesmen as something to be conceded with as good grace as possible, being regarded by them as an embarrassing accompaniment of our modern democracy. But, if conceded, they are apt to try to turn it to party advantage. Consequently, election issues have from time to time been disingenuously selected for their value in attracting votes, or avoided because their prominence might involve loss of office. The unsystematic manner in which issues are authenticated is one of the chief defects in the system. Issues are bandied about in irresponsible fashion during election campaigns. (Halfway through a recent campaign the Prime Minister expressed himself as uncertain what was the predominant issue.) It therefore happens that both the identity and the validity of issues are frequently subjects of debate in the periods following general elections.

It should surely be possible for party leaders to agree prior to a general election what are the issues to be put to the electorate, and furthermore to agree to the form in which the issues should be published to the people. If this procedure were adopted, the unproductive arguments which have hitherto accompanied attempts to interpret popular mandates could be largely avoided.

If the people's mandate is not organized so as to provide the people with a genuine opportunity to express their views on the broad outlines of policy, democracy will suffer a serious set-back. An electorate like ours, growing rapidly in ability to understand political factors, must not be allowed to discover that their alleged influence on politics is ineffective because it is too frequently disclosed as indefinite and disputable. Democracy is too frail a system to survive such a shock. The present makeshift means of enabling the people to have some influence on affairs of State might, even though left unreformed, continue haltingly for a period. But eventually the people's growing disillusionment would probably result in their insufficient co-operation with their rulers. Politicians often say that the people must be made partners in government if there is to be maximum efficiency, welfare, and happiness. But we have not yet gone very far towards achieving this ideal. We must confront the facts. If we should allow the people's part in government to lapse into futility, we might lose democracy beyond recall.

APPENDIX I

'The people'

I⟶T has been remarked, with great authority, that 'the "people" is so indeterminate an expression that its use, let alone its abuse, obscures almost all political discussions'.[1] An even more absolute indictment is that of Disraeli, who once said that, as a political expression, 'the people' is 'sheer nonsense'. He regarded it as belonging rather to the realm of natural history than to that of politics.[2] It was, however, only a few years after making these observations that Disraeli introduced a Bill into the House of Commons 'to amend the representation of the people', without perhaps considering whether the term 'people' in the title of the Bill referred to the electorate or the whole population.

The ambiguities of the present day are fewer than they were before democracy had become a generally accepted principle. Now that the qualification for the franchise is practically that of being an adult, many embarrassments in the use of the expression are removed. Nevertheless the mention of one or two incidents illustrative of earlier ambiguities will help to point the contrast between the past and the present.

Discrimination between the whole population of a State and what used to be known as the commonalty, populace, or masses had its counterpart in the terminology of many centuries ago. The Romans drew a distinction between the class which comprised the whole of the citizens and the class which comprised the citizens without the patricians; and separate words were adopted to describe these two classes. Equivalent expressions have recurred in European countries during medieval times. The result of these early complexities was that, when the introduction of democratic government raised problems requiring the use of accurate terms, the significance of 'the people' was found to be uncertain.

Only a little more than a hundred years ago, Canning protested against members of Parliament speaking of 'the people' in contradistinction to the whole of the citizens. He regarded the people as incomplete without the aristocracy and gentry. Nowadays this protest would hardly be necessary, since the aristocracy and gentry are so diminished as a political force that it is extremely unlikely that it would occur to anyone to exclude them. The decrease in the old class distinction has, in fact, largely helped to dissipate opportunities for confusion in meaning.

[1] A. F. Pollard, *Evolution of Parliament*, 2nd ed., p. 343.
[2] *The Spirit of Whiggism* (1836); cf. a speech by him in 1866 in which he characterized 'the people' as 'a mere indiscriminate multitude' (183 *Parl. Deb.*, 3 s., 103); and see his articles in the *Morning Post* for 26 Aug. and 2 Sept. 1835.

Before democratic government had become firmly established,
politicians of various shades of opinion used the expression 'the
people' to describe the class which they wished to be regarded as
dominant. The expression was applied to some large portion of
the nation which was not sovereign in fact, but to which, in the
opinion of the user, sovereignty ought to be transferred or secured.[1]
At the beginning of the eighteenth century, for instance, Swift
and Defoe both contended that political rights should be confined
to freeholders. Swift asserted that 'law in a free country is, or
ought to be, the determination of those who have property in
land'; and Defoe, in speaking of the 'right of the People', thus
qualified his remarks: 'I would be understood of the freeholders,
for all the other inhabitants live upon sufferance, . . . and have no
title to their living in England, other than as servants.'

Henry Fox, in the middle of the eighteenth century, is reported
as having observed in the House of Commons that, 'when we talk
of people with regard to elections, we ought to think only of those
of the better sort'. The report is not unimpeachable; but, if Fox
did not use these precise words, it is undeniable that they may be
taken as a characteristic exposition of the views of his kind.[2]

Towards the end of his career, Burke indulged in a mathematical
estimate of that section of the inhabitants which was capable of
dealing intelligently with political questions. This body he regarded as truly entitled to the description of 'the people'. 'I have
often endeavoured', he said, 'to compute and to class those who,
in any political view, are to be called the people. . . . In England
and Scotland, I compute that those of adult age, not declining in
life, of tolerable leisure for such discussions, and of some means of
information, more or less, and who are above menial dependence
(or what virtually is such) may amount to about four hundred
thousand.'[3] The chief point of interest in this passage is not,
perhaps, in the figure estimated by Burke, but rather in the
acceptance of the qualification of intelligence as that which entitled citizens to play a part in politics.

It became more apparent in the early nineteenth century that
the claim to political predominance could no longer be put forward on behalf of landowners or of aristocrats in the narrow sense
of that expression. It was advanced on behalf of the more instructed, or, as Canning described them, 'that sound and sober
majority of the nation—that bulk and body of the community
which are truly and legitimately the people'. Brougham, in the
earlier part of his career, was impressed by 'the necessity in the
present times of looking more than formerly may have been essential to the body of the people out of doors, meaning by people

[1] John Austin, A Plea for the Constitution, p. 10 n.
[2] 12 Parl. Hist. 463.
[3] First Letter on Regicide Peace.

the well-informed and weighty parts of the community'.[1] Later
in his career, when speaking in support of the great Reform Bill
in 1831, his interpretation was a little different. When discussing
the attitude of the people towards the Bill, he said: 'I do not mean
the populace—the mob: I have never bowed to them, though I
never have testified any unbecoming contempt of them. . . . But,
if there is a mob, there is the people also. I speak now of the middle
classes—of those hundreds of thousands of respectable persons—
the most numerous, and by far the most wealthy of the community.'[2]

At the time of the first Reform Bill, the expression 'the people'
was generally used to describe what were then known as the
lower classes, as well as the middle classes; but, as a result of the
enlargement of the franchise effected by recent statutes, it is
impossible for there to be more than two opinions at the present
day regarding the meaning to be given to the expression. Either
it means all the inhabitants, or it means the electorate. The latter
is the meaning adopted by the *New English Dictionary*, where,
under the sub-head 'politics', 'the people' is defined as 'the whole
body of enfranchised or qualified citizens, considered as the
source of power; especially in a democratic State, the electorate'.
If this definition is accepted, some other term will be required to
designate the inhabitants as a whole, regarded as a class having
political rights, even though these rights be passive rather than
active.

The distinction between these two meanings was emphasized
in a peculiar way by Siéyès at the beginning of the French Revolution in 1789. He was the first person to draw attention in explicit
terms to a division into active and passive citizens. The former
he described as having political rights, the latter as having merely
natural rights. 'All the inhabitants of a country', he said, 'should
enjoy therein the rights of a passive citizen; all have a right to the
protection of their persons, their property, their liberty and so on;
but all have not the right to take part in the formation of public
authority; all are not active citizens.'[3]

[1] Cf. A. Aspinall, *Lord Brougham and the Whig Party*, p. 82.
[2] 8 *Parl. Deb.*, 3 s., 251. Peel, voicing the Conservative interpretation of
'the people', denied that the expression, as used in the Bill, corresponded with
the earlier meaning, namely 'the great corporate bodies, and those great classes
of the community to whom the franchise was intrusted' (5 *Parl. Deb.*, 3 s.,
114–15). On another occasion in 1831 Peel criticized his opponents for talking
of the people as if they were to be numbered by heads and for forgetting the
influence of wealth and education (3 *Parl. Deb.*, 3 s., 1774).
[3] Aulard, *French Revolution* (translation), vol. i, p. 181. Although Siéyès drew
fresh attention to the distinction between the two kinds of rights, their existence
had given rise to discussion in England many years earlier. See, for instance,
passages in the preface of the famous tract *Jura Populi Anglicani* (1701) and
The Craftsman, 6 July 1734.

At the present day the preponderance, among adults, of active over passive citizens in this country is large. The existence of the latter class does not raise any important problems. It is no longer necessary, as it was two hundred years ago, for liberal-minded persons to make protests on behalf of large sections of the inhabitants, who have no direct representation and no efficient means of making their views known on public matters or of seeking redress in respect of general grievances. But the one remaining ambiguity in the use of the expression 'the people' is sometimes liable to cause inconvenience. Bryce, in his monumental work on *Modern Democracies*, asked: 'Does it [the term "people"] in any given country cover, or ought it to cover, the whole population or only those who are legally citizens, i.e. entitled to share in the government by expressing their mind and will on public questions?'[1] And he did not seem to supply an answer to that question.

One way of evading the difficulty would be to use the term 'electorate', clumsy though it is, to designate the enfranchised and to use the term 'people' to refer to the whole population. Speeches of statesmen and even writings of political scientists frequently contain references to 'the nation', 'the community', 'the public', and 'the country', as alternatives to the terms already mentioned. But one expression is often as good as another; and it is only occasionally that exact terminology is requisite.

[1] Vol. i, p. 162.

APPENDIX II

Instructions to Members of 1660

Seasonable and Healing Instructions humbly tendered to the Free-holders, Citizens and Burgesses, of the respective Counties, Cities and Boroughs of England and Wales, to be seriously recommended by them, to their respective Knights, Citizens and Burgesses, elected and to be elected for the next Parliament. [British Museum, 669 f. 24 (34); Bodleian Library, 13 θ 79 (71)—probably printed in March 1660.]

WE the Freeholders, Citizens, Burgesses, Commons and Freemen of the respective Counties, Cities, and Boroughs of England and Wales, taking into our serious Considerations the many late various Forms and Revolutions of our publick Government, with the miserable Distractions and Oppressions of our ruinated Churches and Realms since the violent changes of our antient established Kingly Government, and Constitution of Parliaments, consisting of King, Lords and Commons, by whose united Counsels and Interests we were happily secured against all treacherous Plots and Conspiracies of forein Enemies and pernicious Domestick Vipers, and advanced to the highest degree of worldly Peace, Prosperity and Felicity. And finding by above eleven years sad Experience, that there is neither Hope nor Probability of restoring our 3. shipwrack'd Nations to their Pristine Tranquillity, Unity, Wealth, Honour, Traffick, Security, but by a speedy Restitution of our antient Form of Parliaments, and publick Regal Government; and with all observing, that in the Writs of Summons now issued for a Parliament to be held at Westminster, on the 25th day of April next, there is no known single Chief Governor, nor yet any real Commissioners nominated, but only Fictitious Utopian Keepers of the Liberties of England, with whom the Members appearing in Parliament can neither conferr nor consult, concerning the difficult and urgent Affairs either of the Realm or Church of England; And that all the Lords and Great Men of the Realm (the antientest hereditary Members of Parliament, the Grand Councellors of the Kingdom, and Chiefest Assertors of our Liberties in all precedent times) are totally omitted out of these new forms of Writs, and all Clauses in them, contrary to all former Presidents without whose concurrent Advice and Assistance with the Commons House in this approaching Parliament, no firm Peace or Settlement can

Y

APPENDIX II

probably be expected, a full and free English Parliament, (from which no legal Members, much lesse the whole English Peerage and Nobility ought to be excluded) being the principal thing the generality of this Nation lately petitioned and declared for, as the only Instrument under God to compose all Differences and dissenting Parties, and put a happy period to our manifold long-lasting Distractions and Confusions: Have thereupon apprehended it our bounden Duty, seriously to recommend these ensuing INSTRUCTIONS to our respective Knights, Citizens, and Burgesses elected, and to be elected and returned by us for our Representatives and Trustees in this approaching Parliament, who receiving full and sufficient Power for themselves, and their respective commonalties of the said Counties, Cities and Boroughs from the said commonalties alone who elect them, to do and consent to all such things as shall be ordained by the Common Council of the Realm in the said Parliament, in their Rights and Behalfs, are thereby obliged in point of Duty and Conscience as their publick servants and Proxies, vigorously to pursue all such just Prescriptions for the Common Welfare and Establishment of our Native Country, as they shall present unto them.

We therefore earnestly desire and require them in pursuance of the Trust reposed by us in them, to improve their uttermost Endeavours and Counsels (there being no particulars prescribed to them in the Writs themselves, as heretofore) to effect these few Individuels.

1. To restore the antient Constitution, Rights, Privileges and Freedom of our English Parliaments, their respective Houses and Members, and to preserve them for all future Mutulations and Violations by armed Force or otherwise, that so they may by free uninterrupted and combined counsels proceed to the speedy settlement of our distracted Churches and Nations, without any Diversions or Obstructions by Souldiers or popular Tumults.

2. To re-establish the antient Fundamental Regal Government of this Kingdom, and the Dominions thereunto belonging (under which we and our Ancestors in former Ages have flourished in great Peace and Prosperity) according to our known Laws, Oaths, Protestations, Covenants, and multiplyed Declarations, and secure it against all future Underminings and Powder-plots of Jesuitical and Fanatick Conspirators.

3. To revive and ratifie the miserably subverted and violated great Charters, Fundamental Laws and Statutes of the Land, made for the preservation of the Persons, Lives, Liberties, Freeholds, Estates, and Properties of all English Freemen, against all Arbitrary and Tyrannycal Judicatures, High Courts of Justice, Proceedings, Tryals, Executions, Judgements, Banishments, Imprisonments, Confinements, Confiscations, Forfeitures, Attainders, Outlawries, Sequestrations, illegal Taxes, Impositions, Excises,

and public Charges whatsoever, not granted by the Common consent in Parliament, and to prevent all future subversions, Contempts and Violations of them, after so vast expences of Treasure and Bloud for their just defence.

4. To establish an able, learned, Orthodox Ministry, and just and righteous Magistracy throughout our Dominions, and to take special care that the Gospel of Christ may be duly and sincerely preached, propagated, the Sacraments and publike justice freely and rightly administered in all places, without neglect or obstruction, to the consolation, protection of all good Christians, and well doers, and the terror and suppression of all Malefactors.

5. To advance all sorts of Trade, Merchandize, and Navigation, by diminishing all excessive Customs, Excises, Imposts at home, by making Peace and holding good correspondence with all forein Kings and Nations abroad, and using all other good means conducing thereto.

6. To redresse all publick Grievances, Oppressions, Frauds, Misdemeanours; to retrench and regulate all exorbitant Taxes, Excises, Imposts, Fees, Extortions, Salaries, superfluous Forces, Garrisons, Officers (civil or military) by Land and Sea, for the peoples ease.

7. To procure a speedy, honourable, safe, Christian Treaty and accord with our long Exiled Protestant King, and Royal posterity, upon moderate, just, righteous terms and Propositions on either side, whereby the bleeding Protestant cause and Religion (much endangered in all places) may be promoted and secured, the Plots and Popish Enemies to extirpate them prevented; the Peace, Government, Laws and Liberties of our Kingdoms, restored, preserved, and perpetuated to posterity; and just publick Debts of the Nation and Souldiers arrears discharged; a general Act of Indempnity, Pardon and Oblivion of all sorts of persons justly capable thereof, procured; all former Inquiries, Feuds, Animosities totally extinguished, and all just sales of duly confiscated Estates, made without Fraud, Covin, Practice of Duresse for valuable considerations, confirmed or recompenced; that so all parties and interests being perfectly reconciled, may henceforth studiously endeavour to keep the unity of the Spirit in the bond of Peace, and to live peaceable and quiet Lives under their lawfull Kings and Governors in all Godlinesse and Honesty being all Members of one and the same Mystical and politick Body, having all one Spiritual and Temporal Lord, one Faith, one Baptism, and one God, and Father; which should both perswade and oblige them to put away all bitternesse, wrath, anger, clamour, evil speaking, with all malice, and to be kind to one another, tenderhearted, forgiving one another, even as God for Christ's sake hath forgiven them, forbearing one another in love. But if we still proceed to bite and devour one another (as we have done for

many years by-past) we shall sodenly be consumed one of another, and made a prey to our common Enemies; which the accomplishment of these instructions by Gods blessing, and the Parliaments wisedom, will prevent, and make us once more THE GLORY AND LADY OF ALL CHRISTIAN KINGDOMS as we are now their reproach.

FINIS

APPENDIX III

Instructions for Members of the Parliament summoned for 21st March, 1681, believed to have been prepared by the Earl of Shaftesbury.

Gentlemen,

We have chosen you two, our knights, to represent this county at the Parliament to be holden at Oxford the twenty-first of March next; and we do give you sufficient power to act on our behalf in all things that shall be found, by joint advice with the Members of Parliament chosen for other places, to be for our public good and welfare; which we must leave to your integrities and prudence. Only there are some particulars so manifestly and indisputably necessary, that we cannot omit to give you our instructions and directions beforehand in them.

First. We all expect that you should, to the last, insist for a bill to exclude the Duke of York by name, and all other Popish successors, from coming to the imperial crown of this realm.

Secondly. That you insist upon an adjustment to be made betwixt the King's prerogative of calling, proroguing, and dissolving Parliaments, and the rights of the people to have annual Parliaments to despatch and provide for those important affairs and business that can nowhere else be taken care of; for, without the certainty of Parliaments meeting in due distance of time from each other, and their sitting so long as shall be necessary for the despatch of the affairs of the nation, it is not possible but that our laws, liberties, lives and estates should become in a short time at the will of the prince.

Thirdly. We expect you should restore to us that liberty we and our forefathers have enjoyed, until these last forty years, of being free from guards and mercenary soldiers; it being the inseparable right of a free nation that they themselves, and no separate number of paid or hired men, should have the guard of their own prince, government, and laws.

Lastly. Although we mention these three particulars as most necessary to us, yet there are several others of great importance which we leave to your wisdoms; assuring ourselves that until you have fully provided for a complete security against Popery and arbitrary power, you will not give any of our money.

APPENDIX IV

Chronological Summary of Parliaments and Ministries

[Dates of Ministries are not given prior to 1770. T = Tory; W = Whig;
C = Conservative; L = Liberal; Lab. = Labour]

Apr.	1660	Parliament met.
Dec.	1660	Parliament dissolved.
May	1661	Parliament met.
Jan.	1679	Parliament dissolved.
Mar.	1679	Parliament met.
July	1679	Parliament dissolved.
Oct.	1679	Parliament met.
Jan.	1681	Parliament dissolved.
Mar.	1681	Parliament met.
Mar.	1681	Parliament dissolved.
May	1685	Parliament met.
July	1687	Parliament dissolved.
Jan.	1689	Parliament met.
Feb.	1690	Parliament dissolved.
Mar.	1690	Parliament met.
Oct.	1695	Parliament dissolved.
Nov.	1695	Parliament met.
July	1698	Parliament dissolved.
Aug.	1698	Parliament met.
Dec.	1700	Parliament dissolved.
Feb.	1701	Parliament met.
Nov.	1701	Parliament dissolved.
Dec.	1701	Parliament met.
July	1702	Parliament dissolved.
Aug.	1702	Parliament met.
Apr.	1705	Parliament dissolved.
Oct.	1705	Parliament met.
Apr.	1708	Parliament dissolved.
Nov.	1708	Parliament met.
Sept.	1710	Parliament dissolved.
Nov.	1710	Parliament met.
Aug.	1713	Parliament dissolved.
Nov.	1713	Parliament met.
Jan.	1715	Parliament dissolved.
Mar.	1715	Parliament met.
Mar.	1722	Parliament dissolved.
Oct.	1722	Parliament met.
Aug.	1727	Parliament dissolved.
Jan.	1728	Parliament met.
Apr.	1734	Parliament dissolved.
Jan.	1735	Parliament met.
Apr.	1741	Parliament dissolved.
Dec.	1741	Parliament met.
June	1747	Parliament dissolved.

Nov.	1747	Parliament met.
Apr.	1754	Parliament dissolved.
Nov.	1754	Parliament met.
Mar.	1761	Parliament dissolved.
May	1761	Parliament met.
Mar.	1768	Parliament dissolved.
May	1768	Parliament met.
Jan.	1770	North (T) took office.
Sept.	1774	Parliament dissolved.
Nov.	1774	Parliament met.
Sept.	1780	Parliament dissolved.
Oct.	1780	Parliament met.
Mar.	1782	North (T) resigned.
Mar.	1782	Rockingham (W) took office.
July	1782	Rockingham (W) died.
July	1782	Shelburne (Coalition) took office.
Feb.	1783	Shelburne (Coalition) resigned, owing to lack of support.
Apr.	1783	Portland, Fox, North (Coalition) took office.
Dec.	1783	Portland, Fox, North (Coalition) dismissed.
Dec.	1783	Pitt (T) took office.
Mar.	1784	Parliament dissolved.
May	1784	Parliament met.
June	1790	Parliament dissolved.
Nov.	1790	Parliament met.
May	1796	Parliament dissolved.
Sept.	1796	Parliament met.
Mar.	1801	Pitt (T) resigned, disagreeing with George III on Roman Catholic question.
Mar.	1801	Addington (T) took office.
June	1802	Parliament dissolved.
Nov.	1802	Parliament met.
May	1804	Addington (T) resigned, owing to lack of support.

May 1804 Pitt (T) took office.
Jan. 1806 Pitt (T) died.
Jan. 1806 Grenville (Coalition) took office.
Oct. 1806 Parliament dissolved.
Dec. 1806 Parliament met.
Mar. 1807 Grenville (Coalition) dismissed, for refusing to give pledge on Roman Catholic question.
Mar. 1807 Portland (T) took office.
Apr. 1807 Parliament dissolved.
June 1807 Parliament met.
Sept. 1809 Portland (T) resigned, owing to ill health.
Oct. 1809 Perceval (T) took office.
May 1812 Perceval (T) died.
June 1812 Liverpool (T) took office.
Sept. 1812 Parliament dissolved.
Nov. 1812 Parliament met.
June 1818 Parliament dissolved.
Jan. 1819 Parliament met.
Feb. 1820 Parliament dissolved (demise of Crown).
Apr. 1820 Parliament met.
June 1826 Parliament dissolved.
Nov. 1826 Parliament met.
Mar. 1827 Liverpool (T) resigned, owing to ill health.
Apr. 1827 Canning (Coalition) took office.
Aug. 1827 Canning (Coalition) died.
Aug. 1827 Goderich (Coalition) took office.
Jan. 1828 Goderich (Coalition) resigned, owing to internal dissensions.
Jan. 1828 Wellington (T) took office.
July 1830 Parliament dissolved (demise of Crown).
Oct. 1830 Parliament met.
Nov. 1830 Wellington (T) defeated in House of Commons on Civil List, and resigned.
Nov. 1830 Grey (L) took office.

Apr. 1831 Grey (L) defeated in House of Commons on Reform Bill (Committee stage).
Apr. 1831 Parliament dissolved.
June 1831 Parliament met.
May 1832 Grey (L) resigned, and resumed office in the same month.
Dec. 1832 Parliament dissolved, to enable the new franchise and distribution to operate.
Jan. 1833 Parliament met.
July 1834 Grey (L) resigned, owing to internal dissensions.
July 1834 Melbourne (L) took office.
Nov. 1834 Melbourne (L) resigned, at the King's suggestion.
Dec. 1834 Peel (C) took office (after Wellington had acted for a short time on his behalf).
Dec. 1834 Parliament dissolved.
Feb. 1835 Parliament met.
Apr. 1835 Peel (C) defeated in House of Commons on motion by Opposition relative to Irish Church revenues and resigned.
Apr. 1835 Melbourne (L) took office.
July 1837 Parliament dissolved (demise of Crown).
Nov. 1837 Parliament met.
May 1839 Melbourne (L) resigned, and resumed office in the same month (Bedchamber question).
June 1841 Melbourne (L) defeated in House of Commons (non-confidence vote).
June 1841 Parliament dissolved.
Aug. 1841 Parliament met.
Aug. 1841 Melbourne (L) defeated in House of

Commons and re-
signed.

Sept. 1841 Peel (C) took office.

Dec. 1845 Peel (C) resigned, and
resumed office in the
same month (Free
Trade question).

June 1846 Peel (C) defeated in
House of Commons
on Irish Coercion
Bill and resigned.

July 1846 Russell (L) took office.

July 1847 Parliament dissolved.

Nov. 1847 Parliament met.

Feb. 1851 Russell (L) resigned,
and resumed office
in the same month.

Feb. 1852 Russell (L) defeated
in House of Com-
mons on Militia Bill
and resigned.

Feb. 1852 Derby (C) took office.

July 1852 Parliament dissolved.

Nov. 1852 Parliament met.

Dec. 1852 Derby (C) defeated in
House of Commons
on Budget and re-
signed.

Dec. 1852 Aberdeen (Coalition)
took office.

Jan. 1855 Aberdeen (Coalition)
defeated in House
of Commons on Se-
bastopol Committee
and resigned.

Feb. 1855 Palmerston (L) took
office.

Mar. 1857 Palmerston (L) defeated in House
of Commons on
Chinese question.

Mar. 1857 Parliament dissolved.

Apr. 1857 Parliament met.

Feb. 1858 Palmerston (L) defeated in House of
Commons on Con-
spiracy to Murder
Bill and resigned.

Feb. 1858 Derby (C) took office.

Mar. 1859 Derby (C) defeated in
House of Commons
on Reform Bill.

Apr. 1859 Parliament dissolved.

May 1859 Parliament met.

June 1859 Derby (C) defeated
in House of Com-
mons on amend-
ment to Address and
resigned.

June 1859 Palmerston (L) took
office.

July 1865 Parliament dissolved.

Oct. 1865 Palmerston (L) died.

Oct. 1865 Russell (L) took office.

Feb. 1866 Parliament met.

June 1866 Russell (L) defeated
in House of Com-
mons on Reform
Bill and resigned.

June 1866 Derby (C) took office.

Feb. 1868 Derby (C) resigned,
owing to ill health.

Feb. 1868 Disraeli (C) took office.

Feb. 1868 Disraeli (C) defeated in
House of Commons
on Disestablishment
of Irish Church.

Nov. 1868 Parliament dissolved.

Dec. 1868 Disraeli (C) resigned,
owing to losses of
his party in general
election.

Dec. 1868 Gladstone (L) took
office.

Dec. 1868 Parliament met.

Mar. 1873 Gladstone (L) defeated in House of
Commons on Irish
University Bill and
resigned, but re-
sumed office in the
same month.

Jan. 1874 Parliament dissolved.

Feb. 1874 Gladstone (L) resigned, owing to
losses of his party in
general election.

Feb. 1874 Disraeli (C) took office.

Mar. 1874 Parliament met.

Mar. 1880 Parliament dissolved.

Apr. 1880 Disraeli (C) resigned,
owing to losses of
his party in general
election.

Apr. 1880 Gladstone (L) took office.

Apr. 1880 Parliament met.

June 1885 Gladstone (L) defeated in House of Commons on Budget and resigned.

June 1885 Salisbury (C) took office.

Nov. 1885 Parliament dissolved.

Jan. 1886 Parliament met.

Jan. 1886 Salisbury (C) defeated in House of Commons on Address and resigned.

Feb. 1886 Gladstone (L) took office.

June 1886 Gladstone (L) defeated in House of Commons on Home Rule for Ireland.

June 1886 Parliament dissolved.

July 1886 Gladstone (L) resigned, owing to losses of his party in general election.

July 1886 Salisbury (C) took office.

Aug. 1886 Parliament met.

June 1892 Parliament dissolved.

Aug. 1892 Parliament met.

Aug. 1892 Salisbury (C) defeated in House of Commons, on vote of non-confidence.

Aug. 1892 Gladstone (L) took office.

Mar. 1894 Gladstone (L) resigned, owing to old age.

Mar. 1894 Rosebery (L) took office.

June 1895 Rosebery (L) defeated in House of Commons on Cordite question and resigned.

June 1895 Salisbury (C) took office.

July 1895 Parliament dissolved.

Aug. 1895 Parliament met.

Sept. 1900 Parliament dissolved.

Dec. 1900 Parliament met.

July 1902 Salisbury (C) resigned, owing to old age.

July 1902 Balfour (C) took office.

Dec. 1905 Balfour (C) resigned.

Dec. 1905 Campbell-Bannerman (L) took office.

Jan. 1906 Parliament dissolved.

Feb. 1906 Parliament met.

Apr. 1908 Campbell-Bannerman (L) resigned, owing to ill health.

Apr. 1908 Asquith (L) took office.

Jan 1910 Parliament dissolved (Relations between the two Houses).

Feb. 1910 Parliament met.

Nov. 1910 Parliament dissolved (Relations between the two Houses).

Jan. 1911 Parliament met.

May 1915 Ministry reconstructed on Coalition basis.

Dec. 1916 Asquith (L) resigned, owing to lack of support.

Dec. 1916 Lloyd George (Coalition) took office.

Nov. 1918 Parliament dissolved.

Feb. 1919 Parliament met.

Oct. 1922 Lloyd George (Coalition) resigned, owing to internal dissensions.

Oct. 1922 Bonar Law (C) took office.

Oct. 1922 Parliament dissolved.

Nov. 1922 Parliament met.

May 1923 Bonar Law (C) resigned, owing to ill health.

May 1923 Baldwin (C) took office.

Nov. 1923 Parliament dissolved.

Jan. 1924 Parliament met.

Jan. 1924 Baldwin (C) defeated in House of Commons on vote of non-confidence and resigned.

Jan. 1924 MacDonald (Lab.) took office.

Oct. 1924 MacDonald (Lab.) defeated in House of Commons, on question of Campbell Case.

Oct. 1924 Parliament dissolved.

Nov. 1924 MacDonald (Lab.) resigned, owing to losses of his party in general election.

Nov. 1924 Baldwin (C) took office.

Dec. 1924 Parliament met.

May 1929 Parliament dissolved.

June 1929 Baldwin (C) resigned, owing to losses of his party in general election.

June 1929 MacDonald (Lab.) took office.

June 1929 Parliament met.

Aug. 1931 MacDonald (Lab.) resigned, owing to internal dissensions.

Aug. 1931 MacDonald (Coalition) took office.

Oct. 1931 Parliament dissolved.

Nov. 1931 Parliament met.

June 1935 MacDonald (Coalition) resigned.

June 1935 Baldwin (Coalition) took office.

Oct. 1935 Parliament dissolved.

Nov. 1935 Parliament met.

May 1937 Baldwin (C) resigned.

May 1937 Chamberlain (C) took office.

Sept. 1939 Ministry reconstructed on Coalition basis.

May 1940 Chamberlain (Coalition) resigned.

May 1940 Churchill (Coalition) took office.

May 1945 Churchill (Coalition) resigned.

May 1945 Churchill (C) took office (Caretaker Ministry).

June 1945 Parliament dissolved.

July 1945 Churchill (C) resigned owing to losses of his party in general election.

July 1945 Attlee (Lab.) took office.

Aug. 1945 Parliament met.

Feb. 1950 Parliament dissolved.

Mar. 1950 Parliament met.

Oct. 1951 Parliament dissolved.

Oct. 1951 Attlee (Lab.) resigned owing to losses of his party in general election.

Oct. 1951 Churchill (C) took office.

Oct. 1951 Parliament met.

Apr. 1955 Churchill (C) resigned.

Apr. 1955 Eden (C) took office.

May 1955 Parliament dissolved.

June 1955 Parliament met.

INDEX

Statutes, illustrations of provisions for consultation on proposed legislation, 69 (n. 1).

Stead, W. T., 99–100.

Strikes, used to influence opinion and policy, 96–97.

Subordinate legislation, publication of, 68.

Swift, Jonathan, 34, 168, 174, 187, 318.

Tamworth Manifesto, 203–5, 286–7.

Tariff reform, 222–5, 257, 262.

Three-party system, effect of, 115, 165, 252, 281, 311.

Tracts, political:
and public opinion, 34–35.
and elections in connexion with policy, 176–80.

Trade unions:
and Members of Parliament as delegates, 25–26.
as political associations, 95.

Trades Union Congress, influence of, 95–98.

Treason, high, offence of, 87.

Treasury, election management by, 169–70.

Trevelyan, G. M., 104, 125, 173.

Unlawful assembly, offence of, 85–87.

Victoria, Queen:
on the party system, 115.
and the choice of Prime Ministers, 150–1.
and dependence of Ministries on results of general elections, 163–4.
and the use of dissolutions of Parliament, 162, 210.
and the official Speech, 283–4.

Virtual representation, 189–90.

Voluntary associations, 66, 95, 98–99, 260.

'Votes' of House of Commons, publication of, 35–36.

Walpole, Horace (after 1791 4th Earl of Orford), 47, 48, 89, 108, 116, 184.

Walpole, Horatio (after 1756 1st Baron Walpole), 20, 132.

Walpole, Sir Robert (after 1742 1st Earl of Orford):
and public opinion, 35.
on publication of parliamentary debates, 37.
and Excise Scheme, 35, 37–42.
and War of Jenkins' Ear, 43–46.
and corporate responsibility, 107–8, 152.
circumstances of resignation of, 108, 116, 156, 160.
and party meetings, 132.
and party organization, 135–6.
other references to, 21 (n. 1), 44, 120–1, 274.

Wars of 1914–18 and 1939–45, see World War I and World War II.

Wellington, 1st Duke of:
on pledges, 18.
and Reform Bill, 1832, 198–9.
and dissolution of 1841, 208, 283.
on men and measures, 238, 240.
his resignation in 1830, 271.

Whips, Party, 134, 137.

Wilkes, John, 2, 17, 21, 27, 50, 89, 110, 283.

William III:
parties under, 103–5.
choice of Ministers by, 147.
election management under, 167–8.
royal influence over elections, 170–3, 267, 283.

William IV:
and public meetings, 83–84.
and choice of Ministers, 150.
and Reform Bill, 1832, 275.

World War I, 127, 128, 252, 308.

World War II, 72, 153, 308.

Wyndham, Sir William, 24, 37, 39, 274.

Yonge, Sir William, 23, 24.

PRINTED IN GREAT BRITAIN
AT THE UNIVERSITY PRESS, OXFORD
BY VIVIAN RIDLER
PRINTER TO THE UNIVERSITY